The Government and Copyright

The Government as Proprietor, Preserver and User of Copyright Material Under the *Copyright Act 1968*

JS Gilchrist

SYDNEY UNIVERSITY PRESS

Sydney University Press
Fisher Library F03
University of Sydney NSW 2006
AUSTRALIA
Email: sup.info@sydney.edu.au
sydney.edu.au/sup

National Library of Australia Cataloguing-in-Publication Data

Title:	The government and copyright : the government as proprietor, preserver and user of copyright material under the *Copyright Act 1968* / John S Gilchrist.
ISBN:	9781743323748 (paperback)
ISBN:	9781743323755 (ebook : epub)
Notes:	Includes bibliographical references and index.
Subjects:	Copyright--Australia.
	Intellectual property--Australia.
	Government publications--Australia.
	Copyright--Official information--Australia.
Dewey Number:	346.940482

Cover design by Miguel Yamin

In memoriam

Ian Steel Gilchrist
and
Violet Cherry Burnell Gregory

Contents

Preface

This book examines the role of government as proprietor, preserver and user of copyright material under the *Copyright Act 1968* (Cth) and the policy considerations that Australian law should take into account in that role.

For the sake of cohesion, it has been necessary to focus discussion in this book on the Australian federal government that is embodied within the term the 'Commonwealth' in the *Copyright Act 1968*. Reference is also made in various chapters of this work to the law and developments in the states and territories of Australia, in some comparable overseas jurisdictions and to international developments in this field.

The book concludes that government copyright law and practice in each of the three governmental roles recognised under the *Copyright Act 1968* has not responded adequately to the information age and to the desire and the ability of individuals to access information quickly and effectively.

The solution offered in this book is reform of the law and of public policy that is in step with access to information policy, the promotion of better communication and interaction with the community, and the enhanced preservation of government and private copyright materials for reasons of government accountability, effective administration and national culture and heritage.

I acknowledge with much thanks the valuable assistance and strong encouragement given to me by various people in the course of preparing this work. Most particularly, I wish to thank Professor Brian Fitzgerald of the Australian Catholic University (ACU) and Dr Anne Fitzgerald, Barrister at Law, whose support and constructive comments aided me immensely, to Neale Hooper of the Queensland University of Technology and formerly of the Office of Economic and Statistical Research, Queensland Treasury, for his valuable knowledge and insights from his pioneering work on the Government Information Licensing Framework (GILF) project and for his ongoing support, and to Ben Atkinson of ACU, for his historiographical and other comments over the life of this work. I also wish to thank my wife who assisted me with a critical review of the text and with proof reading, the Australia Research Council Centre of Excellence for Creative Industries and Innovation (CCI) for their funding support, Sydney University Press, DP Plus document production,

Michael Harrington, and my colleagues at the Academy of Law, ACU, Melbourne, and the University of Canberra.

The law and policy discussed in this book is that available to me at 30 June 2014 but significant developments which have occurred after that date have been included where possible.

John Gilchrist

Foreword

In carrying out their functions, governments deal with a vast and diverse array of copyright materials. These range from legislation and parliamentary documents to cultural and historical artefacts, databases of statistical, mapping, meteorological and scientific data, reports provided by natural resource exploration companies, official reports, and publications and archived public records. Government's role in relation to copyright materials is multifaceted: as well as generating much copyright material itself (through its employees and contractors), government makes extensive use of copyright material created and owned by other parties and is the custodian of copyright materials deposited with it voluntarily or pursuant to legal requirements. In these various roles, government is—to adopt Dr Gilchrist's terminology—the 'proprietor, preserver and user' of copyright materials.

Specific provisions on government (or Crown) copyright have existed in Australian copyright law for more than a century, although they have received little attention until recently, whether from academic researchers, law review bodies or the courts. In the pre-digital or analogue world the position of government with respect to copyright ownership may have been regarded as well settled and of little moment or interest. Indeed, it was not until the mid-2000s that the government copyright provisions of the *Copyright Act 1968* (Cth) were first considered in depth by Australian courts, in a case brought by Copyright Agency Limited seeking compensation from the New South Wales government for its use of survey plans lodged with the Land Titles Registry (*Copyright Agency Limited v New South Wales* [2008] HCA 35). Questions about government ownership and use of copyright materials were raised in the course of inquiries by the Copyright Law Review Committee (CLRC) from the mid-1990s (the Simplification of the *Copyright Act* inquiry [1995–1999]) but were not specifically addressed until the CLRC's Crown copyright inquiry (2003–2005).

With the emergence and widespread adoption of digital technologies during the last quarter of a century, government's role in copyright ownership, use and management has become a dynamic and significant issue. The sheer volume, importance and value of the copyright material produced, used and managed by government ensure that this is the case. The introduction of digital technologies from the mid-1990s saw government materials increasingly being created and distributed in digital form, along with the digitisation of public records and archival holdings. It also saw an increasing demand from citizens, business and the public sector itself to be able to access, use and re-use government information and materials. A feature of early e-government initiatives in the Web 1.0 era was the development of internet portals through which online access was provided to government materials and information in digital form. Web 2.0 technologies spurred Gov 2.0 initiatives as governments responded to calls for greater openness, transparency and accountability. Accompanying these developments has been a growing awareness of the centrality of government information for innovation and public policy and of the need to address the challenges presented to government as owner, user and custodian of copyright materials in the digital, networked environment.

It was against this background that John Gilchrist embarked on the doctoral research project on which this book is based, examining the complexities of the government's interrelated roles as 'proprietor, preserver and user' of copyright and 'the relationship between government copyright law and policy, national cultural policy and fundamental governance values'.

This task is one which Dr Gilchrist is well equipped to undertake, having been involved with intellectual property policy and law during a period spanning four decades, as a government lawyer and legal advisor, academic researcher and participant in major reviews of copyright law. Early in his career as a lawyer in the Commonwealth Attorney-General's Department and the Australian Government Solicitor's Office in the 1970s, he advised on copyright issues and served as Secretary to the Copyright Law Committee on Reprographic Reproduction which was chaired by Justice Franki. Some 30 years later, he was appointed as a member of the CLRC for its Crown copyright inquiry which reported in March 2005. Issues relating to government copyright and the Crown prerogatives to print and publish have been an ongoing, central focus of Dr Gilchrist's academic research, forming the subject of his Master of Laws thesis and several law journal publications. Dr Gilchrist's unparalleled depth of perspective and expertise contribute to a mature, comprehensive and multidimensional examination of the topic.

As the first authoritative treatise on government copyright to be published in Australia, this book will be of immediate interest and relevance to Australian lawyers and policy makers, particularly in the light of ongoing efforts to ensure that the intellectual property system stimulates innovation and fosters trade and investment. Given that government copyright is recognised to some extent in most countries worldwide, this book is a valuable contribution to the international literature on this topic, which remains sparse. Though based primarily on Australian laws and experience, Dr Gilchrist's insights and analyses are globally relevant and will provide guidance in both common and civil law jurisdictions as governments shape their copyright policies, laws and practices for the information age.

Dr Anne Fitzgerald, Barrister
Hobart, Tasmania

Professor Brian Fitzgerald, Dean, Thomas More Academy of Law
Australian Catholic University

30 June 2014

Table of Cases

Australia

Table of Cases

England and Comparative Jurisdictions

Table of Legislation

Australia

England and Comparative Jurisdictions

Introduction

Most people contemplating the modern law of copyright think of it as the embodiment of private rights and the exploitation of those rights—an increasingly pervasive set of rights—that underpin the computer software, music, print and electronic publishing industries, the film and broadcasting industries, and other fields of intellectual endeavour. It touches our daily life and affects the way we behave. Government is seen as the forum for the advancement and further protection of those private rights through legislative enactment.

Nonetheless, government has played a crucial role in the development of copyright law from its beginnings through a system of patronage and grants, control and censorship of the media, through its ownership, production and dissemination of its own intellectual products and through the preservation of, and access to, its own and its society's endeavours. As an institution in society, government has had a unique role and status under copyright law. Today, there are special provisions in the Australian *Copyright Act 1968* (Cth) dealing with the role of government as proprietor, preserver and user of copyright material.

This book examines the role of government as proprietor, preserver and user of copyright material under the *Copyright Act 1968* and the policy considerations that Australian law should take into account in that role. There are two recurring themes arising in this examination that are significant to the recommendations and conclusions. The first is whether the needs and status of government should be different from private sector institutions, which also obtain copyright protection under the law. This theme stems from the 2005 report on *Crown Copyright* by the Copyright Law Review Committee (CLRC) and the earlier Ergas Committee Report, which are discussed in Chapters 1 and 7 of this book. The second is to identify the relationship between government copyright law and policy, national cultural policy and fundamental governance values. This theme goes to the essence of the book. For example, does the law and practice of government copyright properly reflect technological change in the way we now access and use information and does it facilitate the modern information management principles of government? Is the law and practice of government copyright consistent with the greater openness and accountability of government?

Over the last decade and a half, some governments in Australia and overseas have changed their view of their own copyright material, from treating it as a commodity to be licensed and exploited for profit to freely releasing that material for the benefit of government and the community.

The central hypothesis of this book is that each of the three roles of government recognised under the *Copyright Act 1968* should be maintained, but both copyright law and policy should be made more consistent with, and responsive to, the needs of modern democratic governance values and national cultural policy.

The principal questions in this book are:

1. What rights does the government presently have, and what rights should it have, to own copyright in material it produces? Should government-produced material be in the public domain? Does ownership or non-ownership conflict with the principle that all citizens in a liberal democratic society should have fair and open access to government information?
2. Should the government have a role as preserver of its own and privately owned copyright material? If so, what should that role be? How adequate is the present law to achieve this objective? How does preservation accord with the principle that all citizens have fair and open access to government information?
3. What rights does the government presently have, and what rights should it have, to use copyright material owned by other persons? How are these rights justified on information management principles?

The discussion in this book focuses on the Australian federal government that is embodied within the term the 'Commonwealth' in the *Copyright Act 1968*. The scope of that term—and in particular the departments and other emanations of the executive government within the meaning of the 'Commonwealth'—is discussed in detail in Chapter 1. Reference is also made in various chapters of this book to the law and developments in the States and Territories of Australia. These have, in some cases, been innovative and influential in change, particularly in promoting open content policies. Significant developments in accessing and re-using government information in other comparable common law countries and at an international level are also discussed in Chapter 3.

The interests of government as owner, preserver and user of copyright material under the *Copyright Act 1968* are the three principal interests of government beyond its constitutional responsibilities for the administration of copyright as a whole.

The analysis in this book poses questions about the extent to which the interests of government are distinct from the interests of other owners and users of copyright material under the Act and the extent to which the law should accommodate those interests. The analysis also poses broader questions about copyright policy, embodied in the law, concerning the balance of interests between owners and users of copyright material and the relationship the law has to practice. This in turn explores the nature of copyright and the public interest considerations that lie at its heart.

The book seeks to contribute to knowledge of the factors in the development of government copyright law: past, present and prospect. It looks at the copyright origins of the present legal deposit provisions and provides a comprehensive and historical analysis of the role of government across all three copyright interests—as owner, preserver and user of copyright material—and the relationship each bears to the management of information in the information age. The legal and public policy issues are not peculiar to Australia and the book looks beyond Australian developments to those in other comparable common law countries and at a wider international level.

Australian and International Background

This book is written against a background of various Australian and international reports and initiatives into the ownership of, and in accessing and re-using, government copyright material.

Australia

In 2000, the Intellectual Property and Competition Review Committee (Ergas Committee) in its report, *Review of Intellectual Property Legislation under the Competition Principles Agreement*, concluded:

> The Committee does not believe that the Crown should benefit from preferential treatment under the *Copyright Act* as compared with other parties. As a result, we recommend that s 176 of the *Copyright Act* be amended to leave the Crown in the same position as any other contracting party.[1]

In 2004, Stage 1 of a project known as GILF (Government Information Licensing Framework) commenced. It was initiated by the Queensland Spatial Information Council to review licensing practices and options in its business environment. It found inconsistent licensing practices by Queensland Government agencies. In 2005–2006, Stage 2 of the GILF Project resulted in a recommendation that state government agencies pilot the move to an information licensing framework based on Creative Commons for qualifying information where no issues of privacy, confidentiality or other legal or policy constraints applied.

In April 2005, the report of the CLRC on its Crown copyright reference was released by the Australian Government. The committee considered the Ergas Committee's views and recommendation on government ownership of copyright and itself recommended the abolition of the specific government ownership and subsistence provisions in the *Copyright Act 1968*, the abolition of government copyright in certain judicial, executive and legislative materials and changes in the management practices of state, territory and federal governments dealing with Crown copyright material.

In September 2008, a review of the National Innovation System, entitled *Venturous Australia: Building Strength in Innovation* (the Cutler Report), was released. It stated 'Australia

---

1   Australia. Intellectual Property and Competition Review Committee, *Review of Intellectual Property Legislation under the Competition Principles Agreement* (Ergas Committee) (2000) 113, 114.

is behind many other advanced countries in establishing institutional frameworks to maximise the flow of government-generated information and content.[2] Its recommendations included that Australian governments should adopt international standards of open publishing as far as possible and material released for public information by Australian governments should be released under a Creative Commons licence.[3] In its response of May 2009 in *Powering Ideas: An Innovation Agenda for the 21st Century,* the Australian Government stated that it controlled 'mountains of information, and it is determined to make more of this vast national resource accessible to citizens, business people, researchers and policy makers' and announced it would take steps to develop a more coordinated approach to Commonwealth information management, innovation, and engagement involving the Australian Government Information Management Office (AGIMO) and other federal agencies.[4]

The Economic Development and Infrastructure Committee (EDIC) of the Victorian Parliament in its report of June 2009, entitled *Inquiry into Improving Access to Victorian Public Sector Information and Data,* stated:

> The Committee believes that open access should be the default position because:
>
> - PSI [public sector information] is publicly funded and is generated for the purpose of administering the state and undertaking core functions of governance. As a resource created on behalf of all citizens, PSI should be accessible to all citizens; and
> - economic and social benefits arising from the release of the Victorian Government PSI will likely outweigh the benefits of treating it as a commodity.[5]

---

2   Australia. Cutler & Company Pty Ltd, *Venturous Australia: Building Strength in Innovation: Report on the Review of the National Innovation System* (the Cutler Report) Report to Senator the Hon Kim Carr, Minister for Innovation, Industry, Science and Research (August 2008) 94 http://www.industry.gov.au/innovation/InnovationPolicy/Pages/Document%20library/NISReport.aspx or http://www.industry.gov.au/innovation/InnovationPolicy/Documents/Policy/NISReport.pdf.

3   The Cutler Report followed earlier reports that pointed out the advantages to be gained from re-use of government-held materials in the digital content sector, such as Cutler & Company Pty Ltd, *Commerce in Content: Building Australia's International Future in Interactive Multimedia Markets* (1994) 43, which recommended that government provide access to culturally significant data in digital form to IMM content developers and users by early digitalisation of national collections and archives and Department of Communications, Information Technology and the Arts, *Unlocking the Potential: Digital Content Industry Action Agenda, Strategic Industry Leaders Group report to the Australian Government* (2005) 46–7, where it reported that there were insufficiently developed mechanisms for accessing Crown IP for exploitation by digital content firms and proposed work in the area of alternative approaches to intellectual property licensing, such as Creative Commons.

4   Australia. Department of Innovation, Industry, Science and Research, *Powering Ideas: An Innovation Agenda for the 21st Century* (2009) [57] http://apo.org.au/research/powering-ideas-innovation-agenda-21st-century.

5   Victoria. Economic Development and Infrastructure Committee, Parliament of Victoria, *Inquiry into Improving Access to Victorian Public Sector Information and Data: Report* (June 2009) Parliamentary Paper No 198, Session 2006–2009, 19 http://www.parliament.vic.gov.au/edic/inquiries/article/1019.

EDIC also recommended a consistent copyright licensing system over government information for use across all government departments, developed and administered through a central office.[6]

In February 2010, the Victorian Government tabled its response, which agreed that the default position for the management of PSI should be open access. The Victorian Government committed itself to the development of a whole-of-government Information Management Framework (IMF) whereby PSI is made available under Creative Commons licensing by default with a tailored suite of licences for restricted materials.[7]

In July 2007, the Council of Australian Governments, Online and Communication Council commissioned the development of a national information-sharing strategy. This was aimed at promoting better government service delivery and improved policy development through focused interagency collaboration and was widely supported across agencies and jurisdictions. In August 2009, AGIMO published a report, entitled *National Government Information Sharing Strategy*, endorsing nine information-sharing principles aimed at providing benefits to governments and the public. Included among the principles were: agencies should facilitate whole-of-government approaches to information management through inter-departmental communication and collaboration and consistency across government, and should promote information re-use: that is, agencies need to investigate the conditions of use they should apply to the different elements of their information catalogue, for example, legislation, classification, freedom of information and licensing requirements, and to do so ensuring privacy and security requirements are met.[8]

In December 2009, the Australian Government's 2.0 taskforce delivered its final report, entitled *Engage: Getting on with Government 2.0*, whose central recommendation was a declaration of open government by the Australian Government stating that:

- using technology to increase citizen engagement and collaboration in making policy and providing service will help achieve a more consultative, participatory and transparent government
- public sector information is a national resource and that releasing as much of it on as permissive terms as possible will maximise its economic and social value to Australians and reinforce its contribution to a healthy democracy

---

6   Ibid xxvi. **Recommendation 11:** That the Victorian Government develop a consistent copyright licensing system for use across all government departments. **Recommendation 12:** That the Victorian Government establish a central office to develop a copyright licensing system, and provide advice to government on government copyright.

7   Victoria. Department of Innovation, Industry and Regional Development, *Whole of Victorian Government Response to the Final Report of the Economic Development and Infrastructure Committee's Inquiry into Improving Access to Victorian Public Sector Information and Data* (2 February 2010), 8 http://www.parliament.vic.gov.au/images/stories/committees/edic/access_to_PSI/ Response-to-the-EDIC-Inquiry-into-Improving-Access-to-Victorian-PSI-and-Data.pdf.

8   Australia. Department of Finance and Deregulation, Australian Government Information Management Office, *National Government Information Sharing Strategy: Unlocking Government Information Assets to Benefit the Broader Community* (August 2009) [24–34] http://www.finance.gov.au/ files/2012/04/ngiss.pdf.

- online engagement by public servants, involving robust professional discussion as part of their duties or as private citizens, benefits their agencies, their professional development, those with whom they are engaged and the Australian public. This engagement should be enabled and encouraged.[9]

The report noted that meeting these key points at all levels of government was integral to achieving the government's objectives, including public sector reform, innovation and using the national investment in broadband 'to achieve an informed, connected and democratic community'.[10]

In July 2010, the then Minister for Finance and Deregulation released a *Declaration of Open Government,* which implemented this recommendation. Subsequently, the statement of *Intellectual Property Principles for Australian Government Agencies*[11] was amended to reflect government decisions in relation to the ownership of intellectual property in software procured under ICT (Information and Communications Technology) contracts and the free use of PSI. The statement advises agencies to licence PSI under Creative Commons BY licence (otherwise known as the 'attribution licence') or other open content licences[12] and also states that, when Commonwealth records become available for public access under the *Archives Act 1983,* PSI covered by Crown copyright should be automatically licensed under an appropriate open content licence. In January 2011 the Australian Attorney-General's Department released *Guidelines for Licensing Public Sector Information for Australian Government Agencies* to assist agencies in implementing this policy.[13]

On 29 June 2012 the then Australian Attorney-General gave a reference to the Australian Law Reform Commission (ALRC) for inquiry and report into *Copyright and the Digital Economy.* The terms of reference required the ALRC to report by 30 November 2013 on 'whether the exceptions and statutory licences in the *Copyright Act 1968,* are adequate and appropriate in the digital environment', having regard among other things to 'the importance of the digital economy and the opportunities for innovation leading to national economic and cultural development created by the emergence of new digital technologies'.[14] In its report, the ALRC made a number of recommendations for the repeal of a

---

9   Australia. Department of Finance and Deregulation, Australian Government Information Management Office, *Engage: Getting on with Government 2.0* (2009) [xvii] http://gov2.net.au/report/ or http://www.finance.gov.au/publications/gov20taskforcereport/doc/Government20TaskforceReport.pdf.

10   Ibid.

11   Australia. Attorney-General's Department, *Intellectual Property Principles for Australian Government Agencies* (2010) http://www.ag.gov.au/RightsAndProtections/IntellectualProperty/ Documents/StatementofIPprinciplesforAusGovagencies.pdf or [1–7] http://www.ag.gov.au/ RightsAndProtections/IntellectualProperty/Documents/IntellectualPropertyManual.pdf. The statement of intellectual property principles provides a policy for the management of intellectual property across Commonwealth agencies and particularly addresses the contracting practices of the Commonwealth. The statement was amended on 1 October 2010 to reflect government decisions in relation to ownership of IP in software procured under ICT contracts (principle 8(a)) and free use of public sector information (principle 11(b)).

12   Ibid 6.

13   Australia. Attorney-General's Department, *Guidelines for Licensing Public Sector Information for Australian Government Agencies* (28 February 2012) http://www.ag.gov.au/RightsAndProtections/ IntellectualProperty/Documents/GuidelinesforlicensingPSIforAusGovagencies.pdf.

range of specific exceptions and their replacement with a broad 'fair use' exception, covering in a non-exhaustive list, research or study, criticism or review, parody or satire, reporting news, professional advice, quotation, non-commercial private use, incidental or technical use, library or archive use, education, and access for people with disability. The ALRC also recommended the modification of various statutory licences in the *Copyright Act 1968* by making them 'less prescriptive' and making it clear that the institutions to which the statutory licences apply, such as the Crown, may also rely on unremunerated exceptions to infringement including fair use. Under the proposals, whether a use is fair will be determined by factors similar to those presently set out in s 107 of the *Copyright Act of 1976* (US), that is, the purpose and character of the use, nature of the material used, the amount and substantiality that is used and the impact on any potential market for the material.[15] The ALRC also recommended the addition of some specific exceptions to infringement dealing with the government use of copyright material and with orphan works, which are discussed in Chapters 6 and 7 of this book.

International

These Australian developments have occurred against a background of significant international reports and initiatives aimed at promoting better access to public information. The reports and initiatives have originated from a common understanding of the benefits of accessing and re-using environmental, spatial, technological and other scientific information produced by publicly funded institutions, particularly in dealing with common and often global problems. They have widened and gathered momentum in the light of the fundamental technological changes in the way people communicate and access information and are enabled to interact with government.

The 1999 UK Government White Paper, *Future Management of Crown Copyright*, stated that 'opening up access and encouraging public participation in government requires official information to be readily available to all'.[16] Likewise it[17] and the subsequent 2006 review by the Office of Fair Trading, *The Commercial Use of Public Information*,[18] and the 2007 review, *The Power of Information*,[19] spelt out substantial economic and social benefits of opening access to much public information. The Office of Fair Trading in *The*

---

14   Australia. Australian Law Reform Commission, *Copyright and the Digital Economy: Final Report* (ALRC Report 122) (November 2013) 7–8, http://www.alrc.gov.au/publications/copyright-report-122 (tabled in the Parliament of Australia 13 February 2014).

15   Ibid 13–14, 16–17.

16   United Kingdom. Cabinet Office, *Future Management of Crown Copyright*, (1999) [2.1] http://www.opsi.gov.uk/advice/crown-copyright/future-management-of-crown-copyright.pdf.

17   Ibid [1.1], [9.1–9.3].

18   United Kingdom. Office of Fair Trading, *The Commercial Use of Public Information (CUPI)* (2006) Cm 4300, OFT 861 [1.4] http://webarchive.nationalarchives.gov.uk/20140402142426/http://oft.gov.uk/oftwork/publications/publication-categories/reports/consumer-protection/oft861 or http://www.opsi.gov.uk/advice/poi/oft-cupi.pdf.

19   United Kingdom. Cabinet Office, *The Power of Information: An Independent Review by Ed Mayo and Tom Steinberg* (2007) 14–16 [26–38] http://www.opsi.gov.uk/advice/poi/index.htm.

Commercial Use of Public Information summarised its conclusions on the use of PSI in the following terms:

> 1.4 We have concluded that improvements can be made. We estimate that, with these improvements, the sector could double in terms of the value it contributes to the UK economy to a figure of £1 billion annually. This would mean the production of a wider range of competitively priced goods and services for consumers and the generation of wider-spread productivity improvements across the economy.[20]

The *Cross Cutting Review of the Knowledge Economy*, published by HM Treasury in December 2000,[21] and the earlier White Paper, *Future Management of Crown Copyright*[22] in March 1999, were the sources of two key initiatives: the creation of a single point of licensing for most Crown copyright material and the liberalisation of licensing arrangements, with a presumption in favour of public information being made available in digital format. An online class licence for PSI was launched as the Click-Use Licence in 2001. In 2010, a revised policy of access to PSI was introduced, entitled the UK Government Licensing Framework, promoting the use of an Open Government Licence, the terms of which are aligned to be interoperable with any Creative Commons Attribution licence. This further simplified free access to PSI.

In May 2011, the Hargreaves Report, *Digital Opportunity: A Review of Intellectual Property and Growth,* made ten recommendations to the IP framework in the United Kingdom to support innovation and promote economic growth in the digital age. The report recommended measures to improve copyright licensing and to provide copyright exceptions for personal use, format shifting, quotation, parody, non-commercial research and library archiving which were implemented by the UK Government in 2014.[23] These recommendations are discussed in Chapters 4 and 7.

In November 2003, the European Parliament and Council passed a Directive to facilitate the re-use of PSI held by public sector bodies of member states.[24] The Directive was a response to the lack of uniformity on the re-use of public information across the national laws of the European Union. The general principle of the Directive was to ensure that documents held by public sector bodies were re-usable for commercial and non-commercial purposes and, where possible, through electronic means. Article 8(1) of the Directive provides that member states may allow for re-use without conditions

---

20   United Kingdom. Office of Fair Trading, above n 18.

21   United Kingdom. HM Treasury, *Cross Cutting Review of the Knowledge Economy: Review of Government Information* (2000) http://webarchive.nationalarchives.gov.uk/+/http:/www.hm-treasury.gov.uk/spend_sr00_ccr.htm.

22   United Kingdom. Cabinet Office, above n 16.

23   United Kingdom. Intellectual Property Office, 'New Exceptions to Copyright Reflect Digital Age' (Media Release, 1 June 2014) https://www.gov.uk/government/news/changes-to-copyright-exceptions and Intellectual Property Office (UK), 'Changes to copyright exceptions' (Announcement, 30 July 2014) https://www.gov.uk/government/news/changes-to-copyright-exceptions.

24   European Parliament, *Directive 2003/98/EC of the European Parliament and of the Council of 17 November 2003 on the Re-use of Public Sector Information* [2003] OJ L 345/90.

or may impose conditions, where appropriate, through a licence. These conditions shall not unnecessarily restrict possibilities for re-use and shall not be used to restrict competition. By May 2008, all 27 member states had notified complete transposition of the Directive. The Directive was formally implemented in the UK by The Re-use of Public Sector Information Regulations 2005.

At the World Summit on the Information Society held in Geneva in December 2003, representatives from 175 countries declared their common commitment to build a people-centred, inclusive and development-orientated Information Society.[25] One plan of action agreed to at the Summit, and further confirmed in Tunis in 2005, concerned the importance of access to information and knowledge. In particular, paragraph C3 10 (b) stated that '[g]overnments are encouraged to provide adequate access through various communication resources, notably the Internet, to public official information'.[26] In the Tunis Commitment of 2005, the *World Summit* further urged governments 'using the potential of ICTs, to create public systems of information on laws and regulations, envisaging a wider development of public access points and supporting the broad availability of this information'.[27]

The emerging international view around improved access to, and re-use of, PSI is reflected in the Organisation for Economic Co-operation and Development's (OECD) *The Seoul Declaration for the Future of the Internet Economy*, which was endorsed at the ministerial meeting on the future of the internet economy in June 2008.[28] The declaration recommended that PSI and content, including scientific data, and works of cultural heritage be made more widely accessible in digital format. The background document to the declaration also proposed, under the *OECD Recommendation of the Council for Enhanced Access and More Effective Use of Public Sector Information*, that OECD member countries consider other recommendations in the context of improved access to PSI, including:

- maximising the availability of PSI for use and re-use based upon the presumption of openness as the default rule to facilitate access and re-use; and

25 International Telecommunications Union/United Nations, *Declaration of Principles: Building the Information Society: a Global Challenge in the New Millennium*, Document WSIS-03/GENEVA/DOC/4-E (2003), Geneva 2003–Tunis 2005, UN/ITU, 2003, 2005 [A1] Declaration of Principles http://www.itu.int/wsis/docs/geneva/official/dop.html.

26 International Telecommunications Union/United Nations, *Declaration of Principles: Building the Information Society: a Global Challenge in the New Millennium*, Document WSIS-03/ GENEVA/DOC/5-E (2003), Geneva 2003–Tunis 2005, UN/ITU, 2003, 2005 Plan of Action http://www.itu.int/wsis/docs/geneva/official/poa.html.

27 International Telecommunications Union/United Nations, *Tunis Commitment*, Document WSIS-05/TUNIS/DOC/7-E (2005), Geneva 2003–Tunis 2005, UN/ITU, para 17 http://www.itu.int/wsis/docs 2/tunis/off/7.html.

28 OECD, *The Seoul Declaration for the Future of the Internet Economy*, OECD Ministerial Meeting on the Future of the Internet Economy, Seoul, South Korea 17–18 June 2008 [7] http://www.oecd.org/sti/40839436.pdf. Subsequent progress is documented in OECD *The Internet Economy on the Rise: Progress since the Seoul Declaration* (OECD Publishing 2013) http://dx.doi.org/10.1787/9789264201545–en but this work did not investigate the impact of the Internet and ICTs on good governance (176).

- encouraging broad non-discriminatory competitive access and conditions for re-use of PSI, eliminating exclusive arrangements, and removing unnecessary restrictions on the ways in which it can be accessed, used, re-used, combined or shared.[29]

In January 2009, the President of the United States of America, Barack Obama instructed the Director of the Office of Management and Budget (OMB) to issue an Open Government Directive. That Directive, dated 8 December 2009, stated:

> To increase accountability, promote informed participation by the public, and create economic opportunity, each agency shall take prompt steps to expand access to information by making it available online in open formats. With respect to information, the presumption shall be in favour of openness (to the extent permitted by law and subject to valid privacy, confidentiality, security, or other restrictions).[30]

In May 2010, the Administrator, Office of Information and Regulatory Affairs, reported on measures the Obama Administration had taken to promote open government, including:

> Agencies have launched their own open government pages and plans. They have published online previously unavailable high-value data sets. They are adopting new, innovative approaches to public outreach and collaboration.
>
> . . . the Consumer Product Safety Commission [CPSC] launched an initiative that is making important information more accessible to millions of consumers. Families can now find the latest safety information on CPSC's blog, which has articles, videos, podcasts and other information that can keep kids and families safe from a variety of product-related hazards. Among other tools, the site features a 'Recall Search', which provides the latest updates on recalls affecting products families use every day.[31]

In 2014 the US Department of State reported that it was implementing two flagship open government initiatives—Innovating with Geographic Data and Embracing Technologies and Platforms—to increase public access to information.[32]

---

29 OECD, Directorate for Science, Technology and Industry, *Recommendation of the Council for Enhanced Access and More Effective Use of Public Sector Information,* OECD Ministerial Meeting on the Future of the Internet Economy, Seoul, South Korea 17–18 June 2008 [5] http://www.oecd.org/futureinternet/papers.htm.

30 United States of America. Executive Office of the President, Office of Management and Budget, *Memorandum for the Heads of Executive Departments and Agencies* from Peter R Orszag Director, Subject: Open Government Directive (8 December 2009 M-10-06) [2] http://www.whitehouse.gov/sites/default/files/omb/assets/memoranda_2010/m10-06.pdf.

31 United States of America. Executive Office of the President, Office of Management and Budget, *Open Government and Records Management* (12 May 2010) (Cass R Sunstein) http://www.whitehouse.gov/omb/inforeg_speeches/open_government_05122010/.

32 United States of America. United States Department of State, *Open Government Plan* (Summer 2014), 1 http://www.state.gov/documents/organization/231006.pdf.

These reports and initiatives demonstrate that governments see greater efficiencies and better engagement and decision-making in the sharing of information between agencies and between government and the public, which will provide social, political and economic benefits to the community and will contribute to a healthy democracy. They reflect a widespread change in governance values, from treating government information as a commodity to be sold, to an understanding of the benefits to government and to the community at large of the greater sharing of information held by government. This has led to a greater community engagement with government and a strengthening of the goals of government responsiveness and accountability.

About the Book

This book examines the legal and policy basis for government copyright law and related practices of government across all three roles. While it canvasses social, political and economic influences in the development of the law and government policy, it does not seek to analyse the economic merits of arguments nor does it seek to analyse the social and political merits of doing so other than to point to policy inconsistency in these areas and suggest how that should be resolved in the Australian law. Specifically, while the book examines the relationship between government copyright and national cultural policy and governance and democratic values—that is, how copyright law and policy responds to these values—it does not seek to analyse fundamental arguments about why accountability of government is good or why preserving cultural heritage is good, although both are the subject of Australian treaty obligations set out in the *International Covenant on Civil and Political Rights* and the *International Covenant on Economic Social and Cultural Rights*.[33] It assumes the merits and validity of these political and social values. These values make up the public interest considerations that are at the heart of the balance of interests between government and users of its copyright material.

Australian copyright law has developed within a framework of international copyright conventions, which prescribe a system of national treatment and minimum standards of protection for copyright owners. These conventions are discussed in more detail in Chapter 1. While there is little on the protection of government works per se, the conventions contain general provisions that seek to balance the rights of copyright owners against the users of copyright material. While this book discusses Australia's obligations under the provisions of these treaties, it is beyond the scope of this book to address the merits of those standards or reform of these international obligations. Rather, the book argues for domestic reforms that may translate into common international experience and international reform in the long term.

This examination is undertaken within the context of Australian treaty and constitutional obligations, governance values and technological change.

Chapter 1 aims to provide an understanding of the legal and policy framework in which the Australian government operates as proprietor, preserver and user of copyright material and, in particular, its treaty and constitutional obligations. It outlines the scope and

---

33   Refer to Chapter 1, 'Australia's International Civil and Political Treaty Obligations'.

diversity of modern Australian government and the legal scope of 'government' under the *Copyright Act 1968*; that is, what constitutes 'the Commonwealth or a State' under Part VII of the *Copyright Act 1968*.

Chapter 1 then provides a brief historical overview of the role of government under Anglo-Australian law as proprietor, preserver and user of copyright material before turning to legal and policy factors which are important in evaluating the future direction of the role of government in these three areas of governmental interest.

Chapters 2 and 3 explore the first principal question of this book, namely: What rights does the government presently have, and what rights should it have, to own copyright in material it produces? Should government-produced material be in the public domain? Does ownership or non-ownership conflict with the principle that all citizens in a liberal democratic society should have fair and open access to government information?

Chapter 2 is aimed at understanding the rights and policy behind present Crown ownership of copyright in Australia. To provide a deeper understanding of the basis of the present Australian law, Chapter 2 examines the origins of the law vesting copyright in government and the major policy considerations evident in its development; first, by describing the origins and scope of the prerogative right in the nature of copyright, which is preserved by s 8A of the *Copyright Act 1968*, and then by describing the origins and scope of Part VII of the *Copyright Act 1968*, from which government rights mostly derive. It concludes by making some comments on the fragmentation between state and federal governments of official electronic dissemination and licensing of laws, in which the public interest in dissemination is strong.

Chapter 3 further explores the first principal question by comparing Australian rights and policy to those in selected comparable countries as a basis for evaluation of the Australian law. It examines developments in the laws and practices of selected comparable countries in facilitating access to public official information. Of particular relevance to this comparative analysis, for reasons of legal heritage or legal influence, are law and policy developments in the United Kingdom, the European Union, New Zealand, Canada and the United States of America. This chapter examines copyright law and policy in these countries, dealing with both the ownership and management of PSI, and then makes some observations on the open content movement which has been promoting access to public and private information worldwide. It concludes that the open content movement has highlighted fundamental questions facing all governments as to what information should be released or not released and, if released, whether access should be limited in some ways (through price, licensing arrangements or through accessible media). Governments must also decide what proactive steps they must take to disseminate information; that is, to provide access through a 'push' model as opposed to a 'pull' model. This, in turn, provides a basis for evaluation of Australian law and practice.

Chapters 4 and 5 explore the second principal question in this book, namely: Should the government have a role as preserver of its own and privately owned copyright material? If so, what should that role be? How adequate is the present law to achieve this objective? How does preservation accord with the principle that all citizens have fair and open access to government information?

Chapter 4 examines the role of government as preserver of its own copyright records under the *Copyright Act 1968*. It outlines the development of present federal archival practices and laws and the scope of *Copyright Act 1968* provisions relating to the preservation of, and access to, those records and examines the legal and policy aspects of access and re-use of government archival material including policies for the better management of government information. It argues existing laws and practices, which are aimed at promoting an open and accountable government and of preserving national culture and heritage, should be reviewed in the light of technological changes in the way we access, create and communicate works and in the light of further moves towards openness in government.

Chapter 5 further explores the second principal question by examining the long-established role of government as compulsory acquirer and preserver of national copyright material under the *Copyright Act 1968*. What is the justification for these laws? Should these laws as a matter of policy be linked with copyright protection? If there is a justification, should the extent of material deposited under these laws be specific and limited in scope, or should it be all-embracing of everything disseminated to the public?

Chapter 5 also examines the historical and policy basis of these laws. It argues that the laws have, at times, been used for motives of scholarly endeavour and censorship, but in Australia, and some other jurisdictions, they have subsisted as an element of national copyright policy. Nonetheless, this chapter argues that the laws have their most convincing rationale in the preservation of national culture and heritage and that it is important that present deposit laws should therefore embrace a wide range of media.

Chapter 6 explores the third principal question in this book, namely: What rights does the government presently have, and what rights should it have, to use copyright material owned by other persons? How are these rights justified on information management principles? This chapter examines the Crown use of copyright material. Specifically, it examines the rights of government under the *Copyright Act 1968* and related laws to use copyright material owned by other persons for the purposes of government.

The nature, scope and operation of the Crown use provision in the *Copyright Act 1968*, the extent to which licences may be implied to government to reproduce or publish copyright material sent to it, and the breadth of other statutory rights held by government and their relationship to s 183 of the *Copyright Act 1968*, are discussed in more detail in this chapter. In particular, it examines arguments for construing s 183 to complement, rather than override, the special defences to infringement such as s 40 (fair dealing for research or study) which users of copyright material may rely on generally under the *Copyright Act 1968*. It also examines the law in the light of the needs of government information management to transfer information across agency boundaries and to develop access systems for that information.

Chapter 7 argues that the government has roles and responsibilities under the *Copyright Act 1968* which are of significance to society and which should continue to be protected and promoted, and that reform of the law is not in itself the complete solution to rapid changes in the way we communicate with government or in the way we access government information. This chapter commences by examining the wider questions of whether there is any justification for copyright ownership vesting in the government, the extent of the public interest in accessing government information across the spectrum of current government publishing and communication activity and whether copyright protection poses a barrier to access to government information. It then turns to reform of the subsistence and ownership provisions of the Commonwealth and States under the *Copyright Act 1968* and reform of the laws dealing with the role of government as preserver and user of copyright material. It concludes by discussing attempts by proprietors of copyright material to impose contractual and technological restrictions on the use of copyright material and it argues such practices, whether imposed by government or the private sector, should be prohibited where they conflict with public policy established by the *Copyright Act 1968*.

The Conclusion draws together themes which have been examined in earlier chapters and summarises reform proposals to the *Copyright Act 1968* dealing with copyright ownership, archival practices, library deposit and Crown use with a view to an improved legal framework for more effective access to government information and more efficient communication of information within government and between government and the wider community. It concludes government copyright law and practice in each of the roles as owner, preserver and user of copyright material has not responded adequately to the information age and to the desire and the ability of individuals to access information quickly and effectively.

The solution offered in this book is reform of the law and of public policy and, in particular, the introduction of a clearer, more coordinated and consistent licensing policy and one that is in step with access to information policy.

The rate of technological change and evolving views about the role of government in a liberal democracy suggest that laws and policy concerning government ownership, preservation and use of copyright material should be reviewed taking into account the policy considerations mentioned in this book. However, the government's role in all three areas should be continued for reasons of government accountability, effective administration and the preservation of national culture and heritage.[34]

---

34   The recommendations are consistent with the Five Goals in the Australian Government's National Cultural Policy, *Creative Australia,* released by the Australian Government in May 2013; see Australia. Department of Regional Australia, Local Government, Arts and Sport, *Creative Australia:National Cultural Policy* (2013) 44–49 http://creativeaustralia.arts.gov.au/assets/ Creative-Australia-PDF-20130417.pdf. They are: 1. Recognise, respect and celebrate the centrality of Aboriginal and Torres Strait Islander cultures to the uniqueness of Australian identity. 2. Ensure that government support reflects the diversity of Australia and that all citizens, wherever they live, whatever their background or circumstances, have a right to shape our cultural identity and its expression. 3. Support excellence and the special role of artists and their creative collaborators as the source of original work and ideas, including telling Australian stories. 4. Strengthen the capacity of the cultural sector to contribute to national life, community wellbeing and the economy. 5. Ensure Australian creativity thrives in the digitally enabled 21st century, by supporting innovation, the development of new creative content, knowledge and creative industries.

1

Legal and Policy Framework

This chapter aims to provide an understanding of the legal and policy framework in which the Australian government operates as proprietor, preserver and user of copyright material. It is necessary to understand the wide scope and diversity of the nature of modern Australian government, and the copyright material government produces, as well as major legal, policy and technological factors underlying the development and administration of government in order to evaluate the present and future direction of the role of government in these three areas.

This chapter will first describe the scope and diversity of modern Australian government and then examine what constitutes 'the Commonwealth or a State' under Part VII of the *Copyright Act 1968* (Cth): that is, the legal scope of government under the *Copyright Act 1968*. Part VII is headed 'the Crown' and 'the Commonwealth or a State' referred to in Part VII may conveniently be referred to by that title or simply as the 'government'.

This chapter will then provide a brief historical overview of the role of government under Anglo-Australian law as proprietor, preserver and user of copyright material before turning to legal and policy factors that are important in evaluating the future direction of the role of government in these three areas of governmental interest. Those factors are:

- the nature and extent of the protection of government material under Australia's copyright law and Australia's international copyright treaty obligations,
- Australian government administrative and managerial reforms and related Australian civil and political treaty obligations, and
- the impact of technological change on the dissemination of information, and the management of information by government, in this information age.

There are other factors in the 'perennial discourse'[1] of the role of government such as competing political interests and constituencies, and of bargaining and consensus between competing interests, which have an influence on the law and practices of government.[2] It is also evident from an historical analysis of the law that there have been some different policy considerations in the past that have contributed to forming government's

---

1   The Hon JJ Spigelman, 'Citizens, Consumers and Courts' (2001) 60 (4) *Australian Journal of Public Administration* 5.

present role. These are discussed in more depth in later chapters of this book. Nonetheless, an understanding of the listed factors is important in forming a basis for evaluation of the present and future direction of the role of government as proprietor, preserver and user of copyright material.

Scope and Diversity of Modern Australian Government

The Australian system of government is made up of legislative, executive and judicial components that are separately described in the *Australian Constitution* and exist in all state, territory and federal jurisdictions. Under the English common law legal system that Australia inherited at the time of the British colonisation of the territory of Australia, these components have their origins in the absolute power of the sovereign, from whom all legislative, executive and judicial powers emanate. In modern political theory the ultimate source of these component powers is not the sovereign but resides in the people who entrust government to exercise these powers on its behalf.[3]

The scope and complexity of each of the legislative, executive and judicial arms of government have increased over time. The legislative function is presently based on democratically elected representatives in most Houses of Parliament. The numbers of representatives have increased with population and political changes. Parliaments have created more committees and more of their work now relies on committee consideration of legislation or committee-based law reform. Parliaments have their own departments that provide services such as research and library services, Hansard, broadcasting and telecommunications, security and maintenance as well as secretariat support for the Houses of Parliament and for parliamentary committees.

Similarly, the judicial component of power is now exercised by a larger range of courts, some with specialised jurisdictions, and with more extensive judicial administration and training support from the highest to lowest in the hierarchy of courts.

But it is the exercise of executive power that has experienced the most change. Administrative review bodies, human rights and law enforcement review bodies have been established by federal, state and territory governments to exercise a quasi-judicial role. Policing has grown in size and nature and an independent director of public prosecutions in nearly

---

2   See, for example, Peter Drahos, 'Global Law Reform and Rent Seeking: The Case of Intellectual Property' (1996) 7 (1) *Australian Journal of Corporate Law*, where the author points out that sometimes law reform turns out to be 'a product that is generated by the self-interested exchanges that take place in the marketplace of politics' (at 45).

3   Refer, for example, to the judgment of Mason CJ in *Australian Capital Television Pty Ltd and New South Wales v Commonwealth* [1992] HCA 45 [31–42], in which he discussed the concepts of responsible and representative government embodied in the *Australian Constitution* in deciding that the *Constitution* contained an implied freedom of communication on matters relevant to public affairs and political discussion. 'Absent such a freedom of communication, representative government would fail to achieve its purpose, namely, government by the people through their elected representatives; government would cease to be responsive to the needs and wishes of the people and, in that sense, would cease to be truly representative' (38). The majority of the Court were of a similar view: 'The purpose of the Constitution was to further the institutions of representative and responsible government' (McHugh J at 12).

all jurisdictions now carries out the prosecutorial process. All governments have security arms. In the case of the federal government there are four, which focus on external or internal matters. The federal government also has responsibility for the defence forces of the federation—army, navy and air force. The number of federal executive departments (departments of state) has grown with increases in the complexity and size of government. There are currently 18 departments of state.

From the 1970s there has also been a dramatic growth in the number of statutory authorities that are empowered to exercise functions on behalf of government. At the federal level, for example, some are modern statutory emanations of functions formerly undertaken in departments of government such as the Australian Postal Corporation, Airservices Australia, the Civil Aviation Safety Authority, and the Australian Maritime Safety Authority, which are all bodies corporate under their constituent statutes. These authorities have some independence from government control. Some federal authorities established by enactment represent the widening complexities of government and government initiatives, such as the Albury–Wodonga Development Corporation and the Special Broadcasting Service Corporation, as well as the regulatory bodies Australian Prudential Regulation Authority (APRA), the Australian Competition and Consumer Commission (ACCC) and Australian Securities and Investments Commission (ASIC).[4]

In all there are currently around 190 Commonwealth entities and companies subject to the *Public Governance, Performance and Accountability Act 2013* (Cth) ('*PGPA Act*').[5] These include about 70 entities which are bodies corporate and more than 100 non-corporate Commonwealth entities. Among the non-corporate Commonwealth entities are the Australian Sports Anti-Doping Authority (ASADA) and more than 60 other entities whose officials are taken to be employed under the *Public Service Act 1999* (Cth); six prescribed agencies that encompass an 'Executive Agency' under the *Public Service Act 1999*,[6] such as the National Archives of Australia, and five prescribed agencies that engage personnel under their own Act and not the *Public Service Act*, such as the Australian Security Intelligence Organisation and APRA. There are also four parliamentary departments whose officials are employed under the *Parliamentary Service Act 1999* (Cth). [7]

The more than 70 Commonwealth bodies corporate under the *PGPA Act* have separate legal entities from the Commonwealth and have power to hold money on their own account

---

4   Australia. Department of Finance, *Public Governance, Performance and Accountability Act 2013 (PGPA Act) Commonwealth Entities and Companies (189)* 8 December 2014 http://www.finance.gov.au/flipchart/. The *PGPA Act* effectively supersedes the operation of both the *Financial Management and Accountability Act 1997* (Cth) ('*FMA Act*') and the *Commonwealth Authorities and Companies Act 1997* (Cth) ('*CAC Act*') which formerly governed Commonwealth entities. The *CAC Act* has been repealed. Refer to the *Public Governance, Performance and Accountability (Consequential and Transitional Provisions) Act 2014* (Cth), Schedules 2 and 3.

5   Australia. Department of Finance, *Public Governance, Performance and Accountability Act 2013 (PGPA Act) Commonwealth Entities and Companies (189) 8 December 2014* http://www.finance.gov.au/flipchart/.

6   Refer to Part 9 (ss 65–70) of the *Public Service Act 1999* (Cth).

7   Australia. Department of Finance, *Public Governance, Performance and Accountability Act 2013 (PGPA Act) Commonwealth Entities and Companies (189) 8 December 2014* http://www.finance.gov.au/flipchart/.

such as those modern statutory emanations of functions formerly undertaken in departments of government including the Civil Aviation Safety Authority and various primary industries research and development bodies (for example, the Grains Research and Development Corporation, the National Library of Australia, the Australian Government Solicitor, the National Museum of Australia, the Australian Film, Television and Radio School, and the National Film and Sound Archive). There are also 17 Commonwealth companies subject to the *PGPA Act* in which the Commonwealth has a controlling interest such as the Australian Railtrack Corporation Limited, NBN Co Limited and the ASC Pty Ltd (the Australian Submarine Corporation).[8]

Even when one considers the diverse nature of the interests that the departments of state represent, which sometimes conflict, such as those interests represented by the Department of Environment and the Department of Industry and the range of documents emanating from all of these departments, there is a much wider spectrum of governance interests than occurs in a private company or even a company group.

Government does not represent a single interest. It seeks to reconcile and resolve often competing interests in our society. And, unlike a private company, it is also responsible and accountable through its governing party platform and through its behaviour to the populace at large. Philosopher John Locke espoused the concept of a social contract to describe the relationship of citizen to state,[9] but this relationship is much more complex, broader and organic than, for example, the contract between company and shareholder, which is dominated by income and shareholder value and the sharing of economic interests.

Governments also have unique responsibilities. One is the armed defence of the citizens they govern, another is the order, safety and security of its subjects, another is the creation, passing and adjudication of laws governing citizens. The modern state has acquired, by popular will, a variety of responsibilities that no other body shares. They are compulsory state-run education, taxation, social security and public health, the preservation through public institutions of the culture and heritage of the society, the regulation of currency and foreign investment, the regulation of natural resources, employment, communications and transport, and initiatives in respect of indigenous affairs, planning, the environment and overseas aid. In carrying out its responsibilities it is subject to administrative review and to provision of access to documents to the extent no company or private sector body is presently subject.

Ergas Committee Report

In the report entitled *Review of Intellectual Property Legislation under the Competition Principles Agreement* (Ergas Committee), the Committee commented:

---

8 Australia. Department of Finance, *Public Governance, Performance and Accountability Act 2013 (PGPA Act) Commonwealth Entities and Companies (189) 8 December 2014* http://www.finance.gov.au/flipchart/.

9 Peter Laslett (ed), *John Locke: Two Treatises of Government* (Cambridge University Press, 1988) II, Ch VIII, § 95–99, Ch XIX § 212–240.

Rights granted

The Copyright Act provides that the Crown owns the copyright in any works made under the direction or control of the Commonwealth or a State (s 176). This section places the Crown in a more favourable position than other contractors or employers, who only become copyright owners under an assignment in writing, or subject to the terms of a contract of employment (implied or otherwise). The Crown is therefore not subject to normal contractual negotiations.

Cost-benefit analysis

The principles of competitive neutrality as set out in s. 3(1) [sic] of the Competition Principles Agreement provide that:

> The objective of competitive neutrality policy is the elimination of resource allocation distortions arising out of the public ownership of entities engaged in significant business activities: Government businesses should not enjoy any net competitive advantage simply as a result of their public sector ownership. These principles apply only to the business activities of publicly owned entities, not to the non-business, non-profit activities of those entities.[10]

The Ergas Committee concluded:

> The Committee does not believe that the Crown should benefit from preferential treatment under the *Copyright Act* as compared with other parties. As a result, we recommend that s 176 of the *Copyright Act* be amended to leave the Crown in the same position as any other contracting party.[11]

The argument of the Committee can be distilled as follows:

- The Crown is given wider rights than other employers under the law to own copyright.
- Government businesses should not enjoy any net competitive advantage simply as a result of their public sector ownership.
- Section 176 of the *Copyright Act 1968* should be amended to leave the Crown in the same position as any other contracting party.

The argument contains an unstated assumption that the Crown engages in business activities. But the Ergas Committee in its report did not address the question what bodies constituted the Crown under Part VII of the *Copyright Act 1968*. It also did not address the question of what bodies constituted government businesses.

The question of what bodies constituted the Crown under Part VII of the *Copyright Act 1968* was, however, discussed by the CLRC in its report, *Crown Copyright*.

---

10   Australia. Intellectual Property and Competition Review Committee, *Review of Intellectual Property Legislation under the Competition Principles Agreement* (Ergas Committee) (2000) 113.

11   Ibid 114.

What Constitutes the Crown Under Part VII of the *Copyright Act 1968*?

In relation to the way in which ss 176–178 in Division 1 of Part VII of the *Copyright Act 1968* operate, the CLRC in its *Crown Copyright* report expressed concern about the 'uncertainty'[12] created as to who is the Crown and in whom copyright will vest.

The CLRC listed three possible interpretations of the word 'Commonwealth' referred to in the sections.[13] One was that the Commonwealth was referred to as a legal person and includes agents or emanations of the Commonwealth. The second was that an entity that is included as the Commonwealth within the 'shield of the Crown' test would own copyright itself under ss 176–178. The third was that copyright vests in the Commonwealth as a legal person but is exercisable by the relevant authority. This third interpretation adopts the first view but accepts that, for administrative purposes, copyright is exercisable by the arm of government to which it relates.

In 2007, a paper produced by the Parliamentary Library of the Victorian Parliament examined the meaning of the term 'state' and concluded that Crown copyright was applicable to all three arms of government, including the Victorian Parliament and its administrative departments.[14] It based its view on s 15 of the *Constitution Act 1975* (Vic) that refers to the legislative power as part of the State of Victoria.

Section 10(1), in the interpretation section of the *Copyright Act 1968,* provides:

> *the Crown* includes the Crown in right of a State, the Crown in right of the Northern Territory and the Crown in right of Norfolk Island and also includes the Administration of a Territory other than the Northern Territory or Norfolk Island.
>
> *the Commonwealth* includes the Administration of a Territory.

Sections 176–178 in Division 1 of Part VII of the *Copyright Act 1968,* dealing with the vesting of copyright, refer to 'the Commonwealth or a State'. They are collectively referred to in the heading and most of the subheadings of Part VII of the Act as 'the Crown'.

The Scope of 'the Commonwealth or a State'

In most practical respects when we think of the 'Commonwealth' or the 'State', we think of the governments of the Commonwealth or the States or, more precisely, the executive governments of these juristic persons. In essence, the executive governments comprise the departments of government and bodies within ministerial portfolios that are responsible to ministers who in turn are responsible to Parliament and are appointed by the sovereign's

---

12   Australia. Copyright Law Review Committee, *Crown Copyright* (2005) 6, 8, 74, 113.

13   Ibid 74–75.

14   Victoria. Economic Development and Infrastructure Committee, Parliament of Victoria, *Inquiry into Improving Access to Victorian Public Sector Information and Data: Discussion Paper (July 2008)* Parliamentary Paper No 198, Session 2006–2009, 21
http://www.parliament.vic.gov.au/edic/inquiries/inquiry/31.

representative to administer policy portfolios. These executive governments are formally described as the Crown in right of the Commonwealth or State respectively.

However, unlike the headings, the sections in Part VII generally use the term 'the Commonwealth or a State' and not 'the Crown'. There are some exceptions. In Division 1 of Part VII, s 182A refers to 'any prerogative right or privilege of the Crown' that are expressly preserved by the *Copyright Act 1968* in s 8A(1). In Division 2 of Part VII—which is headed 'Use of Copyright Material for the Crown'—s 183(2) uses the expression 'the Government of the Commonwealth'.[15] In the same Division, ss 183A–183C use the terms 'government' and 'government copies'. However, s 182B defines 'government' to mean 'the Commonwealth or a State' for the purposes of that Division. 'State' is defined in s 10(3)(n) of the *Copyright Act 1968*, as modified by the *ACT Self-Government (Consequential Provisions) Regulations*,[16] to include the Australian Capital Territory, the Northern Territory and Norfolk Island.

The use of 'the Commonwealth or a State' suggests that the 'Commonwealth' or the 'State' is not confined to the Crown in right of the Commonwealth, or the Crown in right of the State, that is, the executive government of the Commonwealth or a State. Neither the Commonwealth nor a State is so defined in the *Copyright Act 1968*. Section 2B of the *Acts Interpretation Act 1901* (Cth) defines the Commonwealth to mean the Commonwealth of Australia, which is the body politic of Australia.[17] That body politic established by the *Commonwealth of Australia Constitution Act 1900* (Imp)[18] is divided under that Constitution into three broad arms—the executive, legislative and judicial—that comprise the essential functions of government. Section 6 of the *Commonwealth of Australia Constitution* defines 'the Commonwealth' to mean 'the Commonwealth of Australia as established under this Act'.[19] The view that the use of the term 'the Commonwealth or State' refers to the three arms of government in either case is supported in *Linter Group Ltd (in liq) v Price Waterhouse*[20] in which Justice Harper of the Supreme Court of Victoria expressed the view that the Supreme Court 'as one of the three arms of government of the State of Victoria' is, for the purposes of s 176 of the *Copyright Act 1968*, the State.

---

15 In s 183(2) the reference to 'Government of the Commonwealth' making agreements with the 'Government of some other country' would appear in its context to relate only to the executive government of the Commonwealth, despite the later (1998) insertion of the definition of 'government' in s 182B.

16 Statutory Rules 1989 No 392 (Cth).

17 Section 2B of the *Acts Interpretation Act 1901* (Cth). The '*Commonwealth*', means the Commonwealth of Australia and, when used in a geographical sense, includes the Territory of Christmas Island and the Territory of Cocos (Keeling) Islands, but does not include any other external territory.

18 63 & 64 Vict, c 12, s 9.

19 Section 6 of the *Commonwealth of Australia Constitution Act 1900* (Imp): '*The States* shall mean such of the colonies of New South Wales, New Zealand, Queensland, Tasmania, Victoria, Western Australia and South Australia, including the northern territory of South Australia, as for the time being are parts of the Commonwealth, and such colonies or territories as may be admitted into or established by the Commonwealth as States; and each of such parts of the Commonwealth shall be called a *State*.'

20 [2000] VSC 90 (20 March 2000).

The Broad Test: 'Organisations or Institutions of Government'

In *Deputy Federal Commissioner of Taxation v State Bank of NSW*[21] it was argued by the State Bank of New South Wales that it was the 'State of New South Wales' and was thus not subject to a Commonwealth law that imposed a tax on its property in contravention of s 114 of the *Constitution*. The High Court of Australia rejected arguments that the State Bank must show it is the Crown 'in right of the State' or that it is entitled to the privileges or immunities of the State that is, 'within the shield of the Crown' in respect of the application of the taxing statute. The Full Bench of the High Court stated:

19. The plaintiff submits ... that the question is to be determined by asking whether the State Bank is entitled to 'the privileges and immunities of the Crown' in accordance with the approach adopted in *Townsville Hospitals Board v. Townsville City Council*. Again, this submission has little to commend it. The 'shield of the Crown' doctrine has evolved as a means of ascertaining whether an agency or instrumentality 'represents' the Crown for the purpose of determining whether that agency or instrumentality is bound by a statute enacted by the legislature ... The question which arises here is not to be answered by reference to a doctrine which has evolved with the object of answering questions of a different kind. The question here 'depends upon the meaning and operation of an unalterable constitutional provision which the intention of the legislature cannot affect' *Bank of NSW v The Commonwealth* (1948) 76 CLR per Dixon J at p 359.

20. Once it is accepted that the Constitution refers to the Commonwealth and the States as organisations or institutions of government in accordance with the conceptions of ordinary life, it must follow that these references are wide enough to denote a corporation which is an agency or instrumentality of the Commonwealth or a State as the case may be. The activities of government are carried on not only through the departments of government but also through corporations which are agencies or instrumentalities of government. Such activities have, since the nineteenth century, included the supply on commercial terms of certain types of goods and services by government owned and controlled instrumentalities with independent corporate personalities. Railways are a notable example. As early as 1906, in *The Federated Amalgamated Government Railway and Tramway Service Association v The New South Wales Railway Traffic Employees Association* (the 'Railway Servants Case') [1906] HCA 94; (1906) 4 CLR 488, this Court recognised that the railway undertakings of the colonial governments carried on by incorporated Railway Commissioners were instrumentalities of those governments, ibid., per Griffith CJ at p 535, Likewise, banking activities were conducted by corporations under legislation enacted by the colonial legislatures before federation and the Constitution expressly exempted 'State banking', i.e., 'banks established and conducted by a State or by an authority established under State law and representing a State': *Melbourne Corporation v The Commonwealth* [1947] HCA 26; (1947) 74 CLR 31 per Latham CJ at p 52, from the reach of the legislative power with respect to banking conferred by s.51 (xiii).[22]

---

21   [1992] HCA 6; (1992) 174 CLR 219.

The concept of the Commonwealth or a State 'as organisations or institutions of government in accordance with the conceptions of ordinary life' is wider than the concept of what constitutes a part of the executive government of the Commonwealth or a State. As the majority of the High Court in *Austral Pacific Group v Airservices Australia* stated:

> 10 ... Airservices was established as a body corporate by s 7 of the Airservices Act to perform such functions as the provision of facilities to permit safe aircraft navigation within Australian-administered airspace (s 8(1)(a)). This and other provisions of the statute indicate that Airservices is a Commonwealth agency or instrumentality which is included in the term 'the Commonwealth' in s 75(iii) of the *Constitution*.
>
> ...
>
> 14. Airservices is a body corporate which, while it is charged with the performance of what may be classed as governmental functions, is not part of the executive government of the Commonwealth. Airservices is sued by Austral Pacific as the Commonwealth within the meaning of s 75(iii) of the *Constitution* but it does not necessarily follow that Airservices attracts the preferences, immunities and exceptions enjoyed by the executive government in respect of State laws and identified with the *Cigamatic* doctrine.[23]

Airservices Australia is one of more than 70 bodies corporate established by Commonwealth enactment that are corporate Commonwealth entities subject to the *PGPA Act*.

McHugh J in the same case stated:

> Section 75(iii) of the *Constitution* vests original jurisdiction in the High Court in all matters 'in which the Commonwealth, or a person suing or being sued on behalf of the Commonwealth, is a party'. In a number of cases, the Court has held that various Commonwealth statutory corporations were persons 'suing or being sued on behalf of the Commonwealth' for the purposes of s 75(iii). In *Inglis v Commonwealth Trading Bank of Australia*, however, the Court expressed a difference of opinion on the question whether the Commonwealth Trading Bank was 'the Commonwealth' or 'a person suing or being sued on behalf of the Commonwealth'. In *Maguire v Simpson* the Court decided that the Commonwealth Trading Bank was 'the Commonwealth' for the purposes of s 64 of the *Judiciary Act*. In a number of cases, a Commonwealth statutory corporation was simply held to be within some part of s 75(iii). In *Deputy Commissioner of Taxation v State Bank (NSW)*, the Court said:
>
> 'No doubt [the words 'a person suing or being sued on behalf of the Commonwealth'] were included in order to ensure that the jurisdiction conferred extended to cases in which the Commonwealth itself was not the nominal plaintiff or

---

22   Ibid paras 19–20 (joint judgment of Mason CJ, Brennan, Deane, Dawson, Toohey, Gaudron and McHugh JJ).

23   [2000] HCA 39; (2000) 203 CLR 136, paras 10, 14 per Gleeson CJ, Gummow and Hayne JJ.

defendant. But that circumstance cannot operate as a reason for reading the references to the Commonwealth in the *Constitution* in a restricted sense.'

Although nothing turns on it in this appeal, the better view is that, in both s 75(iii) of the *Constitution* and s 64 of the *Judiciary Act*, 'the Commonwealth' includes Commonwealth statutory corporations or authorities like the third party in the present case.[24]

All those statutory authorities that are presently Commonwealth authorities for *PGPA Act* purposes may thus potentially be included in McHugh J's conception of the scope of the 'Commonwealth' under s 75(iii) of the *Constitution*.[25] While it is relatively easy to identify the legislative and judicial arms of the Commonwealth, it may be seen from these cases that determining the scope of the 'Commonwealth' within the meaning of the *Constitution* is not so clear-cut. The views expressed by the High Court of Australia on the scope of s 75(iii) of the *Constitution* suggest that what constitutes the 'Commonwealth' clearly extends beyond those bodies that constitute the executive government.[26]

Similarly, in *Australian Securities and Investments Commission v Edensor Nominees*, the Full Bench of the High Court of Australia held that the Commission (ASIC) was an agency or instrumentality of the Commonwealth[27] and thus answers the description of 'the Commonwealth' in s 75(iii) of the *Constitution*. This is one of more than 100 Commonwealth agencies presently subject to the *PGPA Act* and the *Public Service Act 1999* (Cth). In the *ASIC* case, Gleeson CJ, Gaudron and Gummow JJ expressed the considerations that led the Court to that conclusion:

> 39. The first question which arises concerns the status of ASIC. It is established by ss 7 and 8 of the ASIC Act as a body corporate. That circumstance does not, of itself, deny the proposition that ASIC falls within the scope of the expression 'the Commonwealth' in s 75(iii) of the *Constitution*. In an appropriate context, those words are of sufficient width to include a corporation which is an agency or instrumentality of the Commonwealth. The ASIC Act provides (s 9) that its members are

---

24 Ibid para 48.

25 McHugh J referred to s 7(1) of the *Commonwealth Authorities and Companies Act 1997* (Cth) ('*CAC Act*') that defined a Commonwealth authority as a body that holds money on its own account and is a body corporate that is incorporated for a public purpose by an Act or by regulations under an Act. McHugh J did not include the 25 Commonwealth (controlled) companies under the *CAC Act*.

26 This wider view extends to 'the State'—refer to *SGH Ltd v Commissioner of Taxation* (2002) 210 CLR 51 (1 May 2002); [2002] HCA 18, para 13: 'Against the background of these other provisions of the Constitution, it is evident that references in s 114 to the Commonwealth and a State are not to be understood narrowly. Reinforcement for that view comes from other provisions of the Constitution and, in particular, s 75. It was in the context of s 75 and its provisions for the original jurisdiction of this Court, that Dixon J referred to the Constitution going 'directly to the conceptions of ordinary life' and said that: "From beginning to end [the Constitution] treats the Commonwealth and the States as organizations or institutions of government possessing distinct individualities. Formally they may not be juristic persons, but they are conceived as politically organized bodies having mutual legal relations and amenable to the jurisdiction of courts upon which the responsibility of enforcing the Constitution rests." ' (per Gleeson CJ, Gaudron, McHugh and Hayne JJ).

27 (2001) 204 CLR 559; [2001] HCA 1, para 39.

appointed by the Governor-General on the nomination of the Minister administering the ASIC Act. Provision is made in s 12 of the ASIC Act for the giving by the Minister of written directions to ASIC respecting the exercise of its functions and powers. Those functions and powers are spelled out in ss 11 and 12A and pertain to the executive functions of government. Section 120 of the ASIC Act provides that the staff of ASIC are appointed as employees under the *Public Service Act 1922* (Cth). The Parliament appropriates money for the purposes of ASIC (s 133) and its activities are inquired into by the Parliamentary Joint Committee on Corporations and Securities appointed pursuant to s 241 of the ASIC Act. ASIC is subjected to audit by the Auditor-General under s 8 of the Commonwealth Authorities and Companies Act 1997 (Cth).

40. This is a clear case of a corporation established by a law of the Commonwealth which answers the description of 'the Commonwealth' in s 75(iii) of the *Constitution*.[28]

There are few court decisions that directly address the question of what constitutes the Commonwealth or a State for the purposes of the *Copyright Act 1968*. All judges of the Full Court of the Federal Court of Australia in *Re Australasian Performing Right Association Ltd; Re Australian Broadcasting Commission* were of the view that the primary task in determining whether a public corporation is an emanation or instrumentality of the Commonwealth for the purposes of the *Copyright Act 1968*, is to determine the intention of the legislature that appears from the statute under which the body is established.[29] In the absence of an express provision on the question, matters to be considered

> include the question whether the corporation fulfills a governmental or non-governmental function; the capacity of the Government to control its activities; financial autonomy; the right of appointment and dismissal of the members of the body and of its staff by the Government; whether it has duties to furnish information or accounts to the Government; and its power over assets in its ownership or control.[30]

The Narrower Test: 'Shield of the Crown'

The Full Court of the Federal Court took the view that the Australian Broadcasting Commission did not fall within the word 'Commonwealth' nor was it an agency or instrumentality of the Commonwealth for the purposes of s 183 of the *Copyright Act 1968*. In reaching that conclusion, the Full Court examined those matters in relation to the *Broadcasting and Television Act 1942* (Cth), the most important of which was the degree of legal control exercisable by the minister or government over the body in question. In reaching their conclusion, however, the judges of the Full Court considered both cases dealing with whether bodies fell within the scope of the 'Commonwealth' under s 75(iii) of the

---

28   Ibid paras 39, 40. Refer also to paras 215, 147, 190 of this case.

29   Refer to (1982) 45 ALR 153 at 158, 167.

30   (1982) 45 ALR 153 at 158, per Bowen CJ and Franki J.

Constitution, such as *Inglis v Commonwealth Trading Bank of Australia*,[31] and whether they were an instrumentality or agent of the Crown in right of the Commonwealth or State, that is, entitled to exercise the privileges and immunities of the Crown, including *Townsville Hospitals Board v Council of the City of Townsville*.[32] While both questions are determined by statutory interpretation based on similar tests, the latter is a narrower question than the former.

The interpretative tests were also applied in *Allied Mills Industries Pty Ltd v Trade Practices Commission (No 1)*[33] where the Federal Court held the Trade Practices Commission was an emanation or agency of the Crown in right of the Commonwealth and thus fell within the meaning of s 183 of the *Copyright Act 1968*.[34]

Sheppard J in that case examined the purposes and objects of the *Trade Practices Act 1974* (Cth) and the power of ministerial control over the Commission set out in s 29 of the Act in reaching the view that the Commission was an emanation or agency of the Crown. He stated:

> 121. Section 183 of the *Copyright Act* provides that the copyright in a work is not infringed by the Commonwealth or a State, or by a person authorised in writing by the Commonwealth or a State, doing any acts comprised in the copyright if the acts are done for the services of the Commonwealth or State. As a matter of precaution the Commission obtained an authority from the Commonwealth to use the various documents. But I have held that the Commission is an agency or emanation of the Crown. The authority was not therefore necessary. I am satisfied that the use to which the Commission has put the documents or to which it will put them in the future has been or will be for the services of the Commonwealth.[35]

The difficulty in the narrower 'shield of the Crown' test is that courts have recognised that it may be possible for an agency or instrumentality to be endowed with the attributes of the Crown for one purpose but not for others or that the legislature could explicitly endow a private corporation carrying on business for private purposes with the privileges and immunities of the Crown and yet that corporation would not answer the description of the 'State' or 'Commonwealth' for constitutional purposes.

Commonwealth and State enactments establishing bodies corporate do not usually include any express provision endowing the attributes of the Crown either in respect of some or all of the functions of the particular body. The few examples in the Commonwealth

---

31   [1969] HCA 44; (1969) 119 CLR 334.

32   (1982) 42 ALR 319 (HC).

33   [1981] FCA 11; (1981) 55 FLR 125.

34   Per Sheppard J, paras 32, 34, 121.

35   Sheppard J stated at para 34. 'Since reserving my decision my attention has been drawn to the joint judgment of Deane and Fisher JJ in *Thomson Publications (Australia) Pty Ltd v Trade Practices Commission* (1979) 40 FLR 257. They reached the conclusion that the Commission was "plainly an instrumentality or agent of the Crown in right of the Commonwealth" (1979) 40 FLR, at p 275. Their decision in that respect is, of course, binding on me'.

sphere where statutory reference is made to the privileges and immunities of the Crown in fact only negate the attributes of the Crown.[36] There are no Commonwealth enactments that contain a specific provision giving a corporation the character of an emanation or agency of the Commonwealth or a State for the purposes of the *Copyright Act 1968*. In a direct sense, the tests of statutory intention whether a body is entitled to be considered the 'Commonwealth' or 'State' for the purposes of the *Copyright Act 1968* have been used to determine the scope of the executive government of the Commonwealth or State and the legal person of the 'Commonwealth' or the 'State'. While there is some lack of clarity in the case law on the question, it is submitted the better view in law is that the terms the 'Commonwealth' or the 'State' comprise the legal persons identified in the *Australian Constitution* 'as organisations or institutions of government in accordance with the conceptions of ordinary life', that is, comprising the three elements of governance identified in the *Constitution* exercising legislative, executive and judicial power.[37]

Ergas Committee Conclusion

It is important to note that regardless of which test is applied to the terms 'Commonwealth' or 'State', many governmental organisations that form a part of the 'Commonwealth' or the 'State' do not engage in business activities. The legislative and judicial organs of government are clearly not engaged in business within meaning of the principles of competitive neutrality set out in clause 3(1) of the Competition Principles Agreement, adopted by the Australian Council of Australian Governments upon which the Ergas Committee relies.[38]

Similarly, it is clear from annual reports of the bodies concerned that the core of the executive government comprising those departments of government may be engaged in the 'business of government' but the essential functions of government are not a 'business' in the commercial competitive sense.

Thus the conclusion that the Ergas Committee expressed is founded on an erroneous assumption. Logically, that committee should have restricted its recommendation to commercial competitive government activities. The irony is that the more likely government bodies are in commercial activities competitive with the private sector the less likely they

---

36 Examples are s 8 of the *Christmas Island Agreement Act 1958* (Cth), s 8 of the *Snowy Hydro Corporatisation Act 1997* (Cth) and s 6 of the *Housing Loans Insurance Corporation (Transfer of Assets and Abolition) Act 1996* (Cth).

37 The Copyright Law Review Committee in its *Crown Copyright* report at 6–7 stated that the scope of what is meant by the Crown is somewhat uncertain and outlined arguments for both the broader view that it encompassed the legislative, executive and judicial arms (an inclusive view) or the narrower view that it refers only the executive arm of government. It did not express a concluded view on the question: Australia. Copyright Law Review Committee, *Crown Copyright*, (Canberra 2005), 6, 7 [paras 2.04–2.06].

38 'The objective of competitive neutrality policy is the elimination of resource allocation distortions arising out of the public ownership of entities engaged in significant business activities: Government businesses should not enjoy any net competitive advantage simply as a result of their public sector ownership. These principles apply only to the business activities of publicly owned entities, not to the non-business, non-profit activities of those entities'. Australia. Council of Australian Governments, *Competition Principles Agreement—11 April 1995* (as amended to 13 April 2007) http://www.coag.gov.au/node/52.

are to fall within the 'Commonwealth' or the 'State' under Part VII of the *Copyright Act 1968* under either test of the scope of those terms.[39]

The Australian Copyright Legal and Policy Framework

Australian copyright law and the provisions dealing with government ownership are derived from the copyright law of the United Kingdom. The Crown in the United Kingdom for centuries exercised control over the dissemination of works through censorship, guild and other laws and exercised its own proprietary rights in the nature of copyright. Shortly after the earliest beginnings of printing in England, it created an Office of King's Printer to publish works of state and of the established religion. Subsequently, under the statutory copyright regime prior to the Imperial *Copyright Act 1911*, the government owned and exercised rights in accordance with the generally applicable copyright statutory provisions, whether in Australia or the United Kingdom. Specific provisions on government ownership were inserted in the 1911 Act, which was applied in Australia by the *Copyright Act 1912* (Cth) and have been continued under the *Copyright Act 1968* (Cth). The major provisions—ss 176 and 178—dealing with the vesting of copyright in government of works by their servants and employees extend slightly beyond the scope of that applicable to other employers, and the government has by virtue of first publication wider rights than those granted to other copyright owners. These provisions are discussed in more detail in Chapter 2 of this book.

In Anglo-Australian practice, governments have preserved their own records and have done so for longer, more extensively and more thoroughly than any other institution in their societies. Present governmental archival practices and laws are discussed in more detail in Chapter 4 of this book. From early times, the British Government has sought to preserve the published culture of its nation by the compulsory deposit of works of its citizens in public libraries. The earliest Anglo common law deposit regime precedes the first British copyright statute, the *Statute of Anne 1709*, by almost a century but was continued and widened in that Act and in later statutory form as part of succeeding copyright laws. This tradition was adopted by Australian colonial laws and is now embodied in Australian federal and state deposit laws. These laws and practices are discussed in detail in Chapter 5 of this book.

Governments have in practice also been users of other copyright material. Until the Australian *Copyright Act 1968*, the legal position of government for acts done over another's copyright material was not clear. Previous statutes were not expressed to bind the Crown and so it is unlikely the government could be held to infringe another's copyright.[40] Under

---

39 Of the more than 70 bodies corporate subject to the *PGPA Act*, a very small proportion are in competition with the private sector, such as Australia Post in respect of most of its postal services, the Australian Broadcasting Corporation and the Special Broadcasting Service Corporation over their broadcasting activities, the Australian Government Solicitor (in part only) and Defence Housing Australia in respect of investment in, and sale of, housing for the defence forces. Some of these statutory authorities such as the CSIRO and primary industry research and development corporations may enter into commercialisation arrangements with the private sector and many receive some funding from the private sector. Of the 17 Commonwealth companies under the *PGPA Act*, a greater proportion are in competition with the private sector.

the *Copyright Act 1968* (Cth) that position changed, and except in relation to offences, the government was bound by its own copyright law.[41] Under that Act, government use of other copyright material has been facilitated by a Crown use provision that enables wider copying of copyright works subject to a claim for compensation by the relevant owners of copyright. Crown use is discussed in detail in Chapter 6 of this book.

Anglo-Australian legal history, from the earliest beginnings to the first copyright statute, shows that government exercised regulatory control over the exploitation of works, exercised its own rights in 'the copy', granted rights and preserved its own works and the works of others through its own archival institutions and through library deposit. In essence the role of government as owner, preserver and user of copyright material has been intertwined with the development of the law of copyright. Government interests and rights in these areas are not alien or recent manifestations of legal policy but represent long recognised aspects of Anglo-Australian law.

Nature and Scope of Government Copyright

Through the grant of exclusive rights, government, like other copyright owners, is able to control the exploitation of a work. Government is also able to claim copyright in all material protected by the law.

The material protected by copyright and the nature and extent of the exclusive rights granted to the copyright owner under the law has expanded in response to technological development.

Copyright law in its initial statutory conception began with the *Statute of Anne*. This enactment—an Act 'for the encouragement of learning'—gave to authors the limited period of protection over the printing of the author's books for 14 years, renewable, if the author was then living, for another 14 years.[42] Under the statute, protection was limited to 'books' and the author was granted the right to print the author's books and to prevent unauthorised importation, publication, sale and exposure to sale of those books.[43] Literary property in unpublished works, that is the right to print and publish those works, continued at common law until publication.[44]

---

40   Refer to Australia. *Report of the Committee Appointed by the Attorney-General of the Commonwealth to Consider what Alterations are Desirable in the Copyright Law of the Commonwealth* (Spicer Committee) (Canberra, 1959) 76, para 401.

41   *Copyright Act 1968* (Cth) s 7.

42   8 Anne, c 19 (1709). The term for books not already printed and published at the time of the statute coming into force.

43   The colonies in Australia—which inherited English laws at the time of their establishment—were subject to later amendments to English laws on copyright. These were the *Copyright Act 1814* (54 Geo 3, c 156), which increased the term of literary copyright to 28 years from the date of publication or the life of the author, whichever was longer, the *Copyright Act 1842* (5 & 6 Vict, c 45), which extended the term of protection to 42 years from first publication or the life of the author plus seven years, whichever was longer, and the *International Copyright Act 1886* (49 & 50 Vict, c 33), the latter two of which extended throughout the British dominions. While four colonies passed laws with concurrent effect to the imperial enactments, the British regime continued after the federation of the Australian states with the adoption of the Imperial *Copyright Act 1911* by the *Copyright Act 1912* (Cth).

From this beginning, the length of protection, the subject matter of protection and the nature of the rights expanded over the next two centuries. The *Copyright Act 1814*[45] increased the term of literary copyright to 28 years or the date of the first publication of the life of the author, whichever was the longer. Subsequently, the *Copyright Act 1842*[46] extended the term to 42 years from first publication, or the author's life plus seven years, whichever was longer. The 1842 Act defined copyright as the sole and exclusive liberty of printing or otherwise multiplying copies of any 'book' that was broadly defined.[47] It included sheet music. Prints and engravings were the subject of copyright enactments in 1735, 1766,[48] 1777, 1836 and 1852.[49] Sculptures were given copyright protection by acts of 1798 and 1814.[50] The *Publication of Lectures Act 1835* was the first occasion in which copyright protection extended to works in oral form.[51] Paintings, drawings and photographs were given protection by the *Fine Art Copyright Act 1862*.[52] Performing rights were first conferred by the *Dramatic Literary Copyright Act 1833*,[53] and were extended from dramatic works to musical works by the *Copyright Act 1842*.

While the Australian Parliament passed the first federal copyright enactment in 1905, this Act effectively supplemented imperial copyright acts operating within Australia. The present law of copyright in Australia is founded on the British *Copyright Act 1911*. This enactment codified the whole law of copyright for the first time. Under the Australian *Copyright Act 1912* (Cth), which implemented the Imperial *Copyright Act 1911*, protection was given to authors generally for a period of the life of the author plus 50 years and to a wider range of material—original literary, dramatic, musical and artistic works and sound recordings—and the exclusive rights included the right to reproduce a work in a material form, to publish the work, to perform the work in public, and to produce a version of the work (such as a translation). Under the current law—the *Copyright Act 1968*—protection has been given to authors generally for the life of the author plus 70 years and the material protected by copyright has expanded to cover television and sound broadcasts, cinematograph films, published editions of works, computer software and the exclusive rights have

---

44   This position was later reaffirmed by the House of Lords decision in *Donaldson v Beckett* (1774) 4 Burr 2408; 98 ER 201. That case established that the common law right to print and publish works ceased upon publication and after publication was governed solely by statute.

45   54 Geo 3, c 156.

46   5 & 6 Vict, c 45.

47   Ibid ss 2, 29. The *International Copyright Act 1886* (49 & 50 Vict, c 33) was passed to enable the bringing of the *Berne Convention* into effect. The Convention came into force on 5 December 1887. Refer generally to K Lindgren, WA Rothnie and JC Lahore, *Copyright and Designs* (LexisNexis, 2004) Vol 1, [4140–4150], specifically [4145].

48   *Engravers' Copyright Act 1735* (8 Geo 2, c13) and *Engravers' Copyright Act 1766* (7 Geo 3, c 38).

49   *Engravers' Copyright Act 1777* (17 Geo 3, c 57), *Copyright in Prints and Engravings (Ireland) Act 1836* (6 & 7 Will 4, c 59) and *International Copyright Act 1852* (15 & 16 Vict, c 12).

50   *Models and Busts Act 1798* (38 Geo 3, c 71); *Sculpture Copyright Act 1814* (54 Geo 3, c 56).

51   5 & 6 Will 4, c 65.

52   25 & 26 Vict, c 68.

53   3 & 4 Will 4, c 15.

widened to include the right to communicate the work to the public, that is to make available online or electronically transmit the work to the public. The material protected by copyright and the exclusive rights enjoyed by copyright owners include copyright material vested in government. The rights apply to government as they do to all other copyright owners. However, under Part VII of the *Copyright Act 1968* the duration of protection given to government works is limited to the life of the author plus 50 years,[54] which is less than the generally applicable term of life plus 70 years for works.[55]

Under Part IX of the *Copyright Act 1968*, there are also rights of a moral nature granted to authors of works and cinematograph films that provide a right of attribution of authorship (the right to be identified as the author), the right to prohibit the false attribution of authorship and the right of integrity of authorship (the distortion, mutilation or alteration of a work that is prejudicial to an author's honour or reputation). Moral rights are recognised in the major multilateral copyright conventions and have their origins in civil law copyright regimes. In Australia, these rights apply to all authors irrespective of whether the copyright is owned by another, such as the government or private employer. The rights cannot be assigned. The author can, however, give permission for any of these acts and a consent may be given by an employee for the benefit of his or her employer in relation to all or any acts or omissions (whether occurring before or after the consent is given) and in relation to all works made or to be made by the employee in the course of his or her employment.[56] If the author of a government submission or report, for example, is a government servant or employee, authorship of a work must be attributed to the employee and must not be attributed to another person unless the consent of the author is obtained.

As a general principle, ownership of copyright vests in the originator or author of the material but if a work is created in the course of employment, copyright in the work will normally vest in the employer and not the author.[57] Under Part VII of the *Copyright Act 1968*, the Crown is the owner of copyright in works, films and sound recordings 'made by, or under the direction or control of' the Commonwealth or State. The scope of this phrase, which appears in ss 176–178 in Part VII, may extend beyond creation in the course of employment with the Crown, and is discussed further in Chapter 2 of this book. These provisions dealing with the vesting of ownership may be modified by agreement between the Crown and the author or maker.[58] Under the *Copyright Act 1968*, copyright is personal property and may be assigned in writing in whole or in part and may be so assigned in respect of future copyright.[59] Copyright may also be licensed in respect of existing or future copyright.[60] The assignment and licensing provisions apply to the government as well as all other copyright owners.

---

54 *Copyright Act 1968* (Cth) pt VII s 180.

55 Ibid pt III s 33.

56 Ibid pt IX s 195AWA(4). In New Zealand, the right to be identified as the author of a work does not apply to work in which Crown copyright exists—*Copyright Act 1994* (NZ) s 97(7).

57 *Copyright Act 1968* (Cth) pt III s 35(6).

58 Ibid pt VII s 179.

59 Ibid pt X s 196.

60 Ibid pt X, ss 196 and 197.

The Notion of Balance

While copyright is statutorily expressed in Australia to grant a number of 'exclusive' rights to the copyright owner that enable the copyright owner to control the exploitation of a work, copyright does not provide absolute rights in the sense that no dealing with the owner's work could ever take place without the owner's consent. This is the position under Australian and other national laws where copyright is protected. It is also the position under the international conventions governing copyright. The most universal exception is when dealing with an insubstantial part of a work. Beyond that, both national and international laws permit more extensive dealings without the permission of the copyright owner for limited purposes of a public benefit nature such as copying by libraries and archives for users and for preservation, and copying by individuals for research or study. The relationship between these limited defences to infringement and the Crown use of copyright material under Australian law is discussed in detail in Chapter 6 of this book.

This notion of a balance between the interest of owners of copyright and users of copyright material is evident in the historical development of copyright law. Similar defences to infringement existed under the *Copyright Act 1912* (Cth) and, prior to that Act, although there were no express statutory defences to infringement contained in the various British enactments that applied to the colonies of Australia, courts developed a doctrine of 'fair abridgment' that later became 'fair dealing', that recognised the utility of such actions.[61] Prior to the *Statute of Anne* of 1709, the law recognised 'rights in the copy' through government regulatory control of printing and publishing, the common law recognition of authors' rights over their unpublished works and through the Crown's exercise of printing privileges, that is, the grant by exercise of the royal prerogative to authors and publishers of exclusive rights to print and publish works. Most of these privileges were of limited duration. There is no evidence that they were absolute in the sense that any dealing without the consent of the copyright holder was an infringement.[62]

Australia's International Copyright Treaty Obligations

Since 1886 the material protected by copyright and the nature and extent of exclusive rights granted to the copyright owner have been governed by multilateral copyright and neighbouring rights treaties that prescribe minimum standards for protection and require

---

61   Refer to *Gyles v Wilcox* (1740) 2 Atkyns 141, *D'Almaine v Boosey* (1835) 1 Younge & Colyer, Exch. 288, 301; and the literary piracy cases *Wilkins v Aikin* (1810) 17 Vesey 422, *Spiers v Brown* (1858) 6 W R 352, *Folsom v Marsh* (1841) 9 F Cas 342, 2 Story (Amer) 100, and *Leslie v Young* [1895] AC 341, and generally TE Scrutton, *The Law of Copyright* (William Clowes and Sons, 3rd edn, 1896) 130–9. The principal Acts affecting the colonies of Australia were the *Copyright Act 1814*, which increased the term of literary copyright to 28 years from the date of publication or the life of the author, whichever was longer, the *Copyright Act 1842*, which extended the term of protection to 42 years from first publication or the life of the author plus seven years, whichever was longer, and the *International Copyright Act of 1886*, the latter two of which extended throughout the British dominions.

62   For an examination of the nature of the prerogative right based on an analysis of original grants (commonly referred to as privileges), refer to JS Gilchrist, *Crown Copyright: An Analysis of Rights Vesting in the Crown under Statute and Common Law and their Interrelationship* (LLM Thesis, Monash University, 1983) 15–21 or John Gilchrist, 'Origins and Scope of the Prerogative Right to Print and Publish Certain Works in England' (2012) 11 (2) *Canberra Law Review* 4.

contracting states to those treaties to recognise copyright in works of nationals of other contracting states and works first published in those states. These standards are themselves derived from national experience. Copyright was then and is now an international form of property, and the age of electronic communications with virtually instant means of accessing information worldwide has highlighted the importance of international treaties to the exploitative and moral rights involved in copyright. The oldest copyright treaty is the *Berne Convention*, concluded on September 9, 1886 and its latest revision is the Paris Act of 1971. That treaty has been augmented by more recent multilateral treaties: the TRIPS Agreement, the *WIPO Copyright Treaty* (WCT) and the *WIPO Performances and Phonograms Treaty* (WPPT). Australia is a party to all these treaties.

Article 2 of the Paris Act of the *Berne Convention* provides for copyright protection in literary and artistic works:

> (1) The expression 'literary and artistic works' shall include every production in the literary, scientific and artistic domain, whatever may be the mode or form of its expression, such as books, pamphlets and other writings; lectures, addresses, sermons and other works of the same nature; dramatic or dramaticomusical works; choreographic works and entertainments in dumb show; musical compositions with or without words; cinematographic works to which are assimilated works expressed by a process analogous to cinematography; works of drawing, painting, architecture, sculpture, engraving and lithography; photographic works to which are assimilated works expressed by a process analogous to photography; works of applied art; illustrations, maps, plans, sketches and three-dimensional works relative to geography, topography, architecture or science.

> (2) It shall, however, be a matter for legislation in the countries of the Union to prescribe that works in general or any specified categories of works shall not be protected unless they have been fixed in some material form.

The Paris Act of the *Berne Convention* expressly encompasses translations, adaptations and arrangements of works, and collective works within the scope of protection.[63] Article 10 of the TRIPS Agreement and Article 4 of the *WIPO Copyright Treaty* require computer programs to be protected as literary works and expressly provide that compilations of data (databases) are protected subject matter which, in the context of the Australian law, amounts to a description more than an extension of the law. These treaties also extend the rights of owners to include the right of communication to the public (that encompasses online dissemination) and the right of authorising the commercial rental of computer programs and certain other works.

None of the above multilateral treaties include any specific provision concerning 'government works' and there are none in the other major multilateral treaties referred to above. However, Article 2(4) of the Paris Act of the *Berne Convention* provides:

---

63 World Intellectual Property Organization. WIPO Database of Intellectual Property Legislative Texts, *Berne Convention for the Protection of Literary and Artistic Works, Paris Act (as amended on September 28, 1979)*, Article 2(3) and (5) http://www.wipo.int/treaties/en/ip/berne/pdf/trtdocs_wo001.pdf. Australia became bound by the Paris Act of the *Berne Convention* on 3 January 1978.

(4) It shall be a matter for legislation in the countries of the Union to determine the protection to be granted to official texts of a legislative, administrative and legal nature, and to official translations of such texts.

The provision accommodates those states parties to the convention who either protect official texts of the kind described as copyright works, or place such texts in the public domain.

Of importance to the future reform of the law and the nature and scope of copyright protection is the three-step test provided in these treaties. This test sets the international standard for copyright exceptions and limitations, and that seeks to draw a limit on the extent of non-infringement exceptions to copyright.

Under this test, exceptions and limitations to the rights of copyright owners must be confined:

- to certain special cases,
- that do not conflict with a normal exploitation of the work, and
- do not unreasonably prejudice the legitimate interests of the right holder.[64]

Interpretation of this test has been closely considered in a decision under the World Trade Organization (WTO) Dispute Settlement System.[65] The three conditions apply on a cumulative basis, each being a separate and independent requirement that must be satisfied. Before any exception can be introduced or extended, consideration must be given to: whether the exception is clearly defined and limited in its field of application or exceptional in its scope, whether it will conflict with actual or potential economic uses of copyright material, and whether the exception causes or has the potential to cause disproportionate prejudice to the economic and personal interests of copyright owners. The non-binding declaration of a group of international experts on the three-step test emphasises that they are to be considered together and as a whole in a comprehensive overall assessment and that the test does not require limitations and exceptions to be interpreted narrowly.[66]

Substantial amendment to our domestic law requires an examination of its impact against these international standards. Non-conformance with those standards would potentially expose Australia to serious economic consequences for Australia such as compensation or the suspension of concessions on trade[67] and potentially prejudice the interests of Aus-

---

64 Article 9(2) of the *Berne Convention*, Article 13 of the TRIPS Agreement, Article 10 of the WCT, Article 16 of the WPPT and Article 17.4.10(a) of the AUSFTA.

65 World Trade Organization, *United States – Section 110(5) of the US Copyright Act: Report of the Panel* (15 June 2000) WT/DS160/R http://www.wto.org/english/news_e/news00_e/1234da.doc.

66 Max Planck Institute for Intellectual Property and Competition Law, *Declaration: A Balanced Interpretation of the 'Three Step Test' in Copyright Law* (July 2008) http://www.ip.mpg.de/en/news/declaration_on_the_three_step_test.html. Refer also to Reto M Hilty, 'Declaration on the "Three-Step Test": Where do we go from here?' (2010) 1 *Journal of Intellectual Property, Information Technology and E-Commerce Law* 83 http://www.jipitec.eu/issues/jipitec-1-2-2010/2614/.

67 Refer to World Trade Organization, *TRIPS (Agreement on Trade-Related Aspects of Intellectual Property Rights)* Part V (Dispute Prevention and Settlement) http://www.wto.org/english/tratop_e/

tralian copyright owners in the exploitation of their rights in other countries.[68] However, the three-step test is expressed in general principles and accordingly is subject to some flexibility in interpretation. The provisions should be understood to permit contracting parties to devise new exceptions and limitations that are appropriate in the digital network environment.[69]

Administration of Government

Australian federal and state governments, like governments in most industrialised democracies, have grown in size substantially since the Second World War. This has occurred despite some redefining of the role of government and the consequent withdrawal of government from some activities.[70] The growth in government has been generated by factors such as population growth, social change, the need for better economic planning and efficiency, technological innovation and administrative and regulatory reform. For example, the last three decades in Australia have brought a burgeoning education sector with far greater secondary education retention rates, the growth of new disciplines to match economic and social change, a huge increase in the proportion of women in the workforce, the passage of anti-discrimination, equal employment opportunity and other human rights legislation and a change from an elite to a mass higher education system. These factors

---

trips_e/t_agm0_e.htm, and Articles 22 and 23 of GATT-Uruguay Round: Understanding on Rules and Procedures Governing the Settlement of Disputes http://www.wto.org/english/docs_e/legal_e/28-dsu_e.htm.

68   Above n 63, Article 6.

69   Refer to *WIPO Copyright Treaty* – 'Agreed statement concerning Article 10: It is understood that the provisions of Article 10 permit Contracting Parties to carry forward and appropriately extend into the digital environment limitations and exceptions in their national laws that have been considered acceptable under the *Berne Convention*. Similarly, these provisions should be understood to permit Contracting Parties to devise new exceptions and limitations that are appropriate in the digital network environment'. http://www.wipo.int/treaties/en/ip/wct/trtdocs_wo033.html#P86_11560. Also refer to Christophe Geiger, 'The Role of the Three-Step Test in the Adaptation of the Copyright Law to the Information Society' (2007) *UNESCO e-Copyright Bulletin* (Jan–March 2007) 2 http://portal.unesco.org/culture/en/files/34481/11883823381test_trois_etapes_en.pdf/test_trois_etapes_en.pdf. It should also be pointed out that the *International Convention for the Protection of Performers, Producers of Phonograms and Broadcasting Organisations* (the Rome Convention) done at Rome on 26 October 1961, to which Australia is a party, provides, in Article 15, permitted exceptions to the protection granted by the Convention that include 'the same kind of limitations' that any Contracting State provides for 'in its domestic laws and regulations, in connection with the protection of copyright in literary and artistic works'. The Convention covers, among other things, protection for the fixation of sounds and for image and sound broadcasts. Refer to http://www.wipo.int/treaties/en/ip/rome/trtdocs_wo024.html#P132_12542. The *Convention for the Protection of Producers of Phonograms against Unauthorised Duplication of their Phonograms* (the Phonograms Convention) of 29 October 1971 has a similar exception (Article 6). Australia is also a party to this Convention. Refer to http://www.wipo.int/treaties/en/ip/phonograms/.

70   'The perennial discourse over the proper role of government can be characterised as a debate between those who emphasize government failure and those who emphasize market failure. Over the last two decades those who emphasize government failure have been in the ascendancy': The Hon JJ Spigelman, 'Citizens, Consumers and Courts' (2001) 60(4) *Australian Journal of Public Administration* 5.

have produced a more educated populace with a consciousness of individual rights and a demand for greater accountability across all sectors of society.[71]

The movement for greater access to government information under e-government reforms and the shift to greater dissemination and licensing of information in Australia and in other developed democracies is in part driven by the desire to promote the greater accountability of government through greater transparency.[72] It is also in part driven by a desire to promote informed participation by the public—to contribute ideas and expertise so that governments can make better informed, effective and efficient decisions. It is also driven by a desire for greater interoperability of information within government and a desire to disseminate information for the social and economic benefit of the public. These policy goals have had a long genesis but social changes and major technological advances in communication have given them impetus and enabled them to be realised with far greater effectiveness.

Accountability and Efficiency

The growing size of government, and the scope and complexity of the activities it engages in, have resulted in a greater concern for accountability and efficiency and a modern reliance upon 'evidence-based'[73] decision-making. In Australia in the 1980s and 1990s, there were financial management reforms in the federal government—first through program budgeting and subsequently largely through the impact of the *FMA Act*, the *CAC Act* and the *PGPA Act* —that emphasised the values of performance, propriety and accountability. Greater information available to decision -makers aids more reliable decision-making and government collects more information than ever before. This occurs across demographic, economic, industrial, agricultural, meteorological, geospatial and other fields.

Throughout the western democracies, freedom of information laws have been introduced over the last few decades to strengthen citizens' access to government information, by providing a right of access to those citizens to information in the possession of government. This right underpins the accountability of government and the ability of citizens to correct or comment on information held about them, to review or question the basis

---

71 'Not only are medical practitioners under scrutiny and subject to criticism much more than they were in times gone by. The same attitude reaches into every section of society. It affects the judiciary, the churches, the political leadership and even the Royal Family. No one is now immune. Everyone is accountable. This tide is unlikely to turn. Consciousness of rights is much more clearly established'. The Hon MD Kirby, 'An International Perspective of Tort System Reforms', *2000 PIAA International Workshop*, The Royal College of Physicians London, England, 11 September 2000) http://www.hcourt.gov.au/assets/publications/speeches/former-justices/kirbyj/kirbyj_tortsystem.htm.

72 The policy circular for federal executive branch departments and agencies OMB Circular A-130 on the Management of Federal Information Resources states among its basic considerations and assumptions: 'Because the public disclosure of government information is essential to the operation of a democracy, the management of Federal information resources should protect the public's right of access to government information'. United States of America. Executive Office of the President, Office of Management and Budget, *OMB Circular A-130 revised* http://www.whitehouse.gov/omb/circulars_a130_a130trans4/.

73 For a critical appraisal of 'evidence-based' policy refer to Richard Mulgan, 'Everyone "Researches". So Why's the Policy so Bad?' *The Public Sector Informant* (Canberra, March 2009) 6.

of government decision-making and simply to obtain information that the government has not published or disseminated. In Australia this is supported by the other administrative law measures, which include an Ombudsman to report on complaints against administrative decisions by government and administrative tribunals to review government decision-making. Each of these measures enables citizens to obtain a clear statement of reasons for decision-making and provide pathways for the resolution of disputes and better administrative decision-making. These measures augment other more traditional forms of accountability through ministers to the Parliament via the use of parliamentary questions, review by parliamentary committee and by auditors responsible to Parliament, as well as via the media.

The Australian Government stated, in its May 2010 *Response to the Report of the Government 2.0 Taskforce*, that it is 'committed to the principles of openness and transparency in Government'.[74] It agreed in principle that the default position would be that government information should be free, based on open standards, easily discoverable, understandable, machine-readable, and freely usable and transformable. In the same year it reformed the *Freedom of Information Act 1982* (Cth) to promote greater access to, and dissemination of, government information.

In the United States of America, in a memorandum for the Heads of Executive Departments and Agencies dated 8 December 2009—'The Open Government Directive'—the Director of the Executive Office of the President stated:

> The three principles of transparency, participation, and collaboration form the cornerstone of an open government. Transparency promotes accountability by providing the public with information about what the Government is doing. Participation allows members of the public to contribute ideas and expertise so that their government can make policies with the benefit of information that is widely dispersed in society. Collaboration improves the effectiveness of Government by encouraging partnerships and cooperation within the Federal Government, across levels of government, and between the Government and private institutions.[75]

Participation and Engagement

The *Report of the Royal Commission on Australian Government Administration* in 1976[76] produced key themes that have been influential in the direction of Australian public administration over the last several decades. One was improved efficiency and effectiveness. Another was greater community participation in government.[77] Efficiency leads to

---

74   Australia. Department of Finance and Deregulation, *Government Response to the Report of the Government 2.0 Taskforce* (May 2010) [3] http://www.finance.gov.au/publications/govresponse20report/doc/Government-Response-to-Gov-2-0-Report.pdf.

75   United States of America. Executive Office of the President, Office of Management and Budget, *Memorandum for the Heads of Executive Departments and Agencies* from Peter R Orszag Director, Subject: Open Government Directive (8 December 2009 M-10-06) [1] http://www.whitehouse.gov/sites/default/files/omb/assets/memoranda_2010/m10-06.pdf.

76   Australia. *Report of the Royal Commission on Australian Government Administration* (Canberra, 1976).

improved service delivery in sectors of government responsibility such as health and other basic needs at less cost to the taxpayer.

In the early part of this century both state and federal governments embarked on e-government initiatives, that is, a range of strategies based on information and communications technologies aimed to achieve more efficient operations, easier access and better engagement.[78] In Victoria, e-government reforms were grounded primarily in a 2002 report entitled *Putting People at the Centre*. Its four objectives were:

- **Substantially improving support services to citizens**—by improving all services, reducing borders between services and increasing the responsiveness of services to the needs of individuals.
- **Providing better community engagement and more effective democracy**—by improving access to information, enhancing community consultation and dialogue and bolstering trust in the privacy of information.
- **Using innovation in finding new opportunities**—by fostering experimentation and investment in innovative opportunities.
- **Creating a framework for ongoing reform within government**—by facilitating holistic policy and services initiatives, building ICT capabilities within agencies and promoting the standardisation and sharing of IC infrastructure and information.[79]

At the federal level, the November 2002 report Better Services, Better Government outlined six key objectives:

- achieve greater efficiency and a return on investment;
- ensure convenient access to government services and information;
- deliver services that are responsive to the needs of individual Australian households, business and civic organisations;
- integrate related services;
- build experience, user trust and confidence in the use of new technologies; and
- enhance closer citizen engagement in policy formulation and processes.[80]

---

77   Australia. Australian Public Service Commission, Lynelle Briggs, *APS Governance – Keynote Address to Department of Employment and Workplace Relations Governance Workshop*, 22 February 2005.

78   Victoria. S Hodgkinson and L Stewart, *Victorian State Government E-Government Landscape Scan: Overview*, Version 3.0 http://web.archive.org/web/20091020023848/http://www.egov.vic.gov.au/index.php?env=-innews/detail:m3086-1-1-8-s-0:n-1647-0-0--.

79   Victoria. *The Victorian eGovernment Resource Centre*, http://web.archive.org/web/20110225204859/http://www.egov.vic.gov.au/victorian-government-resources/e-government-strategies-victoria/putting-people-at-the-centre/putting-people-at-the-centre-executive-summary.html. The egov.vic.gov.au site, including all the information, articles and links the site contained, was discontinued at the end of 2013, and has been superseded by www.digital.vic.gov.au.

80   Australia. National Office of the Information Economy, *Better Services, Better Government* (2002) [1] http://www.finance.gov.au/agimo-archive/__data/assets/pdf_file/0016/35503/Better_Services-Better_Gov.pdf.

E-government reforms have changed the landscape of government administration in many other countries. Canada's Government On-Line initiative was launched in 1999, with the objectives of:

- providing clients with a more accessible government, where information and services are organized according to clients' needs, and are available 24/7, in English or French;
- delivering better and more responsive services by implementing more efficient and timely electronic services; and
- building trust and confidence in on-line service delivery by ensuring that electronic transactions are protected and secure, and that personal information is safeguarded.[81]

In the United States of America, the Director of the Office of Management and Budget (OMB) established an e-government task force in 2001 and that task force produced the federal *E-Government Strategy* in February 2002. In the words of the *E-Government Strategy Report*, its primary goals were to:

- Make it easy for citizens to obtain service and interact with the federal government,
- Improve government efficiency and effectiveness, and
- Improve government's responsiveness to citizens.[82]

Ongoing development of reform in that country mirrors a wider trend across developed democracies.

Similar reforms have occurred in other countries. The OECD has produced two synthesis reports, *The E-Government Imperative* (2003) and *E-Government for Better Government* (2005), and has carried out a series of country reviews to analyse the successes and challenges of e-government in a national context and to make proposals for action that can help countries improve their e-government efforts.[83]

At an international level, the *Declaration of Principles* of the *World Summit on the Information Society* of 2003 affirms the importance to all of access and the ability to contribute information, ideas and knowledge.[84]

---

81   Canada. Government Online (2006) 1
http://publications.gc.ca/collections/Collection/P4-1-2006E.pdf.

82   United States of America. Executive Office of the President, Office of Management and Budget, *E-Government Strategy: Simplified Delivery of Services to Citizens* (2002) [1]
https://www.whitehouse.gov/sites/default/files/omb/inforeg/egovstrategy.pdf.

83   See, for example, OECD, *The OECD E-Government Studies: Belgium* (2008)
http://www.oecd.org/governance/public-innovation/42350611.pdf.

84   International Telecommunications Union/United Nations, *Declaration of Principles: Building the Information Society: a Global Challenge in the New Millennium,* Document WSIS–03/GENEVA/Doc/4-E (2003), Geneva 2003–Tunis 2005, UN/ITU, 2003, 2005, principles 24 and 42, refer to
http://www.itu.int/wsis/docs/geneva/official/dop.html.

The gathering of information by government has also resulted in a consciousness within government of information it possesses as a national strategic asset. Government information is not simply something that government collects and uses to develop and support its policies and decisions. Government information is seen as a repository of information of importance to the individual citizen and to the community at large about government decision-making and about how government behaves. For example, in Australia, the report *Management of Government Information as a National Strategic Resource: Report of the Information Management Steering Committee on Information Management in the Commonwealth Government*—published in August 1997 by the Office of Government Information Technology[85]—expressed the following:

> Our vision is for a government that:
>
> - uses its information fully, as a national strategic asset for government, business and the community;
> - manages information for better policy development and the continuous improvement of services . . . [86]

Government information is also seen as a useful resource that can be applied and mashed-up by the private sector for private and community benefit. However, in Australia and in other countries such as the United States of America during the 1980s, governments commodified information and often adopted a user-pays approach to its release and use by the public.[87] More recently these governments have moved from a user-pays policy to a taxpayer-pays policy and have justified this fundamental change in outlook in the sharing of information with the public by the positive returns of facilitating informed decisions and of maximising innovation and other social and economic returns.[88]

Australia's International Civil and Political Treaty Obligations

Underpinning the Australian legal structure and its administrative and governmental reforms is Australia's recognition of a wide range of civil and political rights embodied in a number of international instruments in this field. The most important of these instruments

---

85   Australia. Office of Government Information Technology, *Management of Government Information as a National Strategic Resource: Report of the Information Management Steering Committee on Information Management in the Commonwealth Government* (August 1997).

86   Ibid xvii.

87   Refer to John Gilchrist, 'The Role of Government as Proprietor and Disseminator of Information' (1996) 7(1) *Australian Journal of Corporate Law* 62, 73, 74.

88   'Public sector information is a national resource and that releasing as much of it on as permissive terms as possible will maximize its economic and social value to Australians and reinforce its contribution to a healthy democracy': Australia. Department of Finance and Deregulation, *Engage: Getting on with Government 2.0* (2009) [xvii] http://gov2.net.au/report/ or http://www.finance.gov.au/publications/gov20taskforcereport/doc/Government20TaskforceReport.pdf. 'Economic and social benefits arising from the release of the Victorian Government PSI will likely outweigh the benefits of treating it as a commodity': Victoria. Economic Development and Infrastructure Committee, Parliament of Victoria, *Inquiry into Improving Access to Victorian Public Sector Information and Data: Report* (June 2009) 19.

are the *International Covenant on Civil and Political Rights* (ICCPR) and the *International Covenant on Economic, Social and Cultural Rights* (ICESCR). Both these treaties are derivative instruments from the *Universal Declaration of Human Rights* (UDHR).[89] They contain principles and standards of conduct espoused over many centuries of human philosophical and political thought and have been to varying extents embodied in national laws such as the revolutionary constitutions of the United States and France in the later part of the 18th century.

From a democratic governance viewpoint, the most significant among all the civil and political rights recognised in domestic and international law is the right of all citizens to vote. Sections 7, 24 and 41 of the *Australian Constitution* collectively provide that all Australians entitled to vote may vote in federal elections. The corresponding international obligation is Article 25 of the ICCPR. That Article provides that:

> Every citizen shall have the right and opportunity,
>
> (a) To take part in the conduct of public affairs, directly or through freely chosen representatives;
>
> (b) To vote and to be elected at genuine periodic elections which shall be by universal and equal suffrage and shall be held by secret ballot, guaranteeing the free expression of the will of the electors;
>
> (c) To have access, on general terms of equality, to public service in his country.[90]

Although the efficacy of the constitutional guarantee is dependent upon the franchise granted by the several states, this Australian democratic governance guarantee is the foundation of accountability and political direction within this society. The High Court of Australia in the electoral advertising case[91] recognised an implied freedom of communication of information and opinions on matters relating to government discerned in the doctrine of representative government in the *Australian Constitution*. This right has also been recognised in state constitutions,[92] and furthers the opportunity of citizens to take part in the conduct of public affairs. Governance determined by the free will of the people underpins the importance of the dissemination of information about social, political and governmental action.

---

89   United Nations. *Universal Declaration of Human Rights* GA Res 217A (III), UN Doc A/810 at 71 (10 December 1948) http://www.ohchr.org/en/udhr/pages/introduction.aspx.

90   United Nations. Office of the United Nations High Commissioner for Human Rights *International Covenant on Civil and Political Rights* (1976) http://www.ohchr.org/en/professionalinterest/pages/ccpr.aspx or http://treaties.un.org/doc/Publication/UNTS/Volume%20999/volume-999-I-14668-English.pdf.

91   *Australian Capital Television Pty Ltd v Commonwealth* (1992) 177 CLR 106; refer also to *Nationwide News Pty Ltd v Wills* (1992) 177 CLR 1.

92   *Stephens v West Australian Newspapers Limited* (1994) 124 ALR 80; *Levy v State of Victoria* (1997) 146 ALR 248.

Under s 51(xxxi) of the *Australian Constitution,* any property acquired by the Commonwealth must be acquired on just terms. The corresponding article is Article 17 of the UDHR.[93] The Constitutional provision encompasses personal property such as copyright.

Another international obligation contained in Article 27(2) of the UDHR and in Article 15(1) of the ICESCR is the right of everyone 'to benefit from the protection of moral and material interests resulting from any scientific, literary or artistic production of which he is the author'.[94] Furthermore, Article 15(2) of the ICESCR provides that the steps to be taken by the states party to the Covenant 'to achieve the full realization of this right shall include those necessary for the conservation, the development and the diffusion of science and culture'. Article 15(2) embraces government archival and library conservation and access activities.[95] Articles 15(1) and 15(2) are both important to the recognition of individual and community identity and achievement. The right to protection of material interests under Article 15(1) resulting from an author's own productions can be traced back many centuries to the flowering of human rights thought in the period of the enlightenment,[96] to the beginnings of copyright law and to biblical times.[97]

In its national report to the United Nations under the ICESCR, the Australian Government points out that it gives effect to Article 15(2) by a number of ways including:

> 604. The Australian Government is committed to creating a copyright regime which balances the rights of copyright owners and creators to receive appropriate rewards for their investment of skill and resources, with the rights of users to access copyright material on reasonable terms.[98]

Article 26 of the ICCPR provides:

---

93   While the UDHR is not a treaty, it is arguable that many of its provisions have obtained the status of customary international law. Article 17 provides: 1. Everyone has the right to own property alone as well as in association with others. 2. No one shall be arbitrarily deprived of his property.

94   Article 27(2) of the UDHR; Article 15(1)(c) of the ICESCR.

95   United Nations. Economic and Social Council, *Third Periodic Report: Australia. 07/23/1998. E/1994/104/Add.22. (State Party Report) Implementation of the International Covenant on Economic, Social and Cultural Rights* (15 June 1998)
http://www.unhchr.ch/tbs/doc.nsf/0/da87cf0d8cdb87708025678500387c12?Opendocument#art15.
Under Article 15 (Heritage) at para 339, 'The Government supports the National Library of Australia, the world's leading documentary resource for learning about and understanding Australia and Australians. The National Library provides leadership to the national system of libraries and information services'.

96   See, for example, the writings of Adam Smith (1723–90) in Adam Smith, *The Wealth of Nations,* Book 1, Chapter V, 1.5.1, 1.5.2 http://www.econlib.org/library/Smith/
smWN2.html#B.I,%20Ch.5,%20Of%20the%20Real%20and%20Nominal%20Price%20of%20Commodities.

97   Genesis 3:19.

98   Australia. Department of Foreign Affairs and Trade, *Common Core Document — Incorporating the Fifth Report under the International Covenant on Civil and Political Rights and the Fourth Report under the International Covenant on Economic, Social and Cultural Rights* (June 2006) 168
http://dfat.gov.au/international-relations/themes/human-rights/Documents/core_doc.pdf.

All persons are equal before the law and are entitled without any discrimination to the equal protection of the law. In this respect, the law shall prohibit any discrimination and guarantee to all persons equal and effective protection against discrimination on any ground such as race, colour, sex, language, religion, political or other opinion, national or social origin, property, birth or other status.[99]

This Article expresses important underlying values of modern liberal democratic societies that have endured and been enhanced for the effective operation of government. These values are the underlying belief in the rule of law and of a common social obligation to observe the law. In the Anglo-Australian legal tradition, rights and liabilities of the citizens and of government are determined by primary sources of the law—legislation and the common law—with disputes resolved by independent tribunals. It is the duty of citizens to observe the law or to face sanctions for disobedience. In order to achieve public order, governments in the English common law tradition have long sought to ensure that the law was disseminated to its citizens. Originally, the law was communicated in manuscript form and orally, later in print and, more recently, in print and electronically. The duty to observe the law entails within it knowledge of the law. There is a legal assumption that every citizen knows the law. That cannot be a realistic assumption unless government uses its best endeavours to disseminate the law. The common law has long recognised a duty on the government to do so.[100] In Australia at least this important governmental role now extends to official documents explaining the law such as explanatory memoranda and statements, second reading speeches and reports of parliamentary debates.

Technological Change and Information Policy

Computers have become the core of our culture. Computers record and store works of literature, music, drama, films, sound recordings and a variety of artistic works and in themselves provide a basis of creativity and the preservation of human endeavour. They transmit and receive information, vision and sound. They are used as tools and repositories of work and research, as sources of entertainment, games and hobbies. They disseminate, and provide access to, information produced by individuals, institutions, commercial and non-commercial organisations, and by governments in nearly all parts of the world.

The dissemination of government information is now embracing the information age. It has undergone revolutionary technological change through the introduction of printing in the 15th century, of the telegraph in the 19th century and of broadcasting and electronic communications in the 20th century. The development and spread of intranet and internet communications in the last two decades of the 20th century, the development of the World

---

99   United Nations. Office of the United Nations High Commissioner for Human Rights, *International Covenant on Civil and Political Rights* (1976) http://www.ohchr.org/en/professionalinterest/pages/ccpr.aspx. There are complementary obligations expressed in Articles 16 and 5 of the ICCPR.

100   Courts in England have regarded the chief object of the duty imposed on the Crown is to ensure that works of state and religion are published and preserved in a correct and authentic form: refer to Chapter 2 of this book and *Universities of Oxford and Cambridge v Richardson* (1802) 6 Ves Jun 689, 711 (31 ER 1260, 1271); *Manners v Blair* (1828) 3 Bli NS 391, 405 (4 ER 1379, 1384).

Wide Web from its beginnings in 1991 and the subsequent growth of sophisticated web search engines have enabled convenient access to an enormous amount of information worldwide by an enormous number of people. This has changed the way individuals and institutions communicate and do business. It has affected the way individuals work, the way they research, the way they are educated and their home activities. More information is being produced and more information is being disseminated than ever before.

While there have been profound changes in these technologies over the latter part of the 20th century and the early 21st century, the past spread of,[101] and existing reliance upon,[102] these technologies and the future projections and planning by governments suggest that:

- the total amount of data and the variety of material in electronic form,
- the accessibility and use of data in that form,
- the number of electronic transactions, and
- the number of communications and interactions between individual and individual and between citizen and government, will very substantially increase.[103]

These technological changes affect the way governments inform, administer and interact with citizens. In particular, technology has provided greater opportunities for administrative efficiency and effectiveness within government, and for better government service delivery. It has also provided greater opportunities to better inform and to be informed and be responsive to individual submissions. Among the modern information principles of government there is a concern about government interoperability and information sharing and a whole-of-government approach to administering policies. The democratic value of accountability to the citizen has been strengthened by easier and greater connectivity between government and the governed. In 2005, overwhelmingly, Australians made contact with government in person. By 2008, the internet was the most common way people made contact with government.[104] Parliaments are also seeing a shift from the broadcasting of their information to the community to the imparting of their information through interaction with the community. For example, there were 77 million users of the Australian Parliament website in 2009.[105]

---

101   The number of worldwide internet users grew by approximately 676 percent from 2000 to 2014 representing a growth of approximately 361 million users to 2.8 billion users (compiled from United Nations, government, consulting and research organisations). *Internet Usage Statistics: The Internet Big Picture* http://www.internetworldstats.com/stats.htm.

102   By 2008, close to 75 percent of Australian households had a computer and, of those, 90 percent were connected to the internet (i.e. 67 percent of all households). Of the 67 percent with internet, close to 78 percent had a broadband connection. This compares to 29 percent with a broadband connection in 2004–05, and illustrates the rapid take-up of broadband internet by Australians. Australia. Department of Broadband Communications and the Digital Economy, *Australia's Digital Economy: Future Directions* (2009) [4] http://pandora.nla.gov.au/pan/102861/20090717-1104/www.dbcde.gov.au/__data/assets/pdf_file/0003/117786/DIGITAL_ECONOMY_FUTURE_DIRECTIONS_FINAL_REPORT.pdf.

103   These factors will be ultimately balanced against the cost of online access including costs imposed by the ICT service providers for time and data limits, the costs imposed by hosts, the cost of software and hardware and upgrades, the cost of power, and poor design of sites.

104   Australia. Department of Finance and Deregulation, Australian Government Information Management Office, *Interacting with Government: Australians' Use and Satisfaction with E-Government Services — 2008* http://www.finance.gov.au/publications/interacting-with-government/index.html.

These technology-induced changes have provided greater opportunities and ability to pursue those values, and the future connectivity between the community and government will in turn further enhance those values.

Changes in technology have changed our capacity to access information and have led to heightened expectations about faster, more mobile and easier access to information.[106] Changes in technology will also change community expectations about how effective government is in delivering its services and how government should go about its business. The community is likely to demand more of its government as it envisions its ability to do more.

This trend is a continuing one and the ability of individuals to access information conveniently and easily will increase and will influence how government treats information in its possession and develops its policy towards others reproducing and communicating to the public or undertaking other acts comprised in the copyright in the information.

Over the last decade, the importance of managing government information in Australia has been recognised through the establishment of institutions like the Australian Government Information Management Office (AGIMO) and official policies like that Government's Online Information Service Obligations.[107] There has also been a substantial growth in the literature dealing with the management of government information and in particular reports on that topic, for example, *Management of Government Information as a National Strategic Resource*—previously referred to[108]—and *Venturous Australia: Building Strength in Innovation* (the Cutler Report)[109] that recommended a National Information Strategy to optimise the flow of information in the Australian economy and to maximise the flow of government-generated information, as well as reports on the commercial and competition policy aspects of the use of government information.[110] In a report by Dr Ian Reinecke entitled *Information Policy and E-Governance in the Australian Government*,[111] a

---

105   Roxanne Missingham, 'Case Study: Australian Parliament' (Paper presented at the *Using Creative Commons in the Public Sector* Seminar, Canberra, Parliament House, 26 November 2010).

106   Garry Barker, 'Get Remote Control: Access your Apple from Anywhere in the World' *The Age Green Guide* (Melbourne) 28 January 2010, 21.

107   Australia. Information Management Office (2007) *Online Information Service Obligations (OISOs)*, http://www.finance.gov.au/agimo-archive/oiso.html.

108   Australia. Office of Government Information Technology, *Management of Government Information as a National Strategic Resource: Report of the Information Management Steering Committee on Information Management in the Commonwealth Government* (August 1997).

109   Australia. Cutler & Company Pty Ltd, *Venturous Australia: Building Strength in Innovation: Report on the Review of the National Innovation System* (the Cutler Report) Report to Senator the Hon Kim Carr, Minister for Innovation, Industry, Science and Research (August 2008) Recommendation 7.7 http://www.industry.gov.au/innovation/InnovationPolicy/Pages/Document%20library/NISReport.aspx or http://www.industry.gov.au/innovation/InnovationPolicy/Documents/Policy/NISReport.pdf.

110   For example, Australia. Intellectual Property and Competition Review Committee, *Review of the Intellectual Property Legislation under the Competition Principles Agreement* (Ergas Committee) (Canberra, September 2000) 113–4.

111   Australia. Department of Prime Minister and Cabinet, *Information Policy and E-Governance in the Australian Government: A Report for the Department of the Prime Minister and Cabinet* Dr Ian Reinecke

survey of Australian Government agencies revealed that there was a wide diversity of information management practice across government including a lack of consistency across government in making PSI available for re-use.[112] The report proposed a more coordinated approach for licensing PSI for re-use and proposed a central point of responsibility to enhance information policy and development, which would bring together the Offices of the Privacy Commissioner and the Freedom of Information Commissioner.[113] These proposals were adopted by the Australian Government through the establishment, by Commonwealth enactment, of the Office of Australian Information Commissioner tasked with 'promoting a pro-disclosure culture' and of 'achieving a coordinated approach to information management policy across government'.[114] That Office published in May 2011 its *Principles on Open Public Sector Information* to guide compliance by Australian Government agencies with the publication objectives of the *Freedom of Information Act 1982* (Cth). The principles included open access:

> Agencies should use information technology to disseminate public sector information, applying a presumption of openness and adopting a proactive publication stance.[115]

and engagement with the community:

> Agencies should:
>
> • consult the community in deciding what information to publish and about agency publication practices.[116]

(March 2009) http://www.dpmc.gov.au/publications/information_policy/docs/information_policy_e-governance.pdf.

112   Ibid 30, para 5.1.

113   Ibid 35, 46, paras 6.3, 9.1, 9.2.

114   Australia. *Parliamentary Debates*, House of Representatives, Parliament of Australia, Information Commissioner Bill 2009, Second Reading Speech (26 November 2009) 12970, http://parlinfo.aph.gov.au/parlInfo/genpdf/chamber/hansardr/2009-11-26/0017/hansard_frag.pdf; refer also to s 7 of the *Australian Information Commissioner Act 2010* (Cth): **Definition of information commissioner functions** The *information commissioner functions* are as follows: (a) to report to the Minister on any matter that relates to the Commonwealth Government's policy and practice with respect to: (i) the collection, use, disclosure, management, administration or storage of, or accessibility to, information held by the Government; and (ii) the systems used, or proposed to be used, for the activities covered by subparagraph (i); (b) any other function conferred by this Act or another Act (or an instrument under this Act or another Act) on the Information Commissioner other than a freedom of information function or a privacy function.

115   Australia. Office of the Australian Information Commissioner, *Principles on Open Public Sector Information* (May 2011) 33, Principle 1, http://www.oaic.gov.au/information-policy/information-policy-resources/information-policy-agency-resources/principles-on-open-public-sector-information or http://www.oaic.gov.au/images/documents/information-policy/information-policy-agency-resources/principles_on_psi_short.pdf.

116   Ibid, Principle 33, Principle 2. As at December 2014, the Abbott Government proposed a Bill that would abolish the Office of Australian Information Commissioner.

Interoperability and Sharing of Information

Governments have also been concerned with the interoperability of information across their many, often physically disparate, agencies to better communicate and coordinate activity across those agencies and to more adequately respond to security threats and other exigencies. E-government reforms in government administration in Australia and elsewhere have generally sought achievement of better coordination and sharing of information on a whole-of-government approach, but greater emphasis on these outcomes has come from a need to deal better with emergency and security exigencies, heightened by the growth of terrorism.[117]

In the United States of America the policy circular for federal executive branch departments and agencies (OMB Circular A-130 on the Management of Federal Information Resources) makes it mandatory for agencies and departments to implement the requirements of the *Computer Security Act of 1987* and the *Federal Information Security Management Act of 2002*. This Circular requires all federal information systems to have security plans and for such systems to have formal emergency response capabilities. Agencies are required to 'develop information systems that facilitate interoperability, application portability, and scalability of electronic applications across networks . . .' in their enterprise architecture.[118] The Information Sharing Environment Implementation Plan (ISE), prepared in November 2006,[119] describes the plan of action the US Federal Government has adopted over three years in response to the requirements of s 1016 of the *Intelligence Reform and Terrorism Prevention Act of 2004*. The President was charged to create the ISE, designate its organisation and management structure, and determine and enforce the policies and rules to govern the ISE's content and usage. The law further required the ISE be 'a decentralized, distributed, and coordinated environment' that 'to the greatest extent practicable, . . . connects existing systems . . .; builds upon existing systems capabilities currently in use across the Government; . . . facilitates the sharing of information at and across all levels of security; . . . and incorporates protections for individuals' privacy and civil liberties.'[120]

In addition, s 1016(b)(1)(A) of that Act required the President to establish an information-sharing environment 'for the sharing of terrorism information in a manner consistent with national security and with applicable legal standards relating to privacy and civil liberties.'

---

117 In a 2002 speech, former US Senate majority leader Tom Daschle criticised the US government for failing to put together various elements of evidence that could have prevented the 9/11 terrorist attacks and attributed the problem to 'stovepipe syndrome' that refers to the difficulty of information sharing faced by large, geographically dispersed companies with large staffs. 'Important information from one corner of the building is not shared with others, and becomes stuck up an information chimney or stovepipe'. Ben Macintyre, 'WikiLeaks Dump Alters Rules of Game Forever', *The Australian* (Sydney) 2 December 2010, 8.

118 United States of America. Executive Office of the President, Office of Management and Budget, *OMB Circular A-130 revised* [The Enterprise Architecture (2) (a) (i)] http://www.whitehouse.gov/omb/circulars_a130_a130trans4.

119 United States of America. Office of the Director of National Intelligence, *Information Sharing Environment Implementation Plan* (November 2006) http://www.fas.org/irp/agency/ise/plan1106.pdf.

120 *Intelligence Reform and Terrorism Prevention Act of 2004* (US) Public Law 108–458–Dec.17, 2004, s 1016(b)(2) http://www.justice.gov/olp/pdf/intelligence_reform_and_terrorism_prevention_act.pdf.

A later *National Strategy for Information Sharing* of October 2007 published by the Office of the President supports and supplements the ISE Implementation Plan.[121]

In Australia, in July 2007, the Council of Australian Government's Online and Communication Council commissioned the development of a national information-sharing strategy to provide a standardised approach to information sharing in support of the delivery of government services to the Australian community.[122] It was driven by a growing demand for the sharing of data and information between governments across all portfolio areas, whole-of-government initiatives in the areas of water, health, education and security and the risk of fragmented and inefficient sharing of information.[123] To assist this work, the Australian Government Information Management Office (AGIMO) established communities of practice to facilitate sharing across government of knowledge, expertise and better practice and a national standards framework to support interoperability.[124] In 2008, the *Gershon Report* on the Australian Government's use and management of ICT pointed to the weak governance of pan-government issues relating to ICT and recommended a whole-of-government approach to ICT policies and support.[125] The report recommended AGIMO identify the need for common approaches such as standards, platforms, applications, infrastructure, business process and aggregated ICT procurement.[126]

Together with a greater awareness of the importance of sharing of information within government and the coordination of activity across agencies comes a greater awareness of the benefits of sharing information with the public and encouraging the public re-use of that information. There are a number of reports in Australia and overseas that point to the social and economic benefits of the re-use of that information.

The Australian Bureau of Statistics, which adopted open content Creative Commons Attribution licensing of its statistical data in December 2008 from a past of commodifying information through a user-pays policy, is aware that not all Australian Bureau of Statistics

---

121   United States of America. The White House, National Security Council, *National Strategy for Information Sharing* (October 2007) http://www.fas.org/sgp/library/infoshare.pdf.

122   This was aimed at promoting better government service delivery and improved policy development through focused inter-agency collaboration, and was widely supported across agencies and jurisdictions.

123   Australia. Department of Finance and Deregulation, Australian Government Information Management Office, *National Government Information Sharing Strategy: Unlocking Government Information Assets to Benefit the Broader Community* (August 2009) http://www.finance.gov.au/files/2012/04/ngiss.pdf.

124   Australia. Department of Finance and Deregulation, Australian Government Information Management Office, *A National Standards Framework for Government* (August 2009) http://www.finance.gov.au/publications/national-standards-framework/docs/nsf.pdf.

125   Australia. Department of Finance and Deregulation, Australian Government Information Management Office, *Review of the Australian Government's Use of Information and Communication Technology* (Sir Peter Gershon 16 October 2008) paras 4.1, 5.1 http://www.finance.gov.au/publications/ICT-Review/docs/Review-of-the-Australian-Governments-Use-of-Information-and-Communication-Technology.pdf.

126   Ibid Appendix J. In November 2008, the Australian Government endorsed the recommendations of the review in full.

products are conducive to re-use by the public and has been considering improvement of the metadata of some of its products to promote greater re-use.[127]

In August 2009, AGIMO published a report endorsing nine information-sharing principles aimed at providing benefits to governments and the public:

> Australians should see less red tape, less complex and inconsistent forms and less repetition of processes, such as authentication. Sharing information between and within governments provides more efficient use of public funding through reduction in repetition of tasks associated with information management such as: collection, authentication, validation and storage.
>
> Fostering an environment of access to a better quality and comparable information will help improve evidence-based decision-making and better informed cross-jurisdictional initiatives. This will result in providing more seamless access to government services.
>
> Australians will benefit from improved services across many public service sectors. Better management of natural resources, more effective and efficient emergency services and health services, and improved policy and planning for their communities.[128]

Included among the information-sharing principles are:

- acting collaboratively, that is agencies should 'facilitate whole-of-government approaches to information management through inter-departmental communication and collaboration, and
- promoting information re-use, that is agencies need to investigate the conditions of use they should apply to the different elements of their information catalogue, for example, legislation, classification, freedom of information and licensing requirements, and to do so ensuring privacy and security requirements are met.

Subsequently, the federal government's 2.0 Taskforce delivered its final report entitled *Engage: Getting on with Government 2.0*, whose central recommendation was a declaration of open government by the Australian Government stating that:

- using technology to increase citizen engagement and collaboration in making policy and providing service will help achieve a more consultative, participatory and transparent government
- public sector information is a national resource and that releasing as much of it on as permissive terms as possible will maximise its economic and social value to Australians and reinforce its contribution to a healthy democracy
- online engagement by public servants, involving robust professional discussion as part of their duties or as private citizens, benefits their agencies, their

---

127 Donna Nicholson, 'Case Study: Australian Bureau of Statistics' (Paper presented at the *Using Creative Commons in the Public Sector* Seminar, Canberra, Parliament House, 26 November 2010).

128 Above n 123, [10].

professional development, those with whom they are engaged and the Australian public. This engagement should be enabled and encouraged.

The fulfilment of the above at all levels of government is integral to the government's objectives including public sector reform, innovation and using the national investment in broadband to achieve an informed, connected and democratic community.[129]

In March 2010, the report titled *Ahead of the Game: Blueprint for the Reform of the Australian Government Administration* recommended that the Australian Government become more open and that it develop new approaches to consultation and collaboration using recent advances in technology, most notably Web 2.0, that allow citizens, community groups and business to engage more effectively in how government services could be delivered—including establishing clear expectations around what the government is seeking to consult on or collaborate. The report also recommended that public sector data be made open, accessible and re-usable to the wider public, consistent with privacy and secrecy laws.[130]

In July 2010 the then Minister for Finance and Deregulation released a *Declaration of Open Government* that implemented the central recommendation of the *Engage: Getting on with Government 2.0* report:

> The Australian Government now declares that, in order to promote greater participation in Australia's democracy, it is committed to open government based on a culture of engagement, built on better access to and use of government-held information, and sustained by the innovative use of technology.
>
> . . .
>
> The Australian Government's support for openness and transparency in government has three key principles:
>
> **Informing**: strengthening citizen's rights of access to information, establishing a pro-disclosure culture across Australian Government agencies including through online innovation, and making government information more accessible and usable;
>
> **Engaging**: collaborating with citizens on policy and service delivery to enhance the processes of government and improve the outcomes sought; and
>
> **Participating**: making government more consultative and participative.

---

129   Australia. Department of Finance and Deregulation, Australian Government Information Management Office, *Engage: Getting on with Government 2.0* (2009) [xvii] http://gov2.net.au/report/ or http://www.finance.gov.au/publications/gov20taskforcereport/doc/Government20TaskforceReport.pdf.

130   Australia. Department of Prime Minister and Cabinet, Advisory Group on Reform of Australian Government Administration, *Ahead of the Game: Blueprint for the Reform of the Australian Government Administration* (March 2010) 39 http://apo.org.au/files/Resource/APS_reform_blueprint.pdf or http://apo.org.au/node/20863. On 8 May 2010 the then Prime Minister announced that the Government had accepted all the recommendations of the Blueprint Report http://www.dpmc.gov.au/publications/aga_reform/aga_reform_blueprint/index.cfm.

Supporting Initiatives

The Australian Government's commitment to action on each of these principles is demonstrated by:

- the passage of legislation reforming the Freedom of Information (FOI) Act and establishing the Office of the Australian Information Commissioner;
- the Government's announcement on 3 May 2010 of its response to the Government 2.0 Taskforce report, *Engage: Getting on with Government 2.0*; and
- its response to the *Ahead of the Game: Blueprint for the Reform of Australian Government Administration* report, in which the Government agreed that creating more open government is a key reform for the Australian Public Service.[131]

The declaration and the reports demonstrate that government sees greater efficiencies and better engagement and decision-making in the sharing of information between agencies and between government and the public, which will provide social, political and economic benefits to the community and contribute to a healthy democracy.

These developments preceded the establishment on 1 November 2010 of the Office of Australian Information Commissioner that was tasked under its 2010 enactment with reporting on any matter that relates to the Commonwealth Government's policy and practice with respect to, inter alia, the use, management, administration, disclosure and accessibility of information held by the government.[132]

Conclusion

These trends highlight somewhat competing policy values between government as a proprietor of copyright with rights of reproduction, publication and dissemination to the public and the need to 'take due care to ensure the quality, integrity and authenticity of government information,'[133] and the demands of modern government for greater accountability, efficiency, improved access, participation and engagement of its citizens. While none of these values are in essence new, having had long origins and development, there is now a greater consciousness of the information resources contained within government and the use to which those resources can be put, without and within government, which provide cogent and compelling values for the future reform of the law and practices of government.

---

131   Australia. Department of Finance and Deregulation, Australian Government Information Management Office, *Declaration of Open Government* (16 July 2010) Lindsay Tanner http://www.finance.gov.au/blog/2010/07/16/declaration-open-government/. The 2010 Blueprint Report (above n 130) also recommended that the Australian Government become more open and that public sector data be made more widely available, consistent with privacy and secrecy laws.

132   Refer to s 7 of the *Australian Information Commissioner Act 2010* (Cth). As at December 2014, the Abbott Government proposed a Bill that would abolish the Office of Australian Information Commissioner.

133   Australia. Office of Government Information Technology, *Management of Government Information as a National Strategic Resource: Report of the Information Management Steering Committee on Information Management in the Commonwealth Government* (August 1997) 35, 147.

2

Crown Copyright: The Government as Proprietor of Copyright Material

To provide a deeper understanding of the basis of the present Australian law, this chapter examines the origins of the law vesting copyright in the Crown and the major policy considerations evident in its development. First, it will describe the origins and scope of the prerogative right in the nature of copyright, and the duty that lies behind the right, which is preserved by s 8A of the *Copyright Act 1968*. Then, it will describe the origins and scope of Part VII of the *Copyright Act 1968*—from which government rights mostly derive.

Australian federal and state governments are important gatherers and generators of information. These governments disseminate more information than ever before. In Australia as well as other western countries there is a wide spectrum of government production and dissemination activity. This ranges from legal and parliamentary materials, reports, pamphlets, maps, designs, directories and circulars and official documents such as passports and marriage certificates that have long been the domain of government publishing, to films and audiovisual material, computer software and databases in print and digital form, architectural plans, procedural manuals, educational material, specialised historical works and a variety of commissioned works such as biographies.[1] There are provisions in the Australian *Copyright Act 1968* that grant to Australian federal and state governments proprietary rights in all of that material.

Access to, and the spread of, information has been aided by the development of digital databases and electronic communication technologies. More and more information is now disseminated in electronic form. Australian federal and state governments also produce a wide range of unpublished material including file and database material that is presently accessible by the public only through FOI or government archival requests. All these forms of material produced by the Australian federal and state governments are presently protected by the *Copyright Act 1968* (Cth).

In the words of the Australian Information Management Steering Committee, in its report entitled *Management of Government Information as a National Strategic Resource*, 'access

---

1   Refer to John Gilchrist, 'The Role of Government as Proprietor and Disseminator of Information' (1996) 7 (1) *Australian Journal of Corporate Law* 62 and Australia. Copyright Law Review Committee, *Crown Copyright* (2005) 11, para 2.18.

to publicly releasable government information is a fundamental right of all citizens in a democratic society'.[2] Does this role as proprietor of copyright material conflict with the principle that all citizens in a modern liberal democratic society should have fair and open access to government information? Do different policy considerations arise across the wide range of materials in facilitating access to those materials? Ought the needs and status of government be different from private sector institutions, which also obtain copyright protection under the law?

This chapter concludes with comments on the fragmentation between state and federal governments of official electronic dissemination and licensing of laws, in which the public interest in dissemination is strong.

Government Ownership: Legal Basis

Australian copyright law and the provisions dealing with government ownership are derived from the copyright law of the United Kingdom. Government ownership can be found in two separate but analogous kinds of rights. One concerns those rights existing in certain works and other subject matter by virtue of the operation of provisions of the *Copyright Act 1968*, essentially Part VII of the *Copyright Act 1968*, which vest those rights in the Commonwealth or a State, and the other concerns those rights existing in works that are the subject of one of the prerogative rights of the Crown, which are expressly preserved by s 8A(1) of the *Copyright Act 1968*. These rights are sometimes referred to as 'prerogative copyright'[3] and are variously referred to in the *Copyright Act 1968* as 'prerogative right or privilege of the Crown in the nature of copyright'[4] or 'prerogative right or privilege of the Crown by way of copyright'.[5] This prerogative right is a common law right that has been inherited by the Crown in the right of the Commonwealth and in right of the several States from the British Crown. Each of these rights form a basis of government ownership and will be discussed below in historical order.

Prerogative Copyright

The prerogative right of the Crown in the nature of copyright is the oldest basis of Crown ownership of works. This right extends to the printing and publication in Australia of various works of state. These works include Acts of Parliament, proclamations, orders in

---

2   Australia. Office of Government Information Technology, *Management of Government Information as a National Strategic Resource: Report of the Information Management Steering Committee on Information Management in the Commonwealth Government* (August 1997) xxviii, 34.

3   Refer to William Blackstone, *Commentaries on the Laws of England*, Book II (Clarendon Press, 1766) 410; Joseph Chitty, *A Treatise on the Law of the Prerogatives of the Crown* (Butterworth and Son, 1820) 238; Australia. Copyright Law Committee on Reprographic Reproduction, *Report of the Copyright Law Committee on Reprographic Reproduction* (Franki Committee) (1976) 58.

4   Section 182A.

5   Section 8A(2).

council and instruments made under an Act of Parliament such as regulations and ordinances. Judgments of the Crown's judicial officers also arguably fall within the right.

The prerogative right is a common law right and is derived from the prerogative right in the nature of copyright held by the British Crown that dates back in time to the early development of printing.[6] As a consequence of the reception of English law into the Australian colonies, the prerogative right has been inherited by the Crown in right of the colonies before federation and by the Crown in right of the several States and the Commonwealth of Australia upon federation.

As Griffith CJ stated in *The King v Kidman*:

> The laws so brought to Australia undoubtedly included all the common law relating to the rights and prerogatives of the Sovereign in his capacity as head of the Realm and the protection of his officers in enforcing them . . . When the several Australian colonies were erected this law was not abrogated, but continued in force as the law of the respective Colonies applicable to the Sovereign as their head.[7]

The law applicable to the prerogatives of the Crown continued as the law of the respective States at the time of the establishment of the Australian Commonwealth and, in respect of the Commonwealth, the Crown in that capacity succeeded to all those prerogatives subsisting at the time the Commonwealth came into being as were appropriate to a federal government of limited competence and that were not inconsistent with provisions of the *Commonwealth Constitution*.[8] The nature of the proprietary right of the Crown to print and publish certain works, which is derived from the Crown's position as head of a self-governing territorial unit, in itself suggests it vests in the Crown in right of Commonwealth and in right of the several States. English and Australian case-law authority supports this view.[9]

The origins of the right lie in the Crown's practice of granting exclusive rights to print and publish works that commenced shortly after the advent of printing in England. The grants formed one instrument of the Crown's exercise of control over all forms of publication in the 16th and 17th centuries.[10] The exercise of the Crown's right in England has always been

---

6 William Caxton established the first press in the precincts of Westminster Abbey c1474/5. The first King's Printer—the printer to legitimately use that title—appears to have been Richard Pynson, who was appointed to the position around 1508/9. His earliest dated proclamation was that of a general pardon issued on the accession of Henry VIII and dated Westminster, May 1509. He described himself as 'prenter unto the kynges noble grace': Henry R Plomer, *Wynkyn de Worde & His Contemporaries from the Death of Caxton to 1535* (London, Grafton & Co, 1925) 138. Refer also to Thomas Frognall Dibdin's Edition of Ames' *Typographical Antiquities* (London, William Miller, 1812) Vol II, 400, vii.

7 *The King v Kidman* (1915) 20 CLR 425, 435.

8 *Australian Communist Party v Commonwealth* (1951) 83 CLR 1, 230; *New South Wales v Commonwealth* (1975) 135 CLR 337, 497–498.

9 *Manners v Blair* (1828) 3 Bli NS 391, 404 (4 ER 1379, 1383); *Attorney-General for New South Wales v Butterworth and Company* (1938) 38 SR (NSW) 195.

10 This control was exercised by Crown grants of privileges to print books, most of which included penalties for contravention of the privileges, which were enforced by the Star Chamber, the grant of a charter by the Crown to the Stationers Company in 1557 that gave the Company a virtual monopoly

by the grant in letters patent—commonly referred to as 'privileges'—of exclusive licences to print and publish those works, most of which have been granted to persons holding the Office of King's Printer.[11]

Reported cases dealing with the prerogative right date back to 1666[12] and while early cases were not consistent in their approach, courts in England eventually adopted the now settled view that the basis of the right lies in

> the character of the duty imposed upon the chief executive officer of the Government, to superintend the publication, of the Acts of the Legislature, and Acts of State of that description, and also of those works, upon which the established doctrines of our religion are founded, that it is a duty imposed upon the first executive magistrate, carrying with it a corresponding prerogative.[13]

In the words of Skinner LCB the right is based on 'a trust reposed in the King, as executive magistrate . . . to promulgate to the people all those civil and religious ordinances which were to be the rule of their civil and religious obedience'.[14] This trust or duty has also been referred to as a 'matter of public care'.[15]

Courts in England have regarded the chief object of the duty imposed on the Crown as to ensure that works of state and religion are published and preserved in a correct and authentic form.[16] It is also implicit from the nature of the works falling within the prerogative and the practice of granting exclusive rights to print and publish that the duty entails an obligation to satisfy public demand for those works since, without this, the state could not expect citizens to be aware of the law and to faithfully observe the tenets of the established religion. Such an obligation was recognised in Skinner LCB in *Eyre and Strahan v Carnan*[17] and Lord Eldon LC in *Universities of Oxford and Cambridge v Richardson*.[18] There are also suggestions in some cases that the duty to superintend the publication of acts of state and of works of the established religion may entail an obligation to ensure that an unreasonable price was not charged for those works. Lord Eldon in *Universities of Oxford and*

---

over printing and various Star Chamber decrees regulating printing until 1640 (when the Star Chamber was abolished), a control perpetuated under the *Licensing Act* of 1662.

11 Throughout the centuries, the Office of King's Printer has been concerned with the public dissemination of the law and other works of church and state. The grants of Office have carried with them the exclusive right to print and publish those works. Examples of the grants of Office are set out in the appendix entitled 'Manuscript Privileges' to this book.

12 *Stationers v Patentees about the Printing of Roll's Abridgment* (also known as *Atkins case*) (1666) Carter 89 (124 ER 842) (HL).

13 *Lord Lyndhurst LC in Manners v Blair* (1828) 3 Bli NS 391, 402–3 (4 ER 1379, 1383).

14 *Eyre and Strahan v Carnan* (1781) Bac Abr 7th edn vol VI (1832) 509, 510.

15 *Roper v Streater* (1672) Bac Abr 7th edn vol VI (1832) 507 (HL).

16 Refer, for example, *Universities of Oxford and Cambridge v Richardson* (1802) 6 Ves Jun 689, 711 (31 ER 1260, 1271); *Manners v Blair* (1828) 3 Bli NS 391, 405 (4 ER 1379, 1384).

17 *Eyre and Strahan v Carnan* (1781) Bac Abr 7th edn vol VI (1832), 509, 512.

18 *Universities of Oxford and Cambridge v Richardson* (1802) 6 Ves Jun 689, 704 (31 ER 1260, 1267).

Cambridge v Richardson, for example, stated that where fees for prerogative works were not ascertained by reference to the privilege 'the benefit shall be reasonable; and if an unreasonable price should be placed on these works, these authorities and patents would be put in considerable hazard'.[19] Such a notion would be consistent with the object of the duty but there are no recorded instances in the cases of the Crown having repealed a privilege for that reason. Some grants to the King's Printer, which were expressed to be made 'for and during Our will and pleasure', contained a condition that the pricing of works be 'just and reasonable' at least in respect of purchases for the services of the state.[20] However, there is scant evidence of the revocation of these grants for this reason. During the 19th century when concerns about the cost of printing under the King's Printers' patents led to a parliamentary inquiry, the sanction that was ultimately employed was to not renew the grant of rights and to have the printing of Acts of Parliament undertaken directly by the state, through its emanation, Her Majesty's Stationery Office (HMSO).[21]

However, there is clear evidence of the imposition of sanctions for not publishing in a correct and authentic form. In *Roper v Streater* the writ of scire facias to repeal a grant appears to have been regarded as an appropriate remedy for abuses of a grant such as 'unskilfulness, selling dear, printing ill etc'.[22] In the Calendar of Patent Rolls, there is a reference in the record of grant of the office of Queen's Printer to John Cawood dated 29 December 1553, to the office having become void because Richard Grafton who held it beforehand 'forfeited it by printing a proclamation in which was contained that a certain Jane, wife of Guildeford Dudley, was queen of England'.[23] Counsel for the defendant in *Basket v University of Cambridge* referred to the publication of Lady Jane Gray's proclamation by stating merely that Queen Mary 'obliged' Grafton to resign his patent but precisely how this was achieved was not discussed.[24] In 1631 the then King's Printers, Robert Barker and the assigns of John Bill, were fined for printing an octavo Bible in which the word 'not' was left out of the seventh commandment (Exodus XX, v 14, Authorised Version) so that it read 'Thou shalt commit adultery'. Copies bearing the misprint were recalled and almost all of the 1000 copies of the edition destroyed. The King's Printers were fined £300.[25]

---

19 *Universities of Oxford and Cambridge v Richardson* (1802) 6 Ves Jun 689, 712 (31 ER 1260, 1271). A control over the price of books was contained in the *Statute of Anne*, 8 Anne c 19 (1709/10), which contained a complaint mechanism against booksellers who 'set a price upon or sell or expose to sale any Book or Books at such a price or rate as shall be conceived by any person or persons to be too high and unreasonable' and provided power to set prices where the price was found to be 'inhanced or any wise to [sic] high or unreasonable' under pain of a penalty of £5 for every book sold or exposed to sale in excess of the set price: refer to University of Cambridge, *Primary Sources on Copyright (1450-1900)* Statute of Anne, London (1710) 3, 4 http://copy.law.cam.ac.uk/cam/index.php.

20 Refer John Gilchrist, 'The Office of King's Printer and the Commercial Dissemination of Government Information—Past and Prospect' (2003) 7 *Canberra Law Review* 145, 151, 154.

21 Ibid 145, 154–60.

22 (1672) Bac Abr 7th edn Vol VI, 1832, 507.

23 United Kingdom. Public Record Office, *Calendar of Patent Rolls, Philip and Mary* Vol 1 (1553–54) (1937) 53.

24 (1758) 1 Black W 105, 116 (96 ER 59, 63).

25 Peter Heylen, *Cyprianus Anglicus* (London, Printed for A Seile, 1668) 228; PM Handover, 'The "Wicked" Bible and the King's Printing House, Black Friars' (1958) *Times (London) House Journal* 215.

While grants to the King's Printer provided a licence to print and publish Acts of Parliament and other laws of the realm, the Crown also granted other privileges over what were described as 'law books'. The privilege in law books is the earliest example of a class monopoly in printing grants made by the Crown and various grants were made for well over two centuries. From an examination of both published and unpublished British public records it appears that the last grant was made in 1788 for a term of 40 years.[26]

In 1553 the first recipient of a grant, Richard Tottel, who was licensed to print 'almaner bokes of oure temporall lawe called the Common lawe' was able to list 25 legal works in his stock, apart from year books, which he considered fell within the grant.[27] Included were Brooke's *Newe Cases* and Littleton's *Tenures*. In the first case dealing with this right, *Stationers v Patentees about the Printing of Roll's Abridgment*, the House of Lords held that a privilege to print 'all law-books that concern the common law' included within it the right to print Roll's *Abridgment*, which was in the nature of a digest of statute and case law as well as parliamentary records.[28] In the second major case, a grant to the defendant of the right to print law books 'touching and concerning the common or statute law' was regarded as including a right to print the third part of Croke's *Reports*, a right that the plaintiff had specifically purchased from the executors of Mr Justice Croke.[29]

The Crown's right over law books was accepted by the courts in *Company of Stationers v Seymour*[30] and *Company of Stationers v Partridge*[31] (although both concern the pirating of almanacs) and appears to have been accepted by one judge in *Millar v Taylor*.[32] However, in the light of the 20th century decision in *Universities of Oxford and Cambridge v Eyre and Spottiswoode Ltd*,[33] which held that the prerogative did not cover the right to print, or authorise others to print, any works the printing of which would be an infringement of copyright, the right over law books cannot presently be considered to cover secondary sources such as original textbooks, original headnotes, annotations, abridgments, or compilations of cases prepared by a reporter, as well as published editions of law reports, the printing of which would be an infringement of copyright. If the Crown's right over law books still exists, it can only do so in relation to the written judgments of its judges.

---

26   United Kingdom. Public Record Office, *MSS Calendars and Indexes to the Patent Rolls: 1 Elizabeth I – 7 William IV* (1965) 90. The grant commenced on 30 April 1789. No subsequent grant has been found by the author in manuscript patent rolls held by the Public Record Office, London. This grant over 'law books' is set out in the appendix entitled 'Manuscript Privileges' to this book.

27   United Kingdom. Public Record Office, *Calendar of Patent Rolls: Edward VI*, Vol V (1547–1553) (1926) 47.

28   (1666) Carter 89 (124 ER 842). Sometimes 'Rolle's—Un Abridgment des plusiers Cases et Resolutions del Common Ley, Alphabeticalment Digest desouth severall Titles'.

29   (1672) Bac Abr 7th edn Vol VI (1832) 507.

30   (1677) 1 Mod 256, 257, 258 (86 ER 865, 866).

31   (1712) 10 Mod 105, 107 (88 ER 647, 648).

32   (1769) 4 Burr 2303, 2315, 2316, 2329 (98 ER 201, 208, 215).

33   [1964] Ch 736.

Whether the Crown's prerogative right extends to the judgments of its judicial officers is not free from doubt. Taggart has argued that the 17th century cases upholding privileges to publish law reports can be 'simply explained by the then extant prerogative control over all printing', and contends that the prerogative extends only to the duty to publish statutes.[34] However that does not explain the continuation of grants over law books into the late 18th century, long after the *Statute of Anne*. On the other hand, Ricketson and Creswell,[35] and Lindgren, Rothnie and Lahore[36] have argued that the prerogative right in relation to the sole printing of judgments continues to exist, separate from any statutory copyright in secondary source material such as law reporters' headnotes.

The arguments for Crown rights over the judgments of its judicial officers can be briefly put as follows:

- the prerogative is not lost by disuse and must be expressly or implicitly removed by statute[37]
- there has been no removal by statute
- judges derive their authority from the Crown, by commission, and judicial power is deemed to be exercised in the Crown's name
- judgments are an exercise of judicial power, and
- there is some evidence of the exercise of a duty, through the Crown's judicial officers, to superintend the publication of judgments to ensure that they are disseminated in a correct and authentic form over many centuries, from the time of the licensing by judges of 'books of the common law' under the Star Chamber decrees of 1586 and 1637 and the *Licensing Act* of 1662[38] through to the development of authorised reports in the late 18th century.[39]

For these reasons it is arguable that Crown prerogative rights still subsist over judgments and that these rights represent the last vestiges of the law book monopoly, which the Crown exercised until the 19th century.

---

34   M Taggart, 'Copyright in Written Reasons for Judgment' (1984) 10 *Sydney Law Review* 319, 320, 324–5. M Perry, 'Judges' Reasons for Judgments – To Whom Do They Belong?' (1998) 18 *New Zealand University Law Review* 257, 273 takes a similar view: 'The only basis for a Crown prerogative over the printing of law reports is on the same footing as the Crown prerogative over all printing, as exercised in the seventeenth century'.

35   S Ricketson and C Creswell, *The Law of Intellectual Property: Copyright, Designs & Confidential Information* (Thomson Legal & Regulatory, Sydney 2nd edn, 2002) vol 2 looseleaf [14.200].

36   K Lindgren, WA Rothnie and JC Lahore, *Copyright and Designs* (LexisNexis Butterworths Sydney, 2004–) vol 1 looseleaf [20.235].

37   Above n 35.

38   *Universities of Oxford and Cambridge v Richardson* (1802) 6 Ves Jun 689, 710 (31 ER 1260, 1270); *Toy v Musgrove* (1888) 14 VLR 349, 378; see above n 35. Refer to John Gilchrist, 'Origins and Scope of the Prerogative Right to Print and Publish Certain Works in England' (2012) 11 (2) *Canberra Law Review* 4, 23–6.

39   Edward Arber, *A Transcript of the Registers of the Company of Stationers of London 1554–1640* (5 vols) (London, Privately Printed, 1875–1894), Vol II 807–12 (Decree of 1586) (s 4); Vol IV 529–36, (Decree of 1637) (s 111); *Licensing Act 1662* (13 & 14 Car II c 33, s III). Refer to John Gilchrist, 'Origins and Scope of the Prerogative Right to Print and Publish Certain Works in England' (2012) 11 (2) *Canberra Law Review* 4, 23–6.

In a 2007 decision of the Federal Court of Australia *Copyright Agency Limited v New South Wales*,[40] Justice Finkelstein commented:

> 185. I also incline to the view that a judge's reasons for judgment should be attributed to the Crown. I am familiar with some of the academic writings on the topic of copyright in judgments. Most writers consider this issue by enquiring whether it can possibly be said that a judge is acting under the direction or control of the Crown. If I might say so, that approach may be misconceived. It is simply beyond argument that a judge does not act under the direction or control of the Crown. On the other hand, if the question is: 'Whether, as a matter of the construction of s 176, a judgment should be attributed to the Crown as a work made by the Crown?' I see no reason why that should not carry an affirmative answer.

With respect to that judge, it has been suggested elsewhere by this author that the preserved prerogative right is unaffected by the statutory right, and in particular s 176 of the *Copyright Act 1968*, and that statutes, judgments and other legal works are not the subject of rights provided by the *Copyright Act 1968* that pertain to their protection as literary works. Inconsistency in the nature of the prerogative right from those statutory rights subsisting under the *Copyright Act 1968*, inconsistency in the principles relating to infringement of the rights and inconsistency in the ownership of rights support this conclusion.[41] Nonetheless, if judgments are no longer the preserve of the prerogative right then Finkelstein J's comments provide some support for concluding that judgments may be the subject of the statutory right. Finkelstein J was not joined by the majority of the Federal Court in these comments that were strictly obiter dicta.

The prerogative right of the Crown in the nature of copyright over statutes has been upheld in Australia in the case of *Attorney-General for New South Wales v Butterworth and Co (Australia) Ltd* where Long Innes CJ in Eq concluded that the exclusive right to print and publish was a prerogative right in the nature of a proprietary right and thus fell within the same broad category as the Crown's right to the ownership of vacant lands in a new colony.[42] The Crown's trust or duty to print and publish certain religious works in England is based on a duty that emanates from the Crown's position as head of the Church of England.[43] There is no established church in Australia[44] and the Crown in right of the Commonwealth or of a State could not have this duty and therefore this right.

---

40   [2007] FCAFC 80 (5 June 2007) http://www.austlii.edu.au/au/cases/cth/FCAFC/2007/80.html.

41   Refer to JS Gilchrist, *Crown Copyright: An Analysis of Rights Vesting in the Crown and Common Law and their Interrelationship*, (LLM thesis, Monash University, 1983) 117–23.

42   (1938) 38 SR (NSW) 195, 246–47.

43   *Manners v Blair* (1828) 3 Bli NS 391, 404 (4 ER 1379, 1383) (HL).

44   *Wylde v Attorney-General for New South Wales* (1948) 78 CLR 224, 286; *Australian Constitution* s 116 – Commonwealth not to legislate in respect of religion – 'The Commonwealth shall not make any law for establishing any religion, or for imposing any religious observance, or for prohibiting the free exercise of any religion, and no religious test shall be required as a qualification for any office or public trust under the Commonwealth'.

The Crown's right to print and publish Acts of Parliament and their abridgments has clear case-law authority[45] and, consistent with the basis of the right, proclamations, orders in council, and instruments made under an act such as regulations and ordinances should, in principle, be encompassed by it. It is unlikely, however, that bills before Parliament would be regarded as falling within it since they are not acts of state that, to use Skinner LCB's phrase in *Eyre and Strahan v Carnan,* determine a subject's civil obedience.[46] The Crown's duty of dissemination, which is the basis of the right, could not therefore be present in this material. But there is no case-law authority to clarify the position.

In summary, at the basis of the extant prerogative right of the Crown in Australia at federal and state levels lies a duty to disseminate certain works of state, to ensure that the publication of these works is done in a correct and authentic form and to ensure that it satisfies public demand for those works. By its terms, this duty serves to promote citizens' access to this information. To the extent that the Crown fulfils this duty, Crown ownership is consistent with citizens obtaining fair and open access to this information. The duty on the Crown that lies at the basis of the prerogative right is an early recognition by government that there are certain works of government in which there is an overriding public interest in citizens accessing information. While the right in Australia is restricted to the law, there are other activities of modern government, such as the administration of public registries, where the interests of the public in accessing works are similarly strong.

Present Scope of Prerogative Copyright

The precise extent of the prerogative right and the duty behind it, however, is not clear. While commentators commonly use the phrase 'printing and publication'[47] to describe the nature of the right, the wording of the privileges have usually only referred to an exclusive right to print and cause to be printed the works in question. However, the privileges normally contained separate prohibitions on others printing, uttering, selling and importing the works into the country.[48] Accordingly, it is implicit in the nature of the exclusive authority to print granted by the privileges and the prohibitions contained within them that the prerogative right was exercised and can be regarded as the right to print and publish in the present-day meaning of these words.

The extant prerogative right of the Crown in Australia is the sole right to print and publish a small number of works of state and it is clear that it includes the right to print and publish abridgements of those works and most probably translations of those works.[49] Neverthe-

---

45 *Attorney-General for New South Wales v Butterworth and Company* (1938) 38 SR (NSW) 195; *Basket v University of Cambridge* (1758) 1 Black W 105 (96 ER 59), 2 Keny 397 (96 ER 1222).

46 (1781) Bac Abr 7th edn Vol VI, 509, 511.

47 Above n 36 [20.205]; see above n 35 [14.195].

48 Refer, for example, to the text of privileges contained in *Stationers Company v Carnan* (1775) 2 Black W 1004 (96 ER 590), *Manners v Blair* (1828) 3 Bli NS 391 (4 ER 1379) and *Universities of Oxford and Cambridge v Eyre and Spottiswoode Ltd* [1964] Ch 736.

49 Crown practice included the grant of rights to print prerogative works in languages other than English (refer, for example, to the grant in *Universities of Oxford and Cambridge v Eyre and Spottiswoode Ltd* [1964] Ch 718, and to the grant by Charles II in 1662, 'Oct. 6 Order by the King that John Durel's

less, the rights of printing and publication are not as extensive as the rights comprised in modern statutory copyright. The prerogative right extends simply to printing and publication and it is uncertain whether the right is infringed by reproduction and dissemination in another medium. For example, would the prerogative extend to the right of communicating the work to the public, which encompasses online dissemination of works? This is a right in literary and other works by virtue of s 31(1)(vi) of the *Copyright Act 1968* (Cth).

Ricketson and Creswell argue that the prerogative is flexible and can extend to new non-print technologies such as online dissemination,[50] while others have argued that it cannot because in the words of Diplock LJ in *BBC v Johns* 'it is 350 years and a civil war too late for the Queen's courts to broaden the prerogative.[51] The grants of exclusive rights were directed at mass reproduction and circulation of works with the objective of providing a commercial monopoly in the exploitation of the works. To the extent that new technologies achieve this object then it is arguable that the Crown's prerogative right will encompass mass reproduction and circulation in those forms.

So, in addition to whatever law and order, democratic or other public policy reasons for the dissemination of the laws of the land including the promotion of what the World Summit on the Information Society called the creation of public systems of information on laws and regulations,[52] there is an existing legal duty on the Crown in Australia that forms the basis of its proprietary right and that requires the dissemination of those laws. This duty exists in perpetuity.[53]

French translation of the Prayer Book be used as soon as printed, in all the French congregation of the Savoy, and all others conformed to the Church of England, with licence to him for the sole printing of the said translation'. *SP Dom 1661–1662* (1861), 508. Refer also to the grant to Bonham Norton of the Office of King's Printer in Latin, Greek and Hebrew (1613) set out in the appendix entitled 'Manuscript Privileges' to this book. Translation rights would seem to be necessary for the adequate dissemination of works, particularly where there may be indigenous languages, as in the case of the United Kingdom, Cymraeg or Scottish Gaelic.

50   See above n 35 [14.205]: 'that the promulgation of statutes etc. in non-printed form comes within existing prerogative rights as a necessary adaptation to changing circumstances, rather than their extension into a new field altogether'; '[the prerogative] should be capable of being applied in a flexible way so as to accommodate changing circumstances and conditions, so long as the fundamental object of the exercise remained the same'. 'Historically, only print technologies were relevant to the question of the prerogative rights, but there is a good argument that the foundation of these rights was not the control of an emergent new industry (printing), but was the Crown's right and obligation to supervise and disseminate the laws of the land'.

51   [1965] Ch 32, 79.

52   International Telecommunications Union/United Nations, *Tunis Commitment*, Document WSIS-05/ TUNIS/Doc/7-E 18 November 2005, Geneva 2003–Tunis 2005, UN/ITU, para 17 http://www.itu.int/wsis/docs 2/tunis/off/7.html.

53   Another important difference between the prerogative copyright and modern statutory copyright is that prerogative copyright exists in perpetuity regardless of publication while the statutory regime under Part VII of the Act grants copyright only for a limited time (generally 50 years from publication).

Part VII of the *Copyright Act 1968*

Statutory provisions in the *Copyright Act 1968* provide the major basis of Crown owner-ship of copyright material in Australia. The special Crown ownership provisions in Part VII of the *Copyright Act 1968* have their origin in similar provisions under the *Copyright Act 1912* (Cth). This Act adopted the British *Copyright Act 1911*, an Act of the British Parliament that sought 'utmost uniformity for Imperial copyright'[54] by being adopted or applied by colonies and self-governing dominions of the British Empire.

Section 18 of the *Copyright Act 1911* provided:

> Without prejudice to any rights or privileges of the Crown, where any work has, whether before or after the commencement of this Act, been prepared or published by or under the direction or control of His Majesty or any Government depart-ment, the copyright in the work shall, subject to any agreement with the author, belong to His Majesty, and in such case shall continue for a period of fifty years from the date of the first publication of the work.

The coming into force of this enactment was the first time in Australian and British copyright law that special provision was made for Crown ownership of copyright. Previously, the Crown claimed ownership under the general provisions of the law, as any other legal person.

Why was a special provision dealing with Crown ownership inserted in the *Copyright Act*? The reasons for the insertion of the clause that became s 18 are not expressed in any of the British Parliamentary deliberations on the Copyright Bill. There was no clause equiv-alent to s 18 in the Copyright Bill 1911 when it was introduced into the British House of Commons. The clause was inserted by the British Government through Standing Commit-tee A when the Bill was referred to committee. The report of that Committee contains no reasons or argument in relation to the provision.[55] Like all other deliberations of the Com-mittee it merely stated what was proposed, by whom and what was agreed. Nor is there any later parliamentary record of discussion or debate over the clause through either House of Parliament.[56]

Nonetheless, the insertion of the provision dealing with Crown ownership occurred against a background of ongoing concern about the costs to the taxpayer of the publication of government works and of unfettered use of government publications by private publish-ers, who were taking a free ride on the products of government for their own profit.

The former is reflected in the 19th-century inquiries into the cost of the private publication of government works and the expansion of the role of Her Majesty's Stationery Office as a

---

54   United Kingdom. *Parliamentary Debates* House of Commons, 7 April 1911 (Official Report) Fifth Series, vol XXIII, 2589 – second reading speech of Mr Buxton, President of the Board of Trade, Friday 7 April 1911: 23 HC Deb 5 s 2589.

55   United Kingdom. *Report from Standing Committee A on the Copyright Bill* (11 July 1911) 36.

56   The amendment was moved by Mr H J Tennant, Parliamentary Secretary to the Board of Trade. The President of the Board of Trade, the Rt Hon Sydney Buxton, introduced the Bill. Mr Tennant was a brother–in–law of the Prime Minister of the time, Mr H H Asquith.

printer and publisher of government works.[57] The picture prior to this expansion was one of rather costly, inefficient and fragmented arrangements for the printing, sale and storage of departmental and parliamentary publications. In 1886, arrangements were put in place for the bringing together of all the important government bookwork printing contracts—including printing for Parliament and public departments. The work was divided into groups and tenders were invited by public advertisement.[58] The only exception had been for printing for the Parliamentary Counsel, for the printing of Bills and orders of either House, and Acts of Parliament. The costs savings arising from this reform were substantial.[59]

At this time some private publishers had begun to realise the commercial potential of some of the titles being issued by HMSO and made reproductions of the material. Consequently, on 23 November 1886 the Treasury published a notice in the *London Gazette*, on advice from Crown law officers:

> Printers and Publishers are reminded that anyone reprinting without due authority matter which has appeared in any Government publication renders himself liable to the same penalties as those he might under like circumstances have incurred had the copyright been in private hands.[60]

These concerns were reflected in the Treasury Minute of 31 August 1887 and in its successor the Treasury Minute of 28 June 1912 dealing with copyright in government publications.

The Treasury Minutes of 1887 and 1912 identified proprietorial interests in the material published by the Crown. The Treasury Minute of 1887 stated:

> The law gives the Crown, or the assignee of the Crown, the same right of copyright as to a private individual. Consequently, if a servant of the Crown, in the course of his duty for which he is paid, composes any document, or if a person is specially employed and paid by the Crown for the purposes of composing any document,

---

57   United Kingdom. *Report from the Select Committee on printing done for the House*, London 1828, 4 Accounts and Papers (House of Commons) 520 (Sess 1828); United Kingdom. *Report from the Select Committee on King's Printers' Patents*, London, 1832, in 18 Accounts and Papers (House of Commons) 713 (Sess 1831–1832); *First Report from the Select Committee on the best means of affording Members information to be derived from Public Documents, with a view to economy, facility of access, and clearness of arrangement* (Select Committee on Printed Papers) London 1833, 12 Accounts and Papers (House of Commons) 15; United Kingdom. *First Report of the Controller of Her Majesty's Stationery Office* (1881) 5.

58   United Kingdom. *Second Report of the Controller of Her Majesty's Stationery Office* (1887) 5.

59   In the order of 39,576l /year for parliamentary papers comparing the costs of production between 1875 and 1888: refer to United Kingdom. *Third Report of the Controller of Her Majesty's Stationery Office* (1890) 4, 5, 23. 'It is well within the mark to say that—going back at farthest to the year 1875 for a comparison of prices—the cost of a first-class battleship, complete with its armament, with an attendant flotilla of half-a-dozen gunboats, has during the last 10 years been saved, without inconvenience to the public, on Government printing and stationery.' (23).

60   G Robbie, 'Crown Copyright – Bete Noire or White Knight?' (1996) 2 *Journal of Information Law and Technology* 1.

the copyright in the document belongs to the Crown as it would in the case of a private employer.

. . .

In other cases the Government publishes at considerable cost works in which few persons only are interested, but which are published for the purpose of promoting literature and science.

These works are of precisely the same character as those published by private enterprise.

In order to prevent an undue burden being thrown on the taxpayer by these works, and to enable the Government to continue the publication of works of this character to the same extent as heretofore, it is necessary to place them, as regards copyright, in the same position as publications by private publishers. If the reproduction of them, or of the most popular portions of them, by private publishers, is permitted, the private publisher will be able to put into his own pocket the profits of the work, which ought to go in relief of the general public, the taxpayer.[61]

The Treasury Minute dated 28 June 1912 stated:

My Lords read section 18 of the Copyright Act, 1911 (1 & 2 Geo. 5. ch.46), which enacts that—

Without prejudice to any rights or privileges of the Crown, where any work has, whether before or after the commencement of this Act, been prepared or published by or under the direction or control of His Majesty, or any Government department, the copyright in the work shall, subject to any agreement with the author, belong to His Majesty, and in such case shall continue for a period of fifty years from the date of the first publication of the work.

The above statutory provision renders it necessary to reconsider the Treasury Minute of the 31st of August, 1887 (presented to the House of Commons No 335 of 1887), and to define anew the practice to be followed with regard to Crown Copyright.

. . .

A considerable and increasing number of Government works fall into the three last classes above set forth, [Official Books, Literary or quasi-literary works, Charts and Ordnance Maps] and My Lords see no reason why such works—often produced at considerable cost—should be reproduced by private enterprise for the benefit of individual publishers.[62]

---

61   United Kingdom. XLIX *Accounts and Papers (House of Commons)* (1887) 224 (No 335, Sess 27 Jan 1887–16 Sept 1887).

62   United Kingdom. LXIX *Accounts and Papers (House of Commons)* (1912) 13 (No 292, Sess 27 Feb 1912–7 March 1913).

The Treasury Minutes of 1887 and 1912 also acknowledged that the Crown published a broad range of material and that the public interest in the dissemination of some material, such as parliamentary reports and Acts of Parliament, demanded 'that it is desirable that the knowledge of their contents should be diffused as widely as possible'[63] and consequently 'no steps will ordinarily be taken to enforce the rights of the Crown in respect of copyright'.[64] Both Minutes reserved the rights of the Crown to assert rights in such material in 'exceptional circumstances', in the words of the 1912 Minute.

These expressed policy considerations—the minimisation of costs that the government and ultimately the taxpayer bears in the printing and publication of government works and the recognition of the overriding public interest and social value in the dissemination of some government works—permeated the development of Crown copyright policy in Britain and Australia until the end of the 20th century.

Another recurring policy consideration evident from the British Treasury Minutes is that of the integrity of government material. The Treasury Minute of 1887 stated that 'Acts of Parliament and official books should not, except when published under the authority of the Government, purport on the face of them to be published by authority'.[65]

The policy expressed by the British Treasury was adopted in Australia shortly after s 18 became Australian law by incorporation into the *Copyright Act 1912*. In a letter dated 27 January 1914 the Prime Minister of Australia wrote to the various State premiers as follows:

> By the Commonwealth *Copyright Act 1912* (No 20 of 1912) the *Imperial Copyright Act 1911*, referred to in the Treasury Minute [dated 28 June 1912], was adopted in Australia, subject to certain modifications set out in the Commonwealth Act, which are not material to the subject of Crown Copyright.
>
> I may mention that the Commonwealth Government proposes to follow the practice which has been adopted in the United Kingdom, and instructions have been issued to the several Departments that immediately upon the publication of works in which it is desired to reserve copyright, application for registration should be made to the Commonwealth Registrar of Copyrights, Melbourne.[66]

These considerations have been later manifest in the Crown's approach to the enforcement of rights in both Commonwealth and State jurisdictions. A more liberal approach has been taken where there is a strong and identifiable public interest in ensuring wide dissemination. A more proprietary approach has been taken where those interests were not as strong.

For example, in 1969 the Commonwealth Government established the Australian Government Publishing Service (AGPS) following the first Erwin Report[67] to provide more

---

63 Ibid.

64 Ibid.

65 United Kingdom. XLIX *Accounts and Papers (House of Commons) (1887)* 225 (No 335, Sess 27 Jan 1887–16 Sept 1887).

66 Australian Archives, Circular Letter W 14/3164 dated Melbourne, 27 January 1914 sent to all States signed by Joseph Cook, Prime Minister (unpublished).

coherent and coordinated government publishing from what was a department-based publishing regime in which there was a wide variation in quality and standards of presentation and printing and some wastage in expenditure.[68] It was modelled on HMSO lines.

In the 1970s the Commonwealth, through AGPS, issued royalty-free licences to individual commercial publishers to publish legal and related materials. The licences were subject to some conditions, including notifying AGPS of what and when the publisher was publishing. If the publisher reproduced the Commonwealth's published edition, a royalty was imposed. In all circumstances no publication was to claim it was the authorised version.[69] In 1982, partly in response to lobbying from the commercial publishers, the Commonwealth issued standing licences to publishers and to educational users allowing publication and multiple reproduction respectively of Commonwealth legislative material, which were royalty-free, largely unlimited and required no notification. In all circumstances no publication was to claim it was the authorised version.[70]

Similarly, in 1995 and 1996, the State of New South Wales issued public waivers of copyright in judgments and legislation citing in the published waivers 'that it is in the interests of the people of New South Wales that access to such [decisions, legislation and extrinsic materials] should not be impeded except in limited special circumstances'.[71] Limited conditions were imposed including that the publication must not directly or indirectly indicate that it is an official version of the material.[72] By 1998, a similar waiver applied in relation to Northern Territory legislation and written judgments, orders and awards of Northern Territory courts.[73]

The CLRC in its report on Crown copyright in 2005 concluded that the management practices for Crown copyright in Australia varied:

> All State and Territories licence government copyright material. Most States have introduced intellectual property policies and guidelines which aim to provide information and guidance on the identification, management and use of copyright.
>
> . . .

---

67   Australia. *The Joint Select Committee on Parliamentary and Government Publications* (Erwin Committee), Parliamentary Paper 32 (1964).

68   Ibid paras 57–67, 82, 94–100.

69   Australia. Attorney-General's Department, AGPS Copyright Licence Agreement (unpublished, 1993).

70   Australia. (1982) 7 (49) *Commonwealth Record* 1782: JC Lahore, *Intellectual Property in Australia: Copyright Law* (1988) looseleaf [4.12.90].

71   New South Wales. 'Notice: Copyright in Judicial Decisions', NSW Government Gazette no 23 (3 March 1995) 1087 (The Hon John Hannaford); 'Notice: Copyright in Legislation and Other Material', NSW Government Gazette no 110 (27 September 1996) and varied by NSW Government Gazette no 20 (19 January 2001) 6611 (The Hon JW Shaw).

72   Ibid.

73   Northern Territory. 'Copyright Policy Concerning Legislation', *Northern Territory Government Gazette*, G43 (1996); Parliament of Northern Territory, 'Copyright Policy in Judgments of the Courts of the Northern Territory' *Northern Territory Government Gazette*, G48, (1998).

The Victorian Government has issued guidelines for the administration of Crown copyright. The Guidelines provide that a fee or royalty should be charged for the right to reproduce government owned material. However, this may be waived or reduced where reproduction is for 'professional, technical or scientific purposes where profit is not a primary purpose of reproduction' and for educational purposes or where dissemination of official material is paramount and commercial considerations are relatively unimportant.[74]

. . .

In Victoria the guidelines for the administration of Crown copyright state that there should be 'relatively wide access to State legislative materials by means of licences to publishers and educational institutions'.[75]

Over the last decade in all Australian jurisdictions there has been an increasing focus by governments in providing public access to information they produce through the internet. This is consistent with the dramatic proliferation of personal computers and increased usage of the internet as a form of communication in Australia and worldwide.

In particular, federal and state governments have established electronic gateways containing low level access information about the role, functions and operations of each government, with deeper access to a wide range of policy, legal and other information usually structured under agency or portfolio responsibility. The scope and range of this information is very substantial and provides a relatively convenient and publicly accessible source of government information.

In 1997 the federal government introduced a web-based database of primary sources of the law named SCALEplus, which initially contained legislation produced by the federal as well as almost all state governments and was available to the public free online. In 2003 that website was superseded by ComLaw,[76] which was also free online but was limited to the legislation of the federal Parliament and the non-self-governing territories. Free searching of state government legislation must now be undertaken through each official state government website or through the non-government website AustLII, run by the University of New South Wales and the University of Technology, Sydney, to which the federal and state governments and courts supply data.[77]

It is relatively easy to obtain access to the law in an up-to-date form through the use of these websites. In particular access is generally more immediate than awaiting the publication of a reprint of legislation or of the judgment of a court. But the development of electronic access to the law has, to a substantial extent, been at the expense of hard-copy publication of the same government information.

---

74   Australia. Copyright Law Review Committee, *Crown Copyright* (2005) 160, 11.26, 11.28.

75   Ibid 167–8, 11.56.

76   URL: http://www.comlaw.gov.au/.

77   URL: http://www.austlii.edu.au/.

In Australia there has been a growing recognition by government of the commercial potential of intellectual property produced by it, particularly with a desire for cost-cutting and cost recovery and other aspects of fiscal and economic reform. There has also been a long recognition of the public interest in the licensing of government information and of supervening non-economic interests in the dissemination of some of that information. Most recently, Australian governments have placed increasing emphasis on disseminating and improving access to information via electronic means and as a result there is a considerable range of administrative, legislative, parliamentary and other governmental information available from this source. Correspondingly, there has been less emphasis on hard-copy publication and over recent years, for example, the federal government has abolished its own bookshops and its departments have authorised less publication in traditional form.[78]

Present Scope of Crown Ownership

The vesting in the Crown of works prepared by, or under the direction or control, of the Crown or first published by the Crown under s 18 of the *Copyright Act 1911* was continued in the regime of Part VII contained in the present *Copyright Act 1968*.

Section 176(2) of the *Copyright Act 1968* provides:

> The Commonwealth or a State is, subject to this Part and to Part X, the owner of the copyright in an original literary, dramatic, musical or artistic work made by, or under the direction or control of, the Commonwealth or the State, as the case may be.

Section 177 of the same Act provides:

> Subject to this Part and to Part X, the Commonwealth or a State is the owner of the copyright in an original literary, dramatic, musical or artistic work first published in Australia if first published by, or under the direction or control of, the Commonwealth or the State, as the case may be.

Like s 18, these provisions vest ownership in works produced by or under the direction or control of the government (s 176(2)) and works first published by the government (s 177).

These provisions have been augmented in the 1968 Act by a similar provision for the later protected subject matter of sound recordings and cinematograph films (s 178).

Section 178 (2) provides:

---

78   Australia. Department of Finance and Administration, *Publishing Information* http://www.agimo.gov.au/information/publishing. The Australian Government Bookshop Network (also known as the Info Access Network) ceased operations on 17 October 2003; Online Information Service Obligations (OISOs) http://www.finance.gov.au/agimo-archive/oiso.html.

> The Commonwealth or a State is, subject to this Part and to Part X, the owner of the copyright in a sound recording or cinematograph film made by, or under the direction or control of, the Commonwealth or the State, as the case may be.

Each of these provisions relating to ownership are expressed to be subject to any agreement made by, or on behalf of the Commonwealth or a State, with the author or maker to the contrary. This is again consistent with the terms of s 18 of the 1911 Act.

What is the scope of the existing Crown ownership provisions in the *Copyright Act 1968*? Is the Crown treated more favourably under the law than other copyright owners?

This segment will analyse the scope and operation of existing law, and areas of uncertainty or lack of clarity.

Part VII of the *Copyright Act 1968*, which is headed 'The Crown' and extends from s 176 to s 183E, provides for the vesting in the Commonwealth or a State of copyright in all subject matter protected by the *Copyright Act 1968* with the exception of published editions of works and television and sound broadcasts. The exceptions are discussed below.

Section 182 in Part VII provides:

> (1) Part III (other than the provisions of that Part relating to the subsistence, duration or ownership of copyright) applies in relation to copyright subsisting by virtue of this Part in a literary, dramatic, musical or artistic work in like manner as it applies in relation to copyright subsisting in such a work by virtue of that Part.

> (2) Part IV (other than the provisions of that Part relating to the subsistence, duration or ownership of copyright) applies in relation to copyright subsisting by virtue of this Part in a sound recording or cinematograph film in like manner as it applies in relation to copyright subsisting in such a recording or film by virtue of that Part.

It is clear from a reading of Part VII and of the Act as a whole that the subsistence, duration and ownership of Crown copyright in this subject matter are determined by the provisions in Part VII. But the provisions of Part III and Part IV of the Act (other than those provisions relating to subsistence, duration or ownership of copyright)[79] apply in relation to copyright subsisting by virtue of Part VII.

Section 31 in Part III in particular sets out the nature of the rights in literary, dramatic, musical and artistic works. The rights in copyright in works include the right to reproduce the work in a material form, to publish the work, to communicate the work to the public, to perform the work (other than an artistic work) in public, to broadcast the work or, in the case of an artistic work, to include the work in a television broadcast, and to cause the work to be transmitted to subscribers to a diffusion service or, in the case of an artistic work, to cause a television program that includes the work to be transmitted to subscribers to a

---

79   Thus, for example, copyright in an original literary work created by a Commonwealth employee in the course of his/her employment with the Commonwealth would continue to subsist so long as the work is unpublished, and where the work is published would subsist for only 50 years after the year in which it was first published (and not 70 years): *Copyright Act 1968 s* 180(1), cf *Copyright Act 1968* s 33(3).

diffusion service. In the case of literary, dramatic and musical works the Act also gives to the copyright owner the right to make an adaptation of the work. This includes the right to make a translation of the work. The nature of rights in published editions of works, television and sound broadcasts, cinematograph films, and sound recordings is set out in ss 88, 87, 86 and 85 in Part IV of the Act.

Likewise infringement and defences to infringement of Crown copyright are determined by provisions outside of Part VII.

There are two exceptions to the subject matter subsisting by virtue of Part VII. Part VII does not make any provision for copyright subsisting in published editions of works and in television and sound broadcasts. Can the Commonwealth or a State as a publisher of an edition of a work prevent another publisher making a facsimile copy of that edition? Reliance can in most cases be placed on the copyright in the work to prevent the reproduction but what if the work is out of copyright? One example would be the reproduction of an early report or a reproduction of a collection of early government papers. The phrase in s 182(2) 'other than the provisions of that Part relating to . . . ownership of copyright' applies only in relation to copyright subsisting by virtue of Part VII in sound recordings and cinematograph films and does not in itself imply that the ownership provisions in Part IV cannot otherwise apply to the Commonwealth or the States. Further, s 7 in Part I of the Act provides that 'subject to Part VII, this Act binds the Crown . . .' that indicates that all the provisions of the Act apply to the Crown subject to the specific provisions of Part VII and suggests, at least, that the Crown in right of the Commonwealth and in right of the State may own rights in published editions of works. The provisions of Part VII relating to subsistence, duration and ownership of rights followed a recommendation of the Spicer Committee that proposed the enactment of a provision similar to s 39 of the United Kingdom *Copyright Act 1956*, which also does not mention specifically Crown rights in broadcasts and published editions of works. Nonetheless, it is clear from the terms of s 182, and from a reading of the Act as a whole that Part VII does not represent a complete code on Crown copyright. As a matter of statutory interpretation, it would seem that the failure to specifically provide for the protection of published editions of works in Part VII does not of itself preclude the Commonwealth or a State owning rights in published editions. Nothing in Part VII is expressly inconsistent with giving effect to the broad terms of s 100 of the Act. That section provides:

> 100. Subject to Parts VII and X, the publisher of an edition of a work or works is
> the owner of any copyright subsisting in the edition by virtue of this Part.

The word 'publisher' is not qualified in any way and should be read as including the Commonwealth or State as a publisher of a work.

Copyright in television and sound broadcasts vests in the maker of the broadcast by virtue of s 99 of the Act:

> 99. Subject to Parts VII and X, the maker of a television broadcast or sound broadcast is the owner of any copyright subsisting in the broadcast.

Under s 22(5) a broadcast is taken to have been made by the person who provided the broadcasting service by which the broadcast was delivered. Under s 91, copyright only subsists in a broadcast made from a place in Australia under the authority of a licence or class licence under the *Broadcasting Services Act 1992* (Cth) or by the Australian Broadcasting Corporation or the Special Broadcasting Service Corporation. These acts expressly extend to these statutory creations of the Commonwealth but do not extend to enable the Commonwealth or a State of itself to own such rights in broadcasts in so far as either body may directly engage in broadcasting.

In addition to the special provisions dealing with Crown ownership already discussed, there is another Crown ownership provision that has its origins in s 18 of the Imperial *Copyright Act 1911*. Section 177 of the *Copyright Act 1968* (Cth) vests in the Commonwealth or a State the copyright in works first published in Australia or a country to which the Act extends if first published by, or under the direction or control of, the Commonwealth or the State to the extinguishment of the rights of any person who claims the copyright in the unpublished work.

A fundamental issue is whether this section should be read subject to s 29(6) of the *Copyright Act 1968* that provides that in determining whether a work has been published for the purposes of any provision of the Act, any unauthorised publication shall be disregarded.

Section 29 (6) provides:

> In determining, for the purposes of any provision of this Act:
>
> (a) whether a work or other subject matter has been published;
>
> (b) whether a publication of a work or other subject matter was the first publication of the work or other subject matter; or
>
> (c) whether a work or other subject-matter was published or otherwise dealt with in the life-time of a person;
>
> any unauthorized publication or the doing of any other unauthorized act shall be disregarded.

The word 'authorised' in the provision may imply 'consent', that is, with the permission of the copyright owner. Does s 29(6) have the effect of restricting the operation of s 177 to circumstances only where the publication is with the consent of the author?

There are conflicting views on this issue. Monotti argues[80] that s 177 should be read in this way because s 29(6) does not appear to be subject to Part VII and yet s 29(8) specifically mentions that nothing in either of the two preceding subsections (including s 29(6)) affects any provisions of Part IX (dealing with moral rights). Further, she argues that s 177 should be read down to avoid the constitutional limitation on acquisition of property other than on just terms,[81] the two provisions are not inconsistent if first publication arises only

---

80   A Monotti, 'Nature and Basis of Crown Copyright in Official Publications' (1992) 9 *European Intellectual Property Review* 305, 314.

81   Although s 177 may appear on its face to be a law with respect to the acquisition of property without provision for just terms as required by s 51(xxxi) of the *Australian Constitution*, it is difficult to characterize s 177 as a law dealing with the acquisition of property because the *Copyright Act 1968* itself creates that property and itself determines in whom that property vests. The High Court of Australia has

after the author's consent has been obtained, and that other provisions of the Act specifically provide that they are subject to Part VII.

Nonetheless, s 7 of the Act provides that the provisions of the Act bind the Crown subject to the provisions of Part VII and accordingly suggests that s 177 is paramount in its operation over and above the requirements of s 29(6). According to the United Kingdom Committee to Consider the Law on Copyright and Designs (the Whitford Committee), the equivalent United Kingdom provision dealing with the automatic vesting of rights in the Crown on first publication 'is said to be necessary in order to safeguard the right of the Crown to publish, for example, evidence given to committees and commissions and the findings of such bodies'.[82] A narrow interpretation would effectively deny s 177 of much of its force. It would expose the Crown to a claim for compensation or infringement where publication was without consent.

Section 177 deals with the ownership of works on first publication by the Commonwealth or a State. The general provision in the Act dealing with ownership of copyright in works (s 35) is expressed to be subject to Parts VII and Part X. Be that as it may, s 29(6) could be read harmoniously with s 177 if the word authorised in s 29(6) was read as 'authorised by the Act'.

The narrow view was accepted in *Copyright Agency Limited v New South Wales*[83] although the Federal Court of Australia held in that case that the Crown did not 'first publish' (within the meaning of s 177 of the *Copyright Act 1968*) the survey plans registered with it by making the plans available to the public and to local government and authorities.

Emmett J stated in that case:

> 131. Under s 183(8), an act done under s 183(1) does not constitute publication of a work. Thus, if the making available of a work to the public by the State is done under s 183, it does not constitute publication. A fortiori, it is not first publication. On the other hand, if such making available by the State is not done under s 183(1), and there is no other licence taken to have been granted to the State to make a work available, it would follow that those acts of the State would be an unauthorised publication and, accordingly, under s 29(6) must be disregarded in determining whether the work has been published and whether the publication was the first publication of the work.[84]

---

taken the view that to the extent that a law passed under the copyright power, s 51(xviii) of the *Constitution*, conferring rights on authors and other originators of copyright material is concerned with the adjustment of competing rights or obligations of other persons, that impact is unlikely to be characterised as a law with respect to the acquisition of property for the purposes of s 51: refer to *Nintendo Company Limited v Centronics Systems Pty Limited* (1994) 181 CLR 134, 160–1; [1994] HCA 27 per Mason CJ, Brennan, Deane, Toohey, Gaudron and McHugh JJ at [38–39].

82 United Kingdom. *Copyright and Designs Law: Report of the Committee to Consider the Law on Copyright and Designs* (Whitford Committee) Cmnd 6732 (1977) [599].

83 [2007] FCAFC 80 (5 June 2007) http://www.austlii.edu.au/au/cases/cth/FCAFC/2007/80.html.

84 Ibid.

Emmett J held on the facts that the survey plans had previously been published and that by the lodgement of the plans, a surveyor must have been taken to have licensed and authorised the Crown to make available to the public, copy and do any other acts required by the Crown's statutory and regulatory planning regime. Copyright in the plans remained with the surveyor. While the case recognised this notion of implied licence in dealings with government it did not explore arguments for the wider interpretation of s 177 above. The Court did not have to decide whether s 177 effected an acquisition of property otherwise than on just terms within the meaning of s 51(xxxi) of the *Commonwealth Constitution*.

Meaning of 'By, or Under the Direction or Control'

The major provisions that vest ownership of copyright in the Commonwealth or a State, (ss 176 (2), 177 and 178(2)) all contain the vesting phrase 'by, or under the direction or control of, the Commonwealth or the State'. That phrase is not defined in the *Copyright Act 1968* and has only been the subject of limited judicial analysis. In *Linter Group Ltd (in liq) v Price Waterhouse*[85] Justice Harper of the Supreme Court of Victoria held that a transcript of judicial proceedings produced pursuant to the judge's direction under the *Evidence Act 1958* (Vic) had been produced under the direction of the State for the purposes of s 176 of the *Copyright Act 1968*:

> As I understand it, it is common ground that the State of Victoria is the owner of the copyright in such transcript as is produced following a direction made pursuant to s.130 of the *Evidence Act 1958*. That section empowers a person acting judicially to direct, in circumstances that apply to this litigation, that any evidence to be given in the proceeding be transcribed in any manner that the judicial officer directs. Every person who thereafter transcribes the evidence shall, in doing so, be under the direction of the Court: s.134. That position obtains here. By s.176 of the *Copyright Act 1968*, the ownership of the copyright in an original literary work produced under the direction of a State shall inure to that State. As one of the three arms of government of the State of Victoria, the Supreme Court is, for the purposes of this provision, the State.[86]

Another relevant case—involving the equivalent phrase in the British *Copyright Act 1911*—was *British Broadcasting Co v Wireless League Gazette Publishing Co*.[87] In that case, the plaintiff company produced a publication called the *Radio Times* that contained advance daily programs for the ensuing week. The defendant selected and copied numerous items from one of the plaintiff's publications in the Wireless League Gazette. Astbury J held that the plaintiff's publication was a compilation in which copyright subsisted but that it was not a work 'prepared or published by or under the direction or control of His Majesty or the Postmaster-General' within the meaning of s 18 of the *Copyright Act 1911*. Copyright in the compilation of the programs therefore belonged to the plaintiff and not the Crown.

---

85   [2000] VSC 90 (20 March 2000) http://www.austlii.edu.au/au/cases/vic/VSC/2000/90.html.

86   Ibid para 7.

87   [1926] Ch 433.

The plaintiff was required under its broadcasting licence and a supplementary agreement to 'transmit efficiently' every day a program of broadcast matter to the reasonable satisfaction of the Postmaster-General who had the power to revoke the licence if the program included improper matter. Astbury J stated that the plaintiff was a licensed corporation entitled, so long as it complied with the licence, to carry on its broadcasting service for profit and to acquire and hold assets to effect that service. He concluded 'so long as they are allowed to carry on their broadcasting business for their own profit ... the property in the Radio Times, including the programs, brought into existence for the purposes of that business, is their own'.[88] Astbury J did not explore the proper construction of the phrase 'direction or control' although it is clear from the case that the production of a publication by the plaintiff was not the object of the licensing power exercised by the Postmaster-General that was directed towards the censorship of improper matter from broadcast programs. Merely to specify the form of the program did not constitute a direction to prepare it or to control the manner in which it was prepared.

In *Land Transport Safety Authority of New Zealand v Glogau*[89] a local statute required taxi drivers to keep log books of driving hours in a form approved by the Secretary for Transport. The Crown claimed copyright in the log books under s 52(1) of the *Copyright Act 1962* (NZ), the equivalent provision to s 176 of the Australian Act. The New Zealand Court of Appeal held that there was no Crown copyright in the log books even though there was *de facto* direction as to their contents and control over their form and content, because the Crown could not under statute or contract require a driver to produce the log books.

These cases therefore are of limited assistance in interpreting the words 'direction' and 'control'.

Copinger and Skone James have suggested that the phrase 'direction or control' in an equivalent United Kingdom provision is a much wider expression than 'contract of service' and that copyright in works that have been commissioned by the Crown may still vest in the Crown under that section.[90] Lindgren, Rothnie and Lahore have expressed the view that the author may be an independent contractor and a work may still be made 'by, or under the direction or control of' the Commonwealth or a State.[91] Ricketson and Creswell consider that the phrase 'is not confined to works made by authors who are employed by the Commonwealth or a State pursuant to a contract of service ... but appears wide enough to cover works made for the Commonwealth or a State by independent contractors. However it is likely that, in such circumstances, the production of such works will need to be the principal object of the exercise of government direction or control, and not merely an incidental or peripheral consequence of some generalized government licensing or monitoring power'.[92] The Australian CLRC in its report on Crown copyright stated

---

88   Ibid 444.

89   [1999] 1 NZLR 261.

90   EP Skone-James, JF Mummery and JE Rayner-James, *Copinger and Skone James on Copyright* 12th edn, (Sweet and Maxwell, 1980) 846–8 and Kevin Garnett, Gillian Davies and Gwilym Harbottle, *Copinger and Skone James on Copyright*, 15th edn (Sweet and Maxwell, 2005) Vol 1, 588.

91   K Lindgren, WA Rothnie and JC Lahore, *Copyright and Designs* (LexisNexis Butterworths, 2004–) looseleaf [20.190].

'while the term clearly includes works created by government employees in the course of their duties, its exact scope is uncertain. It may include commissioned works and the works of volunteers supervised by government'.[93]

While the purposive approach to statutory interpretation guides the construction of all Commonwealth enactments, there is no clear guidance from the context of the Act itself, or its extrinsic materials and case law to assist in ascertaining the meaning of the provision. The provision should be construed according to the ordinary and natural meaning of the words.[94]

A more helpful case is the Federal Court of Australia decision in *Copyright Agency Limited v New South Wales*.[95] That case concerned certain dealings by the State of New South Wales with survey plans prepared by surveyors who were members of the Copyright Agency Limited, a collecting society for the purposes of the *Copyright Act 1968*. The State argued that the copyright in survey plans deposited for registration in pursuance of statutory land holding regimes within the State was vested in the State pursuant to s 176 or s 177 of the Act. Alternatively, it argued that it was authorised to do certain acts in relation to the survey plans otherwise than in pursuance of the Crown use provision that would attract a claim for remuneration from copyright owners in respect of those acts. The State copied and scanned the plans and incorporated them into a database for statutory as well as administrative reasons. It charged the public access and copying fees for the plans, whether electronically or over the counter.

In the majority judgment, Emmett J, with whom Lindgren J agreed, examined the meaning of the phrase 'by, or under the direction or control of' the Crown. He stated:

> 122 . . . '*By*' is concerned with those circumstances where a servant or agent of the Crown brings the work into existence for and on behalf of the Crown. '*Direction*' and '*control*' are not concerned with the situation where the work is made **by** the Crown but with situations where the person making the work is subject to either the direction or control of the Crown as to how the work is to be made. In the copyright context, that may mean how the work is to be expressed in a material form.
>
> 123. **Direction** might mean order or command, or management or control (Macquarie Dictionary Online). Direction might also mean instructing how to proceed or act, authoritative guidance or instruction, or keeping in right order management or administration (Oxford English Dictionary Online).
>
> 124. **Control** might mean the act or power of controlling, regulation, domination or command (Macquarie Dictionary Online). Control might also mean the fact of controlling or of checking and directing action, the function or power of directing

---

92 S Ricketson and C Creswell, *The Law of Intellectual Property: Copyright, Designs & Confidential Information* (Thomson Legal & Regulatory, 2nd edn, 2002–) (looseleaf) [14.180].

93 Above n 74, para 5.15.

94 Refer to ss 15AA, 15AB *Acts Interpretation Act 1901* (Cth), DC Pearce & RS Geddes, *Statutory Interpretation in Australia* (LexisNexis Butterworths, 7th edn, 2011) 36–40.

95 Above n 83.

and regulating, domination, command, sway: *Shorter Oxford English Dictionary* (5th edn, Oxford University 2002).

125. Thus, when the provisions refer to a work being made **under the direction or control of** the Crown, in contrast to being made **by** the Crown, the provisions must involve the concept of the Crown bringing about the making of the work. It does not extend to the Crown laying down how a work is to be made, if a citizen chooses to make a work, without having any obligation to do so.

126. The question is whether the Crown is in a position to determine whether or not a work will be made, rather than simply determining that, if it is to be made at all, it will be made in a particular way or in accordance with particular specifications. The phrase '*under the direction or control*' does not include a factual situation where the Crown is able, *de facto*, to exercise direction or control because an approval or licence that is sought would not be forthcoming unless the Crown's requirements for such approval or licence are satisfied. The phrase may not extend much, if at all, beyond commission, employment and analogous situations. It may merely concentrate ownership in the Crown to avoid the need to identify particular authors, employees or contracting parties.

127. The Parliament did not intend that the Crown would gain copyright, or share in copyright, simply as a side effect of a person obtaining a statutory or other regulatory approval or licence from the Crown.[96]

In this view of the phrase 'by, or under the direction or control of' the Crown, works of Crown servants and agents are made 'by' the Crown. It would also be consistent with this view that works made by the holder of a public or statutory office who normally exercise independent powers and functions would also be works made 'by' the Crown since, in Emmett J's view, the words 'direction or control' are not concerned with the situation where the work is made by the Crown but are concerned with the situation where the person making of the work is subject to either the direction or control of the Crown.

Finkelstein J, while agreeing with his other two judges in the answers to the questions stated for the Federal Court, took a different view of the operation of the phrase. In his view, works made 'by' the Crown did not include works made by servants or agents of the Crown but were intended to deal with those kinds of works where the author was not subject to the direction or control of the Crown and would include works 'where at least in a legal sense, the work has no author'. He cited judgments as an example of the former and Acts of Parliament as an example of the latter.[97] Nonetheless, it should be pointed out that Acts of Parliament are normally drafted by Parliamentary Counsel and do, in a copyright sense, have authors: commonly joint authors.

Emmett J makes it clear that where a work is made 'under the direction or control of the Crown' the Crown must bring about the making of the work. The meaning of the phrase would not extend to the factual situation where the Crown is able *de facto* to exercise direction or control because an approval or licence would not be forthcoming unless Crown

---

96   Ibid.

97   Ibid, paras 185, 184.

requirements are satisfied. In the majority judgment of the Full Federal Court delivered by Emmett J the phrase 'may not extend much, if at all, beyond commission, employment and analogous situations'.[98] While the Full Court of the Federal Court held on the facts that 'a surveyor must be taken to have licensed and authorised the doing of the very acts that the surveyor was intending should be done as a consequence of the lodgement of the Relevant Plan for registration'.[99] That is, there was an implied licence for the State to do everything that, under the statutory and regulatory framework that governed registered plans,[100] the State is obliged to do with, or in relation to, registered plans. The Court did not consider that any of the registered plans were made under the direction or control of the State within the meaning of s 176(2) of the *Copyright Act 1968*.

Accordingly, the phrase 'by, or under the direction or control of the Crown' in the majority view would encompass works of Crown servants, agents, public office holders, and commissioned works and would extend to other works of independent contractors where the Crown's contract has brought about the making of the work. It would seem consistent with this view that works of independent contractors must either be the central object of the Crown's direction (a commissioned work) or be contemplated by the parties as necessarily arising from that direction. This is consistent with a wider meaning of 'direction' beyond 'control'. Of course, a relationship of independent contractor is often governed by a written contract and ownership of copyright in works or other subject matter produced under a commission, or other form of independent contract, can be the subject of an express agreement between the parties, by virtue of s 179 of the *Copyright Act 1968*.

Conclusion

In summary, the scope of the provisions vesting copyright in the government and the range of subject matter contained in the *Copyright Act 1968*, coupled with the widespread functions of modern government produce a disparate variety of material under Part VII of the *Copyright Act 1968*. The Act also preserves old Crown rights in a range of legal material but the precise scope of that material and the extent of those rights is somewhat uncertain.

In much of this statutory and prerogative copyright material there is a strong and identifiable public interest in wide dissemination and access. In other material the interest is

---

98   Ibid, para 126.

99   Ibid, paras 156, 155.

100   On appeal from the Full Federal Court, the High Court of Australia rejected the implication of a licence: 'a licence will only be implied when there is a necessity to do so. As stated by McHugh and Gummow JJ in *Byrne v Australian Airlines Ltd*, 'This notion of "necessity" has been crucial in the modern cases in which the courts have implied for the first time a new term as a matter of law. Such necessity does not arise in the circumstances that the statutory licence scheme excepts the State from infringement, but does so on condition that terms for use are agreed or determined by the Tribunal (s 183(1) and s 183(5)). The Tribunal is experienced in determining what is fair as between a copyright owner and a user. It is possible, as ventured in the submissions by CAL, that some uses, such as the making of a "back-up" copy of the survey plans after registration, will not attract any remuneration'. *Copyright Agency Ltd v New South Wales* [2008] HCA 35, paras 92, 93 http://www.austlii.edu.au/au/cases/cth/HCA/2008/35.html.

not as strong. Policies of successive Australian governments have sought to retain copyright ownership in that material while at the same time facilitating the licensing of some of that material.

Most recently across the spectrum of Part VII and prerogative copyright material there has been an emphasis on the provision of electronic access to information that commonly provides ready and quick access to that information. In the case of legal information, state and federal governments and courts have supplied data for the free online database AustLII and licensed or waived rights for other private databases such as LexisNexis to promote access to legal information. As outlined in this chapter, governments have also long provided similar licences or waivers to legal publishers in print form for the same reason.

As mentioned in the Introduction to this book, at the World Summit on the Information Society held in Geneva in December 2003, representatives from 175 countries declared their common commitment to build a people-centred, inclusive and development- orientated Information Society.[101] One plan of action agreed to at the Summit and further confirmed in Tunis in 2005 concerned the importance of access to information and knowledge. In particular, paragraph C3 10 (b) stated that 'Governments are encouraged to provide adequate access through various communication resources, notably the Internet, to public official information'.[102] In the Tunis Commitment of 2005 the World Summit further urged governments, 'using the potential of ICTs, to create public systems of information on laws and regulations, envisaging a wider development of public access points and supporting the broad availability of this information'.[103] This information has been supplied for public order, planning, political accountability and other social objectives and constitutes a service that is a non-market activity. Governments should be encouraged to provide ICT access to this information freely in pursuance of these objectives.[104]

Australian state and federal policy outlined in this chapter accords with the plan of action agreed to at the World Summit on the Information Society at Geneva—that 'Governments are encouraged to provide adequate access through various communication resources, notably the Internet, to public official information'. However the fragmentation of electronic dissemination of laws and regulations between state and federal governments, which have been poorly cross-linked, with different search engines,[105] and the piecemeal and uncoordinated promulgation of licences or waivers to private publishers and the public by those governments, has less coherently promoted the Tunis Commitment of creating a public system of information on laws and regulations.

---

101   International Telecommunications Union/United Nations, *Declaration of Principles: Building the Information Society: a Global Challenge in the New Millennium,* Document WSIS–03/GENEVA/Doc/4-E 12 December 2003, and *Tunis Agenda for the Information Society,* Document WSIS-05/TUNIS/DOC/6 (Rev.1)-E, 18 November 2005, Geneva-Tunis, UN/ITU, 2003–2005, para A1 http://www.itu.int/wsis/docs/geneva/official/dop.html.

102   Ibid.

103   Ibid, para 17.

104   Refer to John S Cook 'A Summary View of Government Cost Recovery Policies in Australia and New Zealand Relating to the Supply of Public Sector Information' (2010) *Queensland University of Technology ePrints* http://eprints.qut.edu.au/31609/.

105   Refer to the range of official government sites at http://www.comlaw.gov.au/Home/Othersources.

In the next chapter, Australia's progress towards Tunis Commitment goals is the subject of a comparative assessment through a survey of the laws and practices of selected comparable countries.

3

Crown Copyright: A Comparative Perspective

Copyright is an international form of property and ICT technologies are affecting the way all governments and individuals are communicating and accessing government information. This chapter examines developments in the laws and practices of selected comparable countries in facilitating access to public official information. Of particular relevance to this comparative analysis, for reasons of legal heritage or legal influence, are law and policy developments in the United Kingdom, the European Union, New Zealand, Canada and the United States of America.

The common international understanding of the importance of access to information and knowledge have been reflected in developments in the copyright laws and practices dealing with public information in European countries and elsewhere. There has also been a multinational commitment to build a people-centred, inclusive and development-oriented Information Society at Geneva in 2003 and Tunis in 2005.

In the 2008 review of the National Innovation System—*Venturous Australia: Building Strength in Innovation*—it was stated, 'Australia is behind many other advanced countries in establishing institutional frameworks to maximise the flow of government generated information and content'.[1] It is appropriate therefore to explore developments in the laws and practices of selected comparable countries in facilitating access to public official information.

There are a number of policy considerations evident in these developments. One is the long recognised need to disseminate the law, legislative materials and similar information to the public. The rationales are public order and the rule of law, planning and political accountability. This is evidenced in written policies long before the digital era (for example, the UK Treasury Minutes of 1887 and 1912). Outside legislative materials, access to wider Public Sector Information (PSI) is sought to aid transparency of government and may provide

---

1 Australia. Cutler & Company Pty Ltd, *Venturous Australia: Building Strength in Innovation: Report on the Review of the National Innovation System* (the Cutler Report) Report to Senator the Hon Kim Carr, Minister for Innovation, Industry, Science and Research (August 2008) 98 http://www.industry.gov.au/innovation/InnovationPolicy/Pages/Document%20library/NISReport.aspx or http://www.industry.gov.au/innovation/InnovationPolicy/Documents/Policy/NISReport.pdf.

citizens with a heightened capacity to critically assess and to participate in the general workings of government.[2]

Another policy consideration is the more modern concern—prompted by growth of the internet—to facilitate access to government information in order to encourage economic and social benefits to the wider society,[3] or in the words of *The Seoul Declaration for the Future of the Internet Economy*, 'to make public sector information and content, including scientific data, and works of cultural heritage, more widely accessible in digital format'.[4] These benefits are effected by granting wider access to public official information, to enable the public to directly benefit from information in the government's hands and to indirectly benefit from information assembled and developed into new and more valuable information by the private sector.

A third consideration is that the public sector itself seeks to benefit from granting wider access to PSI. Facilitating access to PSI promotes effective and efficient public administration by assisting the work of other public institutions, by eliminating or reducing redundant public investments and by lessening the administrative burden on government services. Better communication of information across often large and physically disparate organs of government promotes these goals and lessens the administrative burden on government and on users.

The common factor in these developments is that there has been a movement from a 'pull' model to a 'push' model of government information management:

> The pull approach to information management is nevertheless dominant in Victoria, and indeed internationally. It is characterised by policies that allow for the release of information to individuals or organisations on request, provided access is not restricted for specific reasons (such as privacy or security).
>
> . . .
>
> The push model emphasises proactive publication of information by government. Under this model, government does not rely on requests for information, and instead identifies and publishes information proactively.[5]

---

2   Victoria. Economic Development and Infrastructure Committee, Parliament of Victoria, *Inquiry into Improving Access to Victorian Public Sector Information and Data: Report* (June 2009) Parliamentary Paper No 198, Session 2006–2009, 3 http://www.parliament.vic.gov.au/edic/inquiries/article/1019.

3   Australia. Office of the Australian Information Commissioner, *Understanding the Value of Public Sector Information in Australia – Issues Paper 2* (November 2011) 16–33 http://www.oaic.gov.au/information-policy/information-policy-engaging-with-you/previous-information-policy-consultations/information-policy-issues-paper-2-november-2011/issues-paper-2 or http://www.oaic.gov.au/images/documents/information-policy/engaging-with-you/previous-information-policy-consultations/issues-paper-2/issues_paper2_understanding_value_public_sector_information_in_australia.pdf.

4   OECD, *The Seoul Declaration for the Future of the Internet Economy*, OECD Ministerial Meeting on the Future of the Internet Economy, Seoul, South Korea 17–18 June 2008, 7 http://www.oecd.org/sti/40839436.pdf.

5   Above n 2, 17–8.

This chapter will conclude that the open content movement has highlighted fundamental questions facing all governments as to what information should be released or not released, and if released, whether access should be limited in some ways (through price, licensing arrangements, or through accessible media). Governments must also decide what proactive steps it must take to disseminate information, that is, to provide access through a 'push' model as opposed to a 'pull' model. This is turn provides a basis for evaluation of Australian law and practices.

The Meaning of Access

The term 'access' is used in this book to describe being able to find and retrieve information in a way that would otherwise often amount to an infringement of copyright; for example, by reproducing or copying material containing information.[6] Where retrieved information is used to reproduce and build upon it, to use it, for example, for economic gain and for a range of public goods, this is referred to as re-use of information. The two steps are sometimes referred to as rights to access and re-use information. A 2008 OECD recommendation used the term 'better access and wider use and re-use'[7] of PSI. The term 'open content' is also used to describe information that is subject to these two rights. Access is sometimes used in other senses.

The term 'open access' is presently applied to unrestricted access via the internet to scholarly and scientific articles and other works, without normally involving an infringement of copyright.

For many western governments, one common use of the term access is in relation to a public right of access to information in its possession. This is effected through FOI laws and underpins the accountability of government in a democratic society. Access may be given through a reasonable opportunity to inspect a document, or to hear or view sound or images, or by provision of a copy of the document or a transcript of a document.[8]

The term 'access' is also used in a wider sense to describe being able to find, obtain and use information in a way that would otherwise normally amount to an infringement of copyright, to be able to retrieve and use the information to reproduce and build upon it, to use

---

6   The term 'access' is sometimes used in the historical sense, that is, of admittance to something, for example, in obtaining access to information that involves cost, labour and time to search and recover. Prior to the information age this information was often only practically available to a segment of the public and required the physical presence of the person or agent seeking access. In some cases access was intentionally restricted or qualified by the terms of the acquisition of documents, or for preservation, confidentiality, or management reasons.

7   OECD. *Recommendation of the Council for Enhanced Access and More Effective Use of Public Sector Information*, (30 April 2008) OECD Ministerial Meeting on the Future of the Internet Economy, Seoul, South Korea 17–18 June 2008 http://www.oecd.org/internet/ieconomy/44384673.pdf. This includes use by the original public sector generator or holder or other public sector bodies and further re-use by business or individuals for commercial or non-commercial purposes. In general, the term 'use' implies this broad spectrum of use and re-use.

8   Refer, for example, s 20 of the *Freedom of Information Act 1982* (Cth).

it, for example, for economic gain and for a range of public goods; that is, to refer to both access to, and re-use of, information.

International Comparisons with the Australian Law

United Kingdom

The United Kingdom copyright law was reformed in 1988 by the enactment of the *Copyright, Designs and Patents Act 1988* (UK). Prior to that reform the United Kingdom law was similar to Part VII of the *Copyright Act 1968* (Cth). Under the *Copyright, Designs and Patents Act 1988* the notion of Crown copyright has been preserved over all material produced by government, but a novel and separate copyright was created in the Parliament of the United Kingdom. Legislative materials have not, under the reforms, entered the public domain.

Section 163 in Chapter X of that Act provides:

Crown copyright

(1) Where a work is made by Her Majesty or by an officer or servant of the Crown in the course of his duties–

(a) the work qualifies for copyright protection notwithstanding section 153(1) (ordinary requirement as to qualification for copyright protection), and

(b) Her Majesty is the first owner of any copyright in the work.

(2) Copyright in such a work is referred to in this Part as 'Crown copyright', notwithstanding that it may be, or have been, assigned to another person.

(3) Crown copyright in a literary, dramatic, musical or artistic work continues to subsist–

(a) until the end of the period of 125 years from the end of the calendar year in which the work was made, or

(b) if the work is published commercially before the end of the period of 75 years from the end of the calendar year in which it was made, until the end of the period of 50 years from the end of the calendar year in which it was first so published.

(4) In the case of a work of joint authorship where one or more but not all of the authors are persons falling within subsection (1), this section applies only in relation to those authors and the copyright subsisting by virtue of their contribution to the work.

(5) Except as mentioned above, and subject to any express exclusion elsewhere in this Part, the provisions of this Part apply in relation to Crown copyright as to other copyright.

(6) This section does not apply to a work if, or to the extent that, Parliamentary copyright subsists in the work (see sections 165 and 166D).

For the purposes of holding, dealing with and enforcing parliamentary copyright, each House of Parliament is treated as a body corporate.[9]

Section 163(3)(a) extends the period of protection for Crown works from 50 to 125 years from the making of the work. The perpetual copyright that hitherto had existed in an unpublished Crown work was abolished and replaced by that 125 year maximum period of protection under s 163(3)(b).

Copyright subsisting in Acts of Parliament by virtue of the Royal prerogative was also abolished and replaced by a copyright subsisting for 50 years from the time of Royal Assent under s 164(2) of the Act.

Both measures have abolished long-established features of the law, similar to the present position in Australia, and have substituted a more limited copyright protection. Of significance is that copyright protection has been retained, particularly in Acts of Parliament.

Crown ownership in works under s 163(1) above was narrowed from works made 'by or under the direction or control of the Crown' (that was the expression used under the preceding *Copyright Act 1956* (UK)) to works made 'by an officer or servant of the Crown in the course of his duties'. Ironically, parliamentary copyright retains the 'direction or control' formula but assists to explain that formula by expressly including within it 'any work made by an officer or employee' of either House 'in the course of his duties' (s 165(4)).

The former would appear to reduce the scope of the former Crown ownership provision while the latter preserves the formula, but seeks to clarify it at the same time.

Section 165 in Chapter X provides:

Parliamentary copyright

(1) Where a work is made by or under the direction or control of the House of Commons or the House of Lords–

(a) the work qualifies for copyright protection notwithstanding section 153(1) (ordinary requirement as to qualification for copyright protection), and

(b) the House by whom, or under whose direction or control, the work is made is the first owner of any copyright in the work, and if the work is made by or under the direction or control of both Houses, the two Houses are joint first owners of copyright.

(2) Copyright in such a work is referred to in this Part as 'Parliamentary copyright', notwithstanding that it may be, or have been, assigned to another person.

(3) Parliamentary copyright in a literary, dramatic, musical or artistic work continues to subsist until the end of the period of 50 years from the end of the calendar year in which the work was made.

(4) For the purposes of this section, works made by or under the direction or control of the House of Commons or the House of Lords include–

---

9 *Copyright, Designs and Patents Act 1988* (UK) s 167(1).

(a) any work made by an officer or employee of that House in the course of his duties, and

(b) any sound recording, film, live broadcast of the proceedings of that House;

but a work shall not be regarded as made by or under the direction or control of either House by reason only of its being commissioned by or on behalf of that House.

(5) In the case of a work of joint authorship where one or more but not all of the authors are acting on behalf of, or under the direction or control of, the House of Commons or the House of Lords, this section applies only in relation to those authors and the copyright subsisting by virtue of their contribution to the work.

(6) Except as mentioned above, and subject to any express exclusion elsewhere in this Part, the provisions of this Part apply in relation to Parliamentary copyright as to other copyright.

(7) The provisions of this section also apply, subject to any exceptions or modifications specified by Order in Council, to works made by or under the direction or control of any other legislative body of a country to which this Part extends; and references in this Part to 'Parliamentary copyright' shall be construed accordingly.

(8) A statutory instrument containing an Order in Council under subsection (7) shall be subject to annulment in pursuance of a resolution of either House of Parliament.

Parliamentary copyright, which fell previously within the scope of Crown copyright under the 1956 Act, was introduced at House of Commons Committee stage partly as an expression of Parliament's independence from the Crown and partly to give Parliament more direct control of reports of its own proceedings. To vest such copyright in the Crown would have had the effect of vesting control of parliamentary papers with the controller of HMSO rather than with the House in question.[10]

In some respects this separate copyright seems to have arisen as a result of an identification between ownership of copyright and the administration of copyright. The creation of a parliamentary copyright has led to some inventive legal transfers of copyright under the law in literary works that become Bills and then subsequently Acts of Parliament.[11]

Copyright in a public Bill 'belongs in the first instance to the House into which the Bill is introduced, and after the Bill has been carried to the second House in both Houses jointly, and subsists from the time when the text of the Bill in handed in to the House in which it is introduced' (s 166(2)). Copyright in a private Bill belongs to both Houses jointly and subsists from the time when a copy of the Bill is first deposited in either House (s 166(3)). Copyright in a personal Bill belongs in the first instance to the House of Lords and, after the Bill has been carried to the House of Commons, to both Houses jointly and subsists

---

10   United Kingdom. *Hansard*, HC, col.93 (S.C.E.); HL Vol. 501, col.194; Kevin Garnett, Gillian Davies, and Gwilym Harbottle, *Copinger and Skone James on Copyright* (Sweet and Maxwell, 15th edn, 2005) vol 1, 611 (para 10–71).

11   Kevin Garnett, Gillian Davies, and Gwilym Harbottle, *Copinger and Skone James on Copyright* (Sweet and Maxwell, 15th edn, 2005) vol 1, 614 (para 10–77).

from the time when it is given a First Reading in the House of Lords (s 166(4)). However, parliamentary copyright ceases on Royal Assent, or if the Bill does not receive Royal Assent, on 'withdrawal or rejection of the Bill or the end of the Session' (s 166(5)).[12] It would seem that that the ordinary rules about subsistence of copyright in a literary work would apply before a Bill has been introduced. Copyright in a literary work that becomes a Government Bill on its introduction into Parliament would normally vest in the Crown because the authors would normally be Crown servants or officers.[13] Copyright in private members Bills would normally subsist in the author, subject to agreement to the contrary. Copyright in both private and government Bills would become parliamentary copyright on its introduction to a House of Parliament. Copyright would subsequently subsist in the Crown on its enactment (s 164(1)). However, if the Bill does not receive Royal Assent or is withdrawn or rejected then, under s 166(7), the copyright in the Bill ceases entirely.[14]

The *Copyright, Designs and Patents Act 1988* also abolished Crown copyright arising solely by first publication. This was recommended by the Australian CLRC in its report on Crown copyright.[15]

A number of the reforms embodied in the *Copyright, Designs and Patents Act 1988* emanated from the recommendations contained in the report of the Whitford Committee. This committee criticised the special treatment given to the Crown under the 1956 Act:

> 592 . . . Prior to 1911 the Crown would appear to have stood in the same position in relation to copyright as any other employer or commissioner of a copyright work.
>
> . . .
>
> 600 . . . in our view, so far as Crown servants are concerned, any general rule relating to works made in the course of employment should apply, and there should be no special provision in favour of the Crown. In other areas we are of the opinion that the Crown has no case for a claim other than that which might be made by any commissioner of a work and that, beyond this, the Crown, like other persons, should safeguard its position by contractual provisions. We can see no good reason for the making of special provisions in respect of Crown copyright. Accordingly we recommend that all the existing Crown copyright provisions, especially first publication provisions, be brought to an end.[16]

---

12 Provided that, notwithstanding its rejection in any Session by the House of Lords, if, by virtue of the *Parliament Acts 1911* and *1949*, it remains possible for it to be presented for Royal Assent in that Session: s 166(5).

13 Above n 11.

14 Ibid. Section 166(7) states that copyright ceases without prejudice to the subsequent operation of s 166 in relation to a Bill which, not having passed in one Session, is reintroduced in a subsequent Session.

15 Australia. Copyright Law Review Committee, *Crown Copyright* (2005) xxi, 128 (para 9.06).

16 United Kingdom. *Copyright and Designs Law: Report of the Committee to Consider the Law on Copyright and Designs* (Whitford Committee) Cmnd 6732 (1977) 150–2.

While some of the recommendations of the Whitford Committee were adopted in the *Copyright, Designs and Patents Act 1988*, the views expressed by the Whitford Committee are characteristic of an outlook shared by some interested in copyright law and also largely shared by the Australian CLRC in its report on Crown copyright.[17] That is, there is a fundamental view that the position of the Crown is essentially no different to a person or corporation and should not be the subject of special provisions.

Of most significance in the United Kingdom are reforms to the administration and licensing of Crown copyright material. The United Kingdom government initially waived Crown copyright on legislative and administrative instruments and adopted electronic point-and-click licensing on a wide variety of other government material. These measures extended well beyond core government information and far beyond the scope of the material covered by the Treasury Minutes of the past. These measures were preceded by reforms in national policy and they effectively implemented the 2003 re-use Directive of the European Parliament and Council.

The waiver covered material such as Acts of the UK Parliament, explanatory notes, government press notices, court forms, Measures of the General Synod of the Church of England, Birth, Death, Marriage and Civil Partnership Certificates, and unpublished Crown copyright public records open for public inspection.

The click-use licences covered PSI (the 'PSI Licence') that is, public sector information other than that covered by a waiver, the 'Value Added Licence' information from a variety of sources, including core Crown copyright information to which value will often be added by means of commentary, analysis, indexing, search facilities or text retrieval software and, finally, parliamentary copyright information (the 'Parliamentary Licence'). Material covered by the Value Added Licence included official histories, handbooks and customised databases. Of the above material, only Value Added Licences could be subject to a fee. But all—waivers and click-use licences—were subject to conditions.

On 30 September 2010, the waiver and click-use licences were effectively replaced by open content licences covering Crown and parliamentary copyright.

Unlike the click-use licences, the open content licences covering Crown and parliamentary copyright information do not require users to register or formally apply for permission to re-use data, and they enable free re-use of a much broader range of public sector and parliamentary information, including database material, for both commercial and non-commercial purposes. Both licences impose fewer conditions than click-use licences and the terms of the licences are aligned to be interoperable with any Creative Commons Attribution licence (CC-BY). The Open Government Licence covering Public Sector Information (version 3) states:

> You are encouraged to use and re-use the Information that is available under this licence freely and flexibly, with only a few conditions.
>
> **Using information under this licence**

---

17   Above n 15, xxi, 127 (para 9.04).

Use of copyright and database right material expressly made available under this licence (the 'Information') indicates your acceptance of the terms and conditions below.

The Licensor grants you a worldwide, royalty-free, perpetual, non-exclusive licence to use the Information subject to the conditions below.

This licence does not affect your freedom under fair dealing or fair use or any other copyright or database right exceptions and limitations.

You are free to

copy, publish, distribute and transmit the Information;

adapt the Information;

exploit the Information commercially and non-commercially for example, by combining it with other Information, or by including it in your own product or application.

You must (where you do any of the above):

acknowledge the source of the Information by including any attribution statement specified by the Information Provider(s) and, where possible, provide a link to this licence;

If the Information Provider does not provide a specific attribution statement, you must use the following:

Contains public sector information licensed under the Open Government Licence v3.0.

These are important conditions of this licence and if you fail to comply with them the rights granted to you under this licence, or any similar licence granted by the Licensor, will end automatically.

. . .

Exemptions

This licence does not cover:

- personal data in the Information;
- Information that has not been accessed by way of publication or disclosure under information access legislation (including the Freedom of Information Acts for the UK and Scotland) by or with the consent of the Information Provider;
- departmental or public sector organisation logos, crests and the Royal Arms except where they form an integral part of a document or dataset;
- military insignia;
- third party rights the Information Provider is not authorised to license;
- other intellectual property rights, including patents, trademarks, and design rights; and
- identity documents such as the British Passport.[18]

These policy initiatives represent a significant easing of the administrative process in obtaining access to and use of government copyright material and a significant widening of access to government material. The ease of use and extent of coverage of material also makes government licensing practice more consistent and coherent across the broad spectrum of its activity. The Open Government Licence is also a less lengthy and legalistic document than the waiver and click-use licences it replaces.

The default position is that PSI should be licensed for use and re-use free of charge under the Open Government Licence, although the UK Government Licensing Framework also provides for a Non-Commercial Government licence[19] and licences where charges apply,[20] licences consistent with the Re-use of Public Sector Information Regulations 2005 and INSPIRE Regulations 2009. The vast majority of UK Parliamentary copyright material can similarly be reproduced under the terms of the Open Parliament Licence.[21]

It is clear from the policy documents that preceded these reforms that there are express economic and social reasons for accessing as well as political accountability reasons.[22] The 1999 UK Government White Paper *Future Management of Crown Copyright* stated that 'opening up access and encouraging public participation in government requires official information to be readily available to all'.[23] This White Paper,[24] the 2006 review by the Office of Fair Trading, *The Commercial Use of Public Information*[25] and the 2007 review, *The*

---

18   United Kingdom. The National Archives, *Open Government Licence for Public Sector Information* (v3.0) http://www.nationalarchives.gov.uk/doc/open-government-licence/version/3.

19   United Kingdom. The National Archives, *UK Government Licensing Framework* (2014) http://www.nationalarchives.gov.uk/documents/information-management/ uk-government-licensing-framework.pdf; http://www.nationalarchives.gov.uk/ information-management/re-using-public-sector-information/licensing-for-re-use/; or http://www.nationalarchives.gov.uk/information-management/re-using-public-sector-information/ re-use-and-licensing/ukglf/; *Non-Commercial Government Licence for public sector information* http://www.nationalarchives.gov.uk/doc/non-commercial-government-licence/ non-commercial-government-licence.htm.

20   United Kingdom. The National Archives, *UK Government Licensing Framework* (2014) *The Charged Licence* 15 http://www.nationalarchives.gov.uk/documents/information-management/ charged-licence.pdf.

21   The information licensed under the Open Parliament Licence (v3.0) includes Parliamentary information in which Crown copyright subsists (i.e. before 1 August 1989—the commencement of the *Copyright, Designs and Patents Act 1988* (UK)): refer to United Kingdom. *Open Parliament Licence v 3.0* http://www.parliament.uk/site-information/copyright/open-parliament-licence/.

22   United Kingdom. The National Archives, *UK Government Licensing Framework: Policy Context* (2014) 5,6 http://www.nationalarchives.gov.uk/information-management/government-licensing/ policy-context.htm.

23   United Kingdom. Cabinet Office, White Paper: *Future Management of Crown Copyright*, (1999) [para 2.1] http://www.opsi.gov.uk/advice/crown-copyright/future-management-of-crown-copyright.pdf.

24   Ibid paras 1.1, 9.1–9.3.

25   United Kingdom. Office of Fair Trading, *The Commercial Use of Public Information (CUPI)* (2006) OFT 861 [para 1.4] http://webarchive.nationalarchives.gov.uk/20140402142426/http://oft.gov.uk/ oftwork/publications/publication-categories/reports/consumer-protection/oft861 or http://www.opsi.gov.uk/advice/poi/oft-cupi.pdf.

Power of Information, spelt out substantial economic and social benefits of opening access to much public information:

> Government itself produces a vast amount of highly valuable information, and the internet increases its potential social and economic value. In terms of scale, the Ordnance Survey, for example, estimates that it underpins £100 billion per year of economic activity in the UK. Direct revenues from PSI are only a fraction of the wider value that this information creates. Revenues to government from the sale and licensing of PSI are around £340 million, and the total market for PSI stands at £590 million per year. The Office of Fair Trading estimates that this could double to £1 billion per year if reforms are implemented.[26]

The Power of Information review also underscored the social benefits of making government information more widely available:

> 30. It can be easy to forget that government releases and uses public sector information to help large numbers of people. This review has identified a range of studies in which the direct benefits of high quality information were measured.
>
> 31. In a study involving 200,000 patients, it was shown that, by providing clear and useful information when dispensing medication, pharmacists could improve patient adherence and persistence with medication advice by 16–33%. This both increased the welfare of patients, and saved government downstream costs of further unnecessary treatment.
>
> 32. A recent study of the effects of publishing heart surgery mortality rates showed the effect on later mortality rates to be at worst neutral and at best helpful to 26,000 patients studied.[27]

More recently, in a White Paper in December 2012 entitled *Modernising Copyright*, the British Government set out its proposed reforms to widen exceptions to infringement of copyright in line with the 2011 Hargreaves Report.[28] The White Paper stated:

> The copyright system is an important part of the UK's social and economic infrastructure. Not only is it key to the business model of many creative businesses, it also impacts on the sharing of information and culture by researchers, educators and citizens, and on the potential for digital technologies to create new value in the storage, display and transmission of content. The Government wants to ensure

---

26   United Kingdom. Cabinet Office, *The Power of Information: An Independent Review by Ed Mayo and Tom Steinberg* (2007) 4, 14–6 [26–38] http://www.opsi.gov.uk/advice/poi/index.htm.

27   Ibid 15, paras 30–2.

28   United Kingdom. Intellectual Property Office, *Digital Opportunity: A Review of Intellectual Property and Growth* (Hargreaves Report) (May 2011) http://www.ipo.gov.uk/ipreview-finalreport.pdf or https://www.gov.uk/government/publications/ digital-opportunityreview-of-intellectual-property-and-growth.

copyright makes the greatest possible contribution to UK economic growth and to our society.[29]

European Union

The European Union in the 1990s passed landmark laws providing for data privacy and database protection that governed public sector organisations.[30] While some member states had domestic laws governing access to PSI, in May 2001 the European Council and Commission adopted Regulation 1049/2001 on public access to European Parliament, Council and Commission documents[31] to improve public access to these institutions documents and to promote transparency in their proceedings. The recitals to the regulation spell out the rationale for this measure:

(1) The second subparagraph of Article 1 of the Treaty on European Union enshrines the concept of openness, stating that the Treaty marks a new stage in the process of creating an ever closer union among the peoples of Europe, in which decisions are taken as openly as possible and as closely as possible to the citizen.

(2) Openness enables citizens to participate more closely in the decision-making process and guarantees that the administration enjoys greater legitimacy and is more effective and more accountable to the citizen in a democratic system. Openness contributes to strengthening the principles of democracy and respect for fundamental rights as laid down in Article 6 of the EU Treaty and in the Charter of Fundamental Rights of the European Union.

. . .

(4) The purpose of this Regulation is to give the fullest possible effect to the right of public access to documents and to lay down the general principles and limits on such access in accordance with Article 255(2) of the EC Treaty.[32]

Article 2(1) of Regulation 1049 provides any citizen or resident of the Union a right of access to documents of the institutions, subject to the principles, conditions and limits defined in the regulation.

A later Directive of the European Parliament and Council[33] on public access to environmental information was expressed to be based on similar principles:

---

29   United Kingdom. Intellectual Property Office, *Modernising Copyright: A Modern, Robust and Flexible Framework* (December 2012) 8 http://webarchive.nationalarchives.gov.uk/20140603093549/ http://www.ipo.gov.uk/response-2011-copyright-final.pdf. 'Those impact assessments (reviewed and validated by the Government's independent Regulatory Policy Committee) suggest that these measures could contribute over £500m to the UK economy over 10 years on a conservative view, with likely additional benefits of around £290m each year' [3].

30   Data Privacy (Directive 95/46/EC).

31   Regulation (EC) 1049/2001 of 30 May 2001.

32   Regulation (EC) 1049/2001 of 30 May 2001, Recitals 1, 2 & 4 of 17.

33   Directive 2003/4/EC of 28 January 2003.

(1) Increased public access to environmental information and the dissemination of such information contribute to a greater awareness of environmental matters, a free exchange of views, more effective participation by the public in environmental decision-making and, eventually, to a better environment.[34]

In November 2003 the European Parliament and Council passed a Directive to facilitate the re-use of PSI held by public sector bodies of member states.[35] The Directive was a response to the lack of uniformity on the re-use of public information across the national laws of the Union. The rationale was described thus:

(2) The evolution towards an information and knowledge society influences the life of every citizen in the Community, *inter alia*, by enabling them to gain new ways of accessing and acquiring knowledge.

(3) Digital content plays an important role in this evolution. Content production has given rise to rapid job creation in recent years and continues to do so. Most of these jobs are created in small emerging companies.

(4) The public sector collects, produces, reproduces and disseminates a wide range of information in many areas of activity, such as social, economic, geographical, weather, tourist, business, patent and educational information.

(5) One of the principal aims of the establishment of an internal market is the creation of conditions conducive to the development of Community-wide services. PSI is an important primary material for digital content products and services and will become an even more important content resource with the development of wireless content services. Broad cross-border geographical coverage will also be essential in this context. Wider possibilities of re-using PSI should *inter alia* allow European companies to exploit its potential and contribute to economic growth and job creation.[36]

The Directive established a minimum set of rules governing and facilitating the re-use of existing documents held by public sector bodies of member states.

The general principle of the Directive was to ensure that documents held by public sector bodies are re-usable for commercial and non-commercial purposes, and where possible through electronic means. The Directive was amended by Directive 2013/37/EU of the European Parliament and of the Council but the provisions of Article 8 remain essentially unchanged. Article 8(1) of the Directive provides that member states may allow for re-use without conditions or may impose conditions, where appropriate, through a licence. These conditions shall not unnecessarily restrict possibilities for re-use and shall not be used to restrict competition.

---

34   Ibid, Recital 1 of 24.

35   Directive 2003/98/EC of the European Parliament and of the Council on the Re-use of Public Sector Information, of 17 November 2003.

36   Directive 2003/98/EC, Recitals 2–5 of 25.

The Article further provides:

> 2. In Member States where licences are used, Member States shall ensure that standard licences for the re-use of public sector documents, which can be adapted to meet particular licence applications, are available in digital format and can be processed electronically. Member States shall encourage all public sector bodies to use the standard licences.

Later provisions mandate non-discrimination and fair trading in imposing conditions on re-use.

Later, in 2006, the European Commission issued a Decision on the re-use of Commission information. Recital 8 provides:

> (8) An open re-use policy at the Commission will support new economic activity, lead to a wider use and spread of Community information, enhance the image of openness and transparency of the Institutions, and avoid unnecessary administrative burden for users and Commission services.[37]

The operative articles of the Decision provide that documents shall be made available in any existing format or language version, through electronic means where possible (Article 6) and the re-use of documents may be allowed without conditions, or conditions may be imposed, where appropriate, through a licence or through a disclaimer (Article 9). There is also a prohibition on non-discrimination and on exclusive arrangements. The Decision applies to published as well as unpublished documents authored by the Commission, such as studies, reports and other data. As with the November 2003 Directive on re-use of PSI (Article 2(b)), the Decision does not apply to documents for which the Commission is not in a position to allow re-use in view of the intellectual property rights of third parties (Article 2(b)).

In 2007 the European Parliament and Council by Directive established an infrastructure for spatial information in the European Community that builds on the 2003 Directive on public access to environmental information. It lays down general rules aimed at the establishment of the Infrastructure for Spatial Information in the European Community (INSPIRE) for the purposes of Community environmental policies. In its recitals the Directive states:

> (16) Since the wide diversity of formats and structures in which spatial data are organised and accessed in the Community hampers the efficient formulation, implementation, monitoring and evaluation of Community legislation that directly or indirectly affect the environment, implementing measures should be provided for in order to facilitate the use of spatial data from different sources across the Member States. Those measures should be designed to make the spatial data sets interoperable, and Member States should ensure that any data or information needed for the purposes of achieving interoperability are available on conditions

---

37   Decision 2006/291/EC of the European Commission, of 7 April 2006, Recital 8 of 10.

that do not restrict their use for that purpose. Implementing rules should be based, where possible, on international standards and should not result in excessive costs for Member States.[38]

The Directive illustrates that access to PSI is useful for the work of other public institutions as well as the community and the private sector.

Across a multi-lingual and multinational political unit such as the European Union there are some inherent barriers to the re-use of public sector information including the diversity of languages, lack of information on available PSI, different administrative traditions and rules, and lack of common standards and metadata for storing and describing information. Implementation of the 2003 PSI Directive by member states was thus slow, but by May 2008, all 27 member states had notified complete transposition of the Directive. In most states this involved new legislation or legislative instruments, in some cases to augment existing laws.[39] In the United Kingdom, implementing regulations were passed under the *European Communities Act 1972*.[40]

The European Union policy trend for the re-use of PSI is evidenced in amendments to the 2003 Directive made in June 2013. European Union Directive 2013/37/EU strengthens the 2003 regime by providing for the first time a genuine right to re-use public sector information, that is, disclosing PSI data for re-use is now obligatory (and not merely encouraged under the 2003 Directive). It also expands the 2003 Directive to explicitly include libraries, museums and archives.[41] Article 3 is replaced by the following:

Article 3

General principle

1. Subject to paragraph 2 Member States shall ensure that documents to which this Directive applies in accordance with Article 1 shall be re-usable for commercial or non-commercial purposes in accordance with the conditions set out in Chapters III and IV.

2. For documents in which libraries, including university libraries, museums and archives hold intellectual property rights, Member States shall ensure that, where the re-use of such documents is allowed, these documents shall be re-usable for commercial or non-commercial purposes in accordance with the conditions set out in Chapters III and IV.

---

38 Directive 2007/2/EC of the European Parliament and Council, of 14 March 2007, Recital 16 of 35.

39 For an analysis of the implementation of the 2003 PSI Directive refer to Miriam Britton, 'Implementing the Public Sector Information Directive' (2012) 34 (2) *European Intellectual Property Review* 75, 80–6. The author mentions that to date there have been three instances where the incorrect or incomplete transposition of the Directive has resulted in infringement proceedings, at least two of which have been resolved.

40 Re-use of Public Sector Information Regulations 2005 (UK).

41 Directive 2013/37/EU of the European Parliament and of the Council of 26 June 2013 amending Directive 2003/98/EC on the Re-use of Public Sector Information, Recitals (7)–(9), (14)–(15) and Article 1(3) http://eur-lex.europa.eu/LexUriServ/LexUriServ.do?uri=OJ:L:2013:175:0001:0008:EN:PDF.

Chapters III and IV of the Directive deal with conditions of re-use and non-discrimination and fair trading. Revised Article 5 in Chapter III requires:

Article 5

Available formats

1. Public sector bodies shall make their documents available in any pre-existing format or language, and, where possible and appropriate, in open and machine-readable format together with their metadata. Both the format and the metadata should, in so far as possible, comply with formal open standards.

European Union member states are obliged to apply these measures through their own laws, regulations and administrative provisions from 18 July 2015.[42]

New Zealand

New Zealand is a country with a similar Anglo common law legal heritage to Australia. New Zealand copyright law is set out in the *Copyright Act 1994*. The Crown ownership provisions extend widely to cover works produced by servants of the Crown as well as works produced by independent contractors to the Crown.[43] In essence the scope of the Crown ownership provisions extend at least as far as the 'direction or control' formula under the equivalent provision in the Australian *Copyright Act 1968*.[44] The period of protection of 100 years after the making of the work is longer than that under the Australian law.[45]

A particular difference from the Australian law is that under s 27 of the *Copyright Act 1994* (NZ) no copyright exists in core legal and parliamentary information.

26 Crown copyright

(1) Where a work is made by a person employed or engaged by the Crown under a contract of service, a contract of apprenticeship, or a contract for services,—

(a) the work qualifies for copyright notwithstanding section 17(1); and

(b) the Crown is the first owner of any copyright in the work.

(2) Copyright in such a work is referred to in this Act as Crown copyright, notwithstanding that such copyright is assigned to another person.

---

42   Ibid, Article 2.

43   *Copyright Act 1994* (NZ) s 26(1).

44   Although the definition of 'Crown' in s 2 of the *Copyright Act 1994* (NZ), which expressly excludes Crown entities, appears more restrictive than the scope of 'the Commonwealth or a State' under the *Copyright Act 1968*; for the scope of the 'Crown' refer to Susy Frankel, *Intellectual Property in New Zealand* (LexisNexis, 2nd edn, 2011) 252.

45   The period of protection of 25 years for typographical arrangements of published editions of works (*Copyright Act 1994* (NZ) s 25) is the same period of protection for published editions in Australia (*Copyright Act 1968* s 96).

(3) Crown copyright shall expire,—

(a) in the case of a typographical arrangement of a published edition, at the end of the period of 25 years from the end of the calendar year in which the work is made:

(b) in the case of any other work, at the end of the period of 100 years from the end of the calendar year in which the work is made.

(4) In the case of a work of joint authorship where 1 or more, but not all, of the authors are persons employed or engaged by the Crown under a contract of service, a contract of apprenticeship, or a contract for services, this section applies only in relation to those authors and the copyright existing by virtue of their contribution to the work.

(5) Subject to this section and to any other express provision of this Act, the provisions of this Act apply in relation to Crown copyright as to other copyright.

(6) Subsection (1) of this section applies subject to any agreement to the contrary.

(7) This section is subject to section 27.

27 No copyright in certain works

(1) No copyright exists in any of the following works, whenever those works were made:

(a) any Bill introduced into the House of Representatives:

(b) any Act as defined in section 29 of the Interpretation Act 1999:

(c) any regulations:

(d) any bylaw as defined in section 2 of the Bylaws Act 1910:

(e) the New Zealand Parliamentary Debates:

(f) reports of select committees laid before the House of Representatives:

(g) judgments of any court or tribunal:

(h) reports of Royal commissions, commissions of inquiry, ministerial inquiries, or statutory inquiries; or

(i) reports of any inquiry established under section 6 of the Inquiries Act 2013.

(1A) No Crown copyright exists in any work, whenever that work was made,—

(a) in which the Crown copyright has not been assigned to another person; and

(b) that is incorporated by reference in a work referred to in subsection (1).

(1B) Except as specified in subsection (1A), nothing in subsection (1) affects copyright in any work that is incorporated by reference in a work referred to in subsection (1).

(2) Subsection (1) shall come into force on a date to be appointed by the Governor-General by Order in Council; and 1 or more Orders in Council may be made appointing different dates for different paragraphs of that subsection.[46]

Section 27 reflects a decision of policy that access to legal and parliamentary information is best encouraged by eliminating copyright protection over it.[47] In addition, s 4 of the *Acts and Regulations Publication Act 1989* (NZ) places a responsibility on government, through the Chief Parliamentary Counsel, to arrange for the printing and publication of legislation including reprints. Section 27(1B), however, excludes from the operation of the provision, 'any work that is incorporated by reference in a work referred to in subsection (1)' other than a Crown copyright work.[48] This has the effect of excluding third-party material such as standards produced by external standard-setting organisations, such as the Accounting Standards Review Board.[49] Views similar to these New Zealand policy settings were adopted by the Australian CLRC in its report on Crown copyright.[50] Copyright protection in New Zealand was retained over other government information.

The *Policy Framework for Government-Held Information* of 1997 produced by the NZ State Services Commission and the Treasury set out 11 principles for the good management of government-held information across government agencies. The principles spelt out access, coverage, ownership and copyright issues and also express the rationales for these measures. These were:

- to contribute to the effective participation of the people of New Zealand in the making and administration of laws and policies;
- to provide clear accountability of Ministers and officials for good government;
- to give confidence in the integrity of government and public decision-making;
- to reduce the cost of government processes; and
- to support the efficient and effective management of government operations.[51]

The main principles were:

1. Availability

---

46   Section 27(2): subsection (1) was brought into force, on 1 April 2001, by the Copyright Act Commencement Order 2000 (SR 2000/245).

47   Refer to Mark Perry, 'Acts of Parliament: Privatisation, Promulgation and Crown Copyright – is there a Need for a Royal Royalty?' [1998] *New Zealand Law Review* 493, 510: 'it could be argued that a Crown prerogative over publication would still exist in New Zealand, although the consequence of such a prerogative claim is unlikely to have any effect in light of the specific provisions in s 27'. Refer to s 225(1)(b) of the *Copyright Act 1994* (NZ).

48   Section 27(1A).

49   Refer to Susy Frankel, *Intellectual Property in New Zealand* (LexisNexis, 2nd edn, 2011) 253, 254. Section 27(1B) and s 27(1A) came into effect on 15 April 2005, and were inserted on 14 April 2005 by s 3 of the *Copyright Amendment Act 2005* (2005 No 33).

50   Australia. Copyright Law Review Committee, *Crown Copyright* (2005) xxvi–xxvii, 136–8 (paras 9.31–9.39).

51   New Zealand. State Services Commission, *Policy Framework for Government Held Information* (1997) http://www.ssc.govt.nz/Documents/policy_framework_for_Government_.htm.

Government departments should make information available easily, widely and equitably to the people of New Zealand (except where reasons preclude such availability as specified in legislation).

2. Coverage

Government departments should make the following information increasingly available on an electronic basis:

- all published material or material already in the public domain;
- all policies that could be released publicly;
- all information created or collected on a statutory basis (subject to commercial sensitivity and privacy considerations);
- all documents that the public may be required to complete; and
- corporate documentation in which the public would be interested.

3. Pricing

a) Free dissemination of Government-held information is appropriate where:

- dissemination to a target audience is desirable for a public policy purpose; or
- a charge to recover the cost of dissemination is not feasible or cost effective.

b) Pricing to recover the cost of dissemination is appropriate where:

- there is no particular public policy reason to disseminate the information; and
- a charge to recover the cost of dissemination is both feasible and cost effective.

c) Pricing to recover the cost of transformation is appropriate where:

- pricing to recover the cost of dissemination is appropriate; and
- there is an avoidable cost involved in transforming the information from the form in which it is held into a form preferred by the recipient, where it is feasible and cost effective to recover in addition to the cost of dissemination.

d) Pricing to recover the full costs of information production and dissemination is appropriate where:

- the information is created for the commercial purpose of sale at a profit; and
- to do so would not breach the other pricing principles.

4. Ownership

Government-held information, created or collected by any person employed or engaged by the Crown is a strategic resource 'owned' by the Government as a steward on behalf of the public.

. . .

7. Copyright

Information created by departments is subject to Crown copyright but where wide dissemination is desirable, the Crown should permit use of its copyright subject to acknowledgement of source.[52]

There was an emphasis in the *Policy Framework* on the political and governmental aspects of the management of information, that is, community participation in and accountability of government, as well as the reduction of costs to the taxpayer. But in prospect was the greater use of information assets to achieve economic transformation and innovation including commercialisation of official information by the private sector.[53]

On 6 August 2010 a revised policy called NZGOAL (The New Zealand Government Open Access and Licensing framework) was announced by the Minister of State Services.

NZGOAL simplified the licensing of government information by standardising government copyright works for re-use through the use of Creative Commons licences.

As the Minister announced:

> By using Creative Commons licensing we are saving taxpayer funds because Government agencies no longer need to spend money writing specific licences for copyright material that can be widely released for re-use. Creative Commons licensing is internationally recognised and uses icons and other tools that simplify matters for the general public.[54]

Under the policy, State Services agencies should license their copyright works for re-use, which are or may be of interest or use to people, on the most open of licensing terms within NZGOAL—the Creative Commons Attribution (BY) licence—unless a restriction applies. Likewise to the greatest extent practicable they should make such works available online. Agencies are also strongly encouraged to provide public online access to non-copyright material that is or may be of interest to people, for copying and re-use, using a 'no-known rights' statement:

NZGOAL Policy Principles

Introduction

24. State Services agencies are strongly encouraged to apply the following principles in relation to:

(a) licensing their copyright works for re-use; and

(b) enabling public access to and re-use of their non-copyright material.

25. The licences and tools referred to in this section are explained in the next section on NZGOAL licences and tools.

Open access to copyright works with Creative Commons Attribution (BY) licence as default

---

52   Ibid.

53   Keitha Booth, 'New Zealand Policy on Information Access' (Speech delivered at International Summit on Open Access to Public Sector Information, Brisbane 4 March, Canberra 6 March 2008) [slide 27] http://www.osdm.gov.au/Events/182.aspx.

54   New Zealand. State Services Commission/Tony Ryall, *More Government Information for Reuse* (6 August 2010) http://beehive.govt.nz/release/more-government-information-reuse.

26. Unless a restriction in paragraph 29 applies, State Services agencies should make their copyright works which are or may be of interest or use to people available for re-use on the most open of licensing terms available within NZGOAL (the **Open Licensing Principle**). To the greatest extent practicable, such works should be made available online. The most open of licensing terms available within NZ-GOAL is the Creative Commons Attribution (BY) licence.

. . .

Open access to non-copyright material

28. Unless a restriction in paragraph 29 applies, State Services agencies should:

(a) provide online public access to non-copyright material that is or may be of interest or use to people;

(b) allow them to copy and re-use such material without restriction; and

(c) include, at the point of release (and in the released material itself if practicable), the 'no-known rights' statement set out at paragraph 86 below or a statement in broadly equivalent terms

(the Open Access Principle).

Restrictions

29. Neither the Open Licensing Principle nor the Open Access Principle applies where licensing a copyright work with the Creative Commons Attribution (BY) licence (in the case of copyright works) or providing open access to and allowing re-use of other material (in the case of non-copyright material) would:

(a) be contrary to legislation, court order or specific government policy;

(b) constitute a breach of contract, breach of confidence, breach of privacy, disclosure of a trade secret or other actionable wrong;

(c) be contrary to an agency's own legitimate commercial interests or business model (such as Standards New Zealand's charging for standards);

(d) result in the publication of a patentable invention for which the agency proposes or may wish to apply for a patent;

(e) be contrary to the public interest, where it exists, in having a single, authoritative and non-adapted version of a specific data source;

(f) result in the release of an incomplete work or incomplete material where the agency considers, acting reasonably, that:

(i) such release would be:

- materially misleading; or
- likely to cause or contribute to material error on the part of recipients or licensees; and

(ii) such risks could not be adequately mitigated by the use of disclaimers or other statements at the point of release and/or within the work or material regarding the incompleteness of the work or material;

(g) threaten the control over and/or integrity of Māori or other traditional knowledge or other culturally sensitive material;

(h) jeopardise the economic or other potential to Māori or other indigenous groups of Māori or other traditional knowledge or other culturally sensitive material; or

(i) otherwise conflict with the existence of a good reason under sections 6, 7 or 9 of the Official Information Act for withholding release of the work or material if the work or material were requested under that Act.[55]

NZGOAL does not apply to a range of information or works containing personal or other sensitive information set out in the 'Restrictions' (above). These restrictions go beyond those reasons for withholding information under the *Official Information Act 1982* (NZ).[56] However, under the policy, agencies are encouraged to release and license datasets once they are stripped of personal information. Further, where one of the restrictions applies (the restrictions of paragraphs 29(c) and 29(e) being most likely) the policy states agencies should consider adopting other Creative Commons licences or making the work available under a more restrictive licence.[57]

Canada

Another country with a similar Anglo common law tradition is Canada.

Section 12 of the *Copyright Act 1985* (Can) provides a Crown ownership regime in virtually the same terms as s 18 of the Imperial *Copyright Act 1911*. This was adopted by the Australian *Copyright Act 1912*:

12. Without prejudice to any rights or privileges of the Crown, where any work is, or has been, prepared or published by or under the direction or control of Her Majesty or any government department, the copyright in the work shall, subject to any agreement with the author, belong to Her Majesty and in that case shall continue for the remainder of the calendar year of the first publication of the work and for a period of fifty years following the end of that calendar year.[58]

---

55   New Zealand. State Services Commission, *New Zealand Government Open Access and Licensing framework (NZGOAL)* (Version 1) (August 2010) paras 24-29 http://ict.govt.nz/assets/Uploads/Documents/NZGOAL.pdf or http://ict.govt.nz/guidance-and-resources/information-and-data/nzgoal/.

56   *Official Information Act 1982* (NZ) ss 6-11.

57   New Zealand. State Services Commission, *New Zealand Government Open Access and Licensing framework (NZGOAL)* (Version 1) (August 2010) paras 30-31, 34-35 http://ict.govt.nz/assets/Uploads/Documents/NZGOAL.pdf.

58   *Copyright Act*, RSC 1985, c C-42 (Can), s 12.

This vests copyright in Her Majesty in works 'prepared . . . by or under the direction or control of' the government or works 'published by . . . or under the direction or control of' the government. While the definition of 'work' embraces cinematograph films, the subject matter of sound recordings and communication signals are dealt with separately and, as with the former and present Australian Copyright Acts, are not subject to specific Crown ownership provisions.

In 1995 the Final Report of the Information Highway Advisory Council[59] took the view that 'ensuring universal and easy access to public information on the Information Highway does not require the abolition of Crown copyright, but instead requires a more liberal approach to making works of the Crown available to the public'.[60]

> The federal government should adopt a more flexible policy with respect to Crown copyright and should make a greater effort to make public information available on the Information Highway without requiring payment or prior authorization.[61]

It recommended that, while Crown copyright should be retained, the Crown in right of Canada should, as a rule, place federal government information and data in the public domain and, where Crown copyright is asserted to generate revenue, licensing should be based on the principles of non-exclusivity and the recovery of no more than the marginal costs of reproducing the information or data.[62] It would seem from the context of the recommendations of the Advisory Council that 'placing federal government information and data in the public domain' means making public and waiving copyright in this information rather than simply abolishing copyright protection. The Advisory Council went on to recommend:

> In the area of Crown copyright, the federal government should create and maintain an inventory of Crown works covered by intellectual property that is of potential interest to the learning community and the information production sector at large; negotiate non-exclusive licences for their use on the basis of cost recovery for digitization, processing and distribution; and invite provincial and territorial governments to provide similar services.[63]

---

59   The 'Information Highway' was described in the report as follows: 'The term flows from the convergence of once-separate communications and computing systems into a single global network of networks. It also refers to the content carried on these electronic networks. Finally, as an integral part of the Information Highway, the software intelligence available will enable users to navigate pathways to a whole universe of information'. Canada. Department of Industry: Information Highway Advisory Council, *Connection, Community, Content: The Challenge of the Information Highway* (Information Highway Advisory Council Secretariat/Industry Canada, 1995) 2.

60   Canada. Department of Industry: Information Highway Advisory Council, *Connection, Community, Content: The Challenge of the Information Highway* (Information Highway Advisory Council Secretariat/ Industry Canada, 1995) 117.

61   Ibid.

62   Ibid.

63   Ibid.

Section 12 of the Canadian *Copyright Act 1985* expressly preserves rights or privileges of the Crown and thus in the Anglo common law tradition, retains the prerogative rights in the nature of copyright over statutes and certain other legal materials. However, by Federal Order in Council dated 19 December 1996 anyone may, without charge or request for permission, reproduce enactments and consolidations of enactments of the Government of Canada, and decisions and reasons for decisions of federally-constituted courts and administrative tribunals, provided due diligence is exercised in ensuring the accuracy of the materials reproduced and the reproduction is not represented as an official version.[64] The Communications Policy of the Government of Canada that took effect on 1 August 2006 states that 'Government information must be broadly accessible throughout society' and specifically provides that:

> Institutions must provide information free of charge when the information is in their control and it:
>
> a) is needed by individuals to make use of a service or program for which they are eligible;
>
> b) explains the rights, entitlements and obligations of individuals;
>
> c) consists of personal information requested by the individual whom it concerns;
>
> d) informs the public about dangers or risks to health, safety or the environment;
>
> e) is required for public understanding of a major new priority, law, policy, program or service; or
>
> f) is requested under the *Access to Information Act* and fees are waived at the discretion of the head of the institution.[65]

This policy document emphasises the political accountability rationale for access to government information. 'Information must be accessible so citizens, as responsible members of a democratic community, may be aware of, understand, respond to and influence the development and implementation of policies, programs, services and initiatives'.[66]

United States of America

Under United States copyright law, works of the United States Federal Government do not have copyright protection. Section 105 of the US *Copyright Act of 1976* provides:

---

64 *Reproduction of Federal Law Order* (SI/97-5) (Canada) http://laws-lois.justice.gc.ca/eng/regulations/SI-97-5/page-1.html. The free online CanLII database of federal and provincial case law and legislation has been established as a non-profit organisation managed by the Federation of Law Societies of Canada http://www.canlii.org/. CanLII is part of the free access to law movement, which includes AustLII, BAILII and NZLII: http://www.worldlii.org/worldlii/declaration/.

65 Canada.Treasury Board of Canada Secretariat, *Communications Policy of the Government of Canada* (2006) Policy Statement 4 and Policy Requirement 2 http://www.tbs-sct.gc.ca/pol/doc-eng.aspx?id=12316.

66 Ibid, Policy Statement 4.

§ 105 · Subject matter of copyright: United States Government works Copyright protection under this title is not available for any work of the United States Government, but the United States Government is not precluded from receiving and holding copyrights transferred to it by assignment, bequest, or otherwise.

A work of the United States Government is defined in s 101 of the Act to mean:

A 'work of the United States Government' is a work prepared by an officer or employee of the United States Government as part of that person's official duties.

The copyright position of the United States Government is not clear-cut. While it does not own copyright in works produced by its officers or employees in the course of their employment, the US Government can own copyright in works assigned or granted under bequests to it, and s 105 does not apply to works of the US Postal Service or other government-funded corporations such as Amtrak.[67] Section 105 does not apply to works, such as submissions, sent by third parties to government. In addition, copyright in works produced under government grants or contracts is determined by reference to specific legislation, agency regulations and contractual conditions applying in the circumstances. For example, in the case of one commissioned work, the official Ada programing language manual, copyright was assigned to the US Government (Department of Defense).[68] Thus not all federal government publications and federal government records are government works. The provision of access to government information provided by the US Federal Government must take into account government and third-party copyright.[69]

This federal regime does not apply to state or municipal governments within the United States of America and copyright protection for state government works varies greatly between the states. There is inconsistency, for example, between the States of Virginia and Illinois. Virginia claims copyright protection in the Statutes of Virginia. The State of Illinois places its statutes in the public domain.[70]

Even where government information is in the public domain, it does not necessarily follow that the nature or extent of that information is known, or that government will make it available, or disseminate it to the public. The question of whether material is in the public domain or not is not in itself determinative of the question of access to, and re-use of, the government information. Gellman points out that US Federal Government agency non-copyright information controls have included licence agreements and royalties, the

---

67   United States of America. House of Representatives Committee on the Judiciary, *Legislative History for Copyright Act of 1976: Notes for the Committee on the Judiciary,* House Report No 94-1476 (1976) at *Copyright Law Revision* (House Report No 94-1476) http://en.wikisource.org/wiki/Copyright_Law_Revision_(House_Report_No._94-1476).

68   United States of America. Ada Information Clearing House, *The Congressional Ada Mandate* http://archive.adaic.com/pol-hist/policy/mandate.txt.

69   Despite s 105 of the US *Copyright Act 1976* the US Government asserts copyright in its government works in other countries. Refer to CENDI 'Frequently Asked Questions about Copyright: Issues Affecting the US Government' (October 2008) [3.1.7] http://www.cendi.gov/publications/04-8copyright.html.

70   I Dmitrieva, 'State Ownership of Copyrights in Primary Law Materials' (2000) 23 *Hastings Communications and Entertainment Law Journal* 81.

limiting of access to selected recipients, denying or delaying access, agreeing with private companies to restrict access to data, and hiding the data and restricting its use through contracts. Agency justifications for doing so have included data integrity and revenue raising.[71]

Simply put, the fact that government-produced information is in the public domain does not ensure access to government information.[72] Access to, and re-use of, government information requires policy, regulatory or other proactive steps by government to ensure it takes place.

At the US federal level, there have been a number of legal and administrative measures passed that have been designed to facilitate access to government information. The *E-Government Act of 2002* brought new laws governing the federal management and promotion of electronic government services and information security.

The findings of Congress at that time were set out in the legislation:

SEC. 2. FINDINGS AND PURPOSES

. . .

(2) The Federal Government has had uneven success in applying advances in information technology to enhance governmental functions and services, achieve more efficient performance, increase access to Government information, and increase citizen participation in Government.

(3) Most Internet-based services of the Federal Government are developed and presented separately, according to the jurisdictional boundaries of an individual department or agency, rather than being integrated cooperatively according to function or topic.[73]

The purposes of the Act were described as follows:

(1) To provide effective leadership of Federal Government efforts to develop and promote electronic Government services and processes by establishing an Administrator of a new Office of Electronic Government within the Office of Management and Budget.

(2) To promote use of the Internet and other information technologies to provide increased opportunities for citizen participation in Government.

---

71 Robert Gellman, 'Twin Evils: Government Copyright and Government Copyright-Like Controls over Government Information' (1995) 45 *Syracuse Law Review* 999.

72 Some agencies may have additional statutory authority to impose conditions for use. Reasons include ensuring that copyrighted information contained in the government product is recognised, adhering to agreements with other parties and maintaining contact with users to ensure maintenance and updating of critical information. Refer to CENDI 'Frequently Asked Questions about Copyright: Issues Affecting the US Government' (October 2008) [3.1.5] http://www.cendi.gov/publications/04-8copyright.html#315.

73 *E-Government Act of 2002* (Public Law 107-347) (US) s 2(b).

(3) To promote interagency collaboration in providing electronic Government services, where this collaboration would improve the service to citizens by integrating related functions, and in the use of internal electronic Government processes, where this collaboration would improve the efficiency and effectiveness of the processes.

(4) To improve the ability of the Government to achieve agency missions and program performance goals.

(5) To promote the use of the Internet and emerging technologies within and across Government agencies to provide citizen-centric Government information and services.

(6) To reduce costs and burdens for businesses and other Government entities.

(7) To promote better informed decisionmaking by policy makers.

(8) To promote access to high quality Government information and services across multiple channels.

(9) To make the Federal Government more transparent and accountable.

(10) To transform agency operations by utilizing, where appropriate, best practices from public and private sector organizations.

(11) To provide enhanced access to Government information and services in a manner consistent with laws regarding protection of personal privacy, national security, records retention, access for persons with disabilities, and other relevant laws.[74]

Section 207 of the Act set in place an Interagency Committee on Government Information to make recommendations to the Director of the OMB to improve the methods by which government information, including information on the internet, is organised, preserved, and made accessible to the public. In December 2005 a memorandum from the Deputy Director of Management to the Heads of Executive Departments and Agencies set out procedures to organise and categorise information and to make it searchable across agencies to improve public access and dissemination. It stated 'when disseminating information to the public-at-large, publish your information directly to the Internet. This procedure exposes information to freely available and other search functions and adequately organises and categorises your information'.[75]

In the Financial Year 2007 *Report to Congress on Implementation of the E-Government Act of 2002* the OMB stated that the federal government was continuing to improve the methods by which government information was disseminated and made available to the public:

---

74   *E-Government Act of 2002* (Public Law 107-347) (US) s 2(b).

75   United States of America. Executive Office of the President, Office of Management and Budget, *Memorandum to the Heads of Executive Departments and Agencies: December 16 2005* (from Dep Director Clay Johnson III) 2 (para 1A) http://www.whitehouse.gov/omb/memoranda/fy2006/m06-02.pdf.

A good example of an E-Government service helping the public to locate Federal information of pertinence to them is eRulemaking, the government-wide online portal (www.Regulations.gov) and federal docket management system to facilitate public participation in the federal regulatory process. eRulemaking recently celebrated its five year anniversary in January 2008, and in those five years it has transformed access to the Federal government rulemaking process by improving the public's ability to locate, view, and comment on federal regulatory actions affecting them.[76]

Other reforms include the introduction of new tools and technologies to the Federal Internet Portal (www.USA.gov) to aggregate and present information on jobs, weather, congressional contact information, federal forms and frequently asked questions from more than 40 federal agencies. As part of the improvement of agency disclosure under the *Freedom of Information Act*, government agencies have published popular records requests directly to their website in anticipation of additional requests for the same records. There have also been measures to optimise and standardise federal geospatial activities, to improve the interoperability of geospatial data and to promote the sharing of that data throughout all levels of government, the private and non-profit sectors and the academic community. In short, there is an institutional momentum to digitalise and make publicly-searchable much federal government information.

In the Memorandum on Transparency and Open Government, issued on 21 January 2009, the President of the United States of America instructed the Director of the OMB to issue an Open Government Directive. That Directive dated 8 December 2009 stated:

> To increase accountability, promote informed participation by the public, and create economic opportunity, each agency shall take prompt steps to expand access to information by making it available online in open formats. With respect to information, the presumption shall be in favour of openness (to the extent permitted by law and subject to valid privacy, confidentiality, security, or other restrictions).
>
> a. Agencies shall respect the presumption of openness by publishing information online (in addition to any other planned or mandated publication methods) and by preserving and maintaining electronic information, consistent with the Federal Records Act and other applicable law and policy. Timely publication of information is an essential component of transparency. Delays should not be viewed as an inevitable and insurmountable consequence of high demand.
>
> b. To the extent practicable and subject to valid restrictions, agencies should publish information online in an open format that can be retrieved, downloaded, indexed, and searched by commonly used web search applications. An open format is one that is platform independent, machine-readable, and made available to the public without restrictions that would impede the re-use of that information.

---

76   United States of America. Executive Office of the President, Office of Management and Budget, *FY 2007 Report to Congress on Implementation of The E-Government Act of 2002* (1 March 2008) 5 http://www.whitehouse.gov/sites/default/files/omb/assets/omb/inforeg/reports/fy2007_egov_report.pdf.

c. To the extent practical and subject to valid restrictions, agencies should proactively use modern technology to disseminate useful information, rather than waiting for specific requests under FOIA.

d. Within 45 days, each agency shall identify and publish online in an open format at least three high-value data sets (see attachment section 3.a.i) and register those data sets via Data.gov. These must be data sets not previously available online or in a downloadable format.

e. Within 60 days, each agency shall create an Open Government Webpage located at http://www.[agency].gov/open to serve as the gateway for agency activities related to the Open Government Directive and shall maintain and update that webpage in a timely fashion.[77]

In May 2010 the Administrator, Office of Information and Regulatory Affairs, reported on measures the Obama Administration had taken to promote open government:

We have been reshaping government according to three core values:

- Transparency. Government should provide citizens with information about what their government is doing so that government can be held accountable.
- Participation. Government should actively solicit expertise from outside Washington so that it makes policies with the benefit of the best information.
- Collaboration. Government officials should work together with one another and with citizens as part of doing their job of solving national problems.

. . .

Agencies have launched their own open government pages and plans. They have published online previously unavailable high-value data sets. They are adopting new, innovative approaches to public outreach and collaboration.

. . .

. . . the Consumer Product Safety Commission launched an initiative that is making important information more accessible to millions of consumers. Families can now find the latest safety information on CPSC's blog, which has articles, videos, podcasts and other information that can keep kids and families safe from a variety of product-related hazards. Among other tools, the site features a 'Recall Search,' which provides the latest updates on recalls affecting products families use every day.[78]

---

77   United States of America. Executive Office of the President, Office of Management and Budget, *Memorandum for the Heads of Executive Departments and Agencies*, from: Peter R Orszag, Director, Subject: Open Government Directive (8 December 2009) M-10-06 [2] http://www.whitehouse.gov/sites/default/files/omb/assets/memoranda_2010/m10-06.pdf.

78   United States of America. Executive Office of the President, Office of Management and Budget, *Open Government and Records Management* (12 May 2010) (Cass R Sunstein) http://www.whitehouse.gov/omb/inforeg_speeches/open_government_05122010/ or http://www.archives.gov/records-mgmt/pdf/sunstein-raco2010.pdf.

In September 2011 the Obama Administration announced a US National Action Plan and embarked on an Open Government Partnership with other national governments to promote accountability (that can improve performance), transparency (to enable the people to find and use information) and dispersal of knowledge among nations.[79]

This National Plan was expressed to build on, but not replace, the Open Government Initiative inaugurated by the President's Memorandum on Transparency and Open Government. Included in its initiatives were an open source 'We the People' petition platform to enable online petitions, modernising the management of government records, continued improvements to the *Freedom of Information Act* administration, and declassification of national security information. This Plan was developed as part of the US participation in an international Open Government Partnership initiative that seeks to promote government commitments around five 'grand challenges' that governments face. One such agreed challenge is increasing public integrity through access to information, media and civil society freedom.[80] In May 2013, the then Australian Attorney-General announced that Australia would join the Open Government Partnership.[81]

Open Content Movement

The advent of the information age has brought significant technological changes with enormous worldwide growth in the use of computers to store information and to access works via the internet. This has enabled the storage of vast amounts of material and the making of electronic and printed copies of copyright material easily and cheaply. The changes have been accompanied by an emphasis on the rights of the copyright owner and of the strengthening of international and national laws to widen and enforce the rights comprised in copyright. Copyright owners have sought legal reforms as well as technological and contractual means of strengthening their interests.[82] For example, as the Ergas Committee reported:

> With new technologies such as the Internet, it is becoming possible to protect material from unauthorised copying through instantaneous contractual agreements between the publisher and user. Although these may be termed 'licence' agreements, they often appear to be more in the nature of 'access' agreements. For

---

79   United States of America. *The Open Government Partnership: National Action Plan for the United States of America* (20 September 2011) http://www.whitehouse.gov/sites/default/files/us_national_action_plan_final_2.pdf.

80   Open Government Partnership Organisation (2011) http://www.opengovpartnership.org/sites/www.opengovpartnership.org/files/page_files/OGP_Oficial_Brochure_1.pdf. In March 2013 the White House issued a self-assessment report, under that Partnership initiative, for the United States of America. Refer to United States of America. The White House, *Open Government Partnership – Government Self-Assessment Report for the United States of America*, 29 March 2013 http://www.whitehouse.gov/sites/default/files/microsites/ostp/ogp_selfassessment_march2013.pdf.

81   Australia. Attorney-General, Media Release 'Australia Joins Open Government Partnership' http://www.finance.gov.au/blog/2013/05/22/australia-joins-open-government-partnership/.

82   Refer to Chapter 7, 'Excluding or Modifying the Special Defences'.

example, to gain access to a file, the user may agree to certain conditions. These terms may prohibit reproduction or further dissemination of the material, or other limitations imposed by the publisher/ provider. This is known as 'click wrapping', and the rules are claimed to be similar to those that apply for 'shrink-wrap' licences—i.e. licence agreements that impose terms on the use of CDs or software within plastic shrink-wrap surrounding the product, binding once the consumer breaks the packaging seal.[83]

The development of open source software and the open content movement are responses to this 'rights' culture.

Open content is information in the public domain or subject to a licence to distribute and re-use. Open content licensing has 'emerged as a practical alternative to the existing licensing systems adopted by governments as it allows others to obtain access to and re-use copyright material with minimal transactions. This is because the licences are automated and grant permission for others to re-use protected material upon discovery of that material'.[84] The Creative Commons initiative is the most coherent and most widespread form of licensing of rights that seeks to free up access to copyright information and other material.

> Too often the debate over creative control tends to the extremes. At one pole is a vision of total control—a world in which every last use of a work is regulated and in which 'all rights reserved' (and then some) is the norm. At the other end is a vision of anarchy—a world in which creators enjoy a wide range of freedom but are left vulnerable to exploitation. Balance, compromise, and moderation—once the driving forces of a copyright system that valued innovation and protection equally—have become endangered species.
>
> Creative Commons is working to revive them. We use private rights to create public goods: creative works set free for certain uses. Like the free software and open source movements, our ends are cooperative and community-minded, but our means are voluntary and libertarian. We work to offer creators a best-of-both-worlds way to protect their works while encouraging certain uses of them—to declare 'some rights reserved'.[85]

Creative Commons licences enable copyright owners to grant to the public some or all of their rights in their works to promote the sharing of information contained in those works, and ultimately to promote creativity. While the licensing of copyright is not new, what is new are the common forms of approaches (protocols) embodied in the licences that own-

---

83   Australia. Intellectual Property and Competition Review Committee, *Review of Intellectual Property Legislation under the Competition Principles Agreement* (September 2000): Final Report of the Intellectual Property and Competition Review Committee to Senator the Hon Nicholas Minchin, Minister for Industry, Science and Resources, and the Hon Daryl Williams AM QC MP, Attorney-General (Ergas Committee) (2000) 36.

84   Victoria. Economic Development and Infrastructure Committee, Parliament of Victoria, *Inquiry into Improving Access to Public Sector Information and Data: Discussion Paper July 2008*, 2 http://www.parliament.vic.gov.au/edic/inquiries/article/151.

85   Creative Commons, *About* http://creativecommons.org/about/.

ers can quickly adopt and the public can easily understand. They cover in the main, text and images, but also sound (music) and moving images.

The web-based licences enable a copyright owner to retain copyright but to offer a licence to make their copyright material more accessible and freely usable. All the six core licences require attribution of the author. Some enable copying, distribution and other copyright acts for non-commercial purposes only. Inherently, the Creative Commons initiative is dynamic and capable of meeting demands for other licensing as the needs of authors and users of copyright material change.

The licences are provided free of charge and are suitable for online as well as other media. While the origins of the initiative emanate from the United States, the standard form licences are being widely adopted across many countries in the private and public sectors as part of a 'free culture' movement and there are branches of the movement in many regions and countries including Australasia.[86] Increasingly, governments in this region, such as New Zealand, Queensland, Victoria, South Australia and the Australian Government, have adopted this internationally recognised form of licensing.[87] In particular, the statement of *Intellectual Property Principles for Australian Government Agencies*[88] was amended on 1 October 2010 to reflect government decisions in relation to the ownership of intellectual property in software procured under ICT contracts and the free use of PSI. Consistent with the Government 2.0 Taskforce recommendations, the statement advises agencies to license PSI under Creative Commons BY licence or other open content licences[89] and also states that when Commonwealth records become available for public access under the *Archives Act 1983*, PSI covered by Crown copyright should be automatically licensed under an appropriate open content licence.[90]

---

86   Creative Commons licensing is now offered in over 70 countries.

87   In Australia, further impetus has come from the Cross Jurisdictional Chief Information Officers Committee, *Australian Governments Open Access and Licensing Framework (AusGOAL)* http://www.ausgoal.gov.au/.

88   Australia. Attorney-General's Department, *Intellectual Property Principles for Australian Government Agencies* (2010) http://www.ag.gov.au/RightsAndProtections/IntellectualProperty/Documents/StatementofIPpprinciplesforAusGovagencies.pdf or [1–7] http://www.ag.gov.au/RightsAndProtections/IntellectualProperty/Documents/IntellectualPropertyManual.pdf. The statement of intellectual property principles provides a policy for the management of intellectual property across Commonwealth agencies and particularly addresses the contracting practices of the Commonwealth. *11(b). Consistent with the need for free and open re-use and adaptation, public sector information should be licensed by agencies under the Creative Commons BY standard as the default.* An agency's starting position when determining how to license its public sector information should be to consider Creative Commons licences (http://creativecommons.org.au/) or other open content licences. Agencies should license their public sector information under a Creative Commons licence or other open content licence following a process of due diligence and on a case-by-case basis. Before releasing public sector information, for which the Commonwealth is not the sole copyright owner, under a Creative Commons BY standard or another open content licence, an agency may need to negotiate with any other copyright owners of the material. *11(c). At the time at which Commonwealth records become available for public access under the Archives Act 1983, public sector information covered by Crown copyright should be automatically licensed under an appropriate open content licence. Agencies will be responsible for the selection and use of an appropriate licence.*

89   Ibid 6.

Conclusion

Until January 2011, the Commonwealth Copyright Administration (CCA), was responsible for the management of copyright in published materials on behalf of Australian Government agencies. Requests for permission to reproduce Commonwealth copyright material could be submitted electronically using a copyright request form on the CCA website. The CCA followed the 'pull' model of dissemination of information—that is an emphasis on dissemination of information in response to individual requests for access. Requests to reproduce unpublished Commonwealth copyright material were directed to the author body. In January 2011, however, the CCA was abolished and Australian Government policy in respect of accessing information has formally been replaced by open content licensing devolved to agencies—the 'push' model—using Creative Commons licensing as the default.

The open content movement highlights fundamental issues facing all governments as to what information should be released or not released and, if released, whether access should be limited in some ways (through price, licensing arrangements, or through accessible media). Governments must also decide what proactive steps it must take to disseminate information, that is, to provide access through a 'push' model as opposed to a 'pull' model. It is clear from this survey of overseas developments that governments are moving to proactive publication of PSI they hold: the 'push' model.

These issues go beyond the question whether the role of government as proprietor of copyright material conflicts with the principle that all citizens in a liberal democratic society should have fair and open access to government information. These issues are being faced by governments whether or not some or all of the information is subject to government copyright or not.[91] There is a strong movement nationally and internationally to release government information unless there are clear public interest grounds opposing release. In essence the movement is described as a right to information or, to use the Obama Administration's phrase, 'in the face of doubt, openness prevails'.[92]

What different policy considerations arise across the wide range of government materials in facilitating access to those materials? The Queensland GILF project estimated that about 15 percent of government information could not be the subject of Creative Commons licensing due to 'issues of privacy, confidentiality or other legal or policy constraints'.[93]

---

90   Ibid.

91   The 2006 *Commercial Use of Public Information* report from the UK Office of Fair Trading concluded that there was no need to abolish Crown copyright in public sector information: 'In fact, the existence of Crown copyright is a key part of the control mechanisms which we want to build on to ensure that PSIHs [public sector information holders] act in a fair and transparent manner': United Kingdom. Office of Fair Trading, *The Commercial Use of Public Information (CUPI)* (2006) [para 4.76] http://webarchive.nationalarchives.gov.uk/20140402142426/http://oft.gov.uk/oftwork/publications/publication-categories/reports/consumer-protection/oft861 or http://www.opsi.gov.uk/advice/poi/oft-cupi.pdf.

92   United States of America. Presidential Documents, *Memorandum for the Heads of Executive Departments and Agencies* of 21 January 2009, 74 (15) Federal Register 4683–4 http://www.justice.gov/oip/foia_guide09/presidential-foia.pdf.

One particular common constraint for government is that a significant component of information held by government emanates from the private sector, that is, in a copyright sense, is subject to third-party rights. Both the 2003 and 2006 European Directives contain an exclusion of information subject to third-party intellectual property rights.

While the public sector is a large generator of information, the aggregation of data from private sector sources some of which, such as statistical data, is legally demanded of the private sector, leads to concerns about the copyright implications about subsequent release of this data for re-use. As further discussed in Chapter 7, it seems to this writer that, in Australia at least, the solution under copyright law lies in providing a statutory right of government to release information submitted from third-party sources, without infringement of copyright.

Beyond the treatment of third-party copyright, there are other potential grounds for denying access, such as commercial confidentiality, national security and privacy protection. The initial defining point for denying access would seem to be the exemptions defined by prevailing FOI laws. Doing so makes for consistent access policy. Adopting such a policy requires training public sector staff to ensure that information is properly released, but jurisdictions that have FOI laws have staff who are familiar with those decisions.

Once a decision is made to release information it is still open to government to 'push' information freely, or to limit access in some ways through price, licensing arrangements and media. Pricing may recoup the costs to the government of compiling and producing information, and licensing conditions may contractually safeguard the integrity and source of the information. These issues are explored further in the concluding chapters of this book.

---

93   Estimate provided in telephone interview by Mr Neale Hooper, Office of Economic and Statistical Research, Queensland Treasury, Brisbane, 31 January 2011. Refer also to Queensland. Queensland Spatial Information Office, Office of Economic and Statistical Research, Queensland Treasury, *Government Information and Open Content Licensing: An Access and Use Strategy* Government Information Licensing Framework Project Stage 2 Report (October 2006) [paras 3.11, 8.8] http://eprints.qut.edu.au/32117/.

4

The Role of National Archives: Accessing and Re-using Copyright Records

The common policy objectives in modern liberal democracies of promoting open and accountable government and of preserving national culture and heritage are reflected in the provision of access to, and the preservation of, unpublished and published works held by government. A wide spectrum of social enquiry is in whole or in part dependent on these government-preserved holdings.

The policy objectives in Australia are manifested in two ways. One is in government archival practices and laws.[1] The other is in the provisions in the Australian *Copyright Act 1968* facilitating access to, and the preservation of, unpublished and published works held by archives and libraries. While preservation of these works and the costs associated with it are in themselves a recognition of the public interest in accessing works held by archives and libraries, existing laws and practices facilitating access should be reviewed in the light of technological changes in the way we access, create and communicate works and in the light of further moves towards openness in government.

This chapter outlines present archival practices and laws in Australia, and the scope of *Copyright Act 1968* provisions, before turning to reform. The focus is on the Australian federal sphere.[2]

---

1   Australian Capital Territory. Auditor-General's Office, Performance Audit Report, Records Management in ACT Government Agencies (June 2008) [3] http://www.audit.act.gov.au/auditreports/reports2008/Report%203-2008%20-%20Records%20Management.pdf. 1.5 The *Territory Records Act 2002* (ACT) establishes a framework for the management and administration of government records. Under Part 1 the principle purposes of the Act are: (a) to encourage open and accountable government by ensuring that Territory records are made, managed and, if appropriate, preserved in accessible form; and (b) to preserve Territory records for the benefit of present and future generations; and (c) to ensure that public access to records is consistent with the principles of the *Freedom of Information Act 1989* (ACT).

2   The federal archival bodies focusing on the collection of non-government records such as the National Film and Sound Archives (which collects the products of Australian private sector media industries) and the Noel Butlin Archives at the Australian National University (which collects business records) have been excluded from this discussion.

Government Archival Practices and Laws

Archives are not peculiar to governments and have been part of human civilisation for millennia.[3] However, governments have preserved records on a greater and more comprehensive scale than any other institution in society. Over the last few centuries in Anglo-Australian history, most of these records have been created by officials in government through filed correspondence, briefings, internal working documents and other material all of which would be the subject of Crown copyright. Some of this government archival material originates from other sources such as letters, submissions and representations received from individuals, corporations, other governments and community groups, the copyright in which would subsist in third parties. Other material preserved in archives includes architectural plans, photographs, films and sound recordings, made by government officials or commissioned by government. A small proportion of the material is published and thus subject to a finite period of copyright protection. Most records are unpublished and are protected by copyright indefinitely while they remain unpublished. Some unpublished records, such as the personal records of public figures, have been donated to archival institutions from non-government sources.[4] While Australian archival records are predominantly on paper, most government recordkeeping is now in electronic form.

Development of Australian Archives

The collection and preservation of archival material by government in Australia has not been coherent. Creation and acquisition of records has been less systematic and more piecemeal, preservation of those documents has sometimes been poor and the destruction of archived records has continued spasmodically until quite recently.[5] Notwithstanding these weaknesses, a valuable heritage of records presently exists back to the beginnings of the British colonisation of Australia.[6]

---

3 'The Sumerians in southern Mesopotamia were using cuneiform markings on clay tablets by the fourth millennium BC and written records were also used by the Egyptian and Persian empires. The records documented a wide range of financial, administrative, property, genealogical and religious matters and both the Egyptian and Persian empires maintained repositories of records', Australia. Australian Law Reform Commission, *Australia's Federal Record: A Review of Archives Act 1983*, Report No. 85 (1998) [2.1]. The Domesday Book—a survey of landholding and tax liability—is the earliest British public record to survive: E M Hallam, 'Nine Centuries of Keeping the Public Records', in Martin, GH and Spufford, P (eds), *The Records of the Nation: The Public Record Office 1938–1988* (The Boydell Press, 1990) 23, 24.

4 Australia. National Archives of Australia, 'Kirby's Personal Records Saved' (2010) 38 *Memento* 30.

5 During the Wilson enquiry hearings in July 1996 into the separation of Aboriginal and Torres Strait Islander children from their families, for example, 'no one could explain the 1938–48 gap in NSW Aboriginal Welfare Board records, but according to State Archives no proof of a rumoured fire in 1952 could be found': M Piggott, 'The History of Australian Record Keeping: A Framework for Research' in BJ McMullin (ed), *Coming Together. Papers from the Seventh Australian Library History Forum* (Melbourne, 1997) 33, 36. Piggott also cites the shredding of records during an inquiry ordered by the Goss government in Qld in 1990 into the administration of the Wacol youth centre.

6 Records held by the British Public Record Office and other British institutions including missionary societies relating to Australia and the Pacific were copied under the Australian Joint Copying Project that

The written record was central to the British colonial administration of Australia from planning and colonisation onwards. In its review of the *Archives Act 1983* (Cth) in 1998, the ALRC stated:

> The colonial administrations were involved not only in the broad management of the colonies' politics, finances and development but also in many of the affairs of individual citizens. In particular, the convict system and the gradual subdivision of the continent into freehold and leasehold properties generated extensive records. In consequence, most aspects of colonial life were reported on in detail and large volumes of written records accumulated in both London and the colonial capitals.

> The process by which the accumulations of records in colonial administrative offices were gradually transformed into what are now the various State archives was a long and haphazard one. Some valuable records were lost through neglect or deliberate destruction . . .[7]

The Commonwealth Government inherited some substantial functions and their records from the States upon federation and the two world wars heightened the need for a coordinated archival function. For many years this was shared between the Commonwealth National Library and the Australian War Memorial. Archival institutions in the States developed out of their library systems and both Commonwealth and the States' archival activities are now subject to what has been described as second generation legislation,[8] characterised by:

- mandatory transfer of records to the archival authority, usually after 25 or 30 years
- some provision for the regulation or guidance of agency record management practices and
- a public right of access to records after a specified period.

At the Commonwealth level, the provision of a public right of access to records after a specified period has mirrored those rights of access, and appeal from decisions on access, that are available under the Commonwealth *Freedom of Information Act 1982*. Under State archival laws, rights of access generally complement rights of access under FOI laws.[9] These laws reflect a consistent policy towards openness of government.

---

began in 1945 and concluded in 1997. See National Library of Australia, *What We Collect, Australian Joint Copying Project* http://www.nla.gov.au/collect/ajcp.html.

7   Australia. Australian Law Reform Commission, above n 3, [2.5], [2.6].

8   Ibid [2.9].

9   NSW: *State Records Act 1998* (NSW) s 56; Tas: *Archives Act 1983* (Tas) ss 15, 18; Commonwealth: *Archives Act 1983* (Cth) ss 31–40; Qld: *Public Records Act 2002* (Qld) ss 15–20; Vic: *Public Records Act 1973* (Vic) ss 10, 10AA, 10A,11; SA: *State Records Act 1997* (SA) ss 25, 26; ACT: *Territory Records Act 2002* (ACT) ss 26–31. The Northern Territory Archives Service (NTAS) has no independent statutory existence. NTAS is part of a Department of the Northern Territory Government. Access to government archives held by the NTAS is determined in accordance with s 142 of the *Information Act 2002* (NT). Section 141 of the *Information Act* provides for the transfer of government archives over 30 years old to the NTAS, where they become part of Territory Archives.

Modern Practices of Selection and Maintenance of Archives

Good records management is the foundation of the effective management of information by government. As the ACT Auditor-General stated in 2008:

> 1.2 Good records management is a fundamental element of good governance, in particular with respect to transparency and accountability. Good recordkeeping supports efficiency and accountability through the creation, management and retention of meaningful, accurate, reliable, accessible and durable records of government activities and decisions.
>
> 1.3 Poor recordkeeping practices negatively affect government administration, and projects are often difficult to implement and sustain effectively in the absence of well-managed records.[10]

There is a cycle of activity in modern archival practice that begins with the capture of full and accurate records of government activity and operations and the classification, appraisal and storage of records by government agencies, and then to the transfer and preservation of records by archival institutions, and the provision of public access to them. Effective access to government information through FOI and archival laws is dependent on the observance of these steps.

Recordkeeping is the subject of Australian and international standards that set out a methodology for managing records known as AS ISO 15489–2002. This has been augmented by a process model for designing and implementing record systems known by the acronym of DIRKS.[11] DIRKS, which was developed by the State Records Authority of New South Wales and the National Archives of Australia, includes a framework for adopting appropriate metadata standards for the control and retrieval of electronic records. Both federal and state governments have adopted DIRKS process methodology.[12] Guidance to public servants on recordkeeping and observance of recordkeeping requirements includes web-based material and ultimate responsibility for the observance of the standards rest with the Chief Executive Officer of the government agency.[13]

The eight step DIRKS methodology[14] recommended in AS ISO 15489–2002 contemplates the capture of records relating to the government agencies' identified business activities

---

10   Above n 1, [3].

11   An acronym for 'designing and implementing recordkeeping systems'.

12   DIRKS remains relevant to most States. However, since 2007, the National Archives has preferred a process of advice on its website rather than adherence to DIRKS.

13   In addition to the *Archives Act 1983* (Cth), recordkeeping requirements are contained in other Commonwealth Acts, standards, policies and guidance including the *Electronic Transactions Act 1999*; the *Evidence Act 1995*; the *Freedom of Information Act 1982*; the *Privacy Act 1988*; the *Protective Security Manual*; and the *Australian Government Information and Communications Security Manual* (ACSI 33).

14   New South Wales. State Records of New South Wales, *Strategies for Documenting Government Business: The DIRKS Manual.* (June 2003) 12, 13 http://www.records.nsw.gov.au/documents/recordkeeping-dirks/DIRKS%20Manual.pdf or http://www.records.nsw.gov.au/recordkeeping/advice/designing-implementing-and-managing-systems/dirks-manual/dirks-manual (June 2003, revised 2007).

and operations (that in turn determines some selection of material captured) but ultimately on an appraisal of the retention period for each class of record, with the object of preserving records of enduring value in archives. Being faced with a mass of material, classification and selection are intrinsically part of the archival process. As the NSW State Archives has stated:

> It is not in the interest of the government or the community to retain records for longer than they are reasonably required to support identified needs. To attempt to preserve and maintain accessibility to all State records indefinitely would be prohibitively expensive and impractical to manage. Even in the electronic environment, where data storage costs continue to fall, the full cost of cataloguing, maintenance, migration and accessibility makes it impossible to keep all State records forever. Moreover, there are certain types of records, such as those containing sensitive personal information, which the community expects will be disposed of when they are no longer required for the purpose for which they were created or for related administrative purposes and where there are no other overriding factors requiring their retention.
>
> All records are created for an identifiable business or administrative purpose and the majority of these records can be disposed of by destruction once that purpose has been fulfilled and all legal and accountability requirements for their retention have been met. There are some types of records however, because of the purpose for which they were created, the activity they document and the information they contain, that have enduring value to the Government, to the community at large or to individuals or groups within it. These records are kept as State archives.[15]

Both good records management and appropriate policies for the preservation of, and public access to, government records are important to the transparency and accountability of government.

Access Provisions Under the Archives Act 1983 (Cth)

At the Commonwealth level, modern organisation, coordination and access to archival records were brought into statutory form by the *Archives Act 1983* (Cth). Unpublished Commonwealth documents in the open access period are subject to public access under that Act under a regime similar to public access under the *Freedom of Information Act 1982* (Cth). There are also special access provisions under the *Archives Act 1983* (Cth) that enable researchers to access more recent government documents subject to certain conditions.

The types of access under the *Archives Act 1983* to preserved records fall into two categories:

- open access period (s 3(7)) and
- access outside the open access period (s 56 access).

The Act has only limited application to documents outside the open access period.

---

15   New South Wales. State Records of New South Wales, *Building the Archives: Policy on Records Appraisal and the Identification of State Archives* (June 2001) [3,4] https://www.records.nsw.gov.au/recordkeeping/rules/policies/building-the-archives.

Open Access Period

The *Archives Act 1983* (Cth) provides a legally enforceable public right of access to Commonwealth records in the open access period under the Act.[16] The open access period is defined by s 3(7) of the *Archives Act 1983*. In 2010, the period before open access is available was reduced from 30 years to 20 years over nearly all Commonwealth records through a 10-year transition period commencing from 1 January 2011 and ending on 31 December 2020.[17]

The widening of access is being implemented progressively over the transition period depending on the date the record came into existence. This widening of access was part of a package of legislative measures contained in the *Freedom of Information Amendment (Reform) Act 2010* (Cth) intended to promote a pro-disclosure culture across government and to build a stronger foundation for more openness in government arising from the Rudd Government's 2007 election commitment to do so. Among the policy objectives expressed in the Act was to increase recognition that information held by the government is a national resource to be managed for public purposes. Both the Commonwealth *Freedom of Information Act 1982* and the *Archives Act 1983* contain exemptions from disclosure for government records, and the exemptions from disclosure of open period access records under the *Archives Act 1983* have largely paralleled exemptions from disclosure under the *Freedom of Information Act 1982*.[18]

Thus, when a member of the public requests to see archives that are in the open access period the National Archives of Australia is required by s 35 of the *Archives Act 1983* to first examine the records to determine whether any exemptions should be claimed. Ideally this should be done just before records are in the open access period, but it is normally left to a request. An exception exists in respect of Cabinet records, which are made public at the beginning of the open access period. An appeal lies to the Administrative Appeals Tribunal in respect of decisions on exempt records.

Under the *Archives Act 1983*, public access may be given in one of the following forms:

- inspection of the record
- a copy of the record
- access to the record through use of computer, projector or other equipment
- a written transcript of a sound record, shorthand or codified record.[19]

---

16   *Archives Act 1983* (Cth) s 31.

17   *Freedom of Information Amendment (Reform) Act 2010* (Cth) sch 3, pt 1. Sections 22A and 22B of the *Archives Act 1983* (Cth) provide separate periods for cabinet notebooks (expanded progressively from 50 years to 30 years) and for records that contain census information from a particular census (99 years) before these records fall into open access.

18   Refer to the *Archives Act 1983* (Cth) s 33. *Freedom of Information Act* exemptions have been amended by the *Freedom of Information Amendment (Reform) Act 2010* (Cth) to include an overriding public interest test for some exemptions, which have not been matched by amendments to s 33 of the *Archives Act 1983* (Cth). Claims for exemption from disclosure of documents held by Archives are fewer due to their age.

19   *Archives Act 1983* (Cth) s 36(2). Where the giving of access in one form would unreasonably interfere with the operations of the Archives or of another Commonwealth institution that has custody

Access Outside the Open Access Period

Section 56(1) and (2) of the *Archives Act 1983* specify two types of closed period access. 'Accelerated release' under s 56(1) enables all records of a certain kind or on a certain subject to be available to the public. For example, records consulted by the Royal Commission into British Nuclear Tests in Australia (covering the period from the mid-1950s to the 1980s) and East Timor records dating from the 1970s.

'Special access' under s 56(2) contemplates access to a person within the closed period. An example would be the grant of access to a retired politician to research records for a memoir or a biography.

'Special access' and 'accelerated release' must be authorised by the responsible minister in accordance with arrangements approved by the Prime Minister.[20] Conditions may be imposed with the grant of special access and the Act provides a penalty for breach of those conditions.[21]

Legal Protection for the Giving of Access

Section 57 of the Act provides protection against actions for infringement of copyright, defamation and breach of confidence by the giving of access under the Act. It expressly covers acts of infringement as well as authorising acts of infringement of copyright and protects officers of the National Archives, the Commonwealth or any other person concerned in the giving or authorising of access.[22] It also protects the author of the record against actions in defamation and breach of confidence for supply of the record to the Commonwealth.[23] No subsequent protection is provided by the *Archives Act 1983* to the publisher of a record that is accessed under the Act.[24] Publication (in the copyright sense) of unpublished works is subject to the restrictive rules set out in s 52 of the *Copyright Act 1968*, which requires a prescribed notice of intended publication to be given and only applies to works made more than 50 years after the death of the author.[25]

---

of the record, or would not be appropriate having regard to the physical nature of the record or would be detrimental to the preservation of the record or would, but for the Act, involve an infringement of copyright not owned by the Commonwealth, State or Territory, access may be refused and access given in another form (*Archives Act 1983* (Cth) s 36(4)).

20   Ibid, s 56(1), (2).

21   Ibid, s 56(3) prescribes a penalty of 20 penalty units. One penalty unit is currently $100.

22   Ibid, s 57(1)(a). Protection also extends to persons authorising or giving access for criminal offences (s 57(1)(c)).

23   Ibid, s 57(1)(b).

24   However, after access is given to a record, publishing (or other use) of that record is subject to the laws of copyright, defamation and breach of confidence; refer to *Archives Act 1983* (Cth) s 57(2). Conditions may be imposed in the grant of special access under s 56(2) of the *Archives Act 1983*. Refer also to reg 9 of the Archives Regulations 1984.

25   Refer to ss 51 and 52 of the *Copyright Act 1968* (Cth) and 'Access and Preservation under the Copyright Act 1968' in this chapter.

Provisions dealing with the preservation, reproduction and communication of archival and library material are found in the *Copyright Act 1968*.

Provisions in the *Copyright Act 1968*

The basis, history and importance of the provisions of the *Copyright Act 1968* dealing with the library deposit of Australian publications are discussed in Chapter 5.[26] Included as part of this library deposit process are publications of state and federal governments. Deposit of publications and the harvesting of material electronically published on government and other websites take place across all jurisdictions in Australia. Deposit libraries and other Australian libraries are rightly concerned to facilitate access to those collections by researchers and to preserve their collections from deterioration and loss. Most major public libraries in Australia also have donated or acquired collections of unpublished papers or have compiled oral histories of significant public figures, accessible to researchers.

Access and Preservation Under the Copyright Act 1968

Division 5 of Part III of the *Copyright Act 1968* contains provisions enabling libraries and archives to reproduce and communicate both published and unpublished works in their collections for their users and for other libraries or archives. These provisions facilitate access to copyright material held by those institutions. The Act also contains provisions enabling the reproduction and communication of works by archives and libraries of works held by them for preservation and other purposes. All the Division 5 provisions are exceptions to infringement. No remuneration is payable to the relevant copyright owners.[27]

Accessing Works by Users

Division 5 of Part III of the *Copyright Act 1968* is headed 'copying of works in libraries or archives' and ss 49 and 50 contained within it enable copying of published works for users and for other libraries or archives.[28]

Copying of published works by librarians or archives for users under s 49 does not represent any radical departure in the law or a significant shift in the balance between the owners of copyright and the users of copyright material. Copying by libraries and archives for users under s 49 'is analogous to copying by individual persons under the fair deal-

---

26   Refer also to John Gilchrist, 'Copyright Deposit, Legal Deposit or Library Deposit?: The Government's Role as Preserver of Copyright Material' (2005) 5(2) *QUT Law and Justice Journal* 177.

27   Section 112 of the *Copyright Act 1968* (Cth) provides that the copyright in a published edition of a work or works is not infringed by the making of a reproduction of the whole or part of that edition if it is made in the course of the dealings described in ss 40–44, 49, 50, 51A and 51B of the Act that are discussed in this chapter under 'Provisions in the *Copyright Act 1968*'. Section 112 does not extend to dealings under s 51AA of the *Copyright Act 1968*.

28   The Franki Committee recommended the extension to archives of what had hitherto been simply library copying provisions: Australia. *Report of the Copyright Law Committee on Reprographic Reproduction* (Franki Committee) (AGPS, 1976) 36, 40.

ing concept'[29] and emanates from it.[30] The reproduction permitted under s 49 covers up to the whole of a journal article or a reasonable portion of another published work.[31] More than a reasonable portion of another work may be reproduced where the work cannot be obtained within a reasonable time at an ordinary commercial price (in loose terms, is not commercially available).[32] The section enables both hard-copy reproduction and electronic transmittal of reproductions to users of the library or archives.[33] Section 49, however, only applies to reproduction where the user declares that the copy is for the user's research or study.[34]

In practice, many libraries and archives provide machines (such as computers or copying machines) for users of the library or archives that affix in close proximity a prescribed notice warning of the relevant obligations under the *Copyright Act 1968* and in particular a reproduction that is a fair dealing for the purposes of research or study.[35] In these circumstances, by virtue of s 39A and s 104B, a body administering a library or archives is deemed not to have authorised the making of an infringing copy on the machine.[36] Reliance upon the individual user to undertake access copying reduces much of the administrative burden under s 49 from officers of the library or archives.

Section 50 of the *Copyright Act 1968* facilitates inter-library and inter-archive loans.[37] It enables a library or archives, upon request, to supply a copy of a periodical publication or other published work within the same limits as s 49 to another library or archives for users of that recipient library or archives or for the collection of that recipient library or archives. The user must fulfil the declaration requirements under s 49.

Section 50 facilitates access to published works for users at some distance from the library or archives, which is of important practical benefit to libraries and archives given the ra-

---

29   Ibid 32.

30   United Kingdom. *Report of the Copyright Committee* (Gregory Committee) Cmnd 8662 (1952) 17; Australia. *Report of the Committee Appointed by the Attorney-General of the Commonwealth to Consider what Alterations are Desirable in the Copyright Law of the Commonwealth* (Spicer Committee) (1959) 28, 29.

31   *Copyright Act 1968* (Cth) ss 49(5),(6),(7).

32   Ibid, s 49(5)(b).

33   Online user access is limited to the premises of the library or archives, *Copyright Act 1968* (Cth) s 49(5A).

34   All reproduction and supply permitted under *Copyright Act 1968* (Cth) s 49 must be in response to a request and declaration by a user that he or she requires the reproduction for the purpose of research or study and has not been previously supplied with a reproduction of the same work by the library or archives. A library or archives is permitted to make available online within its premises for users, articles or other published works that it holds in electronic form, in such manner that users cannot reproduce or communicate the work: s 49(5A).

35   The notices are prescribed under Regulations 4B and 17A of the Copyright Regulations 1989 (Cth), and the wording is contained in Schedules 3 and 9.

36   Refer also to Copyright Regulations 1969 (Cth) reg 4B and Schedule 3.

37   Unlike most provisions in Div 5 of Part III, where the phrase 'library or archives' is used, *Copyright Act 1968* (Cth) s 50 uses only the term 'library' and defines it to include 'an archives all or part of whose collection is accessible to members of the public'.

tionalisation and collaboration of libraries in collection acquisitions and the focus of their collections.[38] Networking of libraries and archives assists both users and the library and archival institutions themselves. The provision enables electronic transmittal of reproductions between libraries or archives. Nonetheless, in comparison with s 49, s 50 imposes more restrictive access to works held in electronic form by requiring, in the case of a supply of a journal article or a reasonable portion of a work to a user, a condition that the article or portion must not be commercially available.[39]

Section 51 enables the reproduction or electronic communication of an unpublished work kept by a library or archives where it is open to public inspection. The reproduction or communication must be for the purposes of research or study of the user or with a view to publication but is of limited application because the provision only applies where the author of the work in question has been dead for more than 50 years.

Preserving Works

Section 51A enables the reproduction and communication of unpublished and published works held as part of the collection of a library or archives for preservation and other purposes. The section specifically enables the reproduction, or communication,[40] of:

- a work in manuscript form or of an artistic work for the purpose of preserving that work against loss or deterioration, or for the purpose of research carried out in that or another library or archives[41]
- a work in published form that has been damaged or has deteriorated, or has been lost or stolen, for the purpose of replacing the work provided it is not commercially available[42] and
- a work for administrative purposes.[43]

Additionally, wider reproduction rights are available to key cultural institutions'[44] collections under s 51B. That provision applies to bodies administering a library or archive that have, under a law of the Commonwealth or State, the function of developing and maintaining the collection, and to other prescribed bodies and, in either case, where the work in the collection is of historical and cultural significance to Australia. The provision enables

---

38   The policy behind *Copyright Act 1968* (Cth) s 50 is to 'facilitate interlibrary loans particularly in a country, which, as is the case with Australia, is situated at a great distance from many of the centres of publication, and which is so large as to make it obviously impossible to provide elaborate library facilities in the widely separated towns which exist': the Franki Committee, above n 28, 37.

39   Refer to *Copyright Act 1968* (Cth) s 50(7B).

40   The term 'communication' enables electronic transmittal of a work, or the making of digital copies available online within the premises of the library or archives.

41   *Copyright Act 1968* (Cth) s 51A(1)(a).

42   Ibid, s 51(1)(b), (c).

43   Ibid, s 51(2), (3). Defined to be 'directly related to the care and control of the collection', *Copyright Act 1968* (Cth) s 51B(6).

44   Those institutions are defined in s 51B(1) and those expressly prescribed are set out in the Copyright Regulations 1969 (Cth) Schedule 5.

the making of up to three reproductions of a manuscript, artistic work or published work for the purposes of preserving those works against loss or deterioration. This defence to infringement is only available in the case of artistic and published works where a copy of the work[45] cannot be obtained within a reasonable time at an ordinary commercial price (that is, not commercially available). As Hudson has pointed out, the wording of the provision suggests a maximum of three copies can be made, not that only three copies can be held at any one time[46] and, if that is its proper construction, that would restrict the effectiveness of the section. Further, the use of different digital proprietary recordkeeping systems by government agencies and the need to convert them to long-term archival format and to back up to different servers,[47] coupled with the need to translate them to different formats as technology changes, suggests a need for further copies for the purposes of preserving works against loss or deterioration.

Section 51AA is directed specifically at the National Archives of Australia. It contains rather narrow and detailed provisions enabling the National Archives of Australia to make or communicate a single copy of a work (published or unpublished) kept in the collection of that archives, where it is open for public inspection, in various circumstances that extend beyond defences otherwise provided in Division 5. They are the making or communicating of a single:

- working copy of a work[48]
- reference copy of the work for supply to the central office of the archives[49]
- reference copy of that work for supply to a regional office[50]
- replacement copy of a work for supply to a regional office[51] and
- replacement copy of a work for supply to the central office.[52]

---

45   In the case of an artistic work, a photographic reproduction cannot be obtained within a reasonable time at a normal commercial price.

46   Emily Hudson, 'The Copyright Amendment Act 2006—The Scope and Likely Impact of New Library Exceptions' (2006) *University of Melbourne Law School Research Series* 5 http://www.austlii.edu.au/au/journals/UMelbLRS/2006/5.html.

47   The National Archives of Australia converts Microsoft word documents into a long-term open system format and uses more than one server for backup: Interview with Messrs Paul Dalgleish, Assistant Director, Reference Policy and Support and Adrian Cunningham, Director, Strategic Relations and Personal Records, National Archives of Australia (at National Archives of Australia, 6 August 2010).

48   That is, 'a reproduction of the work made for the purpose of enabling the National Archives of Australia to retain the copy and use it for making reference copies and replacement copies of the work': *Copyright Act 1968* (Cth) s 51AA(1)(a) and (2).

49   That is, 'a reproduction of a work from a working copy . . . for use by that office in providing access to the work to members of the public': *Copyright Act 1968* (Cth) s 51AA(1)(b) and (2).

50   Upon a written request by a regional office, provided that the officer in charge is satisfied that a reference copy has not been previously supplied to that regional office: *Copyright Act 1968* (Cth) s 51AA(1)(c).

51   Upon a written request by a regional office, provided that the officer in charge is satisfied that a reference copy of the work is lost, damaged or destroyed: *Copyright Act 1968* (Cth) s 51AA(1)(d).

52   Upon a written request by a regional office, provided that the officer in charge is satisfied that a reference copy of the work is lost, damaged or destroyed: *Copyright Act 1968* (Cth) s 51AA(1)(e).

Section 51AA enables the network of National Archives of Australia offices to behave as one central repository. This facilitates access by individuals to archival records in the major cities of Australia that host regional offices of the National Archives of Australia. While copyright in most of these works will reside in the Commonwealth, a proportion of works kept in the collection of the archives will be the subject of other copyright ownership. However, given the nature of the holdings and the purpose for which they are used, the limitations of the defence to a single copy appear unnecessarily restrictive. It appears inconsistent with the wide protection given to the National Archives of Australia from infringement of copyright through the giving of access to records under the *Archives Act 1983*.

While most government records are protected as 'works' under the *Copyright Act 1968*, the provisions in Part III Division 5 of the *Copyright Act 1968* dealing with the preservation of works held in the collections of libraries or archives described above are mirrored in similar provisions set out in Part IV Division 6 of the Act dealing with subject matter other than works. Section 110A applies to the copying, for research or study or with a view to publication, of unpublished sound recordings and cinematograph films kept in the collection of the library or archives that are more than 50 years old, in a similar way to s 51 dealing with works. Section 110B applies to the copying for preservation or replacement by the library or archives of sound recordings and cinematograph films held in the collection of a library or archives in a similar way to s 51A dealing with works, and s 110BA applies s 51B in a similar way to the copying for preservation by the library or archives of significant recordings and films held in key cultural institutions' collections. While some material held by government archives, such as the National Archives of Australia, is in the form of sound recording or film, these provisions are of utmost importance to institutions such as the National Film and Sound Archive to preserve these important emanations of Australian culture and heritage.[53]

The 'Flexible Exception'

Another exception to infringement that may be relied on by archives and libraries is s 200AB of the *Copyright Act 1968*. It is intended to provide 'a flexible exception to enable copyright material to be used for certain socially beneficial purposes, while remaining consistent with Australia's obligations under international copyright treaties'.[54] The provision applies to libraries and archives, educational institutions and use by, or for, persons with a disability and to published and unpublished works.

---

53 The *International Convention for the Protection of Performers, Producers of Phonograms and Broadcasting Organisations* (the Rome Convention) done at Rome on 26 October 1961, to which Australia is a party, provides (in Article 15) permitted exceptions to the protection granted by the Convention that include 'the same kind of limitations' that any Contracting State provides for 'in its domestic laws and regulations, in connection with the protection of copyright in literary and artistic works'. The Convention covers, among other things, protection for the fixation of sounds and for image and sound broadcasts. Refer to *International Convention for the Protection of Performers, Producers of Phonograms and Broadcasting Organisations* http://www.wipo.int/treaties/en/ip/rome/trtdocs_wo024.html#P132_12542.

54 Explanatory Memorandum, Copyright Amendment Bill 2006 (Cth) 108.

The relevant parts of the section applicable to libraries and archives provide:

200AB Use of works and other subject-matter for certain purposes

(1) The copyright in a work or other subject-matter is not infringed by a use of the work or other subject-matter if all the following conditions exist:

(a) the circumstances of the use (including those described in paragraphs (b), (c) and (d)) amount to a special case;

(b) the use is covered by subsection (2), (3) or (4);

(c) the use does not conflict with a normal exploitation of the work or other subject-matter;

(d) the use does not unreasonably prejudice the legitimate interests of the owner of the copyright.

Use by body administering library or archives

(2) This subsection covers a use that:

(a) is made by or on behalf of the body administering a library or archives; and

(b) is made for the purpose of maintaining or operating the library or archives (including operating the library or archives to provide services of a kind usually provided by a library or archives); and

(c) is not made partly for the purpose of the body obtaining a commercial advantage or profit.

. . .

This section does not apply if under another provision the use does not, or might not, infringe copyright

(6) Subsection (1) does not apply if, because of another provision of this Act:

(a) the use is not an infringement of copyright; or

(b) the use would not be an infringement of copyright assuming the conditions or requirements of that other provision were met.

. . .

Cost recovery not commercial advantage or profit

(6A) The use does not fail to meet the condition in paragraph (2)(c), (3)(c) or (4)(c) merely because of the charging of a fee that:

(a) is connected with the use; and

(b) does not exceed the costs of the use to the charger of the fee.

Definitions

(7) In this section:

conflict with a normal exploitation has the same meaning as in Article 13 of the TRIPS Agreement.

special case has the same meaning as in Article 13 of the TRIPS Agreement.

unreasonably prejudice the legitimate interests has the same meaning as in Article 13 of the TRIPS Agreement.

use includes any act that would infringe copyright apart from this section.

Article 13 of the TRIPS Agreement,[55] referred to in s 200AB(7), sets out a three-step test for exceptions to infringement of copyright. The wording of the three-step test is reflected in s 200AB(1), which in turn governs the application of s 200AB(2)–(4). The origins of the three-step test for limitations and exceptions lie in the Paris Act of the *Berne Convention for the Protection of Literary and Artistic Works,* which also binds Australia, and its scope is described in more detail in Chapter 1 of this book.[56]

Under s 200AB(2), library or archival use must be 'made for the purpose of maintaining or operating' the library or archives and must not be made partly for commercial advantage or profit. Otherwise, the operation of s 200AB(2) is governed by the three-step test, which is aimed at conformity with Australia's obligations under TRIPS.

The three steps are cast in wide and general terms that are cumulative in nature and lack clarity in their application to libraries and archives.[57] To overcome the lack of clarity and complexity of s 200AB, some independently produced guides have been published to assist those wishing to understand its scope, such as that published by the Australian Libraries Copyright Committee and the Australian Digital Alliance.[58] There is yet no Australian case law on s 200AB to support these guides. The Australian Copyright Council has set out a number of factors likely to influence the legitimacy of reliance on the section including the view that it is unlikely to apply if the use is not for a specific and identified need or request, and is more likely to apply if the number of people the use is for is small, the time-frame is short and the proportion of the work used is small.[59] An example where s 200AB(2) may

---

55   The TRIPS (Trade-Related Aspects of Intellectual Property Rights) Agreement is annex 1C of the Marrakesh Agreement Establishing the World Trade Organization, signed at Marrakesh, Morocco on 15 April 1994, see World Trade Organization, *Agreement on Trade-Related Aspects of Intellectual Property Rights* (1994) http://www.wto.org/english/docs_e/legal_e/27-trips.pdf.

56   Article 13 of TRIPS follows the wording of art 9 of the Paris Act of the *Berne Convention for the Protection of Literary and Artistic Works*, opened for signature 24 July 1971, 1161 UNTS 30 (entered into force 15 December 1972). Australia became bound by the Paris Act of the *Berne Convention* on 3 January 1978.

57   For a discussion on what Ricketson describes as 'problems of interpretation' of the three-step test in art 9(2) of the *Berne Convention for the Protection of Literary and Artistic Works*, see S Ricketson, *The Berne Convention for the Protection of Literary and Artistic Works: 1886–1986* (London Centre for Commercial Law Studies, 1987) 482–9; and on art 13 of the TRIPS Agreement, see D Gervais, *The TRIPS Agreement: Drafting History and Analysis* (Sweet and Maxwell, 3rd edn, 2008) 239–43.

58   Australian Libraries Copyright Committee and Australian Digital Alliance, *A User's Guide to the Flexible Dealing Provision for Libraries, Educational Institutions and Cultural Institutions* (2008) http://libcopyright.org.au/sites/libcopyright.org.au/files/documents/FlexibleDealingHandbookfinal.pdf or http://digital.org.au/our-work/publication/section-200ab-flexible-dealing-handbook-online.

apply is in enabling archives and libraries to use orphan works (where copyright owners cannot be identified or located) such as digitising and placing them online.[60]

While the scope of the provision is yet to be tested, it remains a last resort defence to infringement for archives and libraries concerned about their exposure to infringement for use that is not governed by other sections of the *Copyright Act 1968* (Cth). By virtue of s 200AB(6), the section does not apply if, under another provision of the Act, the use does not, or would not, (assuming the conditions of that other provision were met) constitute an infringement. Accordingly, where there are express provisions already in the *Copyright Act 1968* that may be relied on by archives or libraries as defences to infringement, archives or libraries are not entitled to augment the scope of those provisions by reliance on s 200AB. It would seem that if the government archive were copying 'for the services of the Commonwealth or State' (within the scope of the Crown use provision) reliance on s 200AB would not be possible. The 'flexibility' of the exception for government archives and libraries is thus limited.

International Comparisons

Many of the provisions dealing with library and archival copying have their origins in laws in the United Kingdom and there is a similarity in the statutory defences to infringement available to libraries and archives under the common law regimes of the United Kingdom, New Zealand and Canada. There is a corresponding regime in the United States of America. The balance between the rights of owners and the interests of libraries and archives and their users is broadly similar in each jurisdiction.

Two notable exceptions are that under all of the statutory regimes except Canada, there are no specific provisions dealing with the national archival institution similar to s 51AA of the Australian *Copyright Act 1968*, nor under any of these regimes is there an equivalent fall-back exception to infringement similar to s 200AB. But taking these exceptions into account, the law in Australia dealing with library and archival copying is broadly similar to the copyright laws of these comparable countries.

Under the present *Copyright, Designs and Patents Act 1988* (UK) the provisions enabling the copying of published works for users and for other libraries (ss 37–41) and by libraries and archives for preservation or replacement (s 42), and of unpublished works for research or study (s 43) are similar to ss 49, 50, 51A and 51 of the *Copyright Act 1968* (Cth). Section 75 of the UK Act also enables the recording of broadcasts for placement in an archive maintained by a body, which is not established or conducted for profit.[61] Provisions introduced in June 2014 into the *Copyright, Designs and Patents Act 1988* (UK) by

---

59 Australian Copyright Council, *Section 200AB: the 'Special Case' or 'Flexible Dealing' Exception* (2009) http://www.copyright.org.au/acc_prod/ACC/Information_Sheets/Special_Case_or_Flexible_Dealing_Exceptions__Section_200AB.aspx.

60 Above n 58, 5, 17, 31–3.

61 This widens the scope of the provision beyond previously designated bodies, such as the British Library, the Imperial War Museum and the British Film Institute: refer to The Copyright and Rights in Performances (Research, Education, Libraries and Archives) Regulations 2014, reg 8.

The Copyright and Rights in Performances (Research, Education, Libraries and Archives) Regulations enable libraries, archives, museums and educational establishments to make works available for the purposes of research or private study through dedicated terminals on their premises (s 40B) provided it is in compliance with any licensing terms to which the work is subject. Some provisions such as s 41 (copying by librarians for supply to other libraries), s 42 (replacement copies by libraries, archives and museums) and s 42A (copying by librarians of single copies of published works for users) have been clarified so that they cannot be contracted out.

Under Part 3 of the *Copyright Act 1994* (NZ) provisions enabling the copying of published works for users of libraries and archives and for other libraries (ss 51–54, 56A), by libraries and archives for preservation or replacement (s 55) and of unpublished works for research or study (s 56) are similar to ss 49, 50, 51A and 51 of the *Copyright Act 1968* (Cth). The provisions apply to prescribed libraries and archives and are broadly defined.[62] By virtue of amendments made by the *Copyright (New Technologies) Amendment Act 2008* (NZ) additional conditions are imposed in respect of digital copying under those provisions including a requirement for the destruction of any additional copy made in the process of supplying the digital copy.[63] In addition, s 90 of the Act permits the recording for archival purposes by prescribed bodies including Archives New Zealand, the New Zealand Film Archive and the National Library of New Zealand of broadcast or cable programs transmitted in New Zealand of particular relevance to New Zealand or New Zealanders.[64]

Under the *Copyright Act 1985* (Can) exceptions to infringement enable libraries, archives or museums to make a copy of a work or other subject matter, whether published or unpublished, in its permanent collection, for the maintenance or management of its permanent collection or the permanent collection of another library, archive or museum. This includes copying for restoration, copying in an alternative format if currently in an obsolete format,[65] and copying 'for the purposes of internal record keeping and cataloguing'.[66] The Act also permits copying for users of the library, archives or museum and for users of other libraries, archives or museums for the purposes of research or private study[67] and copying of unpublished works deposited in an archives for the user's research and private study where copying has not been prohibited by the owner of copyright in the work.[68] Under s 30.2 of the Act it is not an infringement for a library, archive or museum or a person

---

62 Refer to s 50 of the *Copyright Act 1994* (NZ). Both the New Zealand and to a lesser extent the UK acts differ from the Australian *Copyright Act 1968* by not fully extending the library copying defences for users and for other libraries, to archival institutions. However, s 56A of the *Copyright Act 1994* (NZ) permits both archives and libraries to communicate a digital copy of a work to an 'authenticated user' subject to conditions.

63 Sections 56A–56C inserted on 31 October 2008 by s 37 of the *Copyright (New Technologies) Amendment Act 2008* (NZ) (2008 No 27).

64 Refer also to Copyright (General Matters) Regulations 1995 (NZ) reg 5A.

65 Section 30.1(2), *Copyright Act*, RSC 1985 c C-42 (Can), (where not commercially available).

66 *Copyright Act*, RSC 1985 c C-42 (Can), section 30.1.

67 Ibid, section 30.2.

68 Ibid, section 30.21.

acting under its authority to do anything on behalf of any person that the person may do personally under s 29 (which includes a fair dealing for research or private study or for the purpose of education) or s 29.1 (fair dealing for criticism or review). While s 30.2 reflects general principles under the law of agency it also provides flexibility to a library, archive or museum in providing access to users. Section 30.3 also enables these institutions to avoid infringement of copyright through the use of copying machines on its premises but, unlike the Australian provision s 39A, is only effective in respect of the reprographic reproduction of works and then only effective if covered by a licence agreement with a collective society authorised by copyright owners.

The *Copyright Act 1985* provides specific rights to the Librarian and Archivist of Canada that deem copying of works and other subject matter in fulfilment of some responsibilities under the *Library and Archives of Canada Act 2004*[69] not an infringement. This includes copying by representative sampling of documentary material of interest to Canada from the internet or similar medium for the purpose of preservation and fixing a copy of a publication provided by telecommunication under the legal deposit provision.[70]

It is not generally an infringement of copyright for a library or archives in the United States of America to make a copy or a phonorecord[71] of a work or to distribute it, provided the library or archives is available to the public or researchers, the copying or distribution is made without any purpose of direct or indirect commercial advantage, and that copying or distribution includes a copyright notice. Copying is restricted to an article in a periodical publication or a small part of another copyright work for users of that or another library or archives, or to an entire work for those users, where the library or archives has determined that a copy or phonorecord cannot be obtained at a fair price.[72] Both restrictions include a proviso that the library or archives has had no notice that the copy would be used for any purpose other than private study, scholarship or research.[73]

The protection against infringement for reproduction or distribution extends to the making of three copies or phonorecords of an unpublished work for the purposes of preservation and security or for deposit for research use in another library or archives.[74] The right of reproduction also extends to three replacement copies or phonorecords of a published work that is damaged, deteriorating, lost or stolen, or to replace an obsolete format, provided the library or archives has determined that an unused replacement cannot be obtained at a fair price.[75] The rights of reproduction and distribution for users do not gen-

---

69   *Library and Archives of Canada Act* SC 2004 c11.

70   *Copyright Act*, RSC, 1985 c C-42 (Can) section 30.5.

71   'Phonorecords' are material objects in which sounds, other than those accompanying a motion picture or other audiovisual work, are fixed by any method now known or later developed, and from which the sounds can be perceived, reproduced, or otherwise communicated, either directly or with the aid of a machine or device. The term 'phonorecords' includes the material object in which the sounds are first fixed: *Copyright Act of 1976* 17 USC §§ 101.

72   *Copyright Act of 1976* 17USC §§ 108(a) (d) (e).

73   Ibid, 108(d) (e).

74   Ibid, 108(b).

75   Ibid, 108(c).

erally apply to musical works or to pictorial, graphic or sculptural works or audiovisual works (except those dealing with news) unless by way of illustration.[76] Some wider rights are provided to archives and libraries in the case of published works within the last 20 years of copyright protection.[77]

The Act also contains a provision similar to s 39A and s 104B of the Australian Act in operation for the unsupervised use of reproducing equipment located on the premises of a library or archives.[78] This provision, s 108 (f), is expressed not to affect the right of fair use or any contractual obligations assumed by the library or archives when it obtained a copy or phonorecord of a work in its collections.[79]

It is clear from the 23rd Session of the WIPO Standing Committee on Copyright and Related Rights in December 2011 that there are ongoing international deliberations aimed at developing an international instrument dealing with exceptions and limitations for libraries and archives on preservation, right of reproduction and safeguarding copies, legal deposit, library lending, parallel importations, cross-border uses, orphan works, retracted and withdrawn works and works out of commerce, and other issues.[80] Libraries and archives groups have been seeking a set of basic minimum limitations and exceptions for the benefit of libraries, archives and their uses under their national copyright laws[81] and not on the basis of a 'one size fits all' approach.[82]

The proposals for reform outlined below assume Australia's present international treaty obligations.

---

76   Ibid, 108(i).

77   Ibid, 108(h).

78   Ibid, 108(f).

79   Ibid, 108(f)(4). For further comments, refer to Chapter 7, 'Excluding or Modifying the Special Defences'.

80   World Intellectual Property Organisation. *SCCR/23/Conclusions* (2 December 2011) http://www.wipo.int/meetings/en/doc_details.jsp?doc_id=190903. Refer, for example, to *eIFL-IP Draft Law on Copyright Including Model Exceptions and Limitations for Libraries and Their Users* (2014) http://www.eifl.net/system/files/resources/201411/eifl_draft_law_2014.pdf.

81   EIFL(Electronic Information for Libraries)/IFLA, *Library and Archive Groups Delighted by Progress at WIPO* (2 December 2011) http://www.eifl.net/library-and-archive-groups-delighted-progress-wipo.

82   This matter was discussed at the 26th–28th sessions of the WIPO Standing Committee on Copyright and Neighbouring Rights from December 2013–December 2014 focusing on a working document towards an appropriate international instrument and an updated international study on limitations and exceptions: refer to WIPO. Standing Committee on Copyright and Neighbouring Rights http://www.wipo.int/policy/en/sccr/.

Reform

Legal and Policy Aspects of Access

One theme of the 1976 recommendations of the Franki Committee was the concern for the free flow of information. To quote from the first section of the committee's report 'Australia is geographically isolated from the major centres of scientific and industrial research and . . . the vast area of the Australian continent raises special problems in relation to the dissemination of information, particularly in the remoter parts'.[83] There are a number of references in the report to the public interest in ensuring the free flow of information for education and for the scientific, technical and social development in Australia. The concern about the free flow of information was and is a concern in Australia and worldwide. We now use the term 'access to information' to describe it.

In his second reading speech on the Copyright Amendment Bill (No 2) 1979, the Minister noted that the Franki Committee viewed libraries as information resource centres with a legitimate need to copy material.[84] It was an example of copying of a public benefit nature provided as part of the balance of interests between owners of copyright and users of copyright material.[85] The provisions have since been amended to enable electronic access and communication of material.

The provisions of the *Copyright Act 1968* dealing with library and archive copying, and the transmission of copyright material, represent a traditional legislative response to the need for access to copyright material and a balancing of the interests of users for access to copyright material against owners of copyright. The scope of the provisions is based on notions of infringement of private property rights and not unfairly prejudicing the interests of those copyright owners in the exploitation of those rights.

In relation to government archives, the provisions largely impact upon government copyright material. The provisions of the *Copyright Act 1968* do not reflect the broader policy objectives of FOI reforms[86] and technological change in accessing material. Thus a tension has arisen between the public interest in ensuring the widest possible access to government information and the copyright interests in that information.

It is evident that the concept of the role of government has been a changing one particularly over the last three decades. While the demand for access to copyright material and government copyright material in particular is not likely to diminish but to grow, govern-

---

83   Above n 28, 15.

84   Parliament of Australia, *Parliamentary Debates,* Second Reading Speech, Senate, 4 June 1979, 2534 (Senator Chaney, Minister for Aboriginal Affairs).

85   Ibid 4.

86   Section 3(3) and (4) of the *Freedom of Information Amendment (Reform) Act 2010* (Cth) provides: (3) 'The Parliament also intends, by these objects, to increase recognition that information held by Government is to be managed for public purposes, and is a national resource'; and (4) 'The Parliament also intends that functions and powers given by this Act are to be performed and exercised, as far as possible, to facilitate and promote public access to information, promptly and at the lowest reasonable cost'.

ment response to that demand and its need to manage information raise questions beyond simply the balancing of interests within the provisions of the *Copyright Act 1968*. The question of access is not simply a legislative one, whether the material is government owned or not.[87] And the question is not simply a copyright one. FOI and archive laws do not purport to be a complete code of access to documents in the possession of government. Neither is copyright law a complete code of interests in the legitimate use of copyright material. The former contemplates the granting of access outside the Act.[88] The latter contemplates the giving of permission to do acts comprised in the copyright beyond the exceptions to infringement contained in the Act.[89]

The resolution of the public interest in accessing and re-using the archival material of government involves issues of law and policy. The public interest in accessing this material is reflected in the principles of open government espoused in the *Archives Act 1983* (Cth) and the *Freedom of Information Act 1982* (Cth). The material in the possession of these institutions is essentially old unpublished material. It is mostly government copyright material. However, a proportion is copyright material vested in other persons. Any reform must therefore take into account the interests of other copyright owners. The government cannot lawfully sanction the use of material in which it does not own copyright, without legislation legitimising this use.

Access and Copyright Law

The law should be reformed to enable an archival institution to reproduce (for example, through digitisation) or communicate a reproduction of a work or other subject matter housed within it such as a sound recording or cinematograph film, for its own internal purposes. This includes preservation, replacement, reference and fixation in another medium, without limit on number. For clarity it may simply be effected through an inclusive definition of 'internal purposes' to express the scope of copying.[90]

This reform would not economically harm the copyright owner since the material involved is largely unpublished, or would otherwise unfairly prejudice the interests of the copyright owner in the material—whether private or government—and the restraints of administrative cost, time and space and the desire to preserve the original would impose practical limits on how much was copied and how many copies were made. It would promote the

---

87   For example, as government policy reflected in the UK Treasury Minutes of 1887 and 1912 shows. United Kingdom. *XLIX Accounts and Papers (House of Commons)* No 335 (1887); United Kingdom. *LXIX Accounts and Papers (House of Commons)* No 292 (1912–13).

88   Refer to the *Freedom of Information Act 1982* (Cth) s 14; and the *Archives Act 1983* (Cth) s 58.

89   Refer to the *Copyright Act 1968* (Cth) s 196(4).

90   EIFL and other library and archival groups are also seeking wider rights for these 'internal purposes': refer, for example, to s 12 of the *eIFL-IP Draft law on copyright Including Model Exceptions and Limitations for Libraries and Their Users* (2014) http://www.eifl.net/system/files/resources/201411/eifl_draft_law_2014.pdf. 12. (1) Archives, public libraries, other libraries, museums and galleries that are publicly funded in whole or in part, may use and distribute copies of works as part of their activities in accordance with subsections (2)–(12) provided this is not done for commercial purposes. (2) Such institutions may make copies of works in their collection for the purpose of back-up and preservation. Such institutions may also make copies of publicly accessible websites for the purposes of preservation.

preservation of, and access to, archival material. It would simplify aspects of the application of the *Copyright Act 1968* to archives.

The *Copyright Act 1968* should also be clarified to ensure government archival institutions may rely fully on those provisions of the Act applicable to archival institutions, including s 200AB, without recourse to the government statutory licence regime—the Crown use provision s 183—of the *Copyright Act 1968*. Section 183 should augment and not override the provisions generally applicable to libraries and archives. Government archives should be entitled to rely on all the defences applicable under the Act to non-government archives. The public interest in the effective maintenance of government archives and in the copyright defences available to government archives is at least as compelling as that for non-government archival institutions.

However, of most importance is the reform of the law to facilitate electronic access to government information: '[i]n the online world the development of virtual archives is not only desirable, but also essential for continued relevance and survival.'[91]

The rights of access to government records should encompass the technology that enables it. Consistent with the principles of open government, and consequent upon the lawful capacity of archives to supply published and unpublished works to users of the archives under ss 49 and 51 of the *Copyright Act 1968* and s 57 of the *Archives Act 1983*, government archives should be able to make available, online, all records that are open to public inspection, that is, material that is in the open access period and for which no exemption to access under the *Archives Act 1983* may be claimed, without infringement of copyright. The protection provided by s 57 of the *Archives Act 1983* against actions for defamation, breach of confidence and infringement of copyright through the giving of access under the Act should extend to the making available of records online. This reform is consistent with the 2010 amendments to the *Freedom of Information Act 1982* (Cth) mandating the publication of documents to which access has been given under the Act and expanding the protection from civil actions for defamation, breach of confidence and infringement of copyright under ss 90 and 91 of that Act to include both the giving of access and publication of those documents by government under the Act. Measures under the *Freedom of Information Amendment (Reform) Act 2010* (Cth) that require agencies to publish information, which includes accessed information under the *Freedom of Information Act 1982* (Cth) to enable downloading from a website,[92] have not been matched by reforms to the *Archives Act 1983* (Cth). The use of website technology in this way is a sensible and significant aid to public access to government records.

It also seems unnecessary and inconsistent with the principles of public access to government information, for a declaration of use for research or study by the person accessing those government records. Nonetheless, such a requirement could be facilitated electronically as a condition of the search for, and access to, those archival records.[93]

---

91 A Cunningham, *Archives—Encyclopedia of Library and Information Science* (Informaword/Taylor & Francis, 3rd edn, 2010) 1:1 [203] 192–207.

92 Refer to the *Freedom of Information Act 1982* (Cth) s 11C.

93 For example, if it was thought necessary to conform to the three-step test of part 13 of the TRIPS Agreement.

Consistent with protection given to the National Archives of Australia under s 57 of the *Archives Act 1983* (Cth), it would be desirable to amend s 51 of the *Copyright Act 1968* (Cth) to make the period of access to unpublished works for other archival institutions consistent with the period in which these works are open to public inspection. That period may vary under the terms of an acquisition or bequest. The period of access should not be dependent on the period of more than 50 years after the death of the author of the work. These reforms in the copyright law would not, it is suggested, be a breach of the three-step test contained in Article 13 of the TRIPS Agreement.[94] Given the nature of the records and their age, the reforms would not conflict with a normal exploitation of a work or unreasonably prejudice the legitimate interests of the copyright owner.

While these reforms seek to improve the preservation of, and access to, archival works, the re-use of works released under the open access period raises wider issues of reform.

Re-use and Copyright Law

There are demonstrable public benefits in facilitating the re-use of government information.[95] Once accessed, copyright law contemplates the re-use of accessed material—whether government and other copyright works—equally.[96] Section 52 of the *Copyright Act 1968* in particular sets out a formal procedure for the publication of unpublished orphan works. It applies only to works made more than 50 years after the author died and requires the giving of notice of intended publication. This is clearly inconsistent with the established principles of open government espoused in the *Archives Act 1983* and the *Freedom of Information Act 1982*.

In so far as unpublished government copyright material is concerned, where access is granted to that material in the open access period, governments can facilitate wider dissemination by the grant of Creative Commons or similar forms of open content licences for the reproduction, communication and publication of government material. This is con-

---

94   European Union. European Commission, *Green Paper – Copyright in the Knowledge Economy* (16 July 2008) http://ec.europa.eu/internal_market/copyright/docs/copyright-infso/greenpaper_en.pdf; United Kingdom. Intellectual Property Office, *UK Government Response to European Commission's Green Paper – Copyright in the Knowledge Economy* (December 2008) [4.5] http://webarchive.nationalarchives.gov.uk/20140603093549/http://www.ipo.gov.uk/c-eupaper.pdf.

95   Refer, for example, Australia. Cutler & Company Pty Ltd, *Venturous Australia: Building Strength in Innovation: Report on the Review of the National Innovation System* (the Cutler Report) Report to Senator the Hon Kim Carr, Minister for Innovation, Industry, Science and Research (August 2008) [41, 93-95] http://www.industry.gov.au/innovation/InnovationPolicy/Pages/Document%20library/NISReport.aspx or http://www.industry.gov.au/innovation/InnovationPolicy/Documents/Policy/NISReport.pdf; Australia. Department of Broadband Communications and the Digital Economy, *Australia's Digital Economy: Future Directions* (2009) [12], [13] http://pandora.nla.gov.au/pan/102861/20090717-1104/www.dbcde.gov.au/__data/assets/pdf_file/0003/117786/DIGITAL_ECONOMY_FUTURE_DIRECTIONS_FINAL_REPORT.pdf; United Kingdom. Office of Fair Trading, *The Commercial Use of Public Information (CUPI)* (2006) OFT 861 [1.4] http://webarchive.nationalarchives.gov.uk/20140402142426/http://oft.gov.uk/oftwork/publications/publication-categories/reports/consumer-protection/oft861 or http://www.opsi.gov.uk/advice/poi/oft-cupi.pdf; Cabinet Office, *The Power of Information: An Independent Review by Ed Mayo and Tom Steinberg* (2007) [14–6] [26–38] http://www.opsi.gov.uk/advice/poi/index.htm.

96   Refer to the *Copyright Act 1968* (Cth) ss 51, 52.

sistent with the established principles of open government espoused in those Acts[97] and the May 2010 announcement of the *Government Response to the Report of the Government 2.0 Taskforce*:

> The Australian government will amend Australia's copyright policy to ensure that, at the time at which Commonwealth records become available for public access under the *Archives Act 1983*, works covered by Crown copyright are automatically licensed under an appropriate open attribution licence. The selection and use of an appropriate open attribution licence will remain the responsibility of agencies on a case-by-case basis. Agencies can use the National Government Information Licensing Framework (GILF) tool to assist them making information licensing decisions.[98]

This is a matter of policy and requires no legislative amendment. Moreover, policy may be implemented through open content licences to take into account the different interests of government in a diverse range of government material and may be adjusted expeditiously in the light of changes in government activities and priorities. In particular, while access to government works is facilitated by Division 5 of Part III of the *Copyright Act 1968* (Cth) dealing with libraries and archives and ss 31, 3(7) and 57 of the *Archives Act 1983* (Cth), open content licences can facilitate the re-use of published as well as unpublished government material held by archives and libraries by persons accessing those works.

While it is commonly argued government ownership of copyright impedes access to government information, open content attribution licensing conveniently identifies the source and ownership of information and enables a level of assuredness about the re-use of that information. In particular, material in the public domain may be not sourced and may in itself become the subject of third-party ownership claims whether in the published edition or in the edited form of the material.[99] Further, such licensing can provide some control over the integrity of material when it is disseminated so that users receive it in its original, unaltered form and as a consequence can place appropriate reliance on it.[100]

---

97   Refer to A Fitzgerald and K Pappalardo, *Report to the Government 2.0 Taskforce: Project 4 Copyright Law and Intellectual Property* (Dec 2009) [16]–[18] http://gov2.net.au/projects/, where the authors argue that the government's exercise of copyright should be consistent with established policy on open access to, and re-use of, public sector information.

98   Australia. Department of Finance and Deregulation, *Government Response to the Report of the Government 2.0 Taskforce* (May 2010), [10] http://www.finance.gov.au/publications/ govresponse20report/ or http://www.finance.gov.au/publications/govresponse20report/doc/ Government-Response-to-Gov-2-0-Report.pdf. The Australian Government later released *Guidelines for Licensing Public Sector Information* that provides that the default or starting position is that PSI should be released free of charge under a Creative Commons 'BY' licence (the most liberal Creative Commons licence). Attorney-General's Department, *Guidelines for Licensing Public Sector Information for Australian Government Agencies* (28 February 2012) 4 http://www.ag.gov.au/RightsAndProtections/ IntellectualProperty/Documents/GuidelinesforlicensingPSIforAusGovagencies.pdf.

99   The dissemination of federal US legislation and case law is dominated by private suppliers who strongly assert copyright in their marked up versions of these laws.

100   Victoria. Economic Development and Infrastructure Committee, Parliament of Victoria, *Inquiry into Improving Access to Victorian Public Sector Information and Data: Public Hearings and Transcripts,*

An open content attribution licence for government information is, however, limited to actions for infringement of copyright. It is questionable whether the protection afforded by s 57 of the *Archives Act 1983* (Cth) to protect the government and its officers from actions for defamation and breach of confidence should extend further to protect persons who wish to communicate or publish government copyright material more widely. While it is not likely there would be a basis for an action for breach of confidence for the publication of unpublished government material given the age of open access material, that may not be the case with an action for defamation and if such an action might arise it would seem equitable for it to be the responsibility of the publisher and not the government. That is, it should be the responsibility of the person publishing or communicating the accessed information to the public.

An impediment to the subsequent re-use of government records in which the Crown is not the copyright owner is the inability to identify or locate the copyright owner of the record. Open content licensing from the government for re-use of works covered by Crown copyright would not extend to these 'orphan' works. Re-use of third-party orphan works, such as letters, submissions and reports to government can, however, be the subject of statutory reform. Fitzgerald and Pappalardo propose that libraries and archives should be able to use s 200AB of the *Copyright Act 1968* ('the flexible exception') to enable dealings with orphan works, with the assistance of guidelines and case studies, to enable those bodies to function effectively within the digital environment.[101] Where public access has been given to orphan works held by government under the *Freedom of Information Act 1982* (Cth) or *Archives Act 1983* (Cth) it would seem appropriate to extend that statutory protection to the re-use of those orphan works to individuals. The restrictions in s 200AB(1) that the use not conflict with a normal exploitation of the work, or unreasonably prejudice the legitimate interests of the copyright owner would still apply. In 2011, the Hargreaves Report in the United Kingdom included a proposal for a Digital Copyright Exchange to bring together rights holders.[102] The proposal has since been adopted by the United Kingdom government. Such a body, if established in Australia, could serve as a clearinghouse for the identification of copyright owners and a facilitator of licensing and thus reduce the difficulty in identifying and locating the copyright owners for the wider re-use of those works.[103]

(12 August 2008) 9 http://www.parliament.vic.gov.au/archive/edic/inquiries/access_to_PSI/transcripts/ EDIC_080812_A_Fitzgerald.pdf.

101   A Fitzgerald and K Pappalardo, *Copyright Law and Intellectual Property: Report to the Government 2.0 Taskforce: Project 4* (Dec 2009) 53 http://gov2.net.au/projects/index.html.

102   United Kingdom. Intellectual Property Office *Digital Opportunity: A Review of Intellectual Property and Growth* (Hargreaves Report) (May 2011) 39 http://www.ipo.gov.uk/ipreview-finalreport.pdf or https://www.gov.uk/government/publications/digital-opportunityreview-of-intellectual-property-and-growth.

103   The United Kingdom government adopted the proposal through copyright licencing reform under the *Enterprise and Regulatory Reform Act 2013* (UK) c 24, s 77 (which inserts ss 116A–116D and Schedule A1 into the *Copyright, Designs and Patents Act 1988 (UK)* c 48) and by the provision of seed money to establish the 'Digital Copyright Hub' https://www.gov.uk/government/news/ government-gives-150-000-funding-to-kick-start-copyright-hub. See Eleonora Rosati, 'The Hargreaves Report and Copyright Licensing: Can National Initiatives Work per se?' (2011) 33 (11) *European Intellectual Property Review* 673, 676, where the author argues for the proposal, if it manages to obtain the objectives indicated in the Report, as a model for future EU legislation.

Access and Information Management

While the economic value of information in the possession of government is likely to be higher for current or recent material than material in archives, ultimately what is common and important in the achievement of access and better, accountable government is good recordkeeping, and the identification, coordination and management of records by government.

Recordkeeping is an integral part of information management and is its critical first step. Its importance is reinforced by the Australian Standard on Records Management:

> Records contain information that is a valuable resource and an important business asset. A systematic approach to the management of records is essential for organisations and society to protect and preserve records as evidence of actions. A records management system results in a source of information about business activities that can support subsequent activities and business decisions, as well as ensuring accountability to present and future stakeholders.[104]

Under the *Archives Act 1983* (Cth) the National Archives of Australia issues guidelines and principles for recordkeeping, but that body has no coercive powers over government agencies, and responsibility for each agency's conformance with its guidelines rests on the Chief Executive Officer of the agency.

In its 1998 review of the *Archives Act 1983*, the ALRC pointed to the 'parlous state of recordkeeping' in many Commonwealth agencies. Since then there have been a number of reviews by the Commonwealth Auditor-General on recordkeeping in Commonwealth organisations. Two reviews expressed concern about the non-capture of records[105] and the failure of physical records to be kept in compliance with National Archives standards, and the third, in 2006, concluded:

> 20. The audit also found that improvements were required in each of the entity's electronic and paper-based recordkeeping practices. This included, in particular, the need to develop further guidance on circumstances where records are created, received and maintained by the entity having regard to its legal and business requirements.
>
> 21. The ANAO [Australian National Audit Office] considered that entities needed to give ongoing, and in some cases, increased commitment to meeting their recordkeeping responsibilities. This is particularly the case for those records that are created electronically, including records held in electronic systems.[106]

---

104   Standards Australia, *Australian Standard for Records Management* AS ISO 15489 (2002) 1, 4.

105   The first audit was Australia. Australian National Audit Office, *Recordkeeping, Audit Report No 45 2001–02* (1 May 2002) http://www.anao.gov.au/uploads/documents/2001-02_Audit_Report_45.pdf. The second was Australia. Australian National Audit Office, *Recordkeeping in Large Commonwealth Organisations, Audit Report No 7 2003–04* (24 September 2003) http://www.anao.gov.au/uploads/documents/2003-04_Audit_Report_7.pdf.

While the *Archives Act 1983* defines a 'record' to include a document in electronic form,[107] most Commonwealth agency files are still paper based, that is, most Commonwealth agencies are still printing to file.[108] In an electronic environment that poses risks to good recordkeeping, simply because it is reliant on the business area's full and faithful observance of that manual task. In addition, the increasing use by agencies of government of web-based records and electronic interactive sites such as blogs,[109] to promote community engagement suggests the classification and appraisal of records needs to be carefully worked through by agencies with training and other systemic approaches to ensure the intelligent appraisal and retention of agency records in this format. One particular concern is that more web-based information is likely to be ephemeral and hard-copy equivalents of that information may not be available.

The present use of different digital proprietary recordkeeping systems by government agencies and the need to convert them to long term archival format, coupled with the need to translate them to different formats as technology changes, pose not simply immediate and medium-term preservation needs, but more substantial and costly ongoing preservation challenges than the use of the vellum, parchment or non-acidic paper-based media of the past. This, in turn, raises data storage and management issues for government to overcome the impact of technological redundancy.

Another concern for the National Archives is that records generated by government agencies using third-party sites for the purposes of collaboration, service delivery or information dissemination may not be captured as Commonwealth records. This suggests that the definition of 'record' in the *Archives Act 1983* be widened along the lines recommended in the *Report of the Government 2.0 Taskforce* to encompass 'any information created or received by the Commonwealth in the course of performing Commonwealth business.'[110] Unless valuable information in electronic form is preserved it will not be accessible to future generations.

Archives New Zealand (as well as government archival institutions in most Australian states) has standard-setting powers with which agencies are bound to comply.[111] However,

---

106   Australia. Australian National Audit Office, *Recordkeeping Including the Management of Electronic Records, Audit Report No 6 2006–07*, (12 October 2006), Summary and Key Findings [18] http://www.anao.gov.au/Publications.

107   *Record* means a document, or an object, in any form (including any electronic form) that is, or has been, kept by reason of: (a) any information or matter that it contains or that can be obtained from it; or (b) its connection with any event, person, circumstance or thing (*Archives Act 1983* (Cth) s 3).

108   Interview with Paul Dalgleish, Assistant Director, Reference Policy and Support, and Adrian Cunningham, Director, Strategic Relations and Personal Records, National Archives of Australia (at National Archives of Australia, 6 August 2010).

109   For example, Australia. Department of Finance and Deregulation, Australian Government Information Management Office, *Government 2.0 Taskforce* http://gov2.net.au/; and Australia. Department of Finance, *Blog* http://www.finance.gov.au/blog/.

110   Australia. Department of Finance and Deregulation, Australian Government Information Management Office, *Engage: Getting on with Government 2.0: Report of the Government 2.0 Taskforce* (December 2009) 73 http://gov2.net.au/report/ or http://www.finance.gov.au/publications/ gov20taskforcereport/doc/Government20TaskforceReport.pdf.

there are no similar provisions in the *Archives Act 1983* (Cth) and the National Archives of Australia simply consults with Commonwealth agencies on their compliance under the Act. If there are continuing failures to meet recordkeeping responsibilities by Commonwealth agencies, more regular audits conducted by the Commonwealth Auditor-General, and a 'name and shame' sanction of reporting to Parliament, could first be considered. If this is less than effective, the interests of promoting an open and accountable government and of preserving national culture and heritage may require the establishment of a compliance monitoring and enforcement arm in the National Archives and the inclusion of an offence provision in the *Archives Act 1983* (Cth) to improve compliance with archival standards.[112] In the deepest sense what is needed is an inculcation of the value of good recordkeeping among all agency personnel.

It is also important that government identifies and coordinates access to all its PSI, as the *Government Response to the Report of the Government 2.0 Taskforce* points out,[113] in order to accelerate the opportunity to achieve a more open, accountable, responsive and efficient government through Web 2.0 technology. This is important for all agencies of government for current and recent records and for those agencies and the National Archives for archival records.

Conclusion

Existing laws and practices dealing with accessing and re-using copyright protected government records should be reviewed in the light of further moves to openness of government and technological changes in the way we access, create and communicate works. Technology now enables greater interaction and greater sharing of information with and within government. Interaction with the community and the sharing of information with the public aids democratic values and has wider cultural, social and economic benefits, and the sharing of information within agencies and between governments provides governments at all levels with improved coordination and effectiveness.[114]

A key element of sound modern public administration and democratic accountability lies in the proper recording and preservation of, and the giving of public access to, the business of government. To the extent that this element is not realised these goals are diminished.

---

111   Refer to the *Public Records Act 2005* (NZ) ss 17–18, 27, 29, 32, 61–2; and, for example, the *Public Records Act 2002* (Qld) ss 24, 25, 46–9, 56.

112   For example, similar to that for the unauthorised destruction of archives (*Archives Act 1983* (Cth) s 24).

113   Australia. Department of Finance and Deregulation, *Government Response to the Report of the Government 2.0 Taskforce* (May 2010) [11] http://www.finance.gov.au/publications/govresponse20report/ or http://www.finance.gov.au/publications/govresponse20report/doc/Government-Response-to-Gov-2-0-Report.pdf.

114   Australia. Department of Finance and Deregulation, Australian Government Information Management Office, *National Government Information Sharing Strategy: Unlocking Government Information Assets to Benefit the Broader Community* (August 2009) [7], [2.4.2] http://www.finance.gov.au/files/2012/04/ngiss.pdf.

5

Legal Deposit: The Government as Acquirer and Preserver of National Copyright Material

This chapter, like Chapter 4, reviews the long-established aspect of government in fostering national culture and heritage. It examines legal deposit under the *Copyright Act 1968*. Legal deposit is sometimes also referred to as copyright deposit or library deposit and at the federal level is governed by s 201 of the *Copyright Act 1968*.

The Australian *Copyright Act 1968* contains what is commonly referred to as a library deposit provision. The provision is s 201. This requires the publisher of library material, which is published in Australia, to deliver a copy of the material at the publisher's own expense to the National Library, within one month after publication. The provision is restricted to material in which copyright subsists under the Act. There is a penalty for non-compliance of $100.

Section 201 is expressed to be not intended to exclude or limit the operation of any law of a State or Territory of similar effect, and each State and one Territory of Australia similarly requires the deposit of library material published in its State/Territory to its prescribed library.[1]

These library deposit provisions have been a part of Australian copyright laws since their inception as colonial laws. Their common law origins can be traced back beyond the first copyright statute in England (the *Statute of Anne* of 1709)[2] and into the licensing regimes that preceded that statute and then into a private agreement between the University of Oxford and the Stationers' Company, the London-based guild of printers, booksellers and publishers, in 1610.

There are similar compulsory deposit laws throughout the common law world. Over recent years, the nexus between copyright laws and deposit provisions has become weaker by the increasing passage of specific laws, outside copyright protection regimes, called library

---

1   A list of the current statutory provisions is set out in the Table at the end of this chapter. The law discussed in this chapter is that available to the author at 30 June 2014.

2   Entitled '*An Act for the Encouragement of Learning, by Vesting the Copies of Printed Books in the Authors or Purchasers of Such Copies, During the Times Therein Mentioned*' 8 Anne c 19. The Act came into force on 10 April 1710.

deposit or legal deposit laws. One example is the United Kingdom *Legal Deposit Libraries Act 2003*. Nonetheless, they are of similar effect.

What is the justification for these laws? Should these laws, as a matter of policy, be linked with copyright protection? If there is a justification, should the extent of material deposited under these laws be specific and limited in scope, or should it be all-embracing of everything disseminated to the public?

This chapter examines the historical and policy basis of these laws. It argues that the laws have, at times, been used for motives of scholarly endeavour and censorship but, in Australia and some other jurisdictions, they have subsisted as an element of national copyright policy. Nonetheless, it argues that the laws have their most convincing rationale in the preservation of national culture and heritage. This rationale embodies human values that Australia is obliged to respect and promote.[3]

Origins of Library Deposit

Library deposit in the Anglo common law world commenced as a private agreement between the University of Oxford and the Stationers' Company in the United Kingdom. This was almost a century before the first copyright statute, the *Statute of Anne*. On 12 December 1610, the Stationers' Company made (by indenture sealed in Convocation at Oxford on 27 February 1611) a grant of one perfect copy of every book printed by them, on condition that they should have liberty to borrow those books if needed for reprinting, and also to examine, collate and copy the books that were given to others.[4] The obligations were essentially one-sided. The deed contained no penalty for non-compliance.

The agreement with the Master of the Stationers' Company was brought into effect by Sir Thomas Bodley, a former diplomat and fellow of Merton College Oxford. This formed an important part of Sir Thomas' great and costly personal quest to restore and improve the

---

3   Refer to Chapter 1, Australia's International Civil and Political Treaty Obligations. Those values are presently reflected nationally and internationally in policies and laws for the conservation and preservation of moveable cultural heritage that stress the importance to current and future generations of access to their own national heritage collections. In particular, refer to Australian Heritage Collections, *National Conservation and Preservation Policy and Strategy* (1998) (Part 2) Policy Statements 4–6 http://www.collectionsaustralia.net/sector_info_item/25 and UNESCO, *Convention on the Means of Prohibiting and Preventing the Illicit Import, Export and Transfer of Ownership of Cultural Property* (1970) http://www.unesco.org/culture/laws/1970/html, to which Australia is a party. Article 5(c) of the Convention obliges contracting states to promote 'the development or the establishment of scientific and technical institutions (museums, libraries, archives, laboratories, workshops . . .) required to ensure the preservation and presentation of cultural property'. 'Cultural property' includes manuscripts, old books, documents and publications of special interest (historical, artistic, scientific, literary, etc.), sound, photographic and cinematographic archives.

4   In Liber C of the *Court Books of the Stationers' Company* appears the following entry: '14 March 1610–11. Received from Oxon by the Delivery of Mr Doctor Kinge Deane of Christ Church and Vicechauncellor of Oxon the Certificate, under the Universitie's Seale, of ane Indenture, before Sealed at Mr Leake's house in Paule's Churchyard, under the comon Seale. 15 Novbr ult. for one booke of every new Copy to be gyven to the publique library at Oxon, that they appoynt Sr. Thomas Bodley to receive the same.' RC Barrington Partridge, *The History of the Legal Deposit of Books throughout the British Empire* (Library Association, 1938) 17, note 3.

university's public library. Sir Thomas, on 23 February 1597/98, wrote a letter to the Vice-Chancellor of the University of Oxford offering that whereas 'there hath bin heretofore a publike library in Oxford, which, you know, is apparant by the roome itself remayning, and by your statute records, I will take the charge and cost upon me, to reduce it again to his former use', first by fitting it up with shelves and seats, next by procuring benefactions of books, and lastly by endowing it with an annual rent. This offer was extraordinarily generous and was accepted with great gratitude.[5]

However, the concept of legal deposit began earlier in France. This would have been known to Sir Thomas Bodley and his librarian, Thomas James, who is credited with conceiving the idea of the deposit agreement with the Stationers' Company. Partridge records that the first system of legal deposit of books was established by the Montpellier Ordinance of 28 December 1537.

> Every printer and publisher in France, without exception, was ordered to forward to the learned Abbe Melin de Saint Gelais, who had charge of the Royal Library at Blois, a copy of every newly published book, irrespective of author, subject, cost, size, date or language, whether illustrated or not.[6] . . . The penalty for non-compliance with the ordinance was the confiscation of the whole edition of a work not deposited, together with a heavy arbitrary fine.[7]

The lack of sanction or penalty underpinning the agreement between the Stationers' Company and the University of Oxford weakened its effectiveness. Attempts were made to remedy this. First, the company, at the commencement of 1612, passed a by-law that made it obligatory on every one of their members to forward their books to the library. Subsequently, an order of the Star Chamber was made on 11 July 1637 in confirmation of the grant.[8] This contained a sanction of imprisonment or a heavy fine for non-compliance. But the Star Chamber was soon after abolished. The 1662 and 1665 Licensing Acts broadened the deposit requirement to add the Royal Library and the Library of the University of Cambridge to the Library at Oxford. This increased the hostility some printer members had to the deposit arrangements and the Acts themselves contained weaknesses that could be exploited by recalcitrant printers. Thus, the extent of compliance by printer members of the Stationers' Company varied over the 17th century.[9]

---

5   How this agreement was brought into effect is unclear. In 1695, the then university librarian Thomas Hyde stated 'We have been told that Sir Thomas Bodley gave to the Company 50 pounds worth of plate when they entered into this Indenture. But it's not mentioned in our counter-part'. WD Macray, *Annals of the Bodleian Library*, (The Bodleian Library, 2nd edn, 1984) (a reprint of the second edition published in 1890 at the Clarendon Press, Oxford) 15, 41.

6   RC Barrington Partridge, *The History of the Legal Deposit of Books throughout the British Empire* (Library Association, 1938) 2.

7   Ibid 3.

8   Clause XXXIII of the Star Chamber decree of 11 July 1637 stated that one copy of every new book or reprint, with additions henceforth published had to be delivered to Stationers' Hall before any sale of the work took place, the copy afterwards being required to be sent to the Bodleian Library for preservation there. The penalty for non-compliance by any printer was to be imprisonment and a heavy fine. Three years later an Act for the abolition of the Star Chamber was passed reluctantly by Charles 1. Legal protection for the Agreement virtually ceased immediately. Above n 6, 22.

In 1709, the first copyright statute—the *Statute of Anne*—was doubly insulting for printers in that it imposed a reduced period of copyright protection for works and, at the same time, increased the number of deposit libraries to nine in England and Scotland.[10] This number was increased, upon the union with Ireland, to eleven but finally reduced to five (British Museum, Oxford, Cambridge, Advocates Library Edinburgh and Trinity College Dublin) by 6 & 7 Will IV, c 110. Presently, under United Kingdom law, there are six deposit libraries—the British Library Board, the University Library at Cambridge, the Bodleian Library at Oxford, the National Libraries of Scotland and Wales and Trinity College Library in Dublin.[11]

Justification and Policy Basis for Library Deposit

The origins of library deposit lie in a mix of rationales. Certainly Sir Thomas Bodley sought to re-found the university library at Oxford—after it had become sadly denuded of works and fallen into disrepair—essentially for the purposes of scholarly endeavour, despite the fact it was, and continues to be to this day, a public library.

Evidence of this motivation lies in the selection of holdings Bodley and his 'Keeper' (librarian), James, made from donated and deposited works. This conscious selection is well documented in Bodley's correspondence with James. In a letter sent to James in Oxford in 1602, Bodley wrote from his London home:[12]

> Sir, For the increase of your stipend, I doe not doubt but to giue yow very good satisfaction, but till your trauels and troubles are seene to euery student, it will be best in my opinion, not to charge the spitte with too muche rostmeat.
>
> . . .

---

9 Ayliffe says that the agreement was very well observed until about 1640. He should rather have said 'about 1630' for in that year, in a paper of notes made by the Librarian for the use of Archbishop Laud, as Chancellor of the University, complaint was made that the Company were very negligent in sending their books, and it is suggested that a message from the Chancellor might quickly remedy that neglect. Infrequent mention of disputes with the London booksellers is made in speeches delivered by Dr Ralph Bathurst as Vice-Chancellor, 60 years afterwards, some of which were printed by T Wharton in 1761 at the end of his *Life*. WD Macray, *Annals of the Bodleian Library,* (The Bodleian Library, 2nd edn, 1984) (a reprint of the second edition published in 1890 at the Clarendon Press, Oxford) 40.

10 'Under the preceding Licensing Acts the registration of a work at Stationers' Hall, and the delivery of three copies, entitled a printer to what amounted to a perpetual copyright in that work, which privilege he could, of course, sell to another if he chose. On the old foundations, however, was built this new act whereby not only was the number of deposit copies increased from three to nine, but curiously enough, the period of copyright in a work was fixed at twenty-one years only for existing works, and at fourteen years for all works printed after 10 April 1710' (with the prospect of a further fourteen years if the author were alive at the end of the first fourteen years). Above n 6, 35.

11 *Legal Deposit Libraries Act 2003* (UK) c 28, ss 1, 14.

12 GW Wheeler (ed), *Letters of Sir Thomas Bodley to Thomas James* (Clarendon Press, 1926) 34–5 (letter no 26).

In any wise take no riffe raffe bookes (for suche will but proue a descredit to our Librarie) but because I knowe not, whether he will be wonne, to pay for the binding of suche as may neede it, and for their cariage to Oxon (in bothe which pointes, yow may be bold to vrge him, as of your self) it will be requisit to take bookes, that we haue already, whereby those charges may the better be defraied.

. . .

Wherewith I commend yow to Gods good tuition.

your owne assured

Tho Bodley.

Marche 31. [1602].

['he' refers to a donor]

Similarly, in 1612 he wrote:[13]

Sir, I would yow had foreborne, to catalogue our London bookes, till I had bin priuie to your purpose. There are many idle bookes & riffe raffes among them, which shall neuer com into the Librarie, and I feare me that the litle, which yow haue done alreadie, will raise scandal vpon it, when it shall be given out, by suche as would disgrace it, that I haue made vp a number, with Almanackes, plaies, & proclamations: of which I will haue none, but such as are singular. As yet Mr Norton hath not taken any order, for the bringing in of their bookes by reason of the sicknes of their Bedel: but he hath promised faithfully, to doe it with speede.

. . .

I thanke yow very muche, & continue as euer

your true assured frind

Tho. Bodley

Fulham. Ian. 1. [1612]

Another letter, written shortly after, expands on his outlook:

Sir'

. . .

I can see no good reason to alter my opinion, for excluding suche bookes as almanackes, plaies, & an infinit number, that are daily printed, of very vnworthy maters & handling, suche as, me thinkes, both the keeper & the vnderkeeper should disdaine to seeke out, to deliuer vnto any man. Happely some plaies may be worthy the keeping: but hardlie one in fortie. For it is not alike in Englishe plaies, & others of other nations: because they are most esteemed, for learning the languages

---

13   Ibid 219, 221–2 (letter no 220–1).

& many of them compiled, by men of great fame, for wisedome & learning, which is seeldom or neuer seene among vs. Were it so againe, that some litle profit might be reaped (which God knows is very litle) out of some of our playbookes, the benefit thereof will nothing neere conteruaile, the harme that the scandal will bring vnto the Librarie, when it shalbe giuen out, that we stuffe it full of baggage bookes. And though they should be but a fewe, as they would be very many, if your course should take place, yet the hauing of those fewe (suche is the nature of malicious reporters) would be mightily multiplied by suche as purpose to speake in disgrace of the Librarie. This is my opinion, wherin if I erre, I thinke I shall erre with infinit others: & the more I thinke vpon it, the more it doth distast me, that suche kinde of bookes, should be vouchesafed a rowme, in so noble a Librarie. And thus at this time, with my kindest commendations.

your very assured frind

Tho. Bodley

London. Ian. 15. [1612]

The motivation was not to obtain a complete bibliographic record of English printed works. Among the 'riffe raffes' and 'baggage' books excluded from the collection were first (quarto) editions of Shakespeare's plays. The first folio edition of Shakespeare's plays does appear in the library's records in 1635 but appears later to have been discarded in favour of the third edition of 1664.[14] The library has continued a selective retention strategy since that time.

Later, much of the impetus behind the first statutory embodiment of library deposit under the Licensing Acts—and its expansion from the Bodleian Library to cover the Royal Library and the University of Cambridge Library—was that of censorship, that is, to prevent blasphemous and seditious works being gradually and secretly put into general circulation.[15] 'The Royal Library . . . was under the inspection of Crown officials. Seditious publications and libels and satires on court morals would there be instantly detected, with dire consequences to their authors.'[16]

But by the time of the *Statute of Anne* and the enlargement of the deposit libraries to nine, something of the modern manifestation or policy basis of library deposit appears. That is, it was not a policy aimed at the enrichment of some public libraries at private expense but an instrument to gather a full and permanent record of the nation's printed works and of a record of all the branches of knowledge contained within those works.

14　'In the Bodleian Catalogues of 1603 and 1620 no entries whatever appear under the name of Shakespeare. In the supplemental Catalogue of 1635 the First Folio of 1623 is duly recorded; but in the catalogue of 1674 we find only the third edition, that of 1664. The inference is that the third edition seemed to the library keepers of those times vastly preferable to the first and second editions, and so the precious volumes supplied by the Company in 1623 and 1632 were doubtless regarded as little more than waste-paper and were discarded'. Above n 6, 21.

15　Ibid 24.

16　Ibid.

The deposit laws were, and are, limited to publications within national boundaries.[17] In the United Kingdom, more than one deposit library was mandated in order to better preserve these works and to provide access for the public from diverse areas. Attempts in the United Kingdom to restrict the number of deposit copies to one have failed. Within Australia, which is geographically more diverse, there are at least two copies required to be deposited under the combined effect of Commonwealth and state/territory deposit laws.

The deposit system has become so widespread that practically every developed country in the world has some form of legal deposit of books.[18]

Should These Laws as a Matter of Policy Be Linked with Copyright Protection?

In Anglo-Australian law, there has been a strong link between copyright law and library deposit provisions, which has been evident from the *Statute of Anne* to the end of the 20th century. In some countries like the United States of America, the deposit requirement was historically linked with the subsistence of copyright but this is not the position in Australia or the United Kingdom (and more recently the United States). In these jurisdictions, which are presently members of the Berne Union, compliance with formalities under national laws as a condition of copyright protection, such as registration, is forbidden.[19]

Copyright law is concerned with the recognition and protection of creative material by the creation of quasi-monopolistic rights. While the rights of copyright owners are termed exclusive rights, they are balanced with those public interests in research, scholarship, criticism and review and in access to, and the encouragement of, the free flow of ideas, which are embodied in the defences contained in the law to the exclusive rights. These interests are recognised in the international copyright conventions. In essence, copyright law is a two-way street between owner and user and, in the language of policy makers, the law strikes a balance between the owners and the users of copyright material.

The deposit provision in the Australian *Copyright Act 1968* is restricted to library material that is published in Australia and in which copyright subsists. It could be argued that there is a copyright rationale for the deposit provision that includes the provision of best copies

---

17   One exception—based on historical grounds—is the reciprocal deposit of material first published in the United Kingdom in the Library of Trinity College, Dublin and the deposit of material first published in the Republic of Ireland in the British Library.

18   Above n 6, 2, 3.

19   In Australia, under the *Copyright Act 1912* (Cth), there was an optional system of registration. This entitled the copyright owner to certain remedies, which were not otherwise available without registration, but registration did not go to the subsistence of copyright. The optional system of registration was abolished by the *Copyright Act 1968* (Cth). Article 5(2) of the Paris Act of the *Berne Convention*, to which Australia is a party, provides that the enjoyment and the exercise of rights granted by the Convention and by national laws shall not be subject to any formality; 'such enjoyment and such exercise shall be independent of the existence of protection in the country of origin of the work'. In none of the surveyed common law countries does compulsory deposit conflict with this principle. Compulsory deposit is not a condition of copyright protection in any of those countries. Under s 201 of the Australian *Copyright Act 1968* (Cth) there is a separate penalty ($100) for non-compliance. The section operates independently and does not call up any of the specific copyright remedies under the Act, simply because failure to deposit does not breach an act comprised within the copyright of the library material described in the section.

by the publisher for the protection of rights granted by the state. In Australia, under the preceding *Copyright Act 1912*, copyright registration of works, though not a condition of protection, was encouraged by giving the copyright owner certain additional remedies in the event of infringement.[20] Registration involved submitting a copy of the work to the Registrar of Copyrights.[21] Under its predecessor enactment, the *Copyright Act 1905* (Cth), copyright registration was required before the owner of copyright was entitled to institute any proceedings for infringement.[22]

The Spicer Committee, which reported to the Australian Attorney-General in 1959, suggested that 'it seems to us that the main purpose of such a provision should be to build up a complete collection of Australian literature'.[23] The Whitford Committee, which reviewed the law in the United Kingdom in 1977, stated:

> The fact that in this country all copyright legislation since the early eighteenth century has also concerned itself with legal deposit indicates that a link originally existed between the establishment of an author's property right and the obligation to deposit. The link is to be found, in sixteenth century England and in France up till the Revolution, in royal attempts to control the printed word by making all publications illegal except under licence (in England through a member of the Stationers' Company) or unless a 'privilege' had first been obtained. This latter took the form, in both countries, of letters patent conferring monopoly rights on the author or printer for a fixed term: the requirement for the deposit of one or more copies of the work served to ensure that the text had been printed as authorised and no doubt was also regarded as part of the fee exacted for the grant of the monopoly. The Copyright Act of 1709, chiefly directed towards giving statutory form to an acknowledged common law right which had become difficult to enforce, required registration of the work at Stationers' Hall as a prerequisite for any claim and also re-enacted and extended the deposit liability: in an 'Act for the encouragement of Learning' the interests of authors and scholars were both to be protected. Later acts dropped the registration requirement but maintained that of deposit. Deposit has thus, in the past, fulfilled a dual function, facilitating claims to copyright (and, ini-

---

20   Section 26 of the *Copyright Act 1912* (Cth) provided that 'Registration of Copyright shall be optional, but the special remedies provided for by sections fifteen, sixteen, and seventeen of this Act can only be taken advantage of by registered owners'. Those provisions deal with unauthorised public performance of musical and dramatic works, seizure of pirated copies of works and forbidding performance of musical and dramatic works in infringement of the public performance right in those works.

21   Section 38(1) of the *Copyright Act 1912* (Cth) provided 'Every person who makes an application for the registration of the copyright in a book shall deliver to the Registrar one copy of the whole book with all maps and illustrations belonging thereto, finished and coloured in the same manner as the best copies of the book are published, and bound, sewed, or stitched together, and on the best paper on which the book is printed'. Section 40(1) of the Act also required the deposit of best copy of the book with the Librarian of the Parliament.

22   *Copyright Act 1905* (Cth) s 74. An exception to this requirement existed in relation to the infringement of lecturing rights.

23   Australia. *Report of the Committee Appointed by the Attorney-General of the Commonwealth to Consider what Alterations are Desirable in the Copyright Law of the Commonwealth* (Spicer Committee) (1959) 87, para 468.

tially, official control over content) and establishing public archival collections for scholars. The first function is now of diminished importance, though the record of deposit of a copy of a book can still serve as evidence in a copyright action where date of publication is at issue; the second function continues to be of major significance in the preservation and advancement of knowledge. There no longer seems to be any good reason, however, why legislation for the maintenance of libraries of deposit should form part of the law of copyright.[24]

The Committee concluded that '[t]he link between the legal recognition of property rights in published literary matter and its deposit in one or more designated libraries ceased to exist at a date now remote'.[25]

With respect to that Committee, copyright has not, through the grant of exclusive rights to the authors of literary and other works, divorced itself from the goal of the encouragement and preservation of learning and knowledge, even if that relationship may now be merely one of a number of goals in the protection granted by the law. Nevertheless, it must be recognised that various national parliaments have broken the nexus between copyright law and legal deposit by the passage of separate legal deposit enactments. These laws are expressed to rest on the preservation of a national documentary heritage. If that concept is distinct, then the encouragement and preservation of learning and knowledge is complementary to it.

The importance of the copyright link at the Australian federal level is of significance because the deposit law must rely on a constitutional head of power to be a valid law. The Commonwealth Parliament has power to pass laws with respect to copyrights, patents of inventions, designs and trademarks under s 51(xviii) of the *Australian Constitution*. Given the broad interpretation given to this power by the High Court of Australia, it is likely a law purporting to be a law with respect to copyright, which requires the compulsory deposit of copyright material in the National Library of the Commonwealth, would be a valid exercise of legislative power under s 51(xviii).[26]

It may be argued from an historical perspective, and in the light of present policy, that library deposit provisions are part of the balance of interests between owners and users of copyright material regulated by the law and that they promote the public interests in the encouragement of learning and other forms of creativity recognised by that law for the benefit of present and future generations.[27] That is, there is a sufficient connection between the

---

24   United Kingdom. *Copyright and Designs Law: Report of the Committee to Consider the Law on Copyright and Designs* (Whitford Committee) Cmnd 6732 (1977) 204, para 807.

25   Ibid 210, para 831.

26   The general principles of interpretation of heads of power have been established in such cases as *Bank of New South Wales v Commonwealth* (1948) 76 CLR 1, 332–3, *Lansell v Lansell* (1964) 110 CLR 353, 366–7, 370, *The Queen v Public Vehicles Licensing Appeal Tribunal (Tas)* (1964) 113 CLR 207, 225, *Western Australia v Commonwealth* (1975) 134 CLR 201, 245–6, *Nintendo Company Limited v Centronics Systems Pty Ltd* (1994) 181 CLR 134, 160 and *The Grain Pool of WA v Commonwealth* (2000) 202 CLR 479, 492–5, 501.

27   The preamble to the *Library and Archives of Canada Act*, SC 2004, c 11, which incorporates the legal deposit provision under Canadian law cites two of its objectives that: '(a) the documentary heritage of

provisions and the head of power.[28] On that basis, s 201 of the *Copyright Act 1968* (Cth), therefore, is a copyright law within the meaning of s 51(xviii).

Alternatively, if that view is wrong, reliance may be placed on s 51(xxxix) that enables Parliament to make laws with respect to matters incidental to the execution of any power vested by the *Australian Constitution* in the Parliament, such as the copyright power s 51(xviii).[29]

Assuming the deposit provision is a valid exercise of power of the Commonwealth Parliament under s 51(xviii) or s 51(xxxix), then a further question arises. Should the compulsory deposit provision require compensation or other just terms by virtue of s 51(xxxi) of the *Australian Constitution*? Publishers, printers and others have argued at various times, almost from their inception, against deposit provisions as an inequitable impost upon their property rights. The level of observance of them has varied over time. In general, deposit copies are supplied at the cost of the paper, printing and binding (the marginal cost) of the material and the cost of doing so is normally passed on to, and borne by, the purchasers of the publication. Publishers in present day practice also make allowance for author's presentation copies and review copies when setting the price of a book. They also distribute free desk copies to academics to encourage sales of some books. However, deposit copies are delivered through an imposed statutory arrangement. The others are delivered through voluntary arrangements.

Under s 51(xxxi), the Commonwealth Parliament is empowered to make laws for the peace, order and good government of the Commonwealth with respect to 'the acquisition of property on just terms from any State or person for any purpose in respect of which Parliament has power to make laws'. 'Property', in this provision, has been broadly defined by the High Court of Australia to include interests in tangible and intangible property.[30]

It is difficult to characterise compulsory deposit as a law dealing with the acquisition of the intangible property (copyright) because the delivery of a copy does not amount to any act comprised in the copyright. That is, the National Library does not acquire a proprietary copyright under the law. Even if it could be said that the Act authorises the publisher to make the copy for a purpose that would otherwise be an infringement of copyright, this

---

Canada be preserved for the benefit of present and future generations; (b) Canada be served by an institution that is a source of enduring knowledge accessible to all, contributing to the cultural, social and economic advancement of Canada as a free and democratic society.'

28   *The Grain Pool of WA v Commonwealth* (2000) 202 CLR 479, 492.

29   Sir Robert Garran was of the view that an earlier deposit provision (s 75(4) of the *Copyright Act 1905* (Cth)) was incidental to copyright: 'it is an obligation of a kind which is commonly dealt with in Copyright Acts, and it can fairly be said to have some relation to copyright, as being a duty imposed in consideration of a right conferred'. Australia. Attorney-General's Department, *Opinions of the Attorneys-General of the Commonwealth of Australia, Vol 1:1901–1914* (1981) 562–3 (Opinion No 430).

30   *Minister of State for the Army v Dalziel* (1944) 68 CLR 261, 290; *Commonwealth v Tasmania* (*'Tasmanian Dam Case'*) (1983) 158 CLR 1, 145, 246–7, 282–3; *Clunies-Ross v Commonwealth* (1984) 155 CLR 193, 201–2; *Australian Capital Television Pty Limited v Commonwealth* (1992) 177 CLR 106, 165–6; *Georgiadis v Australian and Overseas Telecommunications Corporation* (1994) 179 CLR 297, 303–4 (Mason CJ, Deane and Gaudron JJ); *JT International SA v Commonwealth* (*'The British American Tobacco Case'*) [2012] HCA 43, [29, 41–2] (French CJ) and [144–54] (Gummow J) [180–189] (Hayne J and Bell J).

does not amount to acquiring an interest in the property and thus attract s 51(xxxi) of the *Australian Constitution*.[31]

Similarly, it would be difficult to characterise the deposit of the tangible property (that is, the bound paper on which the intangible property is printed) as an acquisition of property without just terms since copyright itself is intrinsically concerned with the material expression of ideas. A work is made under s 22 of the Act when the work is first reduced to writing or to some other material form and a work is published by virtue of s 29 of the Act if reproductions of the work have been supplied (whether by sale or otherwise) to the public. Even if the delivery of the tangible property is not implicitly sanctioned in this way, to the extent that a law passed under s 51(xviii) or s 51(xxxix) of the *Australian Constitution* conferring rights on authors and other originators of copyright material is concerned with the adjustment of competing rights or obligations of other persons, that impact is unlikely to be characterised as a law with respect to the acquisition of property for the purposes of s 51.[32]

Whether the nexus between copyright law and legal deposit will be broken in Australia at the federal level remains to be seen, but the powers discussed provide a basis for constitutional validity. At the state level, the position is quite distinct. State parliaments have plenary power to enact laws in any field (subject to valid federal laws) and may acquire property without just terms.[33] State deposit laws, which are expressly preserved by s 201(4) of the *Copyright Act 1968* (Cth), are thus not subject to those federal constitutional constraints.

Legal deposit law in the United States of America has long been a feature of federal copyright law. The United States *Copyright Act* contains within it a deposit requirement for, among other things, two complete copies of the best edition of the work published in the United States, which are required to be deposited in its Copyright Office 'for the use or disposition of the Library of Congress'.[34] The *Copyright Act* has been passed pursuant to the express copyright power in Article 1, section 8 of the United States Constitution.[35]

Be that as it may, the common law countries of Canada, New Zealand and the United Kingdom, under different constitutional regimes, have, over the past 10 years, passed specific legal deposit laws that are independent of copyright law. In New Zealand, for instance, the *National Library of New Zealand Act 2003* (NZ) was passed with the purpose of:

---

31 *Georgiadis v Australian and Overseas Telecommunications Corporation* (1994) 179 CLR 297, 304, 306; *Commonwealth v WMC Resources* (1998) 194 CLR 1, 15, 50–1.

32 *Nintendo Company Limited v Centronics Systems Pty Limited* (1994) 181 CLR 134, 160–1 (Mason CJ, Brennan, Deane, Toohey, Gaudron, and McHugh JJ).

33 *Durham Holdings Pty Ltd v The State of New South Wales* (2001) 205 CLR 399, 425–6.

34 *Copyright Act of 1976* 17 USC §§ 407.

35 *United States Constitution* art I § 8: 'The Congress shall have Power . . . To promote the Progress of Science and useful Arts, by securing for limited Times to Authors and Inventors the exclusive Right to their respective Writings and Discoveries'. Under US copyright law, deposit was aided by earlier registration requirements as a condition of US copyright protection and more recently as a condition precedent to actions for civil infringement in the United States: refer to *Copyright Act of 1976* 17 USC §§ 408, 411.

the preservation, protection, development, and accessibility, as appropriate, for all the people of New Zealand, of the collections of the National Library . . . and, to this end, to–

. . .

(g) enable the Minister to notify requirements that copies of public documents be provided to the National Library, for the purposes of assisting in preserving New Zealand's documentary heritage; and

(h) ensure that the power to require public documents referred to in (g) extends to Internet documents and authorises the National Librarian to copy such documents.[36]

It is a rationale that has existed since the beginnings of the laws. As Partridge states:

Legal deposit, the copy-tax, or the delivery of printed copies, as it is severally termed, thus acts as a mirror wherein all the glory of a nation's literature is faithfully reflected. More than this, it stands as a permanent record of the thoughts, aspirations, and discoveries of each successive age.[37]

Compulsory deposit preserves these works for their use in certain libraries privileged to receive and store them. Here is, then, an unfailing guide to authors and research workers in all branches of knowledge of the past, present, and future; and it is not surprising, therefore, that the system merits and earns their deepest gratitude, considering what weary searches and endless expense are saved thereby.[38]

It has the practical additional benefit of limiting the costs borne by the taxpayer of maintaining a national collection. This is effected by reducing the costs burden on the library of searching for, and purchasing, copies of everything that is published within the country. In essence, the purchase costs are moved from the public purse to private expense.

Scope Today

If there is a justification for library deposit laws, should the extent of material deposited under these laws be specific and limited in scope or all-embracing of everything disseminated to the public?

In essence, the library deposit provision, s 201 of the *Copyright Act 1968* (Cth), is limited to library material that is defined in s 201(5):

Delivery of library material to the National Library

(1) The publisher of any library material that is published in Australia and in which copyright subsists under this Act shall, within one month after the publication,

---

36   *National Library of New Zealand Act 2003* (NZ) s 3.

37   Above n 6, 5–6.

38   Ibid 6.

cause a copy of the material to be delivered at his or her own expense to the National Library.

Penalty: $100.

. . .

(5) In this section:

. . .

library material means a book, periodical, newspaper, pamphlet, sheet of letter-press, sheet of music, map, plan, chart or table, being a literary, dramatic, musical or artistic work or an edition of such a work, but does not include a second or later edition of any material unless that edition contains additions or alterations in the letter-press or in the illustrations.

There is a requirement for the 'best copy' of the library material to be deposited. This is in the interests of the preservation of that material.

(2) The copy of any library material delivered to the National Library in accordance with this section shall be a copy of the whole material (including any illustrations), be finished and coloured, and bound, sewed, stitched or otherwise fastened to-gether, in the same manner as the best copies of that material are published and be on the best paper on which that material is printed.

The best copy requirement has been a common feature of all library deposit provisions since the Bodleian agreement's 'perfect copy'.[39] It is inevitably linked with print media. The Australian *Copyright Act 1968* deposit provision does not extend beyond print media to electronic media as, for instance, does the present United Kingdom deposit law. This is a serious omission in the light of the comparatively increasing importance of electronic dis-semination of information vis-à-vis print means of doing so. While the need for reform of the deposit law has been pressed for some time,[40] the National Library of Australia has not

---

39   Section 37 of the *National Library of New Zealand Act 2003* (NZ) ('best copy of the document that has been published in New Zealand'); s 4(3) of the *Legal Deposit Libraries Act 2003* (UK) c 28—for the British Library Board—'the copy is to be of the same quality as the best copies which, at the time of delivery, have been produced for publication in the United Kingdom'. For other than the British Library Board, s 5(6)—'the copy is to be of the same quality as the largest number of copies which, at the time of delivery, have been produced for publication in the United Kingdom'; refer also to *Copyright Act of 1976*, 17 USC s 407(a) (USA) 'best edition'; s 201(2) *Copyright Act 1968* (Cth); in Canada the requirement is all-embracing—*Library and Archives of Canada Act*, SC 2004, c 11, s 10(4) ('(4) For the purposes of this section, every version, edition or form of a publication shall be considered a distinct publication').

40   In 1995, the National Library of Australia joined with the National Film and Sound Archive in making a joint submission on deposit law reform and from time to time since 2001, the two agencies have also raised with relevant government departments the desirability of legal deposit provisions for electronic resources to ensure their collection and preservation. (Interview with Margaret Phillips, Director, Digital Archiving, National Library of Australia (Telephone interview, 10 August 2005) and comments via email from Margaret Phillips to John Gilchrist, 11 November 2005). Refer also to Australia. National Library of Australia, *Pandora: Australia's Web Archive: Legal Deposit* (12 August 2014) http://pandora.nla.gov.au/legaldeposit.html.

waited for the slow pace of law reform and has embarked on a program of its own initiative, with the cooperation of ten other Australian libraries and cultural collecting organisations, to skim websites and copy selected material from them with the consent of the publishers. The program is called PANDORA.[41] The National Library effort has focused on archiving Commonwealth and ACT government publications, tertiary institution publications, conference proceedings, e-journals, items referred by indexing and abstracting agencies and topical sites on a rolling three year basis (for example, in 2008–2009 Law (Criminology) Indigenous Australians (Indigenous Art) and History (local history)).[42] In November 2005, this archive held about one terabyte of data.[43] In March 2011, this archive held about 4.95 terabytes of data;[44] in October 2014 it held 13.18 terabytes of data.[45] Approximately 56 percent were government publications.[46] Nonetheless, this is only a tiny proportion of all material published online in Australia.[47]

Law and Policy in Other Jurisdictions

A number of countries have already undertaken legal change to bring communicators of electronic information under equivalent deposit obligations as those borne by traditional print publishers. In the United Kingdom, the *Legal Deposit Libraries Act 2003*[48] provides a

---

41   Australia. National Library of Australia, *Pandora: Australia's Web Archive* http://pandora.nla.gov.au/.

42   Australia. National Library of Australia, *Pandora: Online Australian Publications: Selection Guidelines for Archiving and Preservation by the National Library of Australia* (Revised August 2005) [3.5] http://pandora.nla.gov.au/selectionguidelines.html.

43   Email from Margaret Phillips, Director, Digital Archiving, National Library of Australia, to John Gilchrist, 11 November 2005. In June and July 2005 the NLA undertook a harvest of the Australian web domain through the Internet Archive, a not-for-profit company in the USA. Approximately 189 million documents or files were captured, the equivalent of 6.69 terabytes of data. The NLA estimated that that was approximately 95 percent of the Australia web domain. In October 2007, the Pandora archive represented only approximately 3 percent of the combined harvests made in 2005 (above), 2006 and 2007—refer to Paul Koerbin, National Library of Australia, *The Australian Web Domain Harvests: A Preliminary Quantitative Analysis of the Archive Data* (15 April 2008 revised) 4–6. http://pandora.nla.gov.au/documents/auscrawls.pdf. See also Simon Grose 'Staff Harvest Web for History', *The Canberra Times* (Canberra), 28 March 2005, 17, col 4.

44   Australia. National Library of Australia, *Pandora Fact Sheet* (20 April 2011) and *Pandora Statistics* (12 September 2013) http://pandora.nla.gov.au/overview.html.

45   Australia. National Library of Australia, *Pandora Statistics* (26 October 2014) http://pandora.nla.gov.au/overview.html.

46   Based on May 2013 figures: National Library of Australia, *Pandora Fact Sheet* (12 June 2013) http://pandora.nla.gov.au/overview.html.

47   The harvesting of websites does not encompass all government publications and up to 2008 excluded online daily newspapers for which print versions exist, news sites, datasets, CAMS, weblogs and various other sites: Australia. National Library of Australia, *Pandora: Online Australian Publications: Selection Guidelines for Archiving and Preservation by the National Library of Australia* (Revised August 2005: updated 13 August 2008) http://pandora.nla.gov.au/selectionguidelines.html#s3.7. There has been some change in exclusions over time—refer to Margaret Phillips, *Collecting Australian Online Publications*, version 6 (2003) National Library of Australia http://pandora.nla.gov.au/guidelines.html.

48   *Legal Deposit Libraries Act 2003* (UK) c 28.

statutory regime of deposit for print publications but leaves much of the scheme of deposit of electronic material to regulatory laws under that Act.

Section 1 of the *Legal Deposit Libraries Act 2003* (UK) provides:

> (1) A person who publishes in the United Kingdom a work to which this Act applies must at his own expense deliver a copy of it to an address specified (generally or in a particular case) by any deposit library entitled to delivery under this section.
>
> . . .
>
> (3) In the case of a work published in print, this Act applies to–
>
> (a) a book (including a pamphlet, magazine or newspaper),
>
> (b) a sheet of letterpress or music,
>
> (c) a map, plan, chart or table, and
>
> (d) a part of any such work;
>
> but that is subject to any prescribed exception.
>
> (4) In the case of a work published in a medium other than print, this Act applies to a work of a prescribed description.
>
> (5) A prescribed description may not include works consisting only of–
>
> (a) a sound recording or film or both, or
>
> (b) such material and other material which is merely incidental to it.
>
> (6) Subject to section 6(2)(h), the obligation under subsection (1) is to deliver a copy of the work in the medium in which it is published.
>
> (7) In this section, 'address' means an address in the United Kingdom or an electronic address.

The *Legal Deposit Libraries Act* is the first legislative measure in the United Kingdom to address the deposit of non-print media.

Under the *Copyright Act of 1976* in the United States of America, the deposit provision covers print media as well as sound recordings (phonorecords) and transmission programs.[49]

In Canada, under the *Library and Archives of Canada Act 2004*, the scheme for legal deposit applies simply to publishers who make publications available in Canada.[50] While compul-

---

49   *Copyright Act of 1976* 17 USC §§ 407. 'Phonorecords' are material objects in which sounds, other than those accompanying a motion picture or other audiovisual work, are fixed by any method now known or later developed, and from which the sounds can be perceived, reproduced, or otherwise communicated, either directly or with the aid of a machine or device. The term 'phonorecords' includes the material object in which the sounds are first fixed: *Copyright Act of 1976* 17 USC §§ 101. For the regulations prescribing the acquisition and deposit of audio and audiovisual transmission programs refer to Patents, Trademarks and Copyrights 37 CFR § 202.22.

50   Section 10, *Library and Archives of Canada Act*, SC 2004, c 11.

sory deposit has its origins in Canadian copyright law, this Act also separates compulsory deposit from the subsistence of copyright. Some of the detail of implementation is left to regulations made under the Act, including the definition of 'publisher' and the classes of publications in respect of which the obligation of deposit subsists. The definition of 'publication' in the Act and the regulations expressly extend the obligation to non-print media.[51] Section 11 of the Act also requires the deposit of archival quality 'recordings' that the Librarian and Archivist determine has historic or archival value.[52]

In New Zealand, under s 31(1) of the *National Library of New Zealand Act 2003* (NZ), the Minister, by notice in the *Gazette*, may require a publisher of a public document (other than an internet document) to give to the National Librarian, at the publisher's own expense, a specified number of copies (not exceeding 3) of:

(a) the public document in printed form;

(b) if the document is an electronic document, the medium that contains the document.

Section 31(2) then makes provision for the time period after first publication for the giving of copies (20 working days or a longer notified period) and for format, public access or other matters.

Section 31(3) of the Act also empowers the minister, by *Gazette* notice, to authorise the National Librarian to make a copy, at any time or times and at his or her discretion, of public documents that are internet documents in accordance with any terms and conditions as to format, public access or other matters that are specified in the notice.

The Act also requires the minister,[53] before notifying a requirement, to consult the publishers or representatives of the publishers likely to be affected by the proposed requirement about the terms and conditions referred to in s 31(2).

In Australia, some States extend their deposit requirements from print media to records, disks, film and audio and videotape. Tasmania and the Northern Territory are the only jurisdictions requiring the statutory deposit of a comprehensive range of electronic as well as print material. In Tasmania, the definition of 'book' under the *Libraries Act 1984* (Tas)[54] is so broad that it has been construed to cover both print and all forms of electronic media. Electronic holdings are obtained by electronic deposit of digital publications and by the State Library of Tasmania itself undertaking its own electronic capture of Tasmanian webpages.[55] In the Northern Territory, the deposit requirement under the *Publications (Legal*

---

51   Section 2 of the *Library and Archives of Canada Act*, SC 2004 and regulations 2–4 of the Legal Deposit of Publications Regulations 2006 SOR/2006-337.

52   'Recording' is defined to include sounds, images or other information: ss 11(1), (2), *Library and Archives of Canada Act*, SC 2004, c 11.

53   Under s 36 of the *National Library of New Zealand Act 2003* (NZ).

54   Refer to s 3 of the *Libraries Act 1984* (Tas)—'book' means any book, periodical, newspaper, printed matter, map, plan, music, manuscript, picture, print, motion picture, sound recording, photographic negative or print, microphotograph, video recording, and any other matter or thing whereby words, sounds, or images are recorded or reproduced.

Deposit) Act 2004 (NT), which came into force in 2005, also covers all electronic media, including documents made available to the public on the internet. Nevertheless, where no printed version of an internet publication is published, the Act envisages the copying by government of the internet publication, rather than deposit.[56]

Another gap in Australian laws, at least, is that they generally do not apply to government-produced works, although governments have observed their terms. At the federal level, the obligation of deposit for government-produced works is not imposed by s 201 but is the subject of ministerial directions. Similar ministerial directions exist under most State laws. For example, at the time of writing, the deposit of Western Australia government agency material with the State Library of Western Australia and the National Library of Australia is subject to a Premier's Directive set out in Premier's Circular 2003/17.[57] The reason for this is that the relevant deposit enactments impose penalties.[58] Nothing in the enactments renders the Crown liable for an offence, either expressly or by necessary implication, and rebuts the general statutory presumption that the Crown is not liable to be sued criminally for a wrong.[59] Nonetheless, compliance by government has historically been strong, although over more recent years the trend of devolution in government publishing to individual agencies coupled with proportionately more online publication has brought with it clear diminution in coverage.[60] In the Northern Territory, statutory deposit obligations are imposed on all publishers, including the Northern Territory government.[61] However, no sanction is provided for non-compliance.[62]

---

55   Refer to State Library of Tasmania, *Legal Deposit* (2014) http://www.linc.tas.gov.au/forpublishers/legaldeposit.

56   Sections 13–14, *Publications (Legal Deposit) Act 2004* (NT).

57   Western Australia. Department of Premier and Cabinet, *Premier's Circular* 2003/17 (Reviewed 2014) *Requirements for Western Australian Government Publications and Library Collections* http://www.dpc.wa.gov.au/GuidelinesAndPolicies/PremiersCirculars. This applies to all Western Australian Government agencies. Publications include books, serials, newspapers, newsletters, maps, reports, brochures, pamphlets, videotapes, films, audiocassettes, sound recordings, CDROMs, DVDs, PDF files, websites and other formats through which information is made available unconditionally to the public. In Western Australia, the *Legal Deposit Act 2012* substantially came into force on 1 January 2014 and s 6 of that Act is expressed to bind the Crown. The Act applies to 'public documents' but does not initially apply to documents published on the internet. A requirement for the deposit of a range of digital Western Australian Government publications is specified in the Premier's Circular Number 2003/17.

58   For example, *Copyright Act 1879* (NSW) s 7.

59   And the presumption against such a legislative intent would have to be 'extraordinarily strong': *Bropho v Western Australia* (1990) 171 CLR 1, 23, 26; 'would require the clearest expression of intention' *State Authorities Super Board v Commissioner of State Taxation* (WA) (1996) 189 CLR 253.

60   Australia. Department of Finance and Deregulation, Australian Government Information Management Office, *Commonwealth Library Deposit and Free Issue Schemes (LDS)* (March 2013) http://www.finance.gov.au/librarydeposit/.

61   Section 6 of the *Publications (Legal Deposit) Act 2004* (NT).

62   Section 17 of the *Publications (Legal Deposit) Act 2004* (NT). Refer also to Department of Arts and Museums, Northern Territory of Australia, *Publications Legal Deposit: About Legal Deposit Legislation (2012)* http://artsandmuseums.nt.gov.au/northern-territory-library/about_us/policies_and_legislation/publications_legal_deposit.

At the federal level, there are both Commonwealth-instituted library deposit and free issues schemes that enhance legal deposit beyond the national library to provide copies to libraries of institutions having publicly funded university status as well as to state libraries. The intention is to create collections of Commonwealth Government publications that are freely available to library users and the public. This facilitates access to government information and accords with the principles of open PSI enunciated by the Office of the Australian Information Commissioner (OAIC).[63]

While there are gaps in the scope of the deposit laws, nearly all deposit libraries have developed selective retention strategies. These have been conscious decisions due to factors such as desire to eschew 'riff-raff' or matters of transitory or titillating moment from more serious literature, national goals and priorities, and to limited library holdings space, staff and other resources. Typically, libraries are not substantial repositories of 'grey literature'.[64] In the National Library of Australia, individual ephemera is selectively collected (for example, that relating to a specific event) but is not separately catalogued. Selection strategies are also determined by resources and role. For example, the National Library of Australia's collection strategy for Australian print and electronic materials is consistent with its position of the national library in a federation of states. It reads:

> 2.1 The *National Library Act 1960*, s.6(a) mandates the development of a comprehensive Australian collection, through legal deposit, purchase and donation, in order to fulfil the Library's national documentary heritage role.
>
> . . .
>
> 2.8 In developing its own collections, the Library endeavours to take into account the collecting activities of other collecting institutions interested in Australian materials.
>
> 2.9 The Library retains its responsibility for collecting material covered by legal deposit except for certain publications which are covered by agreements with state and territory libraries. The Library generally does not collect materials of local community interest only. Responsibility for collecting and preserving this material

---

63   Australia. Department of Finance and Deregulation, Australian Government Information Management Office, *Publishing Public Sector Information* (Jan 2012) http://www.finance.gov.au/blog/ 2012/01/05/publishing-public-sector-information-new-advice-released/ and http://webguide.gov.au/ web-2-0/publishing-public-sector-information/. Refer also to Australia. Office of Government Information Technology, *Management of Government Information as a National Strategic Resource – Report of the Information Management Steering Committee on Information Management in the Commonwealth Government* (August 1997) 12, 15–6, 107–9.

64   CP Auger, *Information Sources in Grey Literature*, (Bowker-Saur, 4th edn, 1998) 3–7 cites various definitions of grey literature—'literature which is not readily available through normal book-selling channels, and therefore difficult to identify and obtain' (Chillag (1985), 'non-conventional', 'informal', 'informally published', 'fugitive' and even 'invisible' (Van der Heij (1985)). Auger states that uncertain availability, poor bibliographic information and control, non-professional layout and format, and low print runs are characteristics of grey literature (3). He includes within the categories of grey literature 'ephemera'—works produced for short-term purposes (6), such as leaflets and posters. [Examples of grey literature include reports, technical notes, and specifications, conference proceedings and preprints, supplementary publications and data compilations and trade literature (3)].

will rest with the appropriate state or territory library. In some instances, the state or territory libraries may arrange for local collecting institutions, such as public libraries or community studies centres, to play a role in ensuring state-wide coverage of the material.

2.10 In building a national collection of Australian online publications, the Library formally collaborates with the mainland state libraries, the Northern Territory Library and other collecting agencies with responsibility for information in online formats, including the National Film and Sound Archive, the Australian War Memorial, and the Australian Institute of Aboriginal and Torres Strait Islander Studies. Each partner selects online publications and websites for which they take responsibility, in accordance with their published selection guidelines. They then store and provide access to selected titles (with the publisher's permission) in PANDORA, Australia's Web Archive, which is maintained centrally at the National Library. The State Library of Tasmania builds and maintains its own archives, Our Digital Island: Preserved Tasmanian Websites and STORS: Long-term storage of Tasmanian electronic documents.[65]

The National Library, in its collecting guidelines, lists a number of categories that it selectively collects or omits.[66] For example:

3.34 . . . The Library collects most Australian serials except those that fall into the following categories:

- publications consisting primarily of advertising, promotional or product information;
- special interest newsletters issued by local churches, clubs, hobby groups, amateur societies, sporting groups, community service organisations, schools, etc. These are considered to be more appropriately held within state or territory library collections;
- material of an administrative or social nature dealing with and directed to members of an organisation below the state or territory level, e.g. staff newsletters of branches of state or territory government departments, banks, corporate bodies and associations;
- company interim or quarterly financial statements or prospectuses. Annual reports of publicly listed companies are collected;
- annual reports of local government authorities (except for capital city CBDs), regional health services, schools, university departments or faculties;
- media releases;
- regional phone/business directories. The standard nationally produced phone directories are collected.[67]

---

65 Australia. National Library of Australia, *Collection Development Policy* (December 2008) paras 2.1, 2.8–2.10. http://www.nla.gov.au/policy-and-planning/collection-development-policy.

66 Ibid paras 3.8–3.35, 4.5–4.16.

67 Ibid para 3.34.

The Canadian Library and Archives has a collection development framework policy that states that its mission is, among other things, to develop 'a comprehensive collection of published Canadiana that documents the published heritage of Canada and materials published elsewhere of interest to Canada, and that supports the creation of a comprehensive national bibliography to make that heritage known and accessible'.[68] Canadiana is material published in Canada and material published in another country if the creator is Canadian or the publication has a Canadian subject.[69]

Library and Archives of Canada (LAC), however, excludes some publications of heritage value:

> However, in the development of a representative collection, LAC recognises that in some cases materials of national heritage value are more effectively acquired, made available, used, and preserved by others in either a local or a regional setting. LAC works with partners to ensure that these materials are acknowledged and maintained as part of the documentary heritage of Canada.[70]

The New Zealand National Library collections policy supplements the work of other libraries in New Zealand and selectively addresses its identified user groups and the variant ownership and needs of its collections.[71] The British Library, by far the largest, 'collects widely and in depth in its areas of traditional strength' and, at its core, seeks to represent 'the collective memory of the nation by retaining for posterity the intellectual output of British publishing'.[72]

Conclusion

If library deposit laws seek to preserve our published literary and cultural heritage, then one feature of their practice is that they have never been completely comprehensive. Some selection of material received under deposit laws has been characteristic of library policies in the United Kingdom and other countries. Further, the scope of the deposit laws themselves has hardly been completely comprehensive. Australian law, in particular, has not kept up to date with technological change and, at present, a vast amount of electronic publication is subject to selective voluntary arrangements. Throughout Anglo-Australian history, the laws themselves have not been perfectly observed. The history of deposit observance in the United Kingdom evidences this. The National Library estimates in 2005

68   Canada. Library and Archives of Canada, *Collection Development Framework* (30 March 2005) [2] http://www.collectionscanada.gc.ca/obj/003024/f2/003024-e.pdf and *Digital Collection Development Policy* (1 Feb 2006) http://www.collectionscanada.gc.ca/collection/003-200-e.html.

69   Ibid. *Collection Development Framework: Key Concepts* [4].

70   Ibid. *Collection Development Framework: Collecting Principles* [3].

71   New Zealand. National Library of New Zealand, *Collections Policy* (December 2010) 5–8 http://www.natlib.govt.nz/about-us/policies-strategy/our-policy-about-collections.

72   United Kingdom. British Library, *Collection Development Policy* (2011) http://www.bl.uk/aboutus/ stratpolprog/coldevpol/index.html.

and 2011 are of an 85 percent to 90 percent compliance for all publishing required to be deposited under s 201.[73]

Deposit laws are an instrument to gather a permanent record of the nation's published works and of a record of all the branches of knowledge contained within those works. While those laws in the Australian states and in the other common law countries cited are now more commonly called library deposit or legal deposit laws, Australian national deposit laws are likely to remain within the *Copyright Act 1968* (Cth) for federal constitutional reasons. To that extent, as a manifestation of national copyright policy, deposit laws are consistent with the goal of the encouragement of learning embodied in the first copyright statute in England—the *Statute of Anne* of 1709. It is consistent with Australia's longstanding membership of the Berne Union—to which almost all developed countries are members—that the deposit laws should not be a formality or condition of obtaining copyright protection. What is important is that the laws be made current to take into account all forms of publication and dissemination.

In essence, the deposit laws are an important part of the preservation of national cultural life and heritage. They are manifestations of a human value—the value of human identity; an understanding and respect for who we are. It is inherent in all artistic, social, economic, scientific and intellectual development. To maintain that value, it is important that future generations have access to, and understand, the past to better understand themselves and to better deal with the future. In cultures based on written records, the greater proportion of material that is not preserved, the less likely that value will be respected and promoted.[74]

Table 1 State and territory library deposit provisions

Jurisdiction	Relevant Act	Library
New South Wales	*Copyright Act 1879* s 5	Fisher Library (University of Sydney) State Library Parliamentary Library
Victoria	*Libraries Act 1988* s 49	State Library

73 Interviews with Ann Triffett, Curator, Monographs, National Library of Australia (Telephone interview, 11 August 2005) and Chris Foster, Director, Australian Collection Management Branch National Library of Australia (Telephone interview, 5 July 2011). It is estimated that the National Library collects over 12,000 books through legal deposit annually as well as hundreds of maps, journals and sheet music publications: Australia. Attorney-General's Department, *Consultation Paper: Extending Legal Deposit* (Canberra, 2012) 4 http://www.ag.gov.au/Consultationsreformsandreviews/Pages/Extending-Legal-Deposit.aspx.

74 At the time of going to print, the Australian Parliament had passed the Civil Law and Justice Legislation Amendment Bill 2014 which will amend the *Copyright Act 1968* (Cth) to extend legal deposit under the Act to include Australia's online landscape. The provisions are expected to come into force in early 2016. Publishers of online material will be required to deposit that material only if they receive a request from the National Library.

Jurisdiction	Relevant Act	Library
Queensland	*Libraries Act 1988* s 68	State Library Parliamentary Library
South Australia	*Libraries Act 1982* s 35	Libraries Board Parliamentary Library
Western Australia	*Legal Deposit Act* 2012[†]	State Library
Tasmania	*Libraries Act 1984* s 22	State Library
Northern Territory	*Publications (Legal Deposit) Act 2004* ss 7, 13	Northern Territory Library

[†] The *Copyright Act 1895* (WA), which included a deposit provision s 7, was repealed in 1994 and subsequent deposit with the State Library until 2014 was voluntary. Significant deposit provisions of the replacement legislation—the *Legal Deposit Act 2012* (WA)—came into operation on 1 January 2014. The deposit provisions of that Act (ss 8, 11, 12 and 13) cover deposit of print, electronic (physical) media and internet documents. Sections 11, 12 and 13 of the Act dealing with internet documents have yet to come into operation.

6

Crown Use: The Government as User of Copyright Material Owned by Other Persons

This chapter examines the rights of government under the *Copyright Act 1968* (Cth) and related laws to use copyright material owned by other persons for the purposes of government. Why does the government possess these rights and are they necessary for the effective operation of modern government? It also examines the laws in the light of the needs of modern government information management to transfer information across agency boundaries and to develop access systems for that information.

An important differentiating feature of government under the law of copyright in Australia are those statutory provisions dealing with the government's use of other copyright material it receives or deals with in the course of its work. No similar rights are given to other institutions or persons under the *Copyright Act 1968* (Cth). These Crown use provisions provide wide entitlements to the Commonwealth and the States to do any acts comprised within the copyright without the express permission of the copyright owner, but subject to compensation. Similar Crown use provisions are also found in other intellectual property enactments of the Commonwealth.[1]

The Crown use provisions in the *Copyright Act 1968* emanate from a recognition of the needs of government to use copyright material in the exercise of its fundamental responsibilities to the community it serves, such as defence, policing, essential communications and emergency relief, without the need to seek prior agreement from copyright owners and without the risk of an injunction to restrain it. The Crown use provisions in the

---

1   Refer to s 163 of the *Patents Act 1990* (Cth) and s 96 of the *Designs Act 2003* (Cth). It would appear that the Crown use provision (s 183 of the *Copyright Act 1968*) is consistent with the *Agreement on Trade-Related Aspects of Intellectual Property Rights* (TRIPS). Article 13, Section 1 (Copyright and Related Rights) of this *Agreement*, which is headed *Limitations and Exceptions*, provides that Members shall confine limitations or exceptions to exclusive rights to certain special cases that do not conflict with a normal exploitation of the work and do not unreasonably prejudice the legitimate interests of the right holder, which is consistent with the *Berne Convention* obligations Australia has long adhered to. Article 31(b), Section 5 (Patents) is more limited and stipulates that 'other use' (that is, use without the authorisation of the right holder) is only permitted if, prior to such use, the proposed user has made efforts to obtain authorisation from the right holder on reasonable terms and such efforts have been unsuccessful within a reasonable period of time (except in cases of national emergency or public non-commercial use).

Copyright Act 1968 are couched in broad language that enables any acts done for 'the services of the Commonwealth or State'. This broad language is a reflection of the broad functions of modern government, which has assumed important regulatory, law enforcement and information-gathering roles across a wide spectrum of community activity in pursuit of goals, such as economic efficiency, better planning, budgeting and development. It is impractical and sometimes inappropriate to seek prior agreement with copyright owners if these functions are to be performed effectively.

The government's entitlement to use material for its services without infringement of copyright does not solely arise under the Crown use provisions. It may arise in three ways.

One way is through an implied licence to the Commonwealth or a State to reproduce or even publish copyright material, such as letters, sent to it. For example, a licence to reproduce a letter would normally be implied from the sender of a letter to government, to enable proper consideration of the contents of the letter by ministerial or departmental officers and to assist in the preparation of a reply. This entitlement is further discussed in this chapter under the section heading 'Implied Licences to the Commonwealth or a State to Reproduce or Publish Material'.

There are also a number of statutory provisions in various Australian jurisdictions that enable the Commonwealth or a State to do acts in relation to copyright material that provide immunity from civil and criminal proceedings. One example is s 90 of the *Freedom of Information Act 1982* (Cth), which provides that where access is given to a document under the Act or where access is given in the bona fide belief that access was required to be given under the Act, then no action for defamation, breach of confidence or infringement of copyright lies against the Commonwealth by reason of the authorising or giving of access. Access may be given in the form of a copy of the document.[2] These provisions are discussed further in this chapter under the section heading 'The Statutory Entitlements to Do Acts Comprised in Copyright'.

Of greatest importance, however, is a provision in Part VII, Division 2 of the *Copyright Act 1968* that enables the Commonwealth and the States to do any act comprised in the copyright in a work or other subject matter if the act is done 'for the services of the Commonwealth or State'.[3] This 'Crown use' provision—s 183 of the *Copyright Act 1968*—and its ancillary provision (s 183A) operate as a statutory licence providing an unfettered entitlement to the Commonwealth and the States to do acts comprised in the copyright in works and other subject matter protected by the *Copyright Act 1968*.

The nature, scope and operation of the Crown use provision in the *Copyright Act 1968*, the extent to which licences may be implied to government to reproduce or publish copyright material it receives and the breadth of other statutory rights held by government and their relationship to s 183 of the *Copyright Act 1968*, are discussed in more detail in the remainder of this chapter. In particular, the writer examines arguments for construing s 183 to complement, rather than override, the special defences to infringement, such as s 40 (fair dealing for research or study) that users of copyright material may rely on generally under

---

2   Refer to s 20 of the *Freedom of Information Act 1982* (Cth).

3   Under the Act, 'the Commonwealth' includes the Administration of a Territory: s 10(1), and a reference to a State includes the Northern Territory and Norfolk Island: s 10(3)(n).

the *Copyright Act 1968*. The writer concludes that there are good reasons in law and policy for construing s 183 to complement these special defences.

Acts comprised in the copyright in material and, most importantly, the reproduction of copyright information within government agencies and across them, are a management demand required for the effective review and consideration of material and for government agency coordination and interoperability, and such acts are also necessary to fulfil the basic right of all citizens in a democratic society to be informed of, and to have access to, government information. Increased engagement with the community online and the internal transfer of agency information will inevitably increase. These practices of government may test the effectiveness of relying on an implicit licence from the provider of information and the present defences to infringement under the *Copyright Act 1968*. The writer concludes that the High Court decision in *Copyright Agency Limited v New South Wales*,[4] and the changing technology in the way we communicate, suggest a need for an express special defence outside the operation of s 183 permitting certain public uses of copyright material deposited or registered in accordance with statutory obligations under State or Commonwealth law.

The Scheme of Section 183

The scheme of s 183 is, in essence, set out in ss 183(1), (4) and (5).

The scheme may be summarised as follows. Section 183(1) provides that the copyright in a work or other subject matter is not infringed by the Commonwealth or a State, or by a person authorised by the Commonwealth or a State, doing any acts comprised in the copyright if the acts are done for the services of the Commonwealth or a State.

Section 183(4) provides that where an act comprised in a copyright has been done under s 183(1), the Commonwealth or State shall, as soon as possible, unless it appears to the Commonwealth or the State that it would be contrary to the public interest to do so, inform the owner of the copyright of 'the doing of the act'.

Section 183(5) provides that where an act comprised in a copyright has been done under s 183(1), the terms for the doing of the act are such terms as are, whether before or after the act is done, agreed or as may be fixed by the Copyright Tribunal.

Section 183(1) is thus expressed as a defence to infringement of copyright as are the special defences to infringement provided in Divisions 3, 4, 5 and 7 of Part III of the Act and in Division 6 of Part IV of the Act, but principally ss 40–53 and ss 103A–104A.[5] One example is s 40 (fair dealing for the purposes of research or study).

---

4   *Copyright Agency Limited v New South Wales* [2008] HCA 35.

5   The description 'special defences' is used in this chapter to describe those defences that are available in limited and specified circumstances and which, apart from a few exceptions, do not enable large scale or multiple acts in relation to copyright such as reproduction. The special defences do not provide a right of remuneration to copyright owners. I exclude from the description 'special defences' all the statutory licence schemes under the Act such as those for the manufacture of records of musical works (ss 54–64), multiple copying of works for the teaching purposes of an educational institution (Div 2, Part VB) and copying by institutions assisting handicapped readers (Div 3, Part VB), as well as the Crown use provisions.

Unlike the special defences, the requirements in s 183(4) and s 183(5) oblige the government to inform the copyright owner and to seek agreement on the terms for the doing of the act. This provides a mechanism for securing compensation for the copyright owner. Compensation is also a feature of other statutory licences under the Act, such as those dealing with the copying of works in educational establishments and the copying of works in institutions assisting handicapped readers in Divisions 2 and 3 of Part VB of the Act. It is distinguished from those statutory licences under the Act because the defence to infringement provided by s 183 is not expressed to be conditional on the giving of notice or on any other undertaking to the copyright owner.[6]

The *Copyright Amendment Act (No 1) 1998* (Cth) also inserted provisions aimed at facilitating the payment of equitable remuneration for the copying of material under s 183(1). This is effected through the sampling of copying rather than notifying each instance of copying in accordance with the requirements of ss 183(4) and (5). The principal provision is s 183A, which enables the Commonwealth or a State to enter into arrangements with an approved collecting society acting on behalf of copyright owners to make payments to the collecting society in relation to copying under s 183(1). Where such arrangements have been made, they override the application of ss 183(4) and (5) and are capable of applying to nearly all copyright material covered by s 183(1). A significant exception is the Crown use of computer programs which can only be subject to the requirements of ss 183(4) and (5).

Neither s 183A nor its related provisions inserted by the *Copyright Amendment Act (No 1) 1998* alter the defence to infringement of copyright provided by s 183(1). Section 183A simply provides a sampling scheme for calculating and making payments of equitable remuneration to copyright owners for the copying of their copyright materials in lieu of the notice requirements of ss 183(4) and (5). But other related provisions inserted by the *Copyright Amendment Act (No 1) 1998* facilitate the rights of copyright owners by enabling the recovery of equitable remuneration under the sampling scheme as a debt due to the collecting society. The operation of s 183A and its related provisions is further discussed later in this chapter under the section heading 'The Impact of Section 183A and its Related Provisions'.

The Scope of Crown Use Under the *Copyright Act 1968*

The defences to infringement provided in the *Copyright Act 1968* have historically been a part of copyright law and represent the balance struck between the rights of the copyright owners and the interests of the users of copyright material—the public—in their access to and dissemination of information. This has been a feature of the growth of this quasi-monopolistic right from its inception. That is, the law has, for many years, recognised that there is a strong public interest in the free flow of information in areas covered by these defences. Governments generate large amounts of information from material supplied to them in their regulatory, statistical, research, law enforcement, management,

---

6   Refer, for example, to s 135ZJ or s 135ZL of the Act, where copying is expressed to be conditional on copying being made solely for the educational purposes of the institution (or of another educational institution), a remuneration notice having been given to the relevant collecting society and the body complying with the marking and recordkeeping requirements set out in s 135ZX of the Act.

budgetary, fiscal and other governing roles and also receive large amounts of copyright information and material voluntarily. Information is regularly reproduced into databases, evaluated, dissected and manipulated to produce new information of value to the community or to a segment of it. It is manifestly impractical to seek permission from each copyright owner to use this copyright information in each case, nor should government be fettered in carrying out this work in the public interest by a copyright claim. On the other hand, the use by government of copyright information and material may be substantial and have a significant impact on the exploitation of that material. The balance arrived at in the Crown use provision is to subject the Crown use defence to later agreement on the terms for the doing of the act. The terms almost invariably lead to financial compensation to the copyright owner, although this is not expressed as a requirement in the section.

A fundamental question in relation to the scope of the Crown use is whether the government is obliged to use s 183(1) in circumstances where an act would otherwise fall within the protection of the special defences to infringement provided in Divisions 3, 4, 5 and 7 of Part III of the Act and in Division 6 of Part IV of the Act but principally ss 40–53 and ss 103A–104A (the fair dealing provisions, library copying and acts done for the purposes of a judicial proceeding). One illustration of this question is where an officer of a Commonwealth department copies on a departmental copier a reasonable part of a copyright work for the purpose of that officer's research or study within the scope of the fair dealing provision s 40, and the research or study concerns that person's official duties. In these circumstances, is the officer entitled to rely on s 40 of the *Copyright Act 1968* as a defence to infringement or must the Commonwealth rely on s 183(1) and thus be required to give notice of the copying to the copyright owner in accordance with the requirements of s 183 or have that copying sampled and subject to equitable remuneration in accordance with s 183A?

This question goes to the heart of the balance between copyright owners and government users.

The answer to this question in law is not absolutely clear. As a matter of statutory interpretation, it is arguable from a reading of the *Copyright Act 1968* that acts involving the use of copyright material that fall within the special defences to infringement but that are done for the services of the Commonwealth are nonetheless 'acts comprised in the copyright' in the material within the scope of s 183(1). Thus, the procedural requirements of s 183 or s 183A must be adhered to in relation to such acts.

The alternative view, and it is suggested the better view, is that s 183(1) complements the special defences to infringement so that the Crown and citizen alike can rely on those special defences; and that s 183(1) confers on the Crown entitlements to the use of copyright material that are additional to the special defences available to all. That is, only if the use of copyright material for the services of the Commonwealth or State goes beyond that permitted by the special defences is the Commonwealth or State obliged to rely on s 183(1) as a defence to infringement.

The Copyright Law Committee on Reprographic Reproduction (the Franki Committee) stated in its report in 1976:

> 7.10 We think that the Crown, or a person authorised by the Crown, should be entitled to copy a work in the circumstances where a private individual would be entitled to copy it without obligation to the copyright owners. If it be accepted that

this is the result presently achieved by section 183, no change in the Act would be required.[7]

There have been a small number of minor amendments made to s 183 since the original passage of the 1968 Act, the most significant of which is s 183(11) inserted by the *Copyright Amendment Act 1980* (Cth). This amendment Act implemented much of the Franki Committee recommendations. No amendment to clarify the operation of s 183 was inserted in the *Copyright Amendment Act 1980* in response to the recommendation contained in paragraph 7.10. No subsequent clarification has been made.[8]

The High Court of Australia in *Copyright Agency Limited v New South Wales* appears to have accepted the complementary view of the Crown use provision:

> The State did not suggest that any of the fair dealing provisions (ss 40–42) or other provisions in Pt III, Div 3 (ss 43–44F) which provide that certain acts do not constitute an infringement, had any application to the uses of the survey plans described … In cases where these provisions do apply, Pt VII, Div 2 respecting Crown use and equitable remuneration is not engaged.[9]

However, the joint judgment of the High Court in this case did not explore the question beyond that statement, as the application of the special defences was not argued by counsel for the State of New South Wales. Technically, the statement is obiter dicta and can be read equivocally.

Arguments in Support of the Wide Scope of Crown Use

There are a number of arguments, based on a reading of s 183 in the context of the Act as a whole, which support the interpretation of s 183(1) that it covers all acts comprised in the copyright in a work or other subject matter if done by the Commonwealth or State for the services of the Commonwealth or State.

The test of infringement in works and other subject matter is described in ss 36 and 101 of the Act. These sections are expressed in similar terms and together provide that the copyright in a work or other subject matter is infringed by a person who, not being the owner of the copyright, and without the licence of the owner of copyright, does in Australia, or authorises the doing in Australia of, any act comprised in the copyright. The special defences to infringement (such as s 40 and its equivalent s 103C of the Act) are not expressed to limit the exclusive rights but in various circumstances enable acts comprised within the copyright, such as reproduction or communication to the public, to be undertaken beyond a substantial part of a work or other subject matter.

---

7   Australia. Copyright Law Committee on Reprographic Reproduction, *Report of the Copyright Law Committee on Reprographic Reproduction* (Franki Committee) (Canberra, 1976) 57 [7.10].

8   Section 183A and its related provisions that were inserted by the *Copyright Amendment Act 1998* (Cth) are directed at providing a more practical alternative to the notice requirements under s 183(4) and (5) and do not address this question.

9   *Copyright Agency Limited v New South Wales* [2008] HCA 35 [11].

Part VII of the *Copyright Act 1968* is headed 'The Crown' and Divisions 1 and 2 of that Part purport to define the position of the Commonwealth and the States in relation to copyright. An act done 'for the services of the Commonwealth or State' is the subject of s 183 and such an act would not arguably cease to be so characterised simply because the Commonwealth or a State could rely on a special defence to infringement. Section 183 appears to contemplate that acts done for the services of the Commonwealth or the State may otherwise not be an infringement by the person doing them. Under s 183(3):

> (3) Authority may be given under subsection (1) . . . to a person notwithstanding that he or she has a licence granted by, or binding on, the owner of the copyright to do the acts.

An act done for the services of the Commonwealth or State therefore falls within, and is governed by, s 183(1) even though it may also be for a purpose specified in one of the special defences to infringement. However, if the act was not done for the services of the Commonwealth or State then the Commonwealth or State may be able to rely on the special defences to infringement of copyright if acting in accordance with those defences.

If this was not the proper interpretation of s 183(1), then it may be argued that it would not have been necessary to insert s 183(11) in the *Copyright Act 1968* by the *Copyright Amendment Act 1980*:[10]

> (11) The copying (*now, by later amendment, reproduction, copying or communication*) of the whole or a part of a work or other subject-matter for the educational purposes of an educational institution of, or under the control of, the Commonwealth, a State or the Northern Territory shall, for the purposes of this section, be deemed not to be an act done for the services of the Commonwealth, that State or the Northern Territory.

That is, if s 183(1) did not apply to the doing of acts by the Commonwealth or a State, which would otherwise be excluded from infringement by virtue of the educational copying provisions in the Act, then it would not have been necessary to insert s 183(11). Following the *Copyright Amendment Act 1980*, a Commonwealth or State educational institution could only rely on those educational copying provisions.

Arguments in Support of the Complementary Scope of Crown Use

The alternative view is that s 183(1) complements the special defences to infringement and does not overlap them.

While s 31 and ss 85–88 describe the rights created by those provisions as 'exclusive rights', the operation of each of those provisions is prefaced by the words 'unless the contrary intention appears'. Those special defences in the *Copyright Act 1968* that provide that the doing of certain acts does not constitute an infringement of copyright and do not provide any entitlement to compensation to the copyright owner, such as s 40 (fair dealing with a

---

10   Inserted by s 24 of the *Copyright Amendment Act 1980* (Cth) No 154 of 1980.

work for the purpose of research or study), may be construed as constituting a contrary intention for the purposes of s 31 and ss 85–88 and, therefore, limit the exclusive rights otherwise conferred by those sections. On this basis the doing of an act that by virtue of the special defences does not constitute an infringement of copyright is not the doing of an act comprised in a copyright to which s 183(1) applies. It follows that a notice under s 183(4) is not required to be given in respect of the doing of an act that is not, apart from s 183, an infringement of copyright and that is not, therefore, within the exclusive rights of the copyright owner.

Consistently, while s 183(3) provides that authority to do acts may be given to a person notwithstanding the person has a licence granted by, or binding on, the owner of the copyright, the acts in contemplation are acts comprised in the copyright within the meaning of s 183(1) described. That is, what is done pursuant to a licence granted by the copyright owner would, apart from that licence, amount to an infringement of copyright. It does not follow that because s 183(3) expressly contemplates acts that would not amount to an infringement of copyright as a result of the grant of a licence, the section has the effect of more broadly encompassing acts that would not be an infringement of copyright under the special defences in the *Copyright Act 1968*. There are other rationales for the express contemplation of licensed acts in s 183(3). For example, s 183(3) could be relied on in relation to defence activity when it is in the public interest not to notify the copyright owner of the doing of the acts for some time or when the terms of the licence may be unreasonable in the circumstances. In *Copyright Agency Limited v New South Wales*[11] both the Full Court of the Federal Court of Australia and the High Court of Australia accepted that the Crown may rely on an implied licence to do acts comprised in the copyright in material submitted to it, without reliance on s 183.

Similarly, the insertion of s 183(11) does not suggest the section more broadly encompasses acts that would not be an infringement of copyright under the special defences in the *Copyright Act 1968*. The insertion of s 183(11) followed a Franki Committee recommendation that the Crown should not be permitted to rely on s 183 for the making of multiple copies of copyright works for use in government schools and that their recommendations in respect of multiple copying in non-profit educational establishments (that first became s 53B and is now embodied in ss 135ZJ and 135ZL of the Act) should apply to government and non-government schools alike.[12] The insertion was directed at multiple copying and not at the limited copying that may be undertaken under the special defences to infringement of copyright. Section 183 has unlimited scope and, apart from s 183(11), a Commonwealth or State school would be unfettered in its capacity to use copyright material and subject only to the notice and terms requirements of s 183. The purpose of the recommendation that led to the insertion of s 183(11) was to ensure similar treatment of government and non-government schools.[13]

---

11   [2007] FCAFC 80 (5 June 2007) [152–8] and [2008] HCA 35 [45–7]. This case is discussed under 'Implied Licences to the Commonwealth or a State to Reproduce or Publish Material' in this chapter.

12   *Report of the Copyright Law Committee on Reprographic Reproduction*, above n 7, 57 [7.11].

13   Curiously, s 183(11) does not cover acts by institutions assisting handicapped readers and institutions assisting intellectually handicapped persons that are not educational institutions but that are nevertheless emanations of the Commonwealth or the States.

The complementary view is also taken by Campbell and Monottti in their examination of immunities of agents of government from liability for infringement of copyright:[14]

> If agents of government are sued for infringement of copyright, but are not able to rely on any of the statutory exceptions mentioned above, they may nevertheless rely on the provisions in the Act that allow for fair dealing with copyright material. The circumstances in which the fair dealing exceptions operate are limited but they include cases in which copyright material is reproduced for research or study . . . An act of fair dealing may also be one for the services of the Crown. For example, an officer of a government department may have dealt fairly with copyright material by photocopying an article in a periodical publication for the purposes of the research required of him or her in the course of official duties. In such a case, the fair dealing exception will probably apply rather than the exception created by s 183 of the Act, and its attendant obligation to pay compensation.

The complementary view finds some support from an examination of extrinsic materials concerning the history and purpose of s 183.[15]

Section 183 was inserted in the *Copyright Act 1968* following a Spicer Committee recommendation.[16] The committee considered the Gregory Committee recommendation that the Crown should be empowered to reproduce copyright material in connection with the equipment of the armed forces and possibly also for civil defence and essential communications, subject to compensation.[17] This recommendation had, to a large extent, been given statutory effect in the United Kingdom.[18] A majority of the Spicer Committee agreed with the view expressed by the Solicitor-General of the Commonwealth that the Commonwealth and the States should be empowered to use copyright material for any purposes of the Crown, subject to the payment of just terms to be fixed, in the absence of agreement, by the Court.

---

14   E Campbell and A Monotti, 'Immunities of Agents of Government from Liability for Infringement of Copyright' (2002) 30 *Federal Law Review* 459, 462–3. The major professional works on Australian copyright law, Lahore and Ricketson, do not address the interrelationship between the special defences and s 183—refer to K Lindgren, WA Rothnie and JC Lahore, *Copyright and Designs*, (LexisNexis Butterworths, 2004–) (looseleaf) Vol 1 [28, 561] and S Ricketson and C Creswell, *The Law of Intellectual Property: Copyright, Designs & Confidential Information* (Thomson Legal & Regulatory, 2nd edn, 2002–) (looseleaf) Vol 1 [12, 275].

15   By virtue of s 15AB of the *Acts Interpretation Act 1901* (Cth) extrinsic materials may be referred to in order to determine the meaning of a provision when the provision is ambiguous or obscure.

16   Refer to second reading speech for the Copyright Bill 1968: Australia, *Parliamentary Debates (Hansard)*, House of Representatives, 16 May 1968, 1536 (N Bowen, Attorney-General), and Australia. *Report of the Committee Appointed by the Attorney-General of the Commonwealth to Consider what Alterations are Desirable in the Copyright Law of the Commonwealth* (Spicer Committee) (Canberra, 1959) [404–6].

17   United Kingdom. *Report of the Copyright Committee* (Gregory Committee) Cmnd 8662 (1952) [75].

18   By provisions of the *Defence Contracts Act 1958* (UK).

The occasions on which the Crown may need to use copyright material are varied and many. Most of us think that it is not possible to list those matters which might be said to be more vital to the public interest than others. At the same time the rights of the author should be protected by provisions for the payment of just compensation to be fixed in the last resort by the Court.

. . .

We note that the Commonwealth and the States have a right to use inventions, subject to the payment of compensation, under section 125 of the Patents Act 1952–1955. We recommend the enactment of a provision on similar lines in respect of Crown use of copyright material.[19]

The purpose of the equivalent provision in the *Patents Act 1952* (s 125) was described by Barwick CJ in *General Steel Industries Inc v Commissioner for Railways (NSW)* as providing 'a means of securing the untrammelled use of the invention by the Governments and the authorities of the Commonwealth and of the States'.[20]

The object s 183 would appear to be aimed at is the unfettered use of copyright materials, such as in times of national exigency, where permission of the relevant copyright owners would otherwise need to be obtained.

The basis of the arguments in favour of the wide scope of s 183(1) ultimately lies in the view that Part VII represents the Crown's position under the *Copyright Act 1968* and overrides the operation of other provisions in the Act. That is, if an officer of a Commonwealth department copies on a departmental copier a reasonable part of a copyright work for the purpose of that officer's research or study within the scope of the fair dealing provision s 40 of the Act, and the research or study concerns that person's official duties undertaken within the department, the copying must be characterised as for the services of the Commonwealth rather than for that person's research or study. In the absence of such a view, the insertion of s 183(11) in the Act raises the question whether the copying of the whole or a part of a work or other subject matter for the educational purposes of an educational institution of the Commonwealth or a State could have been undertaken in reliance on the educational copying provisions, rather than s 183(1), where that copying was for the services of the Commonwealth or a State. The insertion simply prevents reliance on s 183(1).

Part VII of the Act does not represent a complete code of the Crown's position under the *Copyright Act 1968*. Evidence in support of that proposition is that at least some of the special defences expressly contemplate the Crown. For example, ss 49–51A enable acts to be undertaken by an officer in charge of a library, such as the making of a copy of an article in a periodical publication for a user or for another library, and the scope of these provisions expressly contemplates that the libraries may be administered by the Crown.[21] In addition, s 48A (and its equivalent provision s 104A) provides that copyright is not in-

---

19   Spicer Committee Report, above n 16, [404–5]. Two members of the committee were of the view that the Crown's right to use copyright material without the consent of the copyright owner should be confined to use for defence purposes only.

20   (1964) 112 CLR 125, 134.

fringed by an officer of a parliamentary library by anything done for the sole purpose of assisting a Member of Parliament in the performance of that person's duties as a member. This does not oblige parliamentary libraries to pay any compensation to copyright owners and would apply to both Commonwealth and State parliamentary libraries.

The consequences of the wide construction of s 183(1) are significant. It would mean that an individual or a person other than the Crown would be able to do certain acts comprised in the copyright free of compensation to the author while, in similar circumstances, the Crown would be subject to agreeing on terms or having terms determined by the Copyright Tribunal.[22] That is, expressed generally, the acts that others may make lawfully without compensation would attract a right to compensation under s 183 or s 183A of the Act if done for the services of the Crown.

It is more reasonable in the light of the non-exclusive nature of Part VII dealing with the Crown to adopt the complementary construction of the operation of s 183(1). That is, those entitlements expressed in s 183(1) in broad terms and that comprise acts that extend far beyond the scope of the limited special defences to infringement are additional to the entitlements enjoyed under other sections of the Act. Further, if it is accepted that s 183(1) conflicts with the specific provisions that comprise those limited special defences to infringement in respect of acts undertaken for the services of the Commonwealth or a State—that is, the doing of an act that by virtue of the special defences does not constitute an infringement of copyright is the doing of an act comprised in a copyright to which s 183(1) applies—it would appear that the maxim of statutory interpretation *generalia specialibus non derogant* applies. This Latin maxim expresses the principle that provisions of general application give way to specific provisions when in conflict. The maxim applies more strictly in the interpretation of provisions in a particular Act, such as the *Copyright Act 1968*, than in the case of conflict between separate enactments.[23] In this case, it follows that s 183(1) gives way to the special defences when in conflict and that s 183(1)

---

21   Section 195A(1)(c) defines 'officer in charge' in relation to a library referred to in the sections to mean 'the officer holding, or performing the duties of, the office or position in the service of the body administering the library the duties of which involve that person having direct responsibility for the maintenance of, and the provision of services in relation to, the collection comprising the library. Section 195A(1)(a) similarly defines 'officer in charge' in relation to archives. By virtue of s 10(3)(b) a reference to a body administering a library or archives shall be read as a reference to the body (whether incorporated or not), or the person (including the Crown), having ultimate responsibility for the administration of the library or archives. Further, s 51AA enables the making of single working, reference and replacement copies of copyright works by the officer in charge of Australian Archives in certain circumstances. The functions, the strong capacity for executive control, budgetary dependency and accountability to Government *inter alia* evidenced under the Australian Archives' constituent legislation, the *Archives Act 1983* (Cth), suggest the Australian Archives is an emanation of the Commonwealth for the purposes of the Part VII of the Act.

22   The United States Government is able to rely on the doctrine of 'fair use' under s 107 of the US *Copyright Act of 1976*. Refer to United States of America. US Department of Justice, Office of Legal Counsel, *Memorandum from Acting Assistant Attorney-General RE: Whether Government Reproduction of Copyrighted Materials Invariably is a 'Fair Use' under Section 107 of the Copyright Act of 1976* (30 April 1999) http://www.loc.gov/flicc/gc/fairuse.html.

23   DC Pearce and RS Geddes, *Statutory Interpretation in Australia* (LexisNexis Butterworths, 7th edn, 2011) 147; *White v Mason* [1958] VR 79; *Purcell v Electricity Commission of New South Wales* (1985) 60 ALR 652.

gives additional benefits to the Commonwealth and the States beyond the scope of the special defences.

If the Commonwealth and the States are unable to rely upon the special defences to infringement, then government would be placed in a disadvantageous position with respect to its use of copyright material when compared with all other copyright users, such as private institutions, corporations and individuals. Despite the breadth of government functions and powers, and the calls and demands upon it in comparison with other legal users of copyright material, governments would be obliged to remunerate copyright owners in circumstances when other users would not. This would amount to inconsistent policy between the private and public users of copyright material.

Notwithstanding these arguments, the Copyright Agency Ltd on behalf of copyright owners in published works has, since the late 1980s, entered into licensing arrangements with the Commonwealth and the States for the reproduction of these works under s 183. The Copyright Agency Ltd's present agreement with the Commonwealth is based on the premise that the Crown is able to rely on the special defence to infringement of copyright under s 43—reproduction for the purposes of a judicial proceeding or for the purposes of the provision of professional legal advice—but the agreement expressly states that reliance is not placed on other exemptions in the *Copyright Act 1968*.[24] The Copyright Agency Ltd's agreements with the States and Territories also do not appear to include the special defences to infringement as 'copying exempt from payment' within the Data Processing

---

24   Copying is recorded on a sampling basis. Clause 12 of Schedule 8 that deals with survey data protocols provides: 'Exempt—this includes all Commonwealth published and unpublished material as well as material for which a licence has been obtained (subject to verification) or is otherwise exempt from payment because of the utilisation of section 43 of the Copyright Act being a reproduction for the purposes of judicial proceedings or for the purposes of the provision of professional legal advice. (Reliance is not placed on other exemptions in the Copyright Act.)' There is also no express allowance presently made for copying of an insubstantial part of a work. Refer: Australia. Attorney-General's Department, *Agreement between Copyright Agency Limited and the Commonwealth for copying of literary works by the Commonwealth – June 2003* (signed 10 June 2003). Refer also to Australia. Attorney-General's Department, *Australian Government Use of Copyright Material* http://www.ag.gov.au/RightsAndProtections/IntellectualProperty/Pages/ Governmentuseofcopyrightmaterial.aspx.

Protocols in those agreements.[25] This appears to be largely attributable to practical diffi-culties in accurately identifying particular defences when surveying copying.[26]

The Effect of Section 183(1) on the Special Defences to Infringement

There is a suggestion in other contexts within the *Copyright Act 1968* that the extent to which Crown servants may be able to rely on one of the special defences to infringement (s 40) could be limited simply because of the existence and effect of s 183(1).

In *Haines v Copyright Agency Ltd*,[27] the New South Wales Director-General of Education had sent a memorandum to school principals containing a statement that s 40 of the *Copyright Act 1968* (fair dealing for research or study) allowed for virtually the same amount and type of copying as s 53B or s 53D without imposing any need to keep records or make payments. Sections 53B and 53D[28] then enabled the multiple copying by an educational establishment of copyright works for teaching purposes but imposed recordmaking and retention requirements and subjected the educational establishment to claims for payment by copyright owners in respect of that copying. Fox J of the Federal Court, in a judgment with which Bowen CJ and Deane J agreed, made it clear that it was wrong to say that s 40 allowed for virtually the same amount and type of copying as s 53B. Fox J stated:

> What is fair dealing is not fixed by reference to the number of copies, but is to be determined by reference to the facts of each case. An answer to the question must take into account the existence and effect of s 53B (and s 53D). Moreover it is important to the proper working of the sections that a distinction be recognised between an institution making copies for teaching purposes and the activities of individuals concerned with research and study. The memorandum was in relevant respects addressing itself to the former situation.[29]

---

25   Refer, for example, to the *Agreement between the Crown in Right of the State of New South Wales and the Copyright Agency Limited* (dated 14 March 2005) Clause 1.1 (definition of copy) and Annexure C to that Agreement, Clause 9 'Copying Exempt from Payment'. http://www.copyright.com.au/states_territories.htm and the *Interim Rate Agreement between Copyright Agency Limited and Crown in Right of the State of New South Wales* [2009] http://www.lawlink.nsw.gov.au/lawlink/legislation_policy/. These Agreements are referred to in Clauses 3.5–3.6 of the current *Remuneration Agreement between the Crown in Right of the State of New South Wales and Copyright Agency Limited* [2010] http://www.lpclrd.lawlink.nsw.gov.au/lpclrd/lpclrd_copyright/lpclrd_agreements.html. 'The experience since 2003 is that disagreements about which uses are remunerable have led to difficult and protracted negotiations over the amounts payable under the statutory licence. The parties (government agencies and collecting societies) have not reached agreement over whether fair dealing and other exceptions are available to governments, or over how surveys should be conducted and what should be counted': Australia. Australian Law Reform Commission, *Copyright and the Digital Economy: Final Report* (ALRC Report 122) (November 2013) 332 [15.14] http://www.alrc.gov.au/publications/copyright-report-122.

26   Email from Peter Treyde, Commonwealth Attorney-General's Department, to John Gilchrist, 31 January 2008. However, the Copyright Agency Ltd takes the wide view of the operation of s 183(1) (email from Phillip Stabile, Copyright Agency Ltd, to John Gilchrist, 4 April 2008).

27   (1982) 42 ALR 549.

28   Section 53B is now embodied in ss 135ZJ and 135ZL of the Act and s 53D is now embodied in ss 135ZP and 135ZQ of the Act.

The Court ordered that the memorandum be withdrawn and destroyed and its reproduction or distribution be restrained.

McLelland J, at first instance, also considered that the availability to schools of the right to make copies under s 53B, upon compliance with conditions designed to provide 'equitable remuneration' to the owners of copyright, must necessarily have an influence upon what amount and type of copying done in a school and could properly be regarded as a fair dealing under s 40. He stated:

> By way of example, it might be anticipated that a teacher who, even if he procured himself to be appointed as agent for every member of his class, made multiple copies for the purpose of classroom study, of substantially the whole of some separately published book, or sheet music, the subject of copyright, would not in ordinary circumstances be likely to be regarded as engaged in 'fair dealing' under s 40, whereas if the teacher were satisfied after reasonable investigation that copies (not being secondhand copies) of the work could not be obtained within a reasonable time at an ordinary commercial price, such multiple copying could legitimately be carried out on behalf of the school under s 53B if the records required by that section were kept.[30]

It is important to note that the Court in *Haines v Copyright Agency Ltd* did not express a view on whether ss 40 and 53B overlapped. It simply stated that it was wrong to say that s 40 allowed for virtually the same amount and type of copying as the statutory licence (s 53B). However, it does not follow from the decision that some copying may not be undertaken legitimately under s 40 that might also be undertaken in pursuance of that statutory licence or in pursuance of s 183. The issue is essentially whether, on the facts of the case, the dealing is fair and for the purposes described; and this must take into account the number of persons a copier is acting on behalf of as well as the extent of the copying. Both are relevant to the factors set out in s 40(2) of the Act in determining whether a dealing is fair.

It may be fair to make a copy of a reasonable portion of a book for the purpose of research or study of the copier or to make a copy each for two persons for their research or study in accordance with their request but unfair for the copier to make a copy each for 60 persons for their research or study in accordance with their request, despite the fact that, individually, each person could make such a copy for himself or herself. It is submitted that the nature of the dealing in the last example is not fair because the scale of the copying affects the character of the dealing. It carries it beyond the notion of individual copying contemplated by s 40.

The copying of a journal article or a reasonable portion of another published work by an individual for that individual's research or study is deemed by s 40(3) of the Act to be a fair dealing with that work for the purpose of research or study. If that individual is a Crown servant acting in the course of that servant's work for the Crown and the copying is for either of those purposes of the Crown servant, then the extent to which Crown servants

---

29   *Haines v Copyright Agency Ltd* (1982) 42 ALR 549, 556.

30   *Copyright Agency Ltd v Haines* [1982] 1 NSWLR 182, 191.

may be able to rely on s 40(3) is not limited simply because of the existence and effect of s 183. Likewise, there is nothing in the *Haines* decision to suggest that a Crown servant could not undertake acts that otherwise clearly fall within s 40 of the Act, even if that research or study assisted the Crown servant directly or indirectly in that servant's work for the Crown. What the *Haines* decision does suggest is that courts may be reluctant to construe broadly the scope of the special defences, such as s 40, in their application to the Crown.

The Operation of Section 183 and Section 183A of the Copyright Act 1968

Assuming the dealings in question do not attract any of the special defences to infringement under *Copyright Act 1968*, how does the defence provided by s 183 and its related provision (s 183A) operate?

Section 183(1) applies when the person doing the otherwise infringing act is either the Commonwealth or a State or a person authorised in writing by the Commonwealth or a State, and the act is done for the services of the Commonwealth or a State.[31]

Two rights of a copyright owner whose work or other subject matter is affected by acts under s 183(1) are expressly protected by s 183(8). That subsection provides that any act done under s 183(1) does not constitute publication of a work or other subject matter and is not to be taken into account in relation to the duration of any copyright. As any act done under s 183 is done without the consent of the copyright owner, the effect of subsection (8) is to avoid subsection (1) being unfairly determinative of the subsistence of copyright in works that would have protection only on the basis of first publication in Australia, and unfairly determinative of the duration of copyright, for example, in the case of a cinematograph film or a sound recording that, upon publication, has a limited term of protection to 70 years after the year of publication. Acts done under s 183(1) are simply acts over which the copyright owner has no control.

Successors in title to any articles sold to them under s 183(1) are protected from any possible infringement action from subsequent resale by reason of s 183(7). By virtue of that provision, successors in title are entitled to deal with the article as if the Commonwealth or State were the owner of copyright.[32] These provisions apply regardless of whether the act is notified under s 183(4) or recorded under s 183A.

---

31 An agreement or licence fixing the terms upon which a person other than the Commonwealth or State may do an act comprised in a copyright under s 183(1) is inoperative with respect to the doing of that act after the commencement of the 1968 Act unless it has been approved by the Attorney-General of the Commonwealth or a State (s 183(6)).

32 For the purposes of these and all other provisions in s 183, references to the owner of copyright include references to an exclusive licensee where there is an exclusive licence in force in relation to any copyright (s 183(9)).

The Meaning of 'for the Services of the Commonwealth or State'

Section 183 provides some assistance in determining the meaning of the phrase 'for the services of the Commonwealth or State' by specifying acts that fall within and outside of the phrase. Section 183(2) deems:

- the doing of any act in connexion with the supply of goods in pursuance of an agreement or arrangement between the Government of Commonwealth and the Government of another country for the supply to that country of goods required for the defence of that country and
- the sale to any person of such of those goods as are not required for the purposes of the agreement or arrangement,

to be 'for the services of the Commonwealth'.

On the other hand, s 183(11) excludes from the phrase the copying of the whole or a part of a work for the teaching purposes of an educational institution of, or under the control of, the 'Commonwealth, a State or the Northern Territory'.

There are very few reported cases dealing directly with s 183(1) of the *Copyright Act 1968* or other similar Crown use provisions.[33] Judicial consideration of the scope of the phrase 'for the services of the Commonwealth or State' has been largely confined to patent cases.

In *General Steel Industries Inc v Commissioner for Railways (NSW)*,[34] a single judge of the High Court considered whether the defendants in that action could rely on the Crown use provision (s 125 of the *Patents Act 1952* (Cth)) as a defence to an action for infringement of a patent over certain railway vehicle bearing structures.[35] This Crown use provision was similar in language and operation to s 183 of the *Copyright Act* and the major provisions are set out below. The *Patents Act 1952* (Cth) has since been repealed, but there is a revised Crown use provision (s 163) in the current *Patents Act 1990* (Cth).[36]

Section 125 of the *Patents Act 1952* in part provided:

---

33   Refer to comments by Cooper J in *Stack v Brisbane City Council* (1995) 131 ALR 333 at 345 on the meaning of 'the services of'. In *Allied Mills Industries Pty Ltd v Trade Practices Commission (No 1)* (1981) 55 FLR 125 Sheppard J of the Federal Court of Australia held that the Trade Practices Commission was an emanation or agency of the Commonwealth and simply concluded that the use by the Commission of documents in which copyright might subsist in favour of Allied Mills would not be a breach of the *Copyright Act 1968* (Cth) by reason of s 183 as such acts would have been done for the services of the Commonwealth. Most of the documents were relevant to proceedings brought by the Commission against Allied Mills for penalties for breaches of s 45 of the *Trade Practices Act 1974* (Cth). As a matter of precaution the Commission obtained an authority from the Commonwealth to use the various documents.

34   (1964) 112 CLR 125.

35   'THE COMMISSIONER FOR RAILWAYS . . . HEREBY pursuant to s 125(1) of the *Patents Act* 1952 of the Commonwealth of Australia AUTHORIZES AE GOODWIN LIMITED a Company duly incorporated and carrying on business in the State of New South Wales . . . (hereinafter called the Contractor) and any of its Subcontractors IN RELATION to the supply by the Contractor to the Commissioner of any article to be used by the Commissioner in or in relation to the exercise of his powers and the operation of the said railways TO MAKE USE EXERCISE OR VEND any invention to which the provisions of the said s 125(1) relate AND TO USE any model plan document or information relating to any such invention which may be required for that purpose. . .' (1964) 112 CLR 125, 128.

(1) At any time after an application for a patent has been lodged at the Patent Office or a patent has been granted, the Commonwealth or a State, or a person authorised in writing by the Commonwealth or a State, may make, use, exercise or vend the invention for the services of the Commonwealth or State.

. . .

(3) Authority may be given under sub-section (1) of this section either before or after a patent for the invention has been granted, and either before or after the acts in respect of which the authority is given have been done, and may be given to a person notwithstanding that he is authorised directly or indirectly by the applicant or patentee to make, use, exercise or vend the invention.

(4) Where an invention has been made, used, exercised or vended under sub-section (1) of this section, the Commonwealth or State shall, unless it appears to the Commonwealth or State that it would be contrary to the public interest to do so, inform the applicant or patentee as soon as possible of the fact and shall furnish him with such information as to the making, use, exercise or vending of the invention as he from time to time reasonably requires.

(5) Subject to sub-section (2) of this section, where a patented invention is made, used, exercised or vended under sub-section (1) of this section, the terms for the making, use, exercise or vending of the invention are such terms as are, whether before or after the making, use, exercise or vending of the invention, agreed upon between the Commonwealth or the State and the patentee or, in default of agreement, as are fixed by the High Court.

. . .

(8) No action for infringement lies in respect of the making, use, exercise or vending of a patented invention under sub-section (1) of the section.

Section 132 of the *Patents Act 1952* expressly provided that 'references to the Commonwealth include references to an authority of the Commonwealth and references to a State include references to an authority of the State'. Barwick CJ in *General Steel* took the view that the Commissioner for Railways was an authority of the State within the meaning of ss 125 and 132 of the *Patents Act 1952*.

Barwick CJ summarily terminated the action by the plaintiff with costs after being satisfied that the plaintiff's claim did not disclose a reasonable cause of action and was 'manifestly groundless'. He considered:

Sub-section (8) of s 125, in providing that no action for infringement shall be brought for what would otherwise be an infringement of the letters patent, emphasises the clear intention of sub-s (1) and with sub-s (7) provides a means of securing

---

36   The defence provision is s 163 but ss 163–5 set out a broadly similar notification scheme to that contained in s 183. Exploitation rights are dealt with in Ch 17 Part 2 of the Act: Exploitation by the Crown. Wider rights are provided to the Commonwealth to acquire patents under the Act in Part 3 of Ch 17.

the untrammelled use of the invention by the Governments and the authorities of the Commonwealth and of the States. On the other hand, sub-ss (5) and (6) ensure that proper compensation shall be paid to the owner of the letters patent for the acts of a Government or an authority of Commonwealth or State which makes use of the invention.

. . .

The railway system of the State is, in my opinion, undoubtedly a service of the State and the use of the invention in the construction of railway carriages to be used by the Commissioner in that railway system is a use for a service of the State or for the services of the State within the meaning of the expression in the *Patents Act 1952*, whichever may be the proper way to read the final words of s 125(1). One could scarcely imagine that sections such as ss 125 and 132, with their evident practical purpose, did not extend to include within the expression the use of the services of the Commonwealth or State, the use of an invention for the purposes of one of the Government railway systems in Australia.[37]

The judgment did not consider the phrase 'for the services of the State' beyond this brief conclusion.

Shortly after *General Steel Industries*, the House of Lords in *Pfizer Corp v Ministry of Health*[38] held that the supply of the patented antibiotic drug tetracycline to National Health Service hospitals for administration to out-patients and in-patients was a use 'for the services of the Crown' and accordingly fell within the Crown use provision (s 46 of the *Patents Act 1949* (UK)). The Ministry of Health had selected a tenderer who had obtained supplies of the drug manufactured in Italy. The United Kingdom patentee claimed, first, that the Ministry had no power under that section to authorise this method of supply and, secondly, that the supply was used for the benefit of the patients and not for the benefit of any service of the Crown. It is the second claim that is germane to this discussion.

Lord Reid stated in respect of this claim:

In Victorian times they were the armed services—the navy and the army—the Civil Service, the foreign colonial and consular services, the Post Office, and perhaps some others. Now there are many more Government activities which are staffed and operated by servants of the Crown, and are subject to the direction of the appropriate Minister. But it is not suggested that for this purpose any distinction is to be made between the older and the newer services, and it is not argued that the hospital service is not a service of the Crown.

. . .

The real controversy in the present case turns on the meaning of the word "for"—what is meant by '*for* the services of the Crown'? I think that it is a false dichotomy to treat some patented articles as made or used for the benefit of the

---

37   (1964) 112 CLR 125, 133, 134.

38   [1965] AC 512.

department or service which uses them, and others as made or used for the benefit of those persons outside the service who may derive benefit from their use by the service. Moreover, I think that such a distinction would be unworkable in practice. Most, if not all, activities of government departments or services are intended to be for the benefit of the public, and few can be regarded as solely, or even mainly, for the benefit of the department or of members of the service.

. . .

It appears to me that the natural meaning of 'use . . . for the services of the Crown' is use by members of such services in the course of their duties. Sometimes, as in the case of the armed services, that use will or is intended to benefit the whole community: sometimes such use will benefit a particular section of the community: and sometimes it will benefit particular individuals. I cannot see any good reason for making a distinction between one such case and another.[39]

Lord Evershed concurred stating:

As pointed out by the learned judges in the Court of Appeal, there is not and cannot be in this day and age a true antithesis between services of the Crown in the sense of services related to the functions of Government as such and services of the Crown in the sense of the provision of facilities commanded and defined by Act of Parliament for the general public benefit.[40]

Lord Upjohn was also of a similar view. Two judges, Lords Pearce and Wilberforce, dissented, arguing that accepting that view is to withdraw from the benefit of the patent either a large or a preponderant part of the customers for whom the invention was made (and supposedly protected by a monopoly of the right to vend). They suggested a more limited interpretation—that the invention must be for the use of the Crown (that is, the use must be by the Crown or its servants)—and that the use must be for the benefit of the Crown or its servants.[41] It would not enable the Crown, in competition with the patentee, to enter into the field of supplying the article to the public.[42]

In another patent case, *Stack v Brisbane City Council*,[43] the applicants alleged that they were beneficially entitled to a patent for a water meter assemblies invention. One of the respondents agreed to sell and supply water assembly meters incorporating this invention to the first respondent, the Brisbane City Council (BCC). Another respondent manufactured the meters. The BCC installed the water meters in homes in Brisbane for the purposes of measuring householders' use of the water supply. The water meters were not resupplied to the land owner but remained an asset of the BCC. The applicants sought an injunction restraining the respondents from infringing the alleged patent, damages or an

---

39   Ibid 533, 534, 535.

40   Ibid 543.

41   Ibid 549, 568.

42   Ibid 569.

43   (1995) 131 ALR 333.

account of profits and delivery to them of all water assembly meters in the possession of the respondents.

The respondents relied on ss 162 and 163 of the *Patents Act 1990* (Cth) as a defence to the infringement complaint.

Cooper J of the Federal Court held that the BCC was 'impressed with the stamp of government' and was an authority of the State within the meaning of s 162 of the *Patents Act 1990*. The water meters were not resupplied to the land owner and were not used in the relevant sense by the landowner. They were a component part of the apparatus by which water was supplied by the BCC for consumption in the territorial area, and charged for by the BCC, the supply being a function of local government. He concluded that the use of the water meters by the BCC as part of its supply of water in the Brisbane local authority area was the exploitation by the BCC as an authority of a State of the invention, for the services of it as such an authority. Thus, he held that the use of the water meters by the BCC was for the services of the State.

Cooper J referred to the majority and minority views in *Pfizer Corp*, to *General Steel* and to two English decisions—*Pyrene Co Ltd v Webb Lamp Co Ltd* (1920) and *Aktiengesellschaft fur Autogene Aluminium Schweissung v London Aluminium Co Ltd* (1923)—referred to in *General Steel*:

> In the reasoning of Lord Wilberforce in *Pfizer Corp* it was the re-supply by the government department in competition to the patentee which underpinned the conclusion that the grant of monopoly rights was not by the exception in s 46(1) of the Patents Act 1949 (UK) to derogate from the monopoly to a greater extent than the right of the Crown to exploit the invention for its own immediate purposes: see [1965] AC at 568.
>
> . . .
>
> The law in this country is no narrower than the minority view in that decision. If the facts in the instant case fall within the minority view in *Pfizer Corp* and the first instance cases referred to above, it is unnecessary for present purposes to determine whether the majority view in *Pfizer Corp* is the law of Australia.[44]

In *Re Copyright Act 1968; Re Australasian Performing Right Association Ltd*,[45] a case dealing directly with s 183, there was some judicial consideration of the meaning of 'for the services of the Commonwealth' but no decision on the point.

The Australasian Performing Right Association Ltd (APRA) formulated a licence scheme in which it was willing to grant a licence to the Australian Broadcasting Commission of its members' works that was subject to certain conditions, including the payment of a licence fee calculated with reference to the Commission's gross operational expenditure incurred in the provision of radio and television broadcasting services. The scheme was referred to the Copyright Tribunal pursuant to s 154(1) of the *Copyright Act 1968*. The Commission

---

44 (1995) 131 ALR 333, 348.

45 (1982) 65 FLR 437.

took a preliminary objection to the Tribunal's jurisdiction to consider the scheme and to make orders confirming or varying it under s 154(4) on the ground that the Commission was an agent or instrumentality of the Commonwealth and, as such, was protected by s 183 of the Act from infringing copyright when broadcasting or televising items in which copyright subsists.

The Tribunal referred three questions of law to the Federal Court. One was whether the Commission was an agent or instrumentality of the Commonwealth for the purposes of s 183 of the Act. The second of relevance was whether broadcasts by radio or television that are conducted by the Commission are done for the services of the Commonwealth within the meaning of s 183(1) of the Act.

All judges of the Federal Court—Bowen CJ, Franki J and Sheppard J—were of the view that the Australian Broadcasting Commission did not fall within the word 'Commonwealth' nor was it an agency of instrumentality of the Commonwealth for the purposes of s 183 of the Act.

On the second question, Bowen CJ and Franki J stated at pp 444–445:

> No doubt the broadcasting of radio and television programmes by the Commission constitutes a 'service' in the sense that it falls within the words 'postal, telegraphic, telephonic and other like services' used in s 51(v) of the *Constitution (Jones v Commonwealth (No 2) (1965) 112 CLR 206)*.
>
> It does not follow that because broadcasting by the Commission is a service within s 51(v), any broadcasting undertaken by the Commission is for the services of the Crown. Indeed, if the Commission is not the Crown, it would seem that it could not properly be said that its broadcasting was 'for the services of the Crown'. If the Commission is the Crown, then it could be said its broadcasting was 'for the services of the Crown' if the view of the majority of the House of Lords in *Pfizer Corporation v Ministry of Health* [1965] AC 512 be accepted for Australian conditions. This was that the phrase 'for the services of the Crown' is not restricted to the traditional notion that it relates to services used by the Crown or its servants but in modern times extends also to services provided by the Crown or its servants to members of the public. In view of our conclusion that the Commission is not the Crown it is unnecessary to express a concluded view on this point.

Sheppard J stated at p 457:

> . . . [i]t may be possible for an act to be done for the services of the Commonwealth within the meaning of s 183 of the Act, notwithstanding that the Commission is not the Commonwealth nor an agent or instrumentality thereof. Such a situation might arise if there were broadcast or televised something which was plainly broadcast or televised for the services of the Commonwealth, for example, a radio or television programme put on for the purposes of the Commonwealth Government.

While he also referred to the *Pfizer Corp* case, no opinion was expressed on the majority and minority views in that case.

In *Copyright Agency Limited v New South Wales*, the High Court noted the majority view in *Pfizer Corp* that the formula 'for the services of the Crown' was not limited to the internal activities of government departments but included use by government departments in the fulfilment of duties imposed on them by legislation, and that the expression was broad enough to cover provision of products to the public.[46] The High Court in *Copyright Agency Limited v New South Wales* took a wide view of the scope of s 183 and implicitly adopted the majority view in *Pfizer Corp* of what constitutes 'for the services of the Crown'.

As the High Court stated:

> 61. What is important in respect of the submissions made in this case is that no distinctions are made in s 183(1) between government uses obliged by statute and/or government uses which may be 'vital to the public interest' on the one hand, and government uses which reflect considerations more closely resembling commercial uses, on the other.

> 62. Whilst it is not difficult to understand a preference for a policy framed with an eye to such distinctions, no such policy is evinced in the clear and express terms of s 183(1).

> . . .

> 70. There is nothing in ss 183(1), 183(5) or 183A, or other provisions relating to the statutory licence scheme, which suggests that governments may make, or take the benefit of, arrangements which would have the effect of circumventing those provisions as they apply to the copying, and the communication to the public, of registered survey plans.[47]

That is, the execution of activities by the Commonwealth, or a State, within its lawful powers and authority, constitutes a 'service' of the Commonwealth or State whether that includes a sale or supply to a third party. In other words, an act is done 'for the services of the Commonwealth or State' if it is done for the purpose of performing a duty or exercising a power that is imposed upon or invested in the executive government of the Commonwealth or State by statute or by prerogative. This is consistent with the wide scope of the acts encompassed by s 183(1), the language of ss 183(2) and (7) and with the broad intention behind the provision manifested in extrinsic materials.[48]

The fact that, in times of peace, government chooses to arrange copyright licences in procurements for its armed forces rather than rely on s 183 is a reflection of government policy and practice[49] but s 183(1) is intended to secure the untrammelled use of copyright material by the governments and emanations of the Commonwealth and of the States in all these lawful circumstances. Sections 183(4) and (5) and ss 183A and 183B ensure that proper

---

46 *Copyright Agency Limited v New South Wales* [2008] HCA 35 [56].

47 Ibid [70].

48 Refer to judgment of the High Court in Ibid [8, 55–9, 70].

49 It has for more than two decades generally been the practice of the Commonwealth to rely on the provision as a last resort.

compensation shall be paid to the owner of the copyright for the acts of the Commonwealth or State.

The Notice Requirement in Section 183

Section 183 imposes an obligation on the Commonwealth and the States to inform the relevant owner of copyright of the act undertaken in reliance upon the provision. The prescribed means of doing this are set out in reg 25 of the Copyright Regulations 1989 (Cth).

Regulation 25(5) requires that a notice be given in the name of the Commonwealth or the State and that it state the International Standard Book Number (if any) or the title or description of the work sufficient to enable the work or other subject matter to be identified. It also requires that the notice specify the act to which the notice relates, state whether the act has been done by the Commonwealth or the State or a person authorised by the Commonwealth or the State and, if the latter, state the name of the person, and state that the purpose of the notice is to inform the owner in pursuance of s 183(4) of the doing of the act.

Regulations 25(2)–(4) require the notice to be served on the owner of the copyright or authorised agent or, where the person giving the notice does not know the address, or the name or address, of the owner of copyright or authorised agent, by notice in the *Commonwealth of Australia Gazette* or *Government Gazette* of the State as the case requires. It is a cumbersome and costly procedure for all but large-scale acts comprised within the copyright in material.

Assuming the acts in question fall outside the sampling arrangements contemplated by s 183A, can the defence provided by s 183(1) be relied on if the Commonwealth or a State undertakes acts that, at some time after the acts are undertaken, it considers are for the services of the Commonwealth or State and then fails to inform the relevant copyright owner? That is, if the Commonwealth or the State simply does nothing to notify the owner of the copying.

There is nothing in the language of s 183(1) to suggest that it is necessary to establish an intention to rely on the section at the time of the doing of the act. Indeed, s 183(3) expressly provides that authority may be given under subsection (1) (that is, to a person authorised in writing by the Commonwealth or a State) before or after the acts, in respect of which the authority has been given, have been done. Section 183(1) is not dependent on any subjective intention of the actors involved at the time of the acts but on the objective test of whether the copying is, in fact, done for that purpose. This, therefore, leads to the conclusion that the defence may be relied on at any time after the acts.

The notice requirements in s 183(4) are not, unlike the notice requirements in other statutory licences, such as ss 135ZJ–135ZL, expressed to be a condition of the operation of the defence. Section 183(7) also refers to the sale of an article 'which is not, by virtue of subsection (1), an infringement of a copyright'. This clearly contemplates that an act done for the services of the Commonwealth or a State is not an infringement of copyright and supports the view that the defence to infringement is not dependent on informing the copyright owner of the act.

However, s 183(4) clearly imposes an obligation to inform the copyright owner of the doing of the act 'as soon as possible' unless it appears to the Commonwealth or the State that it would be contrary to the public interest to do so.

There is an ambiguity in the way the notification requirement is expressed in s 183(4). The exception 'unless it appears to the Commonwealth or State that it would be contrary to the public interest to do so' is capable of being read as either qualifying the immediately preceding words 'as soon as possible' or the mandatory verb 'shall' preceding those words. The use of commas after 'shall' and 'possible' promotes this response.[50] Lindgren, Rothnie and Lahore appear to suggest that no notice need be given to the copyright owner where it appears to be contrary to the public interest to do so.[51] There are, for example, public interest circumstances such as the security or defence of the Commonwealth where the Commonwealth may not wish to inform the copyright owner. So long as those public interest circumstances continue to exist, then it would seem from either reading of the provision that no notification need be made. Section 183A(6) defines 'excluded copies' from the streamlined arrangements in terms 'where it appears to the government that it would be contrary to the public interest to disclose information about the making of the copies' that is consistent with this view.

If the public interest ceases to exist, such as the cessation of war or armed hostilities or the investigation of terrorist activities, is the Commonwealth then obliged to inform the copyright owner?

It is submitted that notification is required on a reading of s 183(4) in the light of the section as a whole and the underlying economic purpose or object of the Act, which is to protect and reward the originators of certain kinds of creative material by giving them the power to exploit that material. This applies to all excluded copies under the streamlined arrangements. This view has an echo of the Commonwealth's obligations under s 51(xxxi) of the *Australian Constitution* to acquire property on just terms, in this case to provide just terms in dealings with that property that would otherwise be an infringement of the rights of the copyright owner. Further, two important extrinsic materials—the Spicer Committee Report and the second reading speech of the then Attorney-General on the Copyright Bill—appear to support this view.[52]

---

50 Refer to DC Pearce and RS Geddes, *Statutory Interpretation in Australia* (LexisNexis Butterworths, 7th edn, 2011), 164–5 [4.56], where the authors point out that punctuation is a relevant consideration in determining the meaning of a provision even though at the Commonwealth level at least there is no statutory clarification of this principle and courts have at times shown a reluctance to pay regard to punctuation. In four jurisdictions amendments to their Interpretation Acts provide that punctuation in an Act is part of the Act: *Legislation Act 2001* (ACT) s 126(6); *Acts Interpretation Act 1954* (Qld) s 14(6); *Acts Interpretation Act 1915* (SA) s 19; *Interpretation of Legislation Act 1984* (Vic) s 36(3B).

51 K Lindgren, WA Rothnie and JC Lahore, *Copyright and Designs*, (LexisNexis Butterworths, 2004–) (looseleaf) Vol 1 [28,561).

52 Refer to Spicer Committee Report, above n 16, [404–5]. 'The occasions on which the Crown may need to use copyright material are varied and many. Most of us think that it is not possible to list those matters which might be said to be more vital to the public interest than others. At the same time the rights of the author should be protected by provisions for the payment of just compensation to be fixed in the last resort by the Court . . .' and second reading speech for the Copyright Bill 1968, above n 16: 'The Bill puts beyond doubt that the Crown is bound by the copyright law. Provision is made, however,

The Impact of Section 183A and its Related Provisions

From 30 July 1998, the *Copyright Amendment Act (No 1) 1998* (Cth) amended the *Copyright Act 1968* to streamline the system for owners of copyright to be paid for the copying of their works by government. The amendments followed the regime of the statutory licence schemes for copying by educational establishments by providing for a collecting society to be declared by the Copyright Tribunal to administer sampling, collecting and distributing payments in a similar way to the educational copying schemes.

The amendments avoided the operation of ss 183(4) and (5) of the Act by requiring payments for the reproduction of copyright materials by a government to be made the basis of sampling, rather than the statutory method of full recordkeeping embodied in ss 183(4) and (5), where there is a declared copyright collecting society. The statutory provisions reflected changes in practice that had already occurred between copyright owners and government. These provisions contemplate that a relevant collecting society, which may be declared by the Copyright Tribunal in relation to all government copies or a class of government copies, will distribute the equitable remuneration to the owners of copyright in the material that has been copied and will hold in trust the remuneration for non-members who are entitled to receive it.

The method of working out the equitable remuneration payable may provide for different treatment of different kinds or classes of government copies (s 183A(4)).

Section 183A replicates some of the public interest considerations reflected in s 183. In particular, it does not apply to 'excluded copies' that is defined in s 183A(6) to mean 'government copies in respect of which it appears to the government concerned that it would be contrary to the public interest to disclose information about the making of the copies'. This would include copies made for defence or security purposes. A definition section, s 182B, defines 'government copy' to mean a reproduction in a material form of copyright material made under s 183(1) and, in turn, defines 'copyright material' to cover works and subject matter other than works. Computer programs are specifically excluded from the definition of copyright material and thus from the streamlined arrangements.

Thus, copying of computer programs and copying of any material where there is a public interest in non-disclosure of that copying must be governed by the requirements of ss 183(4) and (5). In addition, acts comprised in the copyright other than reproduction of works and subject matter other than works, which are not done in pursuance of a collective agreement and that are done for the services of the Commonwealth or a State, would also be governed by the notification and determination requirements of ss 183(4) and (5). For example, if a State government department made an adaptation of a work, such as a translation or cartoon of a literary work, for the services of the State, this act would be governed by ss 183(4) and (5). Since 2007, the Commonwealth has had a collective agreement

---

[in Pt VII] for the use of copyright material for the services of the Commonwealth or the States upon payment of compensation to the owner of the copyright.' There was very little change from the original 1967 Bill: second reading speech for the Copyright Bill 1967: Australia. *Parliamentary Debates (Hansard)*, House of Representatives, 18 May 1967, 2334–5 (N Bowen, Attorney-General): 'Provision is made . . . for the use of copyright material for the services of the Commonwealth or the States upon payment of compensation to the owner of the copyright. These provisions are contained in clause 179 of the Bill, which in this respect follows the relevant provisions of the Patents Act.'

with Screenrights for the copying for work purposes of transmissions of television and radio programs based on sampling system under s 183A(3).[53] The Commonwealth also has an agreement with the Australasian Performing Right Association (APRA) for the public performance of musical works by the Commonwealth, based on an annual fee factored to the number of full-time staff, in which APRA waives any right to be notified of the performance of music under s 183.

Implied Licences to the Commonwealth or a State to Reproduce or Publish Material

Under the *Copyright Act 1968* it is a direct infringement of copyright to do or to authorise the doing of any act comprised in the copyright in a work or other subject matter without the licence of the copyright owner.[54] The effect of a licence given by the copyright owner is to permit what would otherwise have been an infringement of copyright. Licences may be implied from the nature of the work and the surrounding circumstances as well as expressly granted by the copyright owner. Licences may be expressly granted either orally or in writing. Other than in respect of an exclusive licence, there is no requirement under the 1968 Act that a licence be in writing.

An early case dealing with implied licences to government is *Folsom v Marsh*. That case involved the alleged piracy by a commercial publisher, in 'The Life of Washington', of the private and official letters of US President Washington (as well as his messages and other public acts). The letters of Washington had been previously published under an agreement with the private copyright owners. The originals of the letters had been purchased by Congress. In *Folsom v Marsh*,[55] Story J dismissed a defence that, because they were in their nature and character either public or official letters or private letters of business, the letters were not the proper subjects of copyright. He observed that the author of letters, whether they are literary compositions or familiar letters or letters of business, possesses the sole and exclusive copyright therein. Story J went on to say that persons to whom the letters are addressed must have, by implication, the right to publish any letter or letters addressed to them upon such occasions as require or justify the publication or public use of them. He cited as examples:

- to establish a right to maintain a suit at law or in equity or to defend the same, and
- if misrepresented by the writer or accused of improper conduct in a public manner, he may publish such parts of such letters as may be necessary to vindicate his character and reputation, or free him from unjust obloquy and reproach.[56]

---

53   Other than 'excluded copies' and copies for personal use. Screenrights is the trading name of the Audio-Visual Copyright Society Limited that is a declared collecting society under s 182C of the *Copyright Act 1968* (Cth).

54   Sections 36 and 101. A similar position applies to those indirect infringements under the Act, such as importation for sale or hire (s 102). These indirect infringements require proof of knowledge by the person infringing.

55   (1841) 9 F Cas 342, 2 Story (Amer) 100. Refer also to L Bentley and M Kretschmer, (eds), *Primary Sources on Copyright (1450–1900)* http://www.copyrighthistory.org.

56   *Folsom v Marsh* (1841) 9 F Cas 342, 2 Story (Amer) 100, 111.

He went on to state:

> In respect to official letters, addressed to the government, or any of its departments, by public officers, so far as the right of the government extends, from principles of public policy, to withhold them from publication, or to give them publicity, there may be a just ground of distinction. It may be doubtful, whether any public officer is at liberty to publish them, at least, in the same age, when secrecy may be required by the public exigencies, without the sanction of the government. On the other hand, from the nature of the public service, or the character of the documents, embracing historical, military, or diplomatic information, it may be the right, or even the duty, of the government, to give them publicity, even against the will of the writers. But this is an exception in favor of the government, and stands upon principles allied to, or nearly similar to, the rights of private individuals, to whom letters are addressed by their agents, to use them, and publish them, upon fit and justifiable occasions. But assuming the right of the government to publish such official letters and papers, under its own sanction, and for public purposes, I am not prepared to admit, that any private persons have a right to publish the same letters and papers, without the sanction of the government, for their own private profit and advantage. Recently the Duke of Wellington's despatches have, (I believe) been published by an able editor, with the consent of the noble Duke, and under the sanction of the government. It would be a strange thing to say, that a compilation involving so much expense, and so much labour to the editor, in collecting and arranging the materials, might be pirated and republished by another bookseller, perhaps to the ruin of the original publisher, and editor. Before my mind arrives at such a conclusion, I must have clear and positive lights to guide my judgment, or to bind me in point of authority.[57]

In *Copyright Agency Limited v New South Wales*,[58] the Full Court of the Federal Court of Australia held that the State of New South Wales did not infringe copyright in survey plans registered with the Land and Property Information Division of the New South Wales Department of Lands by making the plans available to the public and to local government and authorities.

Emmett J held on the facts that the survey plans had previously been published and that, by the lodgement of the plans, a surveyor must have been taken to have licensed and authorised the Crown to make available to the public, to copy and to do any other acts required by the Crown's statutory and regulatory planning regime. Copyright in the plans remained with the surveyor. The licence was for the State to do everything that, under the statutory and regulatory framework that governs registered plans, the State was obliged to do with, or in relation to, registered plans.

Emmett J, with whom Lindgren J agreed and with whom Finkelstein J agreed generally, accepted the notion that a surveyor who made the plan must be taken to have licensed and authorised the State to do acts comprised in the copyright in consequence of the

---

57   Ibid 100, 113, 114.

58   [2007] FCAFC 80 (5 June 2007).

lodgement of the plan for registration, regardless of the presence of s 183. To quote from Emmett J's judgment in the case:

> 156 The systems of land holding in New South Wales and the statutory and regulatory framework described above depend in no manner upon the existence of the *Copyright Act*. If s 183 did not exist, it is clear that there would be no utility whatsoever for a surveyor in submitting any of the Relevant Plans for registration unless, by doing so, or assenting to that being done, the surveyor authorised the State to do what it is obliged by the statutory and regulatory regime described above to do, as a consequence of registering the Relevant Plan. Whether or not s 183 has the effect that the doing of the acts, because they are done for the services of the State, are deemed not to be an infringement of copyright, a surveyor must be taken to have licensed and authorised the doing of the very acts that the surveyor was intending should be done as a consequence of the lodgement of the Relevant Plan for registration.[59]

However, on appeal, the High Court took a narrow view of the scope of an implied licence in these circumstances.

> 46 . . . On the one hand, the State uses the plans in direct response to lodgement of the survey plans by an applicant to effect, if appropriate, registration, and to issue title. This includes making a working copy of the plans. These uses are directly connected with private contracts for reward between surveyors and their clients for the preparation of plans for the specific purposes of lodgement, registration and the issue of title. On the other hand, there are uses of survey plans by the State which flow from registration and which involve copying the plans for public purposes or communicating them to the public via a digital system.

> 47. Whilst CAL [Copyright Agency Limited] is seeking remuneration and terms only in respect of those latter uses, the submissions did not always distinguish between the two types of uses. As will be explained in these reasons, the statutory licence scheme applies in the circumstances of this case to authorise the State to make copies of the survey plans after registration, for public purposes and for communication to the public, and provides for terms upon which that can be done. The scheme is compulsory in the sense that an owner cannot complain of the permitted use, but the use is allowed on condition that it be remunerated.[60]

The High Court considered that there was nothing in the express terms of s 183(1) (or its history) that could justify reading down the expression 'for the services of the State' so as to exclude reproduction and communication to the public pursuant to express statutory obligations. The High Court further held that:

> 92 . . . a licence will only be implied when there is a necessity to do so. As stated by McHugh and Gummow JJ in *Byrne v Australian Airlines Ltd*:

---

59   Ibid [156].

60   *Copyright Agency Limited v New South Wales* [2008] HCA 35 [46–7].

'This notion of 'necessity' has been crucial in the modern cases in which the courts have implied for the first time a new term as a matter of law.'

93. Such necessity does not arise in the circumstances that the statutory licence scheme excepts the State from infringement, but does so on condition that terms for use are agreed or determined by the Tribunal (ss 183(1) and (5)). The Tribunal is experienced in determining what is fair as between a copyright owner and a user. It is possible, as ventured in the submissions by CAL, that some uses, such as the making of a 'backup' copy of the survey plans after registration, will not attract any remuneration.[61]

This narrow view suggests copies made for internal administrative purposes, as well as backup copies, would be covered by an implied licence. It is clear in the circumstances of that case that the use that involved copying of the plans for public purposes and later selling the rights to access and use those documents to information brokers and other members of the public via a digital system is not.[62]

Two of the factors the High Court thought were significant in its decision were that the State imposed charges for copies issued to the public and that equitable remuneration for government uses, which involved copying and communication of the plans to the public subsequent to registration, did not undermine or impede the use for which the plans were prepared, namely lodgement for registration and issue of title. It is dangerous to generalise from the circumstances surrounding the lodgement of these survey plans under the system set by State planning laws more broadly to copyright works received by government in other circumstances, although the decision of the High Court has wider implications for the digitalisation of registration systems and the wider needs of government to disseminate such information, whether enhanced with other information or not.

One simple outcome is that government could increase registration fees to take into account any remuneration payable to the authors of the plans for any public uses or communication of such copyright material and consequent administrative costs. Alternatively, it could require any party lodging material for inclusion in any public registry to expressly licence their copyright material to permit use of the document by government users or for the public purposes contemplated by the government or, as Fitzgerald has pointed out, to provide 'an open licence which permits use of the document both by government and non-government users, such as a non-exclusive Creative Commons Attribution (CC-BY) licence.'[63] The wider implications for government in its own management of information are discussed in later in this chapter under the section heading 'Information Management and Section 183'.

---

61   Ibid [92–3].

62   'At its narrowest, the High Court's decision in *Copyright Agency Ltd v New South Wales* can be read as holding that where third party copyright documents (in this case the survey plans) are lodged with a government registry and the State later sells rights to access and use of those documents to commercial vendors at commercial rates, the State's rights to reproduce and communicate those copyright materials are governed by the statutory licensing arrangements and payment of equitable remuneration under ss 183 and 183A of the Copyright Act 1968': B Fitzgerald, A Fitzgerald, et al, *Internet and E-Commerce Law, Business and Policy* (Lawbook, 2011) 430.

63   Ibid 431.

Implied licences to reproduce or publish copyright material may also arise in a wide variety of circumstances unconnected with government. Licences have been implied by the courts from conduct or from custom of the trade or to give a dealing between the parties', ordinary business efficacy. For example, the editor of a newspaper would normally be regarded as having an implied licence to publish, and to edit, a letter sent to him on a public matter.[64]

As the High Court stated in *Concrete Pty Ltd v Parramatta Design & Developments Pty Ltd*:

> A nonexclusive licence to use architectural plans and drawings may be oral or implied by conduct, or may be implied, by law, to a particular class of contracts, reflecting a concern that otherwise rights conferred under such contracts may be undermined, or may be implied, more narrowly, as necessary to give business efficacy to a specific agreement between the parties. A term which might ordinarily be implied, by law, to a particular class of contracts may be excluded by express provision or if it is inconsistent with the terms of the contract. In some instances more than one of the bases for implication may apply.[65]

The existence and extent of any implied licence to government to do acts comprised in the copyright in material forwarded to government depends on the nature of the material and the circumstances of its submittal.

Where letters, submissions or other correspondence are sent to government from individuals, organisations and other governments, a licence or consent to officials in government to copy that correspondence would normally be implied to enable it to be given timely and proper consideration by relevant Crown servants, Ministers and ministerial staff. Frequently, the drafting of responses to correspondence requires input from a number of different areas of administrative responsibility and copies of correspondence are made to enable contemporaneous consideration by those areas.

Such a licence could, of course, be negated by an express prohibition on copying. It is unusual, or even rare, for letters or submissions or other correspondence to government to be marked 'not to be copied'. In some more sensitive areas of government, such as the Commonwealth Department of Defence, the confidentiality of material may be expressly marked, access may be expressed to be restricted to particular recipients and there may be an obligation to number copies made, particularly in the case of tender documents. But it would be unrealistic to suggest that governments, like other large institutions and organisations, should not normally copy a document received by it to enable it to receive timely and proper consideration.

It is just as strongly arguable that a licence would normally be implied to make a copy of a letter, submission or other correspondence sent to governments to ensure the immediate preservation of the document.[66] For example, a letter sent to a minister, which is usually forwarded to

---

64 *Springfield v Thame* (1903) 89 LT 242; *De Garis v Neville Jeffress Pidler Pty Ltd* (1990) 18 IPR 292, 302-3.

65 [2006] HCA 55; (2006) 229 CLR 577 at 595–6 [59] per Kirby and Crennan JJ; see also Gummow ACJ at 584 [16].

66 This gives business efficacy to the relationship established by the submission of the correspondence.

the minister's department for the preparation of a reply, may be copied in the minister's office for that purpose. When the letter ceases to have currency and is placed in archives, governments may rely on ss 51AA and 51A of the *Copyright Act 1968* to undertake such copying.[67]

In some limited circumstances, governments may have an implied licence to publish or to place publicly online. One circumstance where a licence may be implied is in respect of a public submission on a matter of public moment sent to, or given before, a government committee or commission by a Member of Parliament or a peak body representing a community interest. An example is a submission on a law reform issue. The implication of a licence could only arise in the case of a public submission, that is, a submission made in response to the calling of public submissions by the committee or body concerned and that is submitted on that basis. This is akin to the implication of a licence to an editor of a newspaper to publish a letter on a public matter sent to the editor.[68]

There are other circumstances where correspondence received from Members of Parliament or constituents on matters of public moment may carry an implied licence to publish or place online. An implied licence would almost certainly not extend to cover correspondence sent on private constituent affairs or private commercial matters. A claim of confidentiality on a letter or a submission would negate any such licence simply because it is inconsistent with publication. A licence to publish or to place publicly online would clearly not be implied where there was an express restriction placed on the publication of a document, or more broadly, on its use within government.

Similarly, it may still be open to government to publish official letters addressed to government, or any of its departments, by public officers embracing historical, military, or diplomatic information, as Story J in *Folsom v Marsh* suggests,[69] on the basis of an implied licence, but many of these documents in the present Australian context are likely to be Crown copyright material, having been made by, or under the direction or control of, the Commonwealth or a State. In the case of documents emanating from its own public officers of government, no question of an implied licence to government could possibly arise.

Inevitably, from the very nature of something that is implied, there are likely to be uncertainties about the existence of such a licence. In practice, this deters reliance upon such a licence. Section 183(1) offers protection from infringement to the Commonwealth and the States where the position is not clear. Section 183(3) goes even further in that it extends the protection of the provision to a private licencee where written authority is given by the Commonwealth or a State to that person to do acts comprised in the copyright.[70]

---

67   The former permits a single working copy and a single reference copy of a published or an unpublished work kept in the collection of the National Archives of Australia to be made by the Archives where the work is open to public inspection. The latter, which has application to all non-profit archival institutions (as well as libraries), *inter alia* permits a copy of a work in manuscript form or an original artistic work that forms part of the collection of the archives to be made by the archives for the purpose of preserving the manuscript or original artistic work against loss or deterioration.

68   Refer to *Springfield v Thame* (1903) 89 LT 242 and *DeGaris v Neville Jeffress Pidler Pty Ltd* (1990) 18 IPR 292. An implied licence to publish public submissions sent to parliamentary and other public inquiries would normally subsist in the convenor of such inquiries.

69   *Folsom v Marsh* 9 F Cas.342, 2 Story (Amer) 100, 113, 114.

The Statutory Entitlements to Do Acts Comprised in Copyright

There are a number of statutory provisions in various Australian jurisdictions that enable the Commonwealth or a State to do acts in relation to copyright material that provide immunity from civil and criminal proceedings.[71]

Commonwealth enactments, other than the *Copyright Act 1968*, include laws dealing with FOI, archives and parliamentary proceedings in which there are express legal entitlements of government to copy material in its possession without infringing the copyright in the material.[72]

Access to a document may be given to a person under s 20 of the *Freedom of Information Act 1982* (Cth) in one of a number of forms including the provision by the agency or minister of a copy of the document. Measures passed under the *Freedom of Information Amendment (Reform) Act 2010* (Cth) also require the publication of documents to which access has been given under the Act (and other specified government information) to enable downloading from a website. Under ss 90, 91 and 92 of the *Freedom of Information Act 1982* where access has been given to a document in good faith in the belief that access was required to be given under the Act, or when publication of a document is undertaken in good faith in the belief publication is required under the Act or otherwise, then no action for defamation, breach of confidence or infringement of copyright nor any criminal action lies against the Commonwealth by reason of the giving of access or the publication of the document.

The measures that require agencies to publish information under the *Freedom of Information Act 1982* have not yet been matched by reforms to the *Archives Act 1983* (Cth). Consequently, there is at present no equivalent in the *Archives Act 1983* to ss 90–92 of the *Freedom of Information Act 1982*. Section 57 of the *Archives Act 1983* merely provides protection from copyright infringement, for defamation, breach of confidence and criminal actions for the giving of access under the *Archives Act 1983*.[73]

---

70 The agreement or licence providing the authority must be approved by the relevant Commonwealth or State Attorney-General (s 183(6)).

71 The *Copyright Act 1968* includes special defence provisions enabling the doing of acts comprised in the copyright in works and other subject matter by the judicial and parliamentary arms of government. Section 48A and s 104A are defences to infringement that enable a parliamentary library to do acts comprised in the copyright for the sole purpose of assisting a member of parliament in the performance of that person's duties as a member. Section 43 and s 104 are defences to infringement that enable anything done for the purpose of a judicial proceeding or a report of a judicial proceeding. No compensation is provided to the copyright owner under these provisions.

72 Other examples are ss 720 and 743 of the *Offshore Petroleum and Greenhouse Gas Storage Act 2006* (Cth) that enable the responsible Commonwealth Minister or Titles Administrator in exercise of their powers under the Act to do any acts comprised in the copyright in a literary or artistic work that are applicable documents (that include lodged applications, reports and returns under the Act). Refer to the discussion in Brian Fitzgerald, Cheryl Foong and Anne Fitzgerald, 'Copyright Exceptions beyond the *Copyright Act 1968* (Cth)' (2012) 11 (2) *Canberra Law Review* 160.

73 State Freedom of Information Acts contain bars on actions for defamation and breach of confidence in respect of the giving of access under their several enactments but not bars on actions for copyright infringement although all contemplate the provision of a copy of a document as a form of access. Section 23(3)(c) of the *Freedom of Information Act 1982* (Vic) provides that if the form of access to a document would involve an infringement of copyright, access in that form may be refused and access given in

No compensation is contemplated by any of these Commonwealth provisions. They operate independently and irrespective of s 183. Neither does s 183 expressly or implicitly refer to these provisions nor do the provisions expressly or implicitly refer to s 183. They have different objects or purposes and are not so wholly inconsistent or repugnant that they cannot stand together.[74] Effect can be given to each provision at the same time.[75] These acts should thus be accorded independent operation within their given spheres.

Article 9 of the English Bill of Rights 1689, which applies to the Commonwealth and to the Australian States by statute or by the common law, provides absolute protection against liability for reproduction of copyright material in debates or proceedings of Parliament.[76] Another widely-expressed provision is s 4 of the *Parliamentary Papers Act 1908* (Cth), which provides that no civil or criminal action or proceeding shall lie against a person for publishing any document or evidence pursuant to an authorisation given by a House of the Commonwealth Parliament, or a committee thereof, under ss 2 or 3 of that Act. Similar provisions exist in State jurisdictions under various State enactments.[77]

No compensation is contemplated by any of these statutory provisions applying in the Commonwealth and States.

In the case of the State enactments, the operation and proceedings of State Parliaments are not immune from the laws of the Commonwealth but are generally unfettered by them. Section 106 of the *Commonwealth of Australia Constitution Act 1900* specifically deals with the saving of each State constitution and provides for its continuance until altered in accordance with the constitution of the State. However, s 106 is expressed to be subject to the *Australian Constitution* and it has not been treated as invalidating a law that otherwise falls within Commonwealth legislative power.[78] Likewise, s 107 of the *Commonwealth of Australia Constitution Act 1900* provides that every power of the Parliament of a colony that has become or becomes a State shall, unless it is by the *Constitution* exclusively vested

---

another form. The Commonwealth Parliament under the *Australian Constitution* has exclusive legislative power over copyright.

74   As Gaudron J stated in *Saraswati v The Queen* (1991) 100 ALR 193, 204, 'It is a basic rule of construction that, in the absence of express words, an earlier statutory provision is not repealed, altered or derogated from by a later provision unless an intention to that effect is necessarily to be implied. There must be very strong grounds to support that implication, for there is a general presumption that the legislature intended that both provisions should operate and that, to the extent that they would otherwise overlap, one should be read as subject to the other'.

75   Refer to *Rose v Hrvic* (1963) 108 CLR 353, 360.

76   For further discussion see Campbell and Monotti, above n 14.

77   See for example *Parliamentary Papers Act 1891* (WA) s 1; *Parliamentary Papers (Supplementary Provisions) Act 1975* (NSW) s 6 and the *Parliamentary Committees Act 1991* (SA) s 31. Refer also to s 11(1) of the *Parliamentary Privileges Act 1987* (Cth) that provides that no action, civil or criminal, lies against an officer of a House in respect of a publication to a member of a document that has been laid before a House.

78   *Attorney-General (Qld) v Attorney-General (Cth)* (1915) 20 CLR 148, 172; *Amalgamated Society of Engineers v Adelaide Steamship Co ('Engineers Case')* (1920) 28 CLR 129, 154; *Melbourne v Commonwealth* (1947) 74 CLR 31, 66, 75, 83; *Stuart-Robertson v Lloyd* (1932) 47 CLR 482; *Queensland Electricity Commission v Commonwealth* (1985) 159 CLR 192; *Victoria v Commonwealth* (1996) 187 CLR 416.

in the Parliament of the Commonwealth or withdrawn from the Parliament of the State, continue as at the establishment of the State.

The *Copyright Act 1968* clearly falls within a head of Commonwealth constitutional power. The principal question, therefore, is whether s 183 is intended to apply to the publication by State Parliaments of copyright material, that is, to the proceedings of State Parliament. It is clear law that parliamentary privilege is so valuable and essential to the workings of responsible government that express words in a statute are necessary before it may be taken away.[79] In the case of the Parliament of the Commonwealth, s 49 of the *Constitution* requires an express declaration. No express intention to take away either the power of the Commonwealth Parliament or a State Parliament is evident in the *Copyright Act 1968* as a whole or in s 183 specifically and so the provisions of state and federal enactments, which deal with parliamentary publication, stand unfettered by the Act.

Information Management and Section 183

If the Crown can rely on special defences to infringement of copyright, which enable use of private copyright material, why should it also have wider entitlements to use private copyright material? How are these rights justified on information management principles and other policy considerations?

The special defence provisions, augmented by s 183, reflect the peculiar status of government, and the demands on it, to fulfil in the public interest a wider variety of governing powers and functions within a modern liberal democratic society. This is reflected in the growth of most western governments, especially in the years after the Second World War.[80] No other body or institution has the breadth of activity and regulatory, financial, managerial and accountability requirements as modern government.[81]

The information management principles outlined in *Management of Government Information as a National Strategic Resource: Report of the Information Management Steering Committee on Information Management in the Commonwealth Government*, published in August 1997 by the Office of Government Information Technology, stated that:

> In developing systems for the organisation, transmission and transaction of information, agencies should start from the premise that, subject to privacy legislation, all information content will at some time be transferred across agency boundaries, and design access systems accordingly.[82]

---

79 *Duke of Newcastle v Morris* (1870) LR 4 HL 661, 671, 677, 680.

80 As in most industrialised capitalist democracies, refer generally to PS Wilenski, 'Small Government and Social Equity' in Glenn Withers (ed), *Bigger or Smaller Government? Papers from the Sixth Symposium of the Academy of Social Sciences in Australia* (1982) 37.

81 Refer to Chapter 1, 'Scope and Diversity of Modern Australian Government' and 'What Constitutes the Crown under Part VII of the *Copyright Act 1968*'.

82 Australia. Office of Government Information Technology, *Management of Government Information as a National Strategic Resource: Report of the Information Management Steering Committee on Information Management in the Commonwealth Government* (August 1997) xxix, 164.

Acts comprised in the copyright in information and, most importantly, the reproduction of copyright information within government agencies and across them, is a management demand required for the effective review and consideration of material, and is also necessary to fulfil the basic right of all citizens in a democratic society to be informed of, and to have access to, government information.

In 2010, the federal government's *Response to the Report of the Government 2.0 Taskforce*[83] agreed that Australian Government agencies should enable a culture that gives their staff opportunity to experiment and develop new opportunities for online engagement with their customers, citizens and communities of interest in different aspects of the agencies' work and to increase the use of online tools for internal collaboration within and between agencies. Increased engagement with the community online and internal transfer of agency information will increase. These practices may test the effectiveness of relying on an implicit licence from the provider of information and the present defences to infringement under the *Copyright Act 1968*. In particular, the High Court decision in *Copyright Agency Limited v New South Wales* and the changing technology in the way we communicate raise the question whether there is any need for express special defences permitting certain public uses of copyright material deposited or registered in accordance with statutory obligations under state or federal law outside the operation of s 183.[84]

In a 2005 report, the Australian Government's Advisory Council on Intellectual Property recommended that the Crown use provisions in the *Patents Act 1990* (as well as the *Designs Act 2003*) be amended to align with the requirements of the TRIPS Agreement.[85] Article 31(b), Section 5 (Patents) of TRIPS is more limited than the provisions of that agreement dealing with copyright and stipulates that 'other use' (that is, use without the authorisation of the rights holder) is only permitted if prior to such use the proposed user has made efforts to obtain authorisation from the rights holder on reasonable terms and such efforts have been unsuccessful over a reasonable period of time (except in cases of national emergency or public non-commercial use).[86]

The Advisory Council's recommendation has not yet been legislatively adopted. It is inappropriate for copyright usage. For reasons earlier advanced, the requirement of prior consent of the copyright owner for the myriad and complex holdings of rights comprised in most copyright media is impractical and potentially improper for government to exercise. And to restrict exceptions to cases of national emergency, extreme urgency or public non-commercial use is likely to invite disputes over the boundaries of these terms. What

---

83   Australia. Department of Finance and Deregulation, *Government Response to the Report of the Government 2.0 Taskforce* (May 2010) [11] http://www.finance.gov.au/publications/govresponse20report/ or http://www.finance.gov.au/publications/govresponse20report/doc/ Government-Response-to-Gov-2-0-Report.pdf.

84   For example, along the lines of ss 47–50 of the *Copyright, Designs and Patents Act 1988* (UK).

85   Australia. Advisory Council on Intellectual Property, *Review of Crown Use Provisions for Patents and Designs* (November 2005) [3] http://www.acip.gov.au/pdfs/ACIP_Final_Report_Review_of_ Crown_Use_Provisions_Archived.pdf.

86   Refer to World Trade Organization. *Agreement on Trade-Related Aspects of Intellectual Property Rights* (1994) http://www.wto.org/english/tratop_e/trips_e/t_agm0_e.htm and the position under Article 13, Section 1 of TRIPS (Copyright and Related Rights) at n 1.

the majority of the Spicer Committee foresaw in 1959 were that the needs of government to use copyright material 'are varied and many': '[m]ost of us think that it is not possible to list those matters which might be said to be more vital to the public interest than others'.[87]

To suggest that the government pay remuneration to copyright owners every time government reproduces their work for another person or communicates a work online enabling public access to the work, where it is a matter of public record, is counter to recent reforms requiring and enabling publication of documents accessed under the *Freedom of Information Act 1982* (Cth).[88] It also places further administrative burdens on government. The balance between copyright ownership and copyright usage in the information age must take account of the importance of modern access to, and the wide and free dissemination of, information. This involves practical as well as in-principle considerations. There is a public interest in the electronic capture and in dissemination to the public—to councils, public authorities (such as water and telephone) and other interested institutions and persons—of survey plans and of their incorporation into digital cadastral databases with layered and enhanced information from different governmental sources. In the Copyright Agency case, plans could be accessed through Webgov by registered government users only and a licence fee was charged for delivery of particular plans. There is a clear public interest in accessing that information and little public interest in remunerating all authors of all components to the digitalised information that supports the purposes of the deposited works.

What is fair in terms of the use of copyright material—the proper balance of interests between copyright owners and users—must take into account the character of what is done and the extent to which it is done. It should not simply be a question of seeking payment for any use of the material in question. This argument was put, and rejected, in the campaign for remuneration for all photocopying of copyright works.[89] In these circumstances, reliance upon s 183 implies rent seeking and, given the nature of the Crown use provision, which compulsorily enables unfettered use of copyright material, it is in the interests of copyright owners and of government that s 183 be used as a last resort.

Section 48 of the *Copyright, Designs and Patents Act 1988* (UK) provides:

---

87   Spicer Committee Report, above n 16 [404]. In New Zealand, where the Crown use provision in its *Copyright Act 1994* has a restricted scope relating to the needs of national security, periods of emergency, and the safety and health of the public or any member of the public and which is subject to equitable remuneration, the law also provides a number of express non-remunerated provisions enabling copying and other acts by the Crown for administrative and other purposes in addition to acts done under statutory authority: refer to *Copyright Act 1994* (NZ) ss 61–63, 66.

88   Refer to the *Freedom of Information Act 1982* (Cth) s 11C.

89   John Gilchrist, 'The Franki Committee (1976) Report and Statutory Licensing', in Brian Fitzgerald and Benedict Atkinson (eds) *Copyright Future: Copyright Freedom*, (Sydney University Press, 2011) 65, 67. The Australian Copyright Council Ltd had made submissions to the Franki Committee that all copying should be remunerated upon the basis that authors should receive a royalty for each copy page made of any work within copyright. In Britain, the Whitford Committee also reached a similar view by concluding that all reprography be remunerated and that fair dealing be confined to hand or typewritten copies.

48 Material communicated to the Crown in the course of public business

(1) This section applies where a literary, dramatic, musical or artistic work has in the course of public business been communicated to the Crown for any purpose, by or with the licence of the copyright owner and a document or other material thing recording or embodying the work is owned by or in the custody or control of the Crown.

(2) The Crown may, without infringing copyright in the work, do an act specified in subsection (3) provided that—

(a) the act is done for the purpose for which the work was communicated to the Crown, or any related purpose which could reasonably have been anticipated by the copyright owner, and

(b) the work has not been previously published otherwise than by virtue of this section.

(3) The acts referred to in subsection (2) are—

(a) copying the work,

(b) issuing copies of the work to the public, and

(c) making the work (or a copy of it) available to the public by electronic transmission in such a way that members of the public may access it from a place and at a time individually chosen by them.

(4) In subsection (1) 'public business' includes any activity carried on by the Crown.

(5) This section has effect subject to any agreement to the contrary between the Crown and the copyright owner.

A special defence of this kind was recommended by one member of the CLRC in its *Crown Copyright* report.[90] A similar defence also exists under New Zealand law.[91] Such a provision, if adopted in Australian law, should be expressed in a media neutral way so that it encompasses both electronic and hard-copy reproduction and communication of the work.[92] It would facilitate the fulfilment of a public duty on government. It should, nonetheless, be incumbent on government, which requires the deposit of plans or other

---

90 Australia. Copyright Law Review Committee, *Crown Copyright* (2005) 187.

91 *Copyright Act 1994* (NZ) s 62. Section 61 of that Act also provides another public administration defence—namely the specific defence to infringement in relation to copying of material open to public inspection or on an official (statutory) register. This provision is similar to s 47 of the *Copyright, Designs and Patents Act 1988* (UK).

92 Section 48 was amended by The Copyright (Public Administration) Regulations 2014 (UK) to encompass making the work available to the public by electronic transmission, which remedies a limitation of the earlier provision to enable copies to be shared on the internet. Refer to United Kingdom. Intellectual Property Office *Government Policy Statement: Consultation on Modernising Copyright* (July 2012) https://www.gov.uk/government/consultations/copyright. '7.198 The Copyright Act allows a variety of acts to be performed by public bodies to enable them to discharge their duties effectively . . . 7.201 However, although some of these exceptions permit the issuing of copies to the public, this relates only to the issuing of individual copies, for example paper copies. It does not permit copies to be shared on the internet.'

material, to make clear in regulatory, statutory or documentary form the uses of the copyright material contemplated by government. No use beyond the purposes expressed should be authorised. It would also change the character of the dealing if the government was exercising the licence to make a profit from the use of other copyright works rather than simply recouping costs. A proviso could be inserted into this special defence to exclude profit-making activities from the operation of the provision. In this way, the special defence would not unfairly prejudice the legitimate interests of the copyright owner.

Conclusion

The broad scope of the Crown use provision should be retained.[93] There are compelling arguments in law and policy for clarifying the interrelationship between the special defences to infringement and the Crown use provision so that copyright policy is consistent and clear. In particular, it should be made clear that s 183 should complement, rather than override, the special defences to infringement such as s 40 (fair dealing for research or study) that users of copyright material may rely on generally under the *Copyright Act 1968*.

Further, the increased engagement with the community by Australian governments online and the interoperability of information between government agencies, which modern information and communication technologies facilitate, will test the effectiveness of relying on an implicit licence from the provider of copyright material to government and the present defences to infringement under the *Copyright Act 1968*. Reliance by government on s 183 in these circumstances is generally not appropriate. The High Court decision in *Copyright Agency Limited v New South Wales* and the changing technology in the way we communicate suggest a need for an express special defence permitting certain public uses of copyright material deposited or registered in accordance with statutory obligations under state or federal law outside the operation of s 183. Such a provision would recognise the peculiar duties and responsibilities of government.

93　The Australian Law Reform Commission released a discussion paper on its *Copyright and the Digital Economy* reference with a draft recommendation that proposed repeal of the statutory licence in Part VII Div 2 of the *Copyright Act 1968* (Cth) in favour of voluntary licensing arrangements. Australia. Australian Law Reform Commission, *Copyright and the Digital Economy: Discussion Paper* (DP79), 283–297 http://www.alrc.gov.au/inquiries/copyright-and-digital-economy. However in its final Report, it recommended the retention of the statutory licence in an amended form so that it was more flexible and less prescriptive. It recommended detailed provisions such as the setting of equitable remuneration, sampling notices and recordkeeping be removed 'so that more commercial and efficient agreements can be made between the parties'. It did warn, however, that 'the criticism will be that this reduced prescription comes at a cost—namely, uncertainty and litigation'. Australia. Australian Law Reform Commission, *Copyright and the Digital Economy* (ALRC Report 122), 95, 201–202, 206–208 http://www.alrc.gov.au/inquiries/copyright-and-digital-economy. Refer to the discussion in Chapter 7.

7

Reform of the Law: The Government as Proprietor, Preserver and User of Copyright Material

This chapter commences by examining the wider questions of whether there is any justification for copyright ownership vesting in the government, the extent of the public interest in accessing government information across the spectrum of current government publishing and communication activity and whether copyright protection poses a barrier to access to government information. It then turns to reform of the subsistence and ownership provisions of the Commonwealth and States under the *Copyright Act 1968* and reform of the laws dealing with the role of government as preserver and user of copyright material. It concludes by discussing attempts by proprietors of copyright material to impose contractual and technological restrictions on the use of copyright material and it argues such practices, whether imposed by government or the private sector, should be prohibited where they conflict with public policy established by the *Copyright Act*.

It is evident from the previous examination of the roles of government as proprietor, preserver and user of copyright material under the *Copyright Act 1968* that these roles have had early beginnings and are not recent phenomena. In particular, both government preservation roles—in archival and library deposit—precede the *Statute of Anne*.

It is also evident that the current copyright law relating to these areas of government activity is in a number of respects unclear and uncertain, and has failed to respond adequately to technological change and to the practices of the information age. An example of the former is the lack of clarity in the scope of the prerogative right in the nature of copyright preserved by s 8A of the *Copyright Act* and in the scope of the Part VII provisions and, in particular, what government institutions can rely on the Crown provisions and what is meant by 'direction or control'.[1] An example of the latter is the absence of the compulsory deposit of electronic materials to the National Library under the *Copyright Act 1968*.[2]

The longer-term policy emphases on access to government information, and engagement with government, which are reflected in government policy in Australian FOI laws, the Office of Information Commissioner and other administrative laws, and the development of government policy to promote agency interaction and interoperability, have not been

---

1 Discussed in Chapter 2.

2 Discussed in Chapter 5.

fully reflected in the *Copyright Act*. For example, the *Freedom of Information Act 1982* (Cth) requires the publication online of accessed information under the Act, regardless of copyright ownership, and gives government a statutory protection from infringement, but government usage in fulfilment of statutory registration functions imposed on it, which is internally mashed, may attract compensation claims to copyright owners. It is also apparent that the balance of interests under the *Copyright Act 1968* between copyright owners and users of copyright information, reflected in the special defences to infringement of copyright, is not fully shared by government and other users of copyright material. An example is the inability of government archives to rely upon other defences to infringement under s 200AB of the *Copyright Act,* which are nonetheless available to non-government archives, as a result of the presence of the Crown use provision in the Act. In addition, there are doubts about the ability of government to rely on the most important special defences such as fair dealing for research or study when acts comprised in the copyright are undertaken for the services of government.

It has been argued in this book that government has roles and responsibilities of significance to society that should continue to be protected and promoted. It has also been argued that the democratic values that require citizens' access to information, and engagement with government, have undergone and will continue to undergo fundamental change as information and communications technologies transform the capacity of governments and individuals to collect, store, disseminate, access, share and communicate information more expeditiously and in greater quantity than ever before. These trends are likely to continue and are a worldwide phenomena. The capacity of technology to respond to the needs of citizens for information in turn increases the expectations of citizens for more open and accountable government. Responding to these factors raises questions of law and of public policy.

Reform of the law is not in itself the complete solution to rapid changes in the way we communicate with government or in the way we access government information. In some respects law reform lacks the speed and flexibility to respond effectively to rapid technological change. Greater flexibility in achieving policy goals and a stronger capacity to adapt to changes in technology, as well as changing policy emphases, can be achieved through coordinated and consistent open content licensing. In the case of government information there is evidence that this can bring political, social, and economic benefits to society and ease administrative burdens on government through the reduction of labour-intensive specific licensing of government copyright material.

Should the Government Own Copyright in Government Information?

It is not within the scope of this book to argue the merits of copyright protection as a whole. It is, nonetheless, fundamental to the questions raised in the introduction to this book to consider the merits of copyright protection for government-produced material, to consider whether the public interest overrides any copyright protection in government material and to consider whether copyright protection is in itself inconsistent with access to government copyright material.

Government has been a significant owner of copyright or rights in the nature of copyright since the introduction of printing. While government publications in the Anglo-Australian common law tradition were for many centuries largely focused on works of the established religion and of the state, the increasing breadth and complexity of government activity has meant it has published a broader range of works. These works do not simply have a single copyright rationale. The range of government works attracts different rationales.

Those moral rights protecting the integrity of a work are sometimes cited as important to works produced by government, to protect the integrity and source of 'official' government material or of such things as designs in currency. The government is able to use its copyright in such materials to control the way its material is used by the imposition of appropriate licensing conditions. Of great antiquity is the common law duty on the Crown to print and publish certain works of state—and, in particular, legislation—and to ensure that it does so in a correct and authentic form. This is the basis of the Crown's prerogative right in the nature of copyright. Government copyright has its origins in this Crown prerogative right, which is expressly preserved by s 8A of the *Copyright Act 1968*. This justification for Crown copyright was restated in many submissions received by the CLRC and applied broadly across government material.[3] The Victorian Government argued that:

> In some circumstances it is important for a State body to continue to exercise control over State copyright, to ensure confidentiality or quality or consistency with other Government publications or outputs. The State must ensure the continued integrity and authenticity of official government publications so that the public can be aware of the status of each publication. Continuing to maintain Crown copyright is essential to achieving these outcomes.[4]

More recently, the Report of Economic Development and Infrastructure Committee of the Parliament of Victoria stated:

> One of the core objectives for recognising IP protection in PSI is quality control and ensuring that government information is presented in a complete, accurate and authoritative manner.[5]

The then Federal Department of Communications, Information Technology and the Arts (DCITA) argued before the CLRC that Crown copyright can help ensure appropriate use of sensitive published materials that are critical to the health and welfare of the Australian community, such as the use of Commonwealth copyright materials that could risk implying government endorsement of a particular political party, or a commercial product or service, or where immigration forms are used:

---

3   Australia. Copyright Law Review Committee, *Crown Copyright* (2005) 53 (para 4.66).

4   Ibid 53, 54 (para 4.68, Submission 64, 1).

5   Victoria. Economic Development and Infrastructure Committee, Parliament of Victoria, *Inquiry into Improving Access to Victorian Public Sector Information and Data*, Parliamentary Paper 198 Session 2006–2009) (June 2009) 66 (para 6.1.2.1). The committee went on to state: 'While the Committee recognises that copyright protection is not the only mechanism to maintain the integrity of government information and data, copyright does offer governments a simple, effective and established way to maintain the quality and authenticity of their materials' (66–7).

Materials that people rely on in making informed decisions on health, immigration and financial matters are of particularly sensitivity . . . While trade practices, passing off principles may possibly be applicable, copyright is a more immediate and effective tool for the Commonwealth to exercise in these circumstances.[6]

This rationale in relation to government material has also been referred to in reviews in other common law countries. For example, Gordon Robbie, the then Head of Copyright in Her Majesty's Stationery Office (HMSO), explained:

> Another factor not often appreciated is that copyright . . . is also a means by which copyright holders can ensure that their material is used properly and responsibly by third parties. This is of particular importance where that material is authoritative, and where the general public, in one way or the other, are placing reliance on its veracity and accuracy. The Copyright Unit does come across cases of abuse and is able to pursue and prevent them.[7]

The 1999 United Kingdom White Paper entitled the *Future Management of Crown Copyright* stated:

> Many respondents recognised the need to preserve the integrity and official status of government material. It was generally perceived that Crown copyright operates as a brand or kitemark of quality indicating the status and authority of much of the material produced by Government.[8]

Subsequently, the United Kingdom Office of Fair Trading's Report, *The Commercial Use of Public Information* stated:

> Overall, we have concluded that our recommendations . . . will improve the commercial use of public sector information without the need to abolish Crown copyright or other IPR. In fact, the existence of Crown copyright is a key part of the control mechanisms which we want to build on to ensure that PSIHs [Public Sector Information Holders] act in a fair and transparent manner.[9]

Similar views have been expressed in some Canadian reports.[10] For example, in 2001 a Project Report by KPMG Consulting on geospatial data policy noted:

---

6   Above n 3, 53 (para 4.67, Submission 60, 3).

7   G Robbie, 'Crown Copyright—Bete Noire or White Knight?' (1996) 2 *Journal of Information, Law and Technology* 1(current criticisms (iii)) http://www2.warwick.ac.uk/fac/soc/law/elj/jilt/1996_2/special/robbie.

8   United Kingdom. Cabinet Office, White Paper: *Future Management of Crown Copyright*, (1999) para 5.1 http://www.opsi.gov.uk/advice/crown-copyright/future-management-of-crown-copyright.pdf.

9   United Kingdom. Office of Fair Trading, *The Commercial Use of Public Information (CUPI)* (2006) (OFT 861) 58 [para 4.76] http://webarchive.nationalarchives.gov.uk/20140402142426/http://oft.gov.uk/oftwork/publications/publication-categories/reports/consumer-protection/oft861/ or http://www.opsi.gov.uk/advice/poi/oft-cupi.pdf.

A marked difference between the digital data policies and practices between Canada and the US at the national level is the Crown copyright requirements. These requirements, coupled with complex licensing agreements, limit the broader use of geospatial data in Canada when compared to federal US data by preventing redistribution, whether within or between organizations. The use of licensing and copyright to prevent redistribution (i.e., to protect pricing policies) inherently contradicts the goals of maximizing data use and the resulting benefits, and therefore should be minimized.[11]

The report recommended:

Instead of preventing data use, licensing and copyright should be used to protect data integrity, essentially building a 'branding' that can be recognized as a mark of quality data (especially for framework data required to facilitate data integration).[12]

Another justification for copyright protection—and probably the most frequently cited—is that copyright ownership is derived from the 'sweat of the brow'[13] principle, that is the protection of the skill, labour and expense in producing the work, which cannot be appropriated by another to save labour and expense and enable that other person to 'reap where he has not sown'.[14] This principle justifies the protection of the entrepreneur, such as a publisher or cinematograph film producer, as well as the author[15] and as such equally applies to government as entrepreneur, if not as author. Examples are films and audiovisual material produced by departments and agencies of government for educational and other purposes, and commissioned works, such as official histories and biographies. While much material produced by government is a necessary by-product of its day-to-day administration and thus funded by the taxpayer, some material in the vast array of government works would not be produced unless government was able to make a return on investment in them.[16]

---

10   AA Keyes and C Brunet, *Copyright in Canada: Proposals for a Revision of the Law* (April 1977) (Consumer and Corporate Affairs, Ottawa, 1977) 225.

11   KPMG Consulting, *Executive Summary: Geospatial Data Policy Study* (March 2001) (Ottawa, 2001) 24 http://www.geos.ed.ac.uk/~gisteac/proceedingsonline/Source%20Book%202004/SDI/National/ Canada/Canadian%20Geospatial%20Data%20Policy%20Study%20Executive%20Summary.pdf.

12   Ibid 24, 25.

13   Genesis 3:19.

14   '[I]t is a sound principle that a man shall not avail himself of another's skill, labour, and expense by copying the written product thereof. To quote the language of North J in another case: "For the purposes of their own profit they desire to reap where they have not sown, and to take advantage of the labour and expenditure of the plaintiffs in procuring news for the purpose of saving labour and expense to themselves". *Walter v Lane* [1900] AC 539, 552 per Lord Davey. Refer also to Blackstone II, 359.

15   Under Australian and international law copyright protection extends to such persons.

16   Copyright protection may provide an incentive to create government works and copyright protection may ensure public access regardless of commercial considerations. See above n 3, 38, 36 (paras 4.24, 4.16).

The protection that copyright provides for exploitation also enables government to recoup the costs of dissemination and minimise the costs to the government and ultimately to the taxpayer, most significantly in traditional form. In digital form the costs of dissemination are usually small. Cost recovery for the dissemination of copyright works is not simply borne by the Australian public but may be spread to overseas consumers as well.[17] The importance of any one of these theoretical rationales for protection should not be overstated in respect of government, or other copyright owners, since the justifications are broad in nature and their support in arguments for the legal protection of works not previously protected, or for the expansion of rights conferred by the law, are often used collectively as well as individually.[18] However, as the CLRC commented, 'weighed against these rationales is the importance of facilitating access to government material'.[19]

The Public Interest in Accessing Government Copyright Information

Should Australian taxpayers be able to get information from the government free of charge and free of restriction? Should we be able to reproduce and publish it? And should we be able to edit it, sell it and make a profit from it without restriction?

The scope of government publishing in electronic and traditional form in Australia is quite diverse and very substantial. Some government dissemination activity in print or electronic form can be justified on the basis that the market if left to itself would not produce it, or do so in sufficient quantity or widely enough. Information is a merit good. There are positive benefits to society outside the individual consumer of information, which justify government activity. They include:

- social planning, efficiency and productivity objectives,
- political accountability,
- public order and the rule of law, and
- the fostering of cultural and civic values (that justifies government intervention in education and support for the arts).[20]

The strength of the public interest in accessing and re-using government works depends on the nature of the works produced by government.

In much of the material produced by government there is a strong and identifiable public interest in ensuring its widest dissemination, particularly in works of high informational content. In other materials such as commissioned historical works this public interest may

---

17   Above n 3, 56–8 (paras 4.78–4.83). It may be argued that placing government works in the public domain may enable an entrepreneur to publish and thus reap rewards at taxpayers' expense.

18   Lionel Bentley and Brad Sherman, *Intellectual Property Law* (Oxford University Press, 3rd edn, 2009) 33. Those proponents of wider copyright protection are aided by these theoretical perspectives on rights and by the self-interests of sectors of the copyright industry, which sometimes have been accused of 'rent seeking'.

19   Above n 3, xx.

20   CA Kent, 'The Privatizing of Government Information' (1989) 16 (2) *Government Publications Review* 113, 118–22 and John Gilchrist, 'The Role of Government as Proprietor and Disseminator of Information' (1996) 7 (1) *Australian Journal of Corporate Law* 62, 72, 73.

not be as strong. Beyond issues of public interest in accessing copyright material produced by government there are wider issues of confidentiality, security and other considerations that properly restrict access to that material. The GILF project identified approximately 15 percent of material produced by government that should not be accessible by the public. FOI laws provide a list of exceptions to disclosure with which copyright licensing practices ought to be consistent.

The Commonwealth Government's response to the Ergas Committee recommendation that the Crown should not benefit from preferential treatment under the *Copyright Act 1968* as compared with other parties, and that s 176 of the *Copyright Act* be amended to leave the Crown in the same position as any other contracting party,[21] was to first look at developing best practice policy guidelines for Crown ownership of copyright rather than change copyright legislation. A number of submissions to the CLRC supported policy rather than legislative change.[22] But licensing policy was not central to the recommendations of the CLRC, which focused on reform of the provisions of the *Copyright Act*.[23]

The CLRC made some recommendations on the management of Crown copyright 'aimed at promoting consistent copyright management practices in government agencies and increasing the awareness of relevant issues among public service employees and those with whom they interact'.[24] These included the desirability of uniformity in the management of Crown copyright across State and Territory governments and that each State and Territory government consider giving a central agency responsibility for managing Crown copyright, similar to the (then) Commonwealth Copyright Administration (CCA) model.

The CLRC did not promote a vision of wider access to government copyright material through user-friendly licensing steps such as the Open Government Licence adopted by government in the United Kingdom or more widely by governments and other sectors of society through the Creative Commons initiative. Although tasked to consider 'the effect of new technologies'[25] in point 2 of its terms of reference, it did not make any specific recommendations on those technological advances that have enabled wider access online. The Creative Commons initiative was relatively new at the time of the Committee's deliberations, government electronic licensing initiatives in the United Kingdom were in their infancy and implementation of the 2003 European Union Directive on the re-use of PSI was being slowly implemented across European states. In essence, the Committee left

---

21 Australia. Intellectual Property and Competition Review Committee, *Review of Intellectual Property Legislation under the Competition Principles Agreement* (September 2000): Final Report of the Intellectual Property and Competition Review Committee to Senator the Hon Nicholas Minchin, Minister for Industry, Science and Resources, and the Hon Daryl Williams AM QC MP, Attorney-General (Ergas Committee) (2000) 114.

22 Above n 3, 32 (para 4.06).

23 In part this was due to the nature of the terms of reference of the Copyright Law Review Committee that focused in point 1 on 'the appropriateness of the law in Australia in relation to government ownership of copyright material' and raised specific issues in relation to statutory and prerogative material.

24 Above n 3, xxx.

25 Ibid xiii.

detailed consideration of licensing of Crown copyright material to the responsible government administrations.[26]

However, the future direction of public policy for government as proprietor, preserver and user of information, lies in licensing policy as well as law reform to respond to present and future change. The Commonwealth and various State governments have adopted open content licensing policies for much of their government information using Creative Commons licence guidelines. The Commonwealth has devolved licensing of PSI to individual departments and agencies and ceased the functions of the central clearing house model (CCA) for licensing.[27] Instead it has issued guidelines[28] on the licensing of PSI that implement the default model of a free Creative Commons BY licence. There has been no legislative reform of the Crown provisions of the *Copyright Act 1968* since the report of the Committee.

A question related to copyright protection in government material is whether ownership of copyright conflicts with the principle that all citizens in a liberal democratic society should have fair and open access to government information.

Public access to information was a recurring theme in the *Crown Copyright* report. In the CLRC's words:

> Open access to government information is an essential characteristic of modern democracy, as has been increasingly recognised through a range of reforms, such as the introduction of freedom of information legislation throughout Australia in the past two decades. Technological advances in the electronic storage and dissemination of information have also had an impact on access to government material, with governments using the Internet and electronic databases to facilitate cheaper and more efficient access to information. There has been a growth in availability of legal information through a network of legal information institutes that provide free online access.
>
> . . .
>
> Internationally there have been increased efforts to ensure public access to government copyright material, including the United Nations' world summit on the information society in late 2003 and a 2003 European Commission Directive to facilitate the re-use of public sector information.
>
> . . .

---

26   Ibid xxxiii, 184–5. The Copyright Law Review Committee did recommend that the CCA's role be expanded to provide advice and guidance on Commonwealth Crown copyright to assist both Commonwealth agencies and users and stated that the then practice of the Commonwealth compared unfavourably to the HMSO website that provided guidance on a range of topics, such as reproduction of court forms and copyright in public records.

27   The CCA clearing house ceased to function in January 2011.

28   On 28 January 2011 the Australian Attorney-General's Department released *Guidelines for Licensing Public Sector Information for Australian Government Agencies* to assist agencies in implementing this policy (28 February 2012) http://www.ag.gov.au/RightsAndProtections/IntellectualProperty/Documents/GuidelinesforlicensingPSIforAusGovagencies.pdf.

The Committee heard conflicting views on how access to certain public information may be ensured where there is a strong public interest in making it widely available. While some suggested retaining Crown copyright and introducing statutory exceptions or blanket licences, the Committee favours the view expressed in many submissions that called for the abolition of copyright in legislation and other primary legal materials, noting that in many countries there is no copyright in such works. Some suggested that certain executive materials should be treated in the same way, and the Committee considers that appropriate.[29]

In recommending the abolition of copyright in legislation and other legal materials, the Committee also recommended that prerogative rights in the nature of copyright in the right of the Commonwealth and of the States be abolished by amendment to the *Copyright Act 1968*. One criticism of the CLRC's recommendations is that it confused government ownership of copyright material with access to government information. This applies equally to copyright material as well as material subject to the prerogative right in the nature of copyright.

Ownership of copyright information does not *of itself* conflict with the principle that all citizens in a liberal democratic society should have fair and open access to government information. It matters less whether copyright subsists in legal materials if access to those materials including the republication of those materials is freely and openly available. Indeed placing materials in the public domain without a functional obligation to make them available for access or to disseminate those materials would hinder access to them.[30] For example, the independent free access to law site AustLII[31] is reliant on the cooperation of public bodies to deliver an electronic copy of a statute or case for the site to function. Access to, and re-use of, government information requires positive steps—a 'push' model—by government to ensure it takes place. The benefits of licensing are that it is flexible and capable of reflecting the wide variety of material produced by government and the extent of public interest in accessing each kind of government material. Licensing is also capable of adjustment quickly and more easily than statutory amendment.

---

29   Above n 3, xxv–xxvi 138 (para 9.38).

30   Cox has stated that the question of formal ownership of the text of laws and decisions is perhaps secondary to the question of the dissemination of the law: refer to Noel Cox, 'Copyright in Statutes, Regulations, and Judicial Decisions in Common Law Jurisdictions: Public Ownership or Commercial Enterprise' (2006) 27 (3) *Statute Law Review* 185, para 54. The question of whether material is in the public domain or not is not in itself determinative of the question of access to, and re-use of, the government information. Access to, and re-use of, government information requires policy and/or regulatory steps by government to ensure it takes place.

31   AustLII is part of the free access to law movement that includes CanLII, BAILII, and NZLII http://www.worldlii.org/worldlii/declaration/. AustLII's approach is that the obligation of governments and courts to provide access to the law is independent of any questions of ownership 'since the most liberal copyright law still does not deliver an electronic copy of a statute or case to a publisher—and certainly not on a daily or weekly basis—cooperation by public bodies is essential, and such cooperation involves them in licensing the materials to you, even if they do claim copyright': refer to Noel Cox, 'Copyright in Statutes, Regulations, and Judicial Decisions in Common Law Jurisdictions: Public Ownership or Commercial Enterprise' (2006) 27 (3) *Statute Law Review* 185, para 65.

The history of past government licensing in Australia has been lacking in consistency. Submissions to the CLRC by law publishers pointed to the inconsistent approach of the various state and federal jurisdictions to the republication of primary legal materials.[32] It is clearly desirable and possible that the governments of the States and the Commonwealth agree on a consistent regime of licensing across jurisdictions, which makes clear to persons accessing that information their rights to re-use that information and provides a central portal or electronic points of contact for licensing permission. This would facilitate the sharing and re-use of information across all sectors of the society including other governments. It is consistent with the fundamental concept of the present information age that is characterised by the ability of individuals to have access to and to transfer information freely.

In a report to the Department of Prime Minister and Cabinet in 2009 on *Information Policy and E-governance in the Australian Government*, Dr Ian Reinecke stated:

> A survey of Australian government agencies with diverse roles in developing policy reveals the necessity for clearer governance arrangements in order to better coordinate policy development.
>
> . . .
>
> A central theme of the agency survey is a widely held view that there is a need within government for a central point of responsibility to enhance information policy development and practice.[33]

A significant step in this direction was the establishment, by Commonwealth enactment, of the Office of Australian Information Commissioner that was tasked under its 2010 enactment with 'promoting a pro-disclosure culture' and of 'achieving a coordinated approach to information management policy across government'.[34]

Is Access to Information Confused With Access to Copyright Material?

The terms 'information age' or 'information economy' not only reflect the increasing proportion of our gross domestic product in the primary information sector[35] but the present

---

32   Above n 3, 165–74.

33   Australia. Department of Prime Minister and Cabinet, *Information Policy and E-governance in the Australian Government: A Report for the Department of the Prime Minister and Cabinet* [1] Dr Ian Reinecke (March 2009) http://www.dpmc.gov.au/publications/information_policy/docs/information_policy_e-governance.pdf.

34   Australia. *Parliamentary Debates*, House of Representatives. Information Commissioner Bill 2009, Second Reading Speech (26 November 2009) 12970 http://parlinfo.aph.gov.au/parlInfo/genpdf/chamber/hansardr/2009-11-26/0017/hansard_frag.pdf; refer also to s 7 of the *Australian Information Commissioner Act 2010* (Cth): '**Definition of information commissioner functions** The *information commissioner functions* are as follows: (a) to report to the Minister on any matter that relates to the Commonwealth Government's policy and practice with respect to: (i) the collection, use, disclosure, management, administration or storage of, or accessibility to, information held by the Government; and (ii) the systems used, or proposed to be used, for the activities covered by subparagraph (i); ... (b) any other function conferred by this Act or another Act (or an instrument under this Act or another Act) on the Information Commissioner other than a freedom of information function or a privacy function.'

and increasing prevalence of communication and creativity in digital form. 'Works' and 'subject matter other than works' under the *Copyright Act 1968* are now generally captured in digital form.

The Australian Copyright Council, in a submission on the Government 2.0 Taskforce Issues Paper, stated:

> 6. The Terms of Reference for the Taskforce require it to report, among other matters, on issues relating to 'government information' and to 'non-sensitive public sector information'.
>
> 7. It is not in our view clear that, to the extent the Terms of Reference deal with public sector information (PSI), the Taskforce is required to report on copyright material or whether it is required to focus on data (that is, information *per se*).
>
> 8. The Issues Paper indicates that the Taskforce takes the former view. The distinction is nonetheless important.
>
> 9. As members of the Taskforce would be aware, copyright, as such, does not protect information. Rather, copyright protects the way information is expressed or described—for example, in a document, a diagram or a film. Anyone can use another person's information or ideas without infringing copyright, and anyone can produce something new based on another person's information or ideas. Copyright only comes into play if someone wishes, for example, to copy or disseminate material such as a document, photograph, diagram or film in which someone else owns copyright.
>
> 10. The issues that surround access to and re-use of information are thus fundamentally different to the issues that surround access to and re-use of copyright material.[36]

The Council made the essential point that access to, and re-use of, government information is different from the issues that surround access to and re-use of copyright material.[37]

While copyright does not protect ideas, access to government information is now commonly given in an electronic form and copyright is inherent in the form in which it is disseminated. It is quite unrealistic as a norm to expect users seeking to access information to re-express information in their own words and to re-design layout to avoid infringement of copyright of a work or the published edition copyright contained in that work. Requiring this would be a serious practical impediment to access. Downloading of information and its sharing and re-use is done quickly, conveniently and efficiently in its original form, even though its use and dissemination by users may be subject to particular licence conditions.

---

35   S Ricketson and C Creswell, *The Law of Intellectual Property: Copyright, Designs & Confidential Information* (Thomson Legal & Regulatory, 2nd edn, 2002–) (looseleaf) Vol 1 [1.30].

36   Australian Copyright Council, *Response to Government 2.0 Taskforce Issues Paper* (August 2009) 3 http://gov2.net.au/submissions/australian-copyright-council/ or http://gov2.net.au/files/2009/08/Ian-McDonald-Australian-Copyright-Council-Submission.pdf.

37   Ibid 2, 3.

The Economic Development and Infrastructure Committee (EDIC) of the Victorian Parliament stated in its report of June 2009 into improving access to Victorian PSI and data that:

> The Committee believes that open access should be the default position because:
>
> - PSI [public sector information] is publicly funded and is generated for the purpose of administering the state and undertaking core functions of governance. As a resource created on behalf of all citizens, PSI should be accessible to all citizens; and
> - economic and social benefits arising from the release of the Victorian Government PSI will likely outweigh the benefits of treating it as a commodity.[38]

To facilitate discovery of Victorian Government information, EDIC recommended the development of a data directory to allow anyone to identify what information and data exists across government. That is a fundamental starting point in providing access to government information. EDIC also recommended a consistent copyright licensing system over government information for use across all government departments, developed and administered through a central office.[39] It recommended that the Victorian Government adopt the Creative Commons licensing model as the default licensing system but accepted that a tailored suite of licences should be developed for restricted materials.[40]

In making its recommendations EDIC recognised that there were different public access considerations that may apply to some government information. It also recommended that the Victorian Government develop specific guidelines for the pricing of public sector information emphasising that basic information be priced at no cost or marginal cost.[41]

In February 2010 the Victorian Government tabled its response:

> The Victorian Government endorses the committee's overarching recommendation that the default position for the management of PSI should be open access. The Victorian Government further commits to the development of a whole-of-government Information Management Framework (IMF) whereby PSI is made available under Creative Commons licensing by default with a tailored suite of licences for restricted materials

---

38   Above n 5, 19.

39   Ibid xxvi. **Recommendation 11:** That the Victorian Government develop a consistent copyright licensing system for use across all government departments. **Recommendation 12:** That the Victorian Government establish a central office to develop a copyright licensing system, and provide advice to government on government copyright.

40   Ibid. **Recommendation 14:** That the Victorian Government adopt the Creative Commons licensing model as the default licensing system for the Information Management Framework. **Recommendation 15:** That the Victorian Government adopt a hybrid public sector information licensing model comprising Creative Commons and a tailored suite of licences for restricted materials.

41   Ibid. **Recommendation 16:** That the Victorian Government develop specific guidelines for the pricing of public sector information (PSI), emphasising the provision of PSI at no cost or marginal cost. **Recommendation 17:** That all information and data determined to form part of the Victorian Government's basic information product set, as defined by the Productivity Commission, be priced at no cost or marginal costs.

. . .

> In particular, the Victorian Government supports making PSI available at no cost or marginal cost but notes that this pricing structure may not be appropriate in all instances.[42]

The EDIC recommendations and the Victorian Government's response recognise that access is dependent on positive measures by government to identify and make available information for access.

Decisions on access to government information under prevailing FOI and archive laws, with their legally recognised exemptions, are provided in one database of publicly accessible information. Decisions by government departments and agencies leading to electronic or traditional communication of government information by those departments and agencies, are provided in another. These decisions should be communicated and coordinated across all of government. The conditions under which the public is able to re-use government information, however, require identification of the public interest in the material accessed or disseminated and the development of cost-free or marginal cost licensing to maximise the benefits to society of government information. This licensing is best done on a non-exclusive basis and through a coordinated and flexible system, which is clear and capable of simple execution and that reflects the range of different considerations that apply across the spectrum of government dissemination activity. These considerations can be more flexibly reflected in licensing policy than any amendment of the *Copyright Act 1968*. Government ownership of copyright need not inhibit access to, and re-use of, government information provided that licensing policy adequately reflects the social values in the dissemination of information in this information age.

There is a wider argument beyond the accountability, form and other principles outlined.[43] Giving access to information in the possession of government is not something for governments to fear or to commodify but has the positive benefit or public good of stimulating public interaction and engagement with government and wider intellectual activity.[44] That, in turn, promotes an informed, energised and creative society that enhances the cultural, political and social life of the nation. It also benefits government directly by enabling specific policies to be pursued with greater confidence by agencies and by enabling 'service delivery agencies to more effectively build trust with their constituencies, especially in the areas of greater sensitivity such as welfare, child support and health'.[45]

---

42   Victoria. Department of Innovation, Industry and Regional Development, *Whole of Victorian Government Response to the Final Report of the Economic Development and Infrastructure Committee's Inquiry into Improving Access to Victorian Public Sector Information and Data* (2 February 2010) 8 http://www.parliament.vic.gov.au/images/stories/committees/edic/access_to_PSI/
Response-to-the-EDIC-Inquiry-into-Improving-Access-to-Victorian-PSI-and-Data.pdf.

43   Refer also to Chapters 2 and 3.

44   For a survey of reports assessing the social and economic value of public sector information refer to Australia. Office of the Australian Information Commissioner, *Understanding the Value of Public Sector Information in Australia – Issues Paper 2* (November 2011) 16–33 http://www.oaic.gov.au/
information-policy/information-policy-engaging-with-you/previous-information-policy-consultations/
information-policy-issues-paper-2-november-2011/issues-paper-2 or http://www.oaic.gov.au/images/
documents/information-policy/engaging-with-you/previous-information-policy-consultations/
issues-paper-2/issues_paper2_understanding_value_public_sector_information_in_australia.pdf.

Beyond the political, administrative and social benefits of open content licensing outlined in this book,[46] there are within the scope of information in the possession of government, records from sources other than the government. Access to and re-use of this material cannot be legally licensed by the government without a statutory basis. To do so requires law reform.

Reforms of the law discussed in the remainder of this chapter are based on the continued subsistence of Crown ownership of copyright and seek to further facilitate access to, and the dissemination of, government information and to bring government copyright policy in line with government FOI and cultural policy. These proposed reforms seek to clarify the law to enable it to apply with greater certainty, to assist the Commonwealth and the States to better achieve policy goals involved with its roles as owner, preserver and user of copyright material and to achieve a proper balance of interests between owners and users of government copyright material. These reforms of the law should go hand in hand with licensing policy.

Reform of the Special Crown Subsistence and Ownership Provisions

At the basis of the extant prerogative right of the Crown in Australia to print and publish statutes, judgments and certain other works at federal and state levels lies a duty to disseminate certain works of state, to ensure that the publication of these works is done in a correct and authentic form and to ensure that it satisfies public demand for those works. This duty, founded on these public policy objectives, should be maintained.[47] It is important that the duty not be expressed, as it is in New Zealand, as a responsibility simply to arrange for the dissemination of these works,[48] but that there is a further positive duty to satisfy public demand for the works, including reprints of the works. Such a duty serves to promote citizens' access to this information. To the extent that the Crown fulfils this duty, Crown ownership is consistent with citizens obtaining fair and open access to this information.

The CLRC recommended that copyright in certain materials produced by the judicial, legislative and executive arms of government should be abolished. This recommendation covered materials subject to the prerogative right in the nature of copyright as well as copyright subsisting by virtue of Part VII of the *Copyright Act 1968*. The aim was to facilitate access to the materials.

---

45   Above n 33, 46 [para 9.2]: 'There is already evidence that greater accessibility to information in child support is leading to increased online communication to obtain information and transact business more quickly and efficiently'.

46   Above n 44, 33. 'While the OAIC recognises that the benefits of open PSI are often difficult to quantify in contrast to revenue generated by sale or licensing, a minimum cost approach best supports the objects of the FOI Act, which require that PSI be managed for public purposes and recognised as a national resource, by maximising reuse' (*Freedom of Information Act 1982* (Cth) s 3).

47   The Copyright Law Review Committee recommended that the Commonwealth and the States be placed under a statutory duty to disseminate their legislation and judgments: see above n 3, 138 (para 9.39).

48   *Acts and Regulations Publication Act 1989* (NZ) s 4.

The CLRC recommended that abolition of the prerogative right should only be prospective to avoid a possible federal constitutional requirement to provide 'just terms' for the acquisition of State property by the Commonwealth.

> While the Committee is not in a position to state unequivocally that the Commonwealth has the power to legislate to remove the Crown prerogative in the nature of copyright, the Committee notes that there is significant support for the argument that it may validly do so.[49]

In its report, the CLRC admitted the validity of the measure and possible need for compensation was not without doubt. If implemented, the CLRC's recommendation of prospective abolition is likely to raise difficulties in determining the legal protection of newly amended past enactments although this difficulty should recede in the longer term with the passage of new and replacement legislation. The CLRC noted the opposition of several States to the abolition of the prerogative and recommended alternatively, that if the Commonwealth Government should decide that copyright in primary legal materials should be preserved, the prerogative should be replaced by statutory provisions for the sake of clarity and that there should be a statutory waiver of copyright in such materials because of the interest in their broad public dissemination.[50] The creation of such statutory provisions is within the Commonwealth's legislative power under s 51(xviii) of the *Constitution*, and the abolition of the prerogative of the States by the Commonwealth and its replacement through the creation of these statutory rights may eliminate the constitutional requirement of compensation based on an acquisition of State property.

Nonetheless, it is clear that it is within the cooperative capacity of the Commonwealth and the State governments to enact laws abolishing their own Crown prerogative rights in the nature of copyright and to agree to their replacement by a statutory copyright provided under Commonwealth law. This cooperative approach seems more desirable and faces less risk of legal challenge.

The replacement of the prerogative by a statutory right would make clearer the nature and extent of the rights of the Crown. It would also involve identifying with greater clarity the materials subject to the prerogative right. This would match similar reforms in the United Kingdom.[51]

An alternative and more modest reform is to legislatively clarify the subject matter of the prerogative and its application of the rights to modern technology through amendment of the *Copyright Act*. Amendment should also clarify the interrelationship between copyright subsisting under the Act and the prerogative right. A good illustration of this is the protection given to Bills before Parliament and then to subsequent related enactments. These issues of uncertainty and lack of clarity are discussed in more detail in Chapter 2 of this book.

Both steps would involve cooperative Commonwealth and State agreement and action.

---

49 Above n 3, 139.

50 Ibid 140.

51 Refer to *Copyright, Designs and Patents Act 1988* (UK) s 164.

Be that as it may, continuing a copyright regime in 'works of state' does not in itself run counter to the free dissemination of those materials. Access to the law can be achieved through appropriate licensing, which can provide a means of protecting the interests of the Crown in the dissemination of the works and, in particular, ensuring works of state are published in a correct and authentic form by ensuring appropriate licensing conditions are placed on that licensing. This is entirely consistent with the legal duty placed on the Crown and its long practice in England of exercising printing and publication rights of 'works of state and religion' through the Office of King's Printer (a private publisher).

The Crown has a legal duty to disseminate the laws of the land. This legal duty on the Crown in Australia forms the basis of its proprietary right over legal materials. In addition to the law and order, democratic or other public policy reasons for the dissemination of the laws of the land, the Crown is under a duty to do so. This duty exists in perpetuity.[52] This duty is important enough to be expressed fully in statutory form regardless of what licensing practices are adopted by government to allow others to print and publish the laws of the land. However, it would be sensible and consistent with this duty on the Crown to freely licence others to do so.

The open content licensing of others should not permit government to abrogate this fundamental legal responsibility to its citizens. In the United States of America, for example, where no copyright in legal materials subsists at the federal level, private publishers of legal materials have legitimately claimed copyright in edited materials and in the published edition of these works to prevent others obtaining a free ride on their publications.[53]

Meaning of 'the Commonwealth or a State'

In Chapter 1 of this book it was stated:

> the better view in law is that the terms 'the Commonwealth' or 'the State' comprise the legal persons identified in the *Australian Constitution* 'as organisations or institutions of government in accordance with the conceptions of ordinary life', that is comprising the three elements of governance identified in the *Constitution* exercising legislative, executive and judicial power.[54]

The CLRC in its *Crown Copyright* report stated that the scope of what is meant by the Crown is somewhat uncertain and outlined arguments for both the broader view, that it encompassed the legislative, executive and judicial arms, and the narrower view that it refers only the executive arm of government. It did not express a concluded view on the question.

---

52 Another important difference between the prerogative copyright and modern statutory copyright is that prerogative copyright exists in perpetuity regardless of publication whilst the statutory regime under Part VII of the Act grants copyright only for a limited time (generally 50 years from publication).

53 JS Heller, 'Copyright Law and American Law Libraries: A 1994 Status Report' (1994) 25 (3) *The Law Librarian* 128 at 129.

54 Chapter 1, The Narrower Test: "Shield of the Crown".

It is this writer's view that the *Copyright Act 1968* should be amended to make it clear that the references to the Commonwealth or a State in the Act encompass the legislative, executive and judicial arms of those bodies politic. This amendment would remove any uncertainty about application of the Act to all three arms of these bodies politic.

Even with this reform, there remains some lack of clarity whether a statutory body constitutes an emanation of the executive government of the Commonwealth or a State for the purposes of the *Copyright Act*. As a reform measure, the CLRC recommended that the Commonwealth, States and Territories each prepare a non-exhaustive list of government bodies for the purposes of the *Copyright Act*, similar to the Crown bodies list maintained by Her Majesty's Stationery Office (HMSO) in the United Kingdom, to provide greater clarity and certainty.[55] This administrative measure is of its nature more flexible than regulatory or statutory amendment and enables greater clarity to users of copyright material, and to persons entering agreements with government in understanding the scope of the law. Being an administrative list, it can be updated quickly and easily without the need for amending legislation or new regulations. However, it does not have a binding legal status, apart from some estoppel value. It would be open to a court challenge whether a body does constitute 'the Commonwealth' or 'State' for the purposes of the *Copyright Act 1968*.

An option that has not been followed by the Commonwealth is declaring by statute or regulation whether a new body is an emanation of the Commonwealth for the purposes of the *Copyright Act 1968* or otherwise providing legislative or regulatory support to an administrative list. Representatives of the Victorian Government expressed the view before the CLRC that they did not favour giving the Commonwealth Attorney-General power to declare State government entities,[56] but a declaration based on non-exhaustive lists compiled separately by the States and the Commonwealth would provide greater clarity for persons dealing with government.

Apart from these steps, and extending beyond the CLRC's recommendations, it would seem sensible that the *Copyright Act* should clarify whether the 'shield of the Crown' test is to be applied to 'Commonwealth' or 'State' emanations of the executive and the factors to be taken into account in that determination. The *Copyright Act 1968* sets out a list of factors to be considered in determining whether a dealing constitutes a fair dealing for research or study, and there is no harm, and some assistance to users and government bodies, in providing similar guidance in dealings with Commonwealth or State bodies in copyright matters.

Ownership and Subsistence

The CLRC agreed with the Ergas Committee's recommendation that the *Copyright Act 1968* should be amended to leave the Crown in the same position as any other contracting party, expressing the view that the 'there is no justification for government to have a privileged position compared with other copyright owners'.[57] The CLRC also expressed a number of other reasons for reaching that conclusion:

---

55   Above n 3, xxix, 125–6.

56   Ibid 124.

57   Ibid 127–8.

The Committee has concluded that the special Crown subsistence and ownership provisions should be repealed for several reasons. First, the subsistence provisions are not clearly drafted and it is difficult to envisage situations where they would be relied upon today. Second, the ambit of the ownership provisions is uncertain and the committee considers there is no justification for government to have a privileged position compared with other copyright owners.[58]

It considered that the words 'direction or control' in ss 176–8 of Part VII that govern the vesting of ownership in works in the Commonwealth or a State were 'potentially far too broad'.[59] 'Ownership of copyright in works commissioned by government from independent parties should not be determined by default provisions that alter the usual copyright ownership rules'.[60] This gave government a negotiating advantage. The CLRC also heard evidence that 'many creators have been unaware that in the absence of a written contractual provision with government, they have lost copyright in their creations'.[61] Nevertheless, the CLRC thought the Crown should still be able to claim ownership under the general provisions of the Act. That is, government should rely on the copyright vesting in it by virtue of employment (s 35(6)) or the commissioning of works (s 35(5)) under the *Copyright Act* rather than the Crown's 'direction or control' test under ss 176–8.

Secondly, the CLRC thought that retention of the 'first publication' provision in s 177 of the *Copyright Act 1968,* where ownership of copyright vests in the Crown by virtue of the Crown being first to publish material, was not justified. 'The Committee can see no justification for retaining this provision, under which the author's copyright is extinguished merely by the fact of the Crown publishing his or her work first'.[62]

Thirdly, it saw no practical use, given the adherence of most countries to the international copyright conventions, for the vesting provisions (ss 176(1) and 178(1)) that provide that copyright in works, sound recordings or films made by, or under the direction or control of, the Commonwealth or a State would vest in the Commonwealth or a State where the requirements for subsistence of copyright in that material were not otherwise met.[63]

The 'direction or control' test contained in ss 176–8 is potentially broader than the employment test with which the CLRC recommended it be replaced; although there is some uncertainty, expressed in the CLRC's report, about how much broader it is.[64] In its narrower construction, it may extend beyond works produced by servants or employees of the Crown to commissioned works and works of volunteers supervised by government. But the term 'direction' may encompass a wider range of situations to circumstances where government guides, manages, instructs or orders the making of the work.[65]

---

58   Ibid xxi.

59   Ibid.

60   Ibid.

61   Ibid.

62   Ibid.

63   Ibid 66, 67.

64   Ibid 67–73, 128.

An argument against the CLRC's recommendations abolishing the 'direction or control' test contained in ss 176–8 is that simple legislative clarification of the phrase may eliminate its 'potentially far too broad'[66] scope. Further, while there may be many examples of a creator dealing with government, who is either poorly informed or has little negotiating power or both, governments deal with diverse people and bodies many of which are both informed and in respect of which government has no or little negotiating advantage, particularly in major acquisitions involving technology. The negotiating position of creators dealing with government may not be affected by removal of the 'direction or control' test.

A contrary policy that has been expressed at times by some departments of government is that, to the extent that the government funds the production of a work, it should own copyright in it. This policy has formed the basis of intellectual property clauses in standard form defence acquisition contracts that provide for Commonwealth ownership of 'foreground information' produced under the contract.[67] It has some parallels in the policy reflected in s 35(5) of the *Copyright Act* dealing with commissioned works, in which copyright vests in the commissioner and not the author of the work. From a management of rights perspective, authors, as well as government administrators, should be made more aware of the possible transfer of rights in these circumstances, and also be informed that under existing law they may negotiate an agreement to the contrary. By virtue of s 179 of the *Copyright Act 1968*, the vesting of ownership in works under ss 176–8 may be modified by agreement between the Commonwealth or a State and the author of the work.

In the 2008 *Intellectual Property Principles for Australian Government Agencies*, government policy directed federal government agencies to 'maintain a flexible approach in considering options for ownership, management and use of IP'.[68] From October 2010, in respect of information and communication technology contracts for software, agencies should also adopt a default position in favour of the ICT supplier owning the IP in the software developed under the procurement contract.[69] The IP principles also include sample contract clauses that are now a part of Australian government procurement policy.

The CLRC recommended the abolition of s 177 of the *Copyright Act*. That section provides:

> *Crown copyright in original works first published in Australia under direction of Crown*

---

65   Ibid 68. Refer also to Chapter 2, 'Part VII of the *Copyright Act 1968: Meaning of "By, or Under the Direction or Control"*'.

66   Ibid xxi.

67   Ibid 157.

68   Australia. Attorney-General's Department, *Intellectual Property Principles for Australian Government Agencies* http://www.ag.gov.au/RightsAndProtections/IntellectualProperty/Documents/StatementofIPprinciplesforAusGovagencies.pdf, and *Australian Government Intellectual Property Manual* (March 2012) 1–7 http://www.ag.gov.au/RightsAndProtections/IntellectualProperty/Documents/IntellectualPropertyManual.pdf.

69   Ibid. Refer also to Australia. Attorney-General's Department, *Model Clauses on the Ownership of Intellectual Property Rights in Developed Software for use by Commonwealth Agencies* (2010) http://www.ag.gov.au/RightsAndProtections/IntellectualProperty/Documents/Samplemodelcontractclauses.pdf.

Sect 177—Subject to this Part and to Part X, the Commonwealth or a State is the owner of the copyright in an original literary, dramatic, musical or artistic work first published in Australia if first published by, or under the direction or control of, the Commonwealth or the State, as the case may be.

The Whitford Committee considered the equivalent UK provision and noted that it was said to be 'necessary in order to safeguard the right of the Crown to publish, for example, evidence given to committees and commissions and the findings of such bodies',[70] but recommended it be abolished.

It is understandable that it may indeed be desirable to safeguard this right; but we do not see that a right arising because of publication safeguards a right to publish. Further it seems indefensible to provide such a safeguard by a provision enabling the Crown to override an independent copyright in works independently produced.[71]

The justification described by the Whitford Committee could be satisfied by a right to publish material rather than an assignment of the copyright in the work. The CLRC did not recommend such an amendment and, in the practical demands of parliamentary or government inquiries, there are administrative measures that can be implemented to ensure consent to the publication of privately owned copyright material submitted to them. There are also broad statutory rights that government can rely on to publish material given to a house of parliament or to a parliamentary committee contained in the *Parliamentary Privileges Act 1987* (Cth)[72] and equivalent state laws and in the various Parliamentary Papers Acts in the Commonwealth and the States.[73]

As noted in Chapter 2, one legal writer has maintained that s 177 only operates where publication is with the consent of the author.[74] If that is the case, s 177 would operate only

---

70   United Kingdom. *Copyright and Designs Law: Report of the Committee to Consider the Law on Copyright and Designs* (Whitford Committee) Cmnd 6732 (1977) [para 599].

71   Ibid.

72   Section 16(2)—For the purposes of the provisions of Article 9 of the Bill of Rights, 1688 as applying in relation to the Parliament, and for the purposes of this section, 'proceedings in Parliament' means all words spoken and acts done in the course of, or for the purposes of or incidental to, the transacting of the business of a House or of a committee, and, without limiting the generality of the foregoing includes: (a) the giving of evidence before a House or committee, and evidence so given; (b) the presentation or submission of a document to a House or a committee; (c) the preparation of a document for purposes of or incidental to the transacting of any such business; and (d) the formulation, making or publication of a document, including a report, by or pursuant to an order of a House or a committee and the document so formulated, made or published.

73   *Parliamentary Papers Act 1908* (Cth) ss 2–4; *Parliamentary Privileges Act 1987* (Cth) s 16(2)(d); *Defamation Act 2005* (NSW) s 28; Parliamentary Papers (Supplementary Provisions) Act 1975 (NSW) ss 4–6; *Parliament of Queensland Act 2001* (Qld), ch 3, pt 3; *Defamation Act 2005* (SA) s 26; *Defamation Act 2005* (Tas) s 28; *Constitution Act 1975* (Vic) s 73; *Parliamentary Papers Act 1891* (WA) ss 1–3A; *Legislative Assembly (Powers and Privileges) Act 1992* (NT) s 11.

74   A Monotti, 'Nature and basis of Crown Copyright in Official Publications' (1992) 9 *European Intellectual Property Review* 305–16, 314.

where the author consented to publication and in those circumstances the justification for the repeal of s 177 would be largely removed. In the Federal Court decision of *Copyright Agency Limited v State of New South Wales*, Lindgren and Emmett JJ stated in relation to the operation of s 177:[75]

> 150. In essence, the applicability of s 177 depends upon whether or not, by submitting a Relevant Plan for registration, a surveyor must be taken to have authorised the State to reproduce and communicate that Relevant Plan to the public as a registered plan. That is question 5. If the State has such a licence, there is no need to rely on s 183(1) and s 29(6) does not apply. If the State does not have such a licence, it must rely on s 183(1); otherwise, the publication by the State would be unauthorised. However, if it relies on s 183(1), what is done does not constitute publication.

While this is technically *obiter dicta* in relation to the particular decision, it had hitherto not been the generally accepted view. If s 177 is not subject to s 29(6) its effect is tantamount to an acquisition of private property.[76] At the very least, the *Copyright Act* should be clarified so that it is clear that s 177 should be read as subject to s 29(6) or be repealed. If the provision is repealed, in the interests of open access to government information a form of statutory licence should be inserted in the *Copyright Act 1968* along the lines of s 48 of the United Kingdom *Copyright, Designs and Patents Act 1988* as described in Chapter 6 and below, to enable governments to publish online or in any other form non-confidential material submitted to it 'in the course of public business'.

The CLRC also considered that ss 176(1) and 178(1) were not clear in their operation and it was difficult to envisage situations where they could be relied upon today.[77] Section 176(1) has the effect of ensuring copyright protection in works made by, or under the direction or control of, the Commonwealth or a State where the author was not a qualified person. Section 178(1) has a similar effect in relation to sound recordings and films. Thus, for example, copyright in a work made by a Nauruan author who is resident in Nauru but which is made under the direction of the Commonwealth would vest in the Commonwealth under that provision. Nauru is not a member of any of the multilateral copyright conventions and is not a country to which the Copyright (International Protection) Regulations 1969 extend. In the case of the Nauruan national, copyright in that work could still subsist under Australian law provided the work was first published in Australia or another convention country. While it is certainly true that the practical application of this provision has diminished over time as more and more countries become members of the multilateral copyright

---

75   [2007] FCAFC 80 (5 June 2007) [para 150]. This issue was not raised on appeal to the High Court.

76   It is doubtful whether s 177 would amount to an acquisition of private property and thus be invalid under s 51(xxxi) of the *Australian Constitution*. To the extent that a law passed under s 51(xviii) (copyright, patents of inventions and designs, and trade marks) or s 51(xxxix) (matters incidental to the execution of any power) of the *Australian Constitution* conferring rights on authors and other originators of copyright material is concerned with the adjustment of competing rights or obligations of other persons, that impact is unlikely to be characterised as a law with respect to the acquisition of property for the purposes of s 51. (*Nintendo Company Limited v Centronics Systems Pty Limited* (1994) 181 CLR 134, 160–1 (Mason CJ, Brennan, Deane, Toohey, Gaudron, and McHugh JJ)).

77   Above n 3, 64.

conventions, Australia's contribution to regional cooperation and development such as through the Pacific Islands Forum, some members of which are not members of these conventions, or in its other regional government cooperative roles, may justify the retention of these provisions at least in the short term. This role includes research and training and development programs and grants as well as legal and administrative assistance.

In reaching the conclusion that the current special Crown subsistence and ownership provisions in Division 1 of Part VII were undesirable, the CLRC did not think the government was undeserving of copyright protection. It simply considered that the general ownership provisions were sufficient for the government's needs. It did not recommend that government works be placed in the public domain as is the case with much of US Federal Government-produced material, although it did so recommend in relation to primary sources of the law—essentially statutory and judicial material.[78]

The CLRC agreed with the Ergas Committee that there was no justification for government to have a privileged position compared with other copyright owners. For reasons that have been discussed in Chapter 1, this conclusion cannot be justified on the principles of competitive neutrality for most of government that is encompassed within the meaning of 'the Commonwealth or a State' under Part VII of the *Copyright Act 1968*. The justification principally resides in other reasons the CLRC put forward. However, the clarification of other aspects of the Part VII, Division 1 provisions, and the abolition of s 177, could equally be resolved through amendment of that Division, rather than the repeal of Division 1. In the United Kingdom under the *Copyright, Designs and Patents Act 1988*, Crown and parliamentary copyright provisions have not been brought within the general provisions of the Act. Under Part X of that Act the 'direction or control' test of ownership continues in respect of works that are the subject of parliamentary copyright (s 165(1) of that Act)[79] with a clarification of its scope,[80] but has been reduced for works the subject of Crown copyright to an employment test (s 163(1)).[81] Similarly, the Canadian and New Zealand copyright acts have retained separate Crown copyright provisions.

---

78   Ibid 135–8.

79   Section 165(1) Where a work is made by or under the direction or control of the House of Commons or the House of Lords: (a) the work qualifies for copyright protection notwithstanding section 153(1) (ordinary requirement as to qualification for copyright protection), and (b) the House by whom, or under whose direction or control, the work is made is the first owner of any copyright in the work, and if the work is made by or under the direction or control of both Houses, the two Houses are joint first owners of copyright.

80   Section 165(4) For the purposes of this section, works made by or under the direction or control of the House of Commons or the House of Lords include: (a) any work made by an officer or employee of that House in the course of his duties, and (b) any sound recording, film or live broadcast of the proceedings of that House; but a work shall not be regarded as made by or under the direction or control of either House by reason only of its being commissioned by or on behalf of that House.

81   Section 163(1) Where a work is made by Her Majesty or by an officer or servant of the Crown in the course of his duties: (a) the work qualifies for copyright protection notwithstanding section 153(1) (ordinary requirement as to qualification for copyright protection), and (b) Her Majesty is the first owner of any copyright in the work.

The CLRC further acknowledged that s 35(6) of the *Copyright Act 1968* which the government would need to rely on for ownership of copyright may not cover all situations in which government might own copyright, for example:

> ... where the government has appointed officers (such as members of tribunals), or other situations where work is being produced for the government (such as by a committee of inquiry or by an independent party).[82]

The CLRC recommended that the provision 'should be amended to meet the legitimate needs of government'[83] and canvassed some different expressions used in UK, Irish and New Zealand legislation but did not specify a particular form of words. It stated it did not support an extension of the provision to contracts for services, as in New Zealand.

The Commonwealth and the States at present have a distinct position under Australian copyright law compared with other copyright owners by virtue of *both* Divisions 1 and 2 of Part VII of the *Copyright Act 1968*. The Crown use provisions in Division 2 of Part VII have no parallel in the general provisions of the Act dealing with companies or other copyright owners. This in itself is a legal recognition that the needs and responsibilities of government are different from other copyright owners.

It has been argued that clarification of aspects of the Part VII, Division 1 dealing with Crown copyright, and the abolition of s 177, can be resolved through amendment of Part VII, Division 1 of the *Copyright Act*, rather than its repeal. The reforms discussed above assist in identifying ownership of copyright information and in removing unjust acquisition of copyright. The proposed reforms also provide a basis of identifying bodies outside the scope of Part VII. However, the reforms do not go to the heart of calls for greater access to and dissemination of government information. In particular, the abolition of s 177 highlights the need for government to be able to exercise some rights over third-party works in the public interest, that is, in enabling greater public access to information in the possession of government. There are other statutory reforms outlined below that promote these goals and that can be implemented without denying the principle of government ownership of its own copyright information.

Reform of Access and Dissemination Laws

In Chapter 4 it was pointed out that the 2010 amendments to the *Freedom of Information Act 1982* (Cth) mandate the publication of documents to which access has been given under the Act, and expand the protection from civil actions for defamation, breach of confidence and infringement of copyright under ss 90 and 91 of that Act to include both the giving of access and publication of those documents by government under the Act. Measures under the *Freedom of Information Amendment (Reform) Act 2010* (Cth) require agencies to publish information, which includes accessed information under the *Freedom of Information Act,* to enable downloading from a website.[84] These measures will very

---

82   Australia. Copyright Law Review Committee, *Crown Copyright*, Canberra (2005) 132–133.

83   Ibid 134.

substantially facilitate access to information in the possession of government, whether copyright in that information vests in the government or in other parties that have submitted information to government, because it will enable searching online of any accessed information by any member of the public.

The most significant obligations are provided under s 11C of the *Freedom of Information Act 1982* below:

11C Publication of information in accessed documents

Scope

(1) This section applies to information if an agency or Minister gives a person access to a document under section 11A containing the information, except in the case of any of the following:

(a) personal information about any person, if it would be unreasonable to publish the information;

(b) information about the business, commercial, financial or professional affairs of any person, if it would be unreasonable to publish the information;

(c) other information of a kind determined by the Information Commissioner under subsection (2), if it would be unreasonable to publish the information;

(d) any information, if it is not reasonably practicable to publish the information under this section because of the extent of any modifications to a document (or documents) necessary to delete information mentioned in paragraphs (a) to (c).

. . .

Publication

(3) The agency, or the Minister, must publish the information to members of the public generally on a website by:

(a) making the information available for downloading from the website; or

(b) publishing on the website a link to another website, from which the information can be downloaded; or

(c) publishing on the website other details of how the information may be obtained.

. . .

The agency or minister that gives access to a document under the *Freedom of Information Act 1982* must publish the information within ten working days after access is given to the document.[85] The use of website technology in this way is a significant aid to public access to government information and particularly file or unpublished information. This reform of the *Freedom of Information Act* places access to information in the possession of government

---

84 Refer to s 11C of the *Freedom of Information Act 1982* (Cth).

85 Refer to s 11C(6) and (7).

above the interests of copyright ownership in government and other proprietors in the pursuance of the democratic values of openness and accountability of government.

Broader copyright policy in respect of access to government information should as far as practicable be consistent with this policy. To put it more simply, the right of access to government information under FOI laws should be reflected in copyright law and copyright licensing policy and facilitating access should be the default—the position adopted in the Victorian Government Response to the EDIC Inquiry into *Improving Access to Victorian Public Sector Information and Data*[86] and in the Australian Government's *Response to the Report of the Government 2.0 Taskforce*.[87] Exemptions to access may still be claimed consistent with exemptions under the *Freedom of Information Act 1982* but overwhelmingly government should promote free and open access to information in its possession.

Preservation and Access

The *Report of the Government 2.0 Taskforce* recommended:

> 6.7 Copyright policy should be amended so that works covered by Crown copyright are automatically licensed under a Creative Commons BY licence at the time at which Commonwealth records become available for public access under the *Archives Act 1983*.[88]

The Australian Government response to that report recommendation stated:

> **AGREED, WITH MODIFICATION.** The Australian Government will amend Australia's copyright policy to ensure that, at the time at which Commonwealth records become available for public access under the *Archives Act 1983*, works covered by Crown copyright are automatically licensed under an appropriate open attribution licence. The selection and use of an appropriate open attribution licence will remain the responsibility of agencies on a case-by-case basis. Agencies can use the National Government Information Licensing Framework (GILF) tool to assist them making information licensing decisions.[89]

The limitation in the recommendation and the response, is that it is restricted to 'works covered by Crown copyright'. Government archival material includes works in which copyright vests in other persons, bodies and other governments. The Creative Commons

---

86 Above n 42, 8.

87 Australia. Department of Finance and Deregulation, *Government Response to the Report of the Government 2.0 Taskforce: Engage: Getting on with Government 2.0* (May 2010) 10 http://www.finance.gov.au/publications/govresponse20report/ or http://www.finance.gov.au/publications/govresponse20report/doc/Government-Response-to-Gov-2-0-Report.pdf.

88 Australia. Department of Finance and Deregulation, Australian Government Information Management Office, *Engage: Getting on with Government 2.0: Report of the Government 2.0 Taskforce* (December 2009) Recommendation 6.7 http://gov2.net.au/report/ or http://www.finance.gov.au/publications/gov20taskforcereport/doc/Government20TaskforceReport.pdf.

89 Above n 87, 10.

licensing proposed in the recommendation must be limited to works covered by Crown copyright or the government would infringe copyright in other material contained in archival records.

However, consistent with the policy behind the 2010 amendments to the *Freedom of Information Act 1982* and the principles of transparency and accountability of government, it is submitted that by statutory requirement government archives should make available online all records that are open to public inspection, that is, material that is in the open access period and for which no exemption to access under the *Archives Act 1983* may be claimed, without infringement of copyright. The protection provided by s 57 of the *Archives Act 1983* against actions for defamation, breach of confidence and infringement of copyright through the giving of access under the Act should extend to the making available of records online.

The subsequent re-use of works covered by Crown copyright can be encouraged by the use of open attribution licences. Otherwise, subject to the recommendation dealing with the re-use of orphan works below, it should be the responsibility of the person wishing to publish or communicate accessed information to the public more widely to ensure their protection against copyright infringement, breach of confidence or defamation.

Other reforms outlined in Chapter 4 also propose statutory amendments designed to simplify the preservation and administrative work of archives and libraries, to facilitate access and research and to simplify aspects of the application of the *Copyright Act 1968* to libraries and archives. It was pointed out that simplification of the law dealing with internal copying by a library or archives should aid the preservation of, and access to, government archival material.[90]

In that chapter it was also argued that it would also be desirable to amend s 51 of the *Copyright Act*—copying of unpublished works in libraries or archives for research or study or with a view to publication—to make the period of access to unpublished works under that provision consistent with the period in which these works are open to public inspection. That period may vary under the terms of an acquisition or bequest. The period of access should not be dependent on the period of more than 50 years after the death of the author of the work (the period of copyright protection). Given the nature of the records and their age, this reform would not conflict with a normal exploitation of a work or unreasonably prejudice the legitimate interests of the copyright owner.

These reforms would not, it is suggested, be a breach of the three-step test contained in Article 13 of the TRIPS Agreement.[91]

---

90   In Chapter 4, 'Reform: *Access and Copyright Law*', it was argued that the law should be reformed to enable an archival institution to reproduce or communicate a reproduction of a work or other subject matter housed within it for its own internal purposes. This includes preservation, replacement, reference, and fixation in another medium, without limit on number. For clarity, it may simply be effected through an inclusive definition of 'internal purposes' to express the scope of the copying.

91   European Union. European Commission, *Green Paper – Copyright in the Knowledge Economy* (16 July 2008) http://ec.europa.eu/internal_market/copyright/docs/copyright-infso/20091019_532_en.pdf and United Kingdom. Intellectual Property Office, *UK Government Response to European Commission's Green Paper – Copyright in the Knowledge Economy* (December 2008) [4, 5] http://webarchive.nationalarchives.gov.uk/20140603093549/http://www.ipo.gov.uk/c-eupaper.pdf.

The *Copyright Act 1968* should also be clarified to ensure government archival institutions may rely fully on those provisions of the Act applicable to archival institutions, including s 200AB, without recourse to the government statutory licence regime, the Crown use provision (s 183) of the *Copyright Act*. Government archives should be entitled to rely on all the defences applicable under the Act to non-government archives. The public interest in the effective maintenance of government archives and in the copyright defences available to government archives is at least as compelling as that for non-government archives.

Re-use

While open content licensing can facilitate the re-use of government copyright records, in Chapter 4 it is pointed out that an impediment to the subsequent re-use of government records in which the Crown is not the copyright owner is the inability to identify or locate the copyright owner of the record. Open content licensing from the government for re-use of works covered by Crown copyright would not extend to these 'orphan' works. Re-use of third-party orphan works, such as letters, submissions and reports to government can, however, be the subject of statutory reform. Fitzgerald and Pappalardo propose that libraries and archives should be able to use s 200AB of the *Copyright Act 1968* ('the flexible exception') to enable dealings with orphan works, with the assistance of guidelines and case studies, to enable those bodies to function effectively within the digital environment.[92] Where public access has been given to orphan works held by government under the *Freedom of Information Act 1982* (Cth) or *Archives Act 1983* (Cth) it would seem appropriate to extend that statutory protection to the re-use of those orphan works to individuals. The Hargreaves Report's proposal for a Digital Copyright Exchange to bring together rights holders has been implemented by the UK Government[93] and such a body, if established in Australia, could serve as a clearinghouse for the identification of copyright owners and a facilitator of licensing and reduce the difficulty in identifying and locating the copyright owners for the wider re-use of those works and thus the need for reliance on s 200AB.

Reform of Crown Use—Promoting Interactivity and Interoperability

If the Crown can rely on special defences to infringement of copyright, which enable use of private copyright material, why should it also have wider entitlements to use private copyright material? How are these rights justified on information management principles and other policy considerations?

---

92   A Fitzgerald and K Pappalardo, *Report to the Government 2.0 Taskforce: Project 4 Copyright and Intellectual Property* (Dec 2009) 53 http://gov2.net.au/projects/index.html.

93   United Kingdom. Intellectual Property Office, *Digital Opportunity: A Review of Intellectual Property and Growth* (Hargreaves Report) (May 2011) 39 http://www.ipo.gov.uk/ipreview-finalreport.pdf or https://www.gov.uk/government/publications/
digital-opportunityreview-of-intellectual-property-and-growth. The United Kingdom government adopted the proposal through copyright licencing reform under the *Enterprise and Regulatory Reform Act 2013* (UK) c 24, s 77 (which inserts ss 116A–116D and Schedule A1 into the *Copyright Designs and Patents Act 1988* c 48) and by the provision of seed money to establish the 'Digital Copyright Hub' https://www.gov.uk/government/news/government-gives-150-000-funding-to-kick-start-copyright-hub.

In Chapter 6 it was argued that that government should be able to rely on all the special defences to infringement of copyright on which companies and other users of copyright material may rely before the Crown becomes subject to the Crown use provisions. Reform should clarify the interrelationship between the special defences to infringement and the Crown use provisions so that copyright policy is consistent and clear. In present practice, however, it was pointed out that government agreements with the Copyright Agency suggest that almost all the special defences have been eliminated from the recording scheme entered into with Copyright Agency.

The special defence provisions, augmented by s 183, reflect the peculiar status of government and the demands on it to fulfil, in the public interest, a wider variety of governing powers and functions within a modern liberal democratic society. This is reflected in the growth of most western governments, especially in the years after the Second World War.[94] No other body or institution has the breadth of activity and regulatory, financial, managerial, policy and accountability requirements as modern government.

While the origins of the Crown use provisions lie in ensuring the government's capacity to undertake acts comprised in the copyright in works and other subject matter in times of emergency and exigency, the development of Part VII Divisions 1 and 2 of the Act dealing with Crown copyright (and, in particular, the insertion of s 183A) show that the government has acceded to copyright owner demands that it record, on a sampling basis, and pay for almost all copying undertaken by government of other copyright material in the course of its work. In the writer's experience, prior to the insertion of s 183A, the Commonwealth did not generally purport to rely upon s 183 where individual copying took place. The insertion of s 183A and the practical implementation of that provision, have changed the character of the operation of the Crown use provisions—which had been hitherto mainly restricted in an *ad hoc* way to multiple copying of works and the copying of audiovisual material—and in these circumstances it is important that the capacity of government to rely on the special defences be made clear.

In its Discussion Paper of June 2013, the ALRC proposed that the Crown use provision s 183 (and its ancillary provisions) be repealed in favour of voluntary licensing arrangements. In its Final Report of November 2013, the Commission recommended retaining the statutory Crown use licence, but with recommendations designed to encourage and facilitate voluntary licensing. The Final Report also recommended the introduction of 'fair use' as a defence to infringement that applies to any particular use of copyright material and also recommended certain limited defences for government. 'That means that governments . . . will be able to rely on unremunerated exceptions, including fair use . . . to the extent that they apply'.[95] Regardless of whether a broad fair use exception as contemplated

---

94   As in most industrialised capitalist democracies, refer generally to PS Wilenski, 'Small Government and Social Equity' in Glenn Withers (ed), *Bigger or Smaller Government?: Papers from the Sixth Symposium of the Academy of Social Sciences in Australia*, Canberra, (Academy of Social Sciences in Australia 1982) 37.

95   Australia. Australian Law Reform Commission, *Copyright and the Digital Economy: Final Report* (ALRC Report 122) (November 2013) 195 http://www.alrc.gov.au/publications/copyright-report-122. While the Commission's Discussion Paper of June 2013 on this reference proposed repeal of the statutory licence in Part VII Div 2 of the *Copyright Act 1968* (Cth) in favour of voluntary licensing arrangements, in its Final Report of November 2013 the Commission recommended retaining the

by the Commission is eventually introduced into the *Copyright Act 1968*, in this writer's view, a general defence to infringement of copyright 'for the services of the Commonwealth or State' should be retained for the compelling public policy reasons expressed in this book.

As pointed out in Chapter 6, engagement with the community online and internal transfer of agency information by government in the information age will increase. Governments will reproduce and communicate more copyright information through these practices. This may test the effectiveness of relying on an implicit licence from the provider of information and the present special defences to infringement under the *Copyright Act*. The High Court decision in *Copyright Agency Limited v New South Wales*[96] and changing information and communication technology suggest a need for an express special defence permitting certain public uses of copyright material deposited or registered in accordance with statutory obligations under state or federal law, outside the operation of s 183. It should be permissible for government to integrate, enhance, mash, and disseminate copyright information to the public that incorporates deposited material in pursuance of statutory obligations or other public purposes of government and in the public interest, without remuneration to copyright owners.

In Chapter 6, the insertion of a section into the *Copyright Act 1968* similar to s 48 of the *Copyright, Designs and Patents Act 1988* (UK) was proposed.[97] The provision is expressed to apply to works communicated to the Crown 'in the course of public business' that is defined to cover 'any activity carried on by the Crown'. If a provision similar to s 48 is inserted into the *Copyright Act 1968* (Cth), a proviso should also be inserted into this special defence to exclude profit-making activities from the operation of the provision. These measures seek practical levels of assurance that the defence to infringement will not be abused and will not threaten the normal exploitation of copyright owners' material or otherwise unreasonably prejudice the legitimate interests of copyright owners. The insertion of such provision in the *Copyright Act 1968* is also justified by the recommended repeal of s 177 of the Act (ownership of copyright on first publication by the Commonwealth or State).

A narrower non-statutory alternative to the reform suggested above is to require, as a condition of the lodging documents in pursuance of a statutory obligation, an express licence to use the document for the public purposes contemplated by the government. In that case it should be incumbent on government authorities, which require the deposit or registration of plans or other material, to make clear in regulatory, statutory or documentary form the uses of the copyright material contemplated by government. No use beyond the purposes expressed would be authorised. Alternatively, as Fitzgerald has pointed out, the Crown could simply require any party lodging material for inclusion in a public registry

---

statutory licence. Australian Law Reform Commission, *Copyright and the Digital Economy: Discussion Paper* (DP79), 283–297, at 285, 289 http://www.alrc.gov.au/publications/ copyright-and-digital-economy-dp-79 and Australian Law Reform Commission, *Copyright and the Digital Economy: Final Report* (ALRC Report 122) (November 2013) 332 [8.60, 8.88, 15.14, and recommendations 8.1–8.4] http://www.alrc.gov.au/publications/copyright-report-122.

96 [2008] HCA 35.

97 The provision should be expressed in a media-neutral way so that it encompasses electronic and hard copy reproduction and communication of the work.

to provide 'an open licence which permits use of the document both by government and non-government users, such as a non-exclusive Creative Commons Attribution (CC-BY) licence'.[98]

By way of comparison, the New Zealand *Copyright Act 1994* contains a Crown use provision that is narrower in scope than the Australian provision,[99] but that Act also contains a provision (s 62) in similar terms to s 48 of the United Kingdom Act and a further unremunerated defence provision enabling copying of material open to public inspection or on an official register, whether for members of the public or otherwise.[100] The *Copyright Act 1994* (NZ) also provides for an unremunerated defence to infringement for the doing of any particular act specifically authorised by statute (unless the enactment provides otherwise).[101] This provision does not exclude any defence of statutory authority that is otherwise available under an enactment. Unremunerated defences to infringement of copyright works for the purposes of public administration are thus wider than exist under Australian law.

Where government is unable to rely on the special defences to copyright infringement outlined, as a matter of practice it is in the interests of copyright owners and government that the Crown use provision be used as a last resort, and that governments be encouraged where practical to seek licences to use copyright material, unless it would be contrary to the public interest to do so. Where voluntary or contractual licensing is not practical, reliance should be placed on the remunerated statutory licence regime contained in s 183A. The practice for many years in Australian Government defence procurements and other major contracting by that government has been to enter into negotiated licensing arrangements in relation to copyright and other intellectual property rather than rely on s 183. As mentioned earlier in this chapter, the *Intellectual Property Principles for Australian Government Agencies* direct federal government agencies to 'maintain a flexible approach in considering options for ownership, management and use of IP'.[102]

Reform of Cultural and Heritage Deposit Laws

In essence, the deposit laws are a recognition of the same values that lie behind the granting of copyright protection in works and subject matter other than works. Deposit laws are an instrument to gather a permanent record of the nation's published works and a record of all the branches of knowledge contained within those works. These intellectual outputs across the subject matter protected by the *Copyright Act 1968* are to be encouraged, valued

---

98 B Fitzgerald, A Fitzgerald et al, *Internet and E-Commerce Law, Business and Policy* (Lawbook, 2011) 431.

99 *Copyright Act 1994* (NZ) s 63.

100 *Copyright Act 1994* (NZ) s 61 (similar to s 47 of the *Copyright, Designs and Patents Act 1988* (UK)).

101 *Copyright Act 1994* (NZ) s 66.

102 Australia. Attorney-General's Department, *Intellectual Property Principles for Australian Government Agencies*, 3 http://www.ag.gov.au/RightsAndProtections/IntellectualProperty/Documents/StatementofIPprinciplesforAusGovagencies.pdf and *Australian Government Intellectual Property Manual* (March 2012) 1–7 at 4 http://www.ag.gov.au/RightsAndProtections/IntellectualProperty/Documents/IntellectualPropertyManual.pdf.

and protected and they should be preserved. As copyright laws seek, in the words of the US Constitution, to 'promote the progress of science and the useful arts'[103] the deposit laws are an important part of the preservation of national cultural life and heritage. A record of these works and access to them are for these reasons important.

While those laws in the Australian states and in the other common law countries cited are now more commonly called library deposit or legal deposit laws, Australian national deposit laws are likely to remain within the *Copyright Act 1968* for federal constitutional reasons. To that extent, as a manifestation of national copyright policy, deposit laws are consistent with the goal of 'the encouragement of learning' embodied in the first copyright statute in England—the *Statute of Anne* of 1709.[104] It is consistent with Australia's long-standing membership of the Berne Union—to which almost all developed countries are members—that the deposit laws should not be a formality or condition of obtaining copyright protection. What is important is that the laws be made current to take into account all forms of publication and dissemination.

The October 2007 *Discussion Paper on the Extension of Legal Deposit*[105] released jointly by the then Department of Broadband, Communications and the Digital Economy and the Attorney-General's Department outlined the background to its consideration of legal deposit, which is yet to lead to legislative reform:

> 11. The legal deposit scheme was considered by the then Copyright Law Review Committee (CLRC) in 1959. In its report advising the Government on the nature and scope of copyright reforms which led to the Copyright Act[106] the CLRC noted:

> '. . . that the main purpose of such a provision should be to build up a complete collection of Australian literature.'

> That report made no mention of the use to which such a collection should be put.

> 12. The CLRC again considered the legal deposit scheme in 1999 in its report Simplification of the Copyright Act 1968. There the Committee said:

> 'The Committee regards the primary purpose of the legal deposit provisions as ensuring the preservation of aspects of Australia's cultural heritage. At the same time the deposited materials must be accessible to the public whether by being displayed, or being available on site for research or study purposes.'

> This purpose is also reflected in the Guidelines for Legal Deposit Legislation, published by the United Nations Educational Scientific and Cultural Organisation (UNESCO) in 2000.

---

103   Article 1, Section 8 of the *US Constitution*.

104   8 Anne c 19.

105   Australia. Attorney-General's Department, *Discussion Paper on the Extension of Legal Deposit* (2007) http://arts.gov.au/sites/default/files/pdfs/legal_deposit_discussion_paper_2007.pdf.

106   Australia, *Report of the Committee appointed by the Attorney-General of the Commonwealth to consider what Alterations are Desirable in the Copyright Law of the Commonwealth* (Spicer Committee) (1959) 87.

13. A national record of Australia's economic, social, scientific and educational activities helps foster the creation of new intellectual output. The relationship between access to information and the development of new knowledge is acknowledged in international fora such as the UNESCO/ International Federation of Library Associations and Institutions forum. An extension of the existing legal deposit scheme to include audiovisual material and electronic publications could be expected to facilitate further innovation and creative output.

14. An extended legal deposit scheme could have the aim of building up a comprehensive collection of published Australian audiovisual and electronic material to more effectively preserve Australia's cultural heritage.

. . .

24. Most recently, the Joint Committee on Publications, in its May 2006 report on the Distribution of the Parliamentary Papers, recommended that the legal deposit provisions of the Copyright Act be extended to include electronic copies of documents.[107]

Documents published or communicated to the public by the government should continue to be deposited under the deposit provisions of *Copyright Act 1968*. For reasons advanced in Chapter 5, the deposit provisions should be widened to include electronic and audiovisual materials protected by copyright and first published or communicated to the public in Australia.

The deposit requirement for these materials can, to a substantial extent, be effected electronically. While a deposit obligation cannot be imposed as a condition of copyright protection, encouragement to observe the obligation can be achieved through the expansion of the present penal regime and through the preservation of archival quality examples of this nation's cultural output that authors, publishers, producers and later generations can access and view and help foster a new intellectual output. The cost of a best copy of the deposited material to the originators of the material is more than offset by the costs of preservation and storage borne by government. Consistent with UNESCO guidelines, it should continue to be without remuneration.[108]

As Jules Larivière has stated:

> Not only should national legal deposit schemes be maintained, but they should be expanded to include material that traditionally has been considered as 'archival' material and therefore not subject to legal deposit. Dynamic publications, such as databases, existing in one copy that is stored on a main server accessible to any authorised user should also be subject to legal deposit since they now constitute a major portion of the cultural and intellectual heritage of a country. Legal deposit should therefore include material that exists in one copy only, as long as it is publicly accessible material.

> . . .

---

107   Above n 105, 6, 8.

108   UNESCO, Jules Larivière, *Guidelines for Legal Deposit Legislation* (2000) IFLA [7.1.5] http://archive.ifla.org/VII/s1/gnl/chap7.htm.

It is absolutely necessary that all national legal deposit legislation include digital material. National legal deposit agencies have always co-operated with information producers to ensure an efficient legal deposit system, and there is no reason to believe that this would change within a new publishing environment.[109]

The precise scope of deposit laws over copyright media requires consultation with the national institutions that preserve them. Not everything published or communicated to the public has been and can be preserved. But it is important that those deposit requirements capture all government output within the scope of those laws.

It is very important for all national legal deposit agencies to get involved in the discussions, as the sole organizations able to preserve the cultural and intellectual heritage of nations and to be the guardian of the democratic right of freedom of access to information for all citizens.[110]

In March 2012, the Attorney-General's Department issued a further public consultation paper. Its focus was 'solely on a proposal for an extended scheme in the *Copyright Act* for the National Library' and was 'without prejudice to further consultation to be conducted by the Office for the Arts on legal deposit of audiovisual material to the NFSA'[111] (the National Film and Sound Archive). In essence, current mandatory deposit obligations under s 201 of the *Copyright Act 1968* would be extended to physical format electronic publications, while online electronic publications would be subject to a deposit on demand. However, the material would not include sound recordings, films or material that is primarily audiovisual.[112]

It has been argued in this book that an extension to electronic publications is long overdue. Audiovisual material should also be included within the deposit obligations under the *Copyright Act* so that all forms of cultural and intellectual heritage protected by that Act are preserved for future generations.

Excluding or Modifying the Special Defences

The proposals for reform encompass both law and licensing policy to enable greater access to, and re-use of, government information. Government licensing policy on its own cannot lawfully deal with all material in the possession of government. It will not facilitate all the administrative and access reforms discussed in this book.

Reform of the law is necessary to assist access to information in the possession of government and to protect the government in the granting of access to that copyright information, which is subject to Crown and other ownership claims.

---

109   Ibid.

110   Ibid.

111   Australia. Attorney-General's Department, *Consultation Paper: Extending Legal Deposit* (Canberra, 2012) 3 http://www.ag.gov.au/consultations/pages/ExtendingLegalDeposit.aspx.

112   Ibid 6.

Most statutory reforms outlined may be undertaken through amendment to the *Copyright Act 1968*, although some reforms foreshadowed in this chapter are more appropriately undertaken through the *Archives Act 1983*. In so far as Crown ownership is concerned, the reforms are essentially aimed at a clarification of the current law. In so far as the Crown's role as preserver of copyright material is concerned, the reforms seek to widen the notion of library material to bring the deposit requirement up to date to encompass electronic means of publishing and disseminating information. The reforms also seek to facilitate access to preserved works through simplification of internal administrative obligations on libraries and archives and to require government archives to place online unpublished accessed material. In so far as the Crown's role as user of other copyright material is concerned, the reforms proposed seek to clarify the application of the special defences to the use of copyright material within government and to insert a new special defence to enable government, in pursuance of statutory duties placed on it, to copy, remix and disseminate information deposited with it in pursuance of its statutory governance obligations.

A relevant concern for the efficacy of the law reforms proposed in this book is the present reality and prospect of acts comprised in the copyright in material being made subject to licence agreements that purport to exclude or modify the copyright special defences. In the United States, as of March 2011, the publisher HarperCollins reportedly placed a licensing limitation on its eBooks that does not allow borrowing from a library more than 26 times.[113]

Lynne Brindley, the Chief Executive of the British Library, stated in 2006:

> The World Intellectual Property Organisation, the body that frames intellectual property law internationally, is clear that limitations and exceptions such as fair dealing and library privilege are as relevant to the digital environment as they are to the . . . analogue equivalent.

Brindley added,

> However, out of thirty licensing agreements recently offered to the Library for use of digital material, twenty-eight were found to be more restrictive than the rights existing under current copyright law . . . Our concern is that, if unchecked, this trend will drastically reduce public access, thus significantly undermining the strength and vitality of our creative and educational sectors.[114]

The British Library IP Manifesto's key recommendations included:

---

113   Dahleen Glanton,'Publisher e-Lending Restrictions Spark Outrage', *The Canberra Times/Chicago Tribune* (Canberra), 14 March 2011, 13. Section 108 of the US *Copyright Act of 1976* dealing with reproduction by libraries and archives provides: f) Nothing in this section— . . . (4) in any way affects the right of fair use as provided by section 107, or any contractual obligations assumed at any time by the library or archives when it obtained a copy or phonorecord of a work in its collections. (*Copyright Act of 1976* 17USC § 108(f) (2009)).

114   United Kingdom. British Library, *IP Threatens Innovation, Research and our Digital Heritage,-* Intellectual Property: A Balance—The British Library Manifesto (Press Release, 25 September 2006) http://www.web.archive.org/web/20101020110441/http://www.bl.uk/news/2006/pressrelease20060925.html.

Licenses providing access to digital material should not undermine longstanding limitations and exceptions such as 'fair dealing'.[115]

The Copyright Law Review Committee in its report *Copyright and Contract* surveyed the terms of local and overseas online and offline licences and recommended that the *Copyright Act 1968* be amended to provide that an agreement, or the provision of an agreement, that excludes or modifies, or has the effect of excluding or modifying the operation of the listed (special) defences, has no effect.[116] This recommendation has not been adopted by the Australian Government. More recently in the United Kingdom the Hargreaves Report[117] recommended that the government should change the law to make it clear no exception to copyright can be overridden by contract.

5.39 At present it is possible for rights holders licensing rights to insist, through licensing contracts, that the exceptions established by law cannot be exercised in practice.

> 'A recent study analysed 100 contracts offered to the British Library and found numerous examples of the diversity of contracts and licences, as well as demonstrating that contracts and licences often override the exceptions and limitations allowed in copyright law. This imbalance must be addressed, as licences should never substitute for legislation on core maters [sic] such as exceptions and limitations. The licensing framework now underpins much of the content online and contracts rather than copyright dictate how content can be used. Legislation must be amended to ensure that contracts are prevented from overriding copyright exceptions.' *LACA submission (Libraries and Archives Copyright Alliance).*

5.40 Applying contracts in this way means a rights holder can rewrite the limits the law has set on the extent of the right conferred by copyright. It creates the risk that should Government decide that UK law will permit private copying or text mining, these permissions could be denied by contract. Where an institution has different contracts with a number of providers, many of the contracts overriding exceptions

---

115   Ibid.

116   Australia. Copyright Law Review Committee, *Copyright and Contract* (2002) 274 [para 7.49]. Section 47H of the *Copyright Act 1968* operates this way over certain exceptions permitting the reproduction of computer programs for technical study, back-up, security testing and error correction. This was inserted by the *Copyright Amendment (Computer Programs) Act 1999* (Cth) which implemented a recommendation of the Copyright Law Review Committee on *Computer Software Protection* (1995) [10.106].

117   Above n 93. The UK government limited its response to specific new exceptions which expressly provide 'To the extent that a term of a contract purports to prevent or restrict the making of a copy which, by virtue of this section, would not infringe copyright, that term is unenforceable'. Refer to The Copyright and Rights in Performances (Research, Education, Libraries and Archives) Regulations 2014 (UK), The Copyright (Public Administration) Regulations 2014 (UK) and The Copyright and Rights in Performances (Disability) Regulations 2014 (UK).

in different areas, it becomes very difficult to give clear guidance to users on what they are permitted. Often the result will be that, for legal certainty, the institution will restrict access to the most restrictive set of terms, significantly reducing the provisions for use established by law. Even if unused, the possibility of contractual override is harmful because it replaces clarity ('I have the right to make a private copy') with uncertainty ('I must check my licence to confirm that I have the right to make a private copy').[118]

In 2013, the ALRC also proposed a similar but more limited reform.[119] Such licence restrictions may be imposed in a variety of ways—such as through an express supply contract or through 'shrink-wrap' terms—and seek to alter the balance of interests between owners of copyright and users of copyright information established by the *Copyright Act*. While the enforceability of many of these restrictive contractual licences is the subject of some doubt as a matter of domestic law,[120] they are contrary to the public policy established by the *Copyright Act* and for this reason should not be enforceable. Governments in Australia have at times sought to impose restrictions on the use of their copyright material through such means[121] and as a matter of policy, consistent with other measures proposed in this book, it would appear sensible to adopt that recommendation of the CLRC.

The digital environment has also prompted the use of technical systems of protection by copyright owners in order to control copying and to otherwise control the use of information.

Article 11 of the WIPO Copyright Treaty, to which Australia acceded on 26 July 2007, provides:

Contracting Parties shall provide adequate legal protection and effective legal remedies against the circumvention of effective technological measures that are

---

118 Ibid 51.

119 On 30 November 2013, the Australian Law Reform Commission's Final Report on its *Copyright and the Digital Economy* reference recommended that any term of an agreement, that restricts or prevents the doing of an act, which would otherwise be permitted by specific libraries or archives exceptions, is unenforceable. The Commission did not adopt the draft recommendation in its Discussion Paper that similar limitations on contracting out should apply to its fair use exception. However it recommended that if the fair use exception is not enacted, limitations on contracting out should apply to a new fair dealing exception, Australian Law Reform Commission, *Copyright and the Digital Economy: Final Report* (ALRC Report 122) (November 2013) 454–6 [20.92–20.100] and recommendations 20–1, 20–2 http://www.alrc.gov.au/publications/copyright-report-122 cf Australia. Australian Law Reform Commission, *Copyright and the Digital Economy: Discussion Paper* (DP 79) (June 2013) 353, 372–5 http://www.alrc.gov.au/publications/copyright-and-digital-economy-dp-79.

120 Above n 116, 8, 183. Cf the United States case of *MDY Industries, LLC v Blizzard Entertainment Inc* (9th Cir 2010) WL 5141269; 97 USPQ 2nd (BNA) 1001—where users were required to agree to an end user licence agreement before installation of the software for an online role playing game and a terms of use agreement before creating an online account. These were held to be enforceable against MDY who had sold a software 'bot' that automatically plays the early levels of the game. Also *Vernor v Autodesk Inc* (9th Cir 2010): http://cdn.ca9.uscourts.gov/datastore/opinions/2010/09/10/09-35969.pdf where a 'shrink-wrap' licence of software that imposed restrictions on use was enforceable against a purchaser of the software because it was a purported licence of the software, not a sale of the product.

121 For example, Prof C Howard, 'Quoting the Law a Copyright Offence', *The Age*, 19 February 1981, 12; 'Officious Bystander', 'Secrecy in law is a contradiction', *The Bulletin*, 14 September 1982, 52.

used by authors in connection with the exercise of their rights under this Treaty or the *Berne Convention* and that restrict acts, in respect of their works, which are not authorised by the authors concerned or permitted by law.

While access control technological protection measures such as encryption, access codes and copy control measures are aimed to prevent or inhibit the infringement of copyright some measures can amount to restrictions on legitimate purchased copies that restrict or modify the special defences or limit access to a work, such as jurisdictional limitations on their use or pay for use rather than pay for copy. That is, some measures have the effect of restricting acts that are otherwise permitted by law. Provisions of the *Copyright Act 1968* and Copyright Regulations 1989 (Cth) provide some exceptions to the statutory prohibitions on circumventing such access control measures. The *Copyright Act 1968* enables the circumvention of measures for matters such as interoperability, computer security testing, online privacy, law enforcement and national security.[122] Section 116AN(9) of the Act also makes provision for other exceptions, prescribed by regulations, which must be limited to acts that 'will not infringe the copyright in a work or other subject matter'. The Copyright Regulations prescribe certain acts in Schedule 10A, including some special defences to infringement, as other exceptions.[123] The exceptions do not extend to all of the special defences, including s 40 (fair dealing for research or study), yet they expressly cover the equivalent copying to s 40 by a library and archives under s 49 of the *Copyright Act 1968*[124] and would appear to encompass the Crown use provision (s 183).[125] It would be desirable to widen the exceptions listed in the Schedule at least where there is no commercial advantage or profit[126] to strengthen the balance of interests between users and owners of copyright material.[127]

---

122   *Copyright Act 1968* (Cth) s 116AN.

123   Copyright Regulations 1969 (Cth) reg 20Z and Schedule 10A.

124   The House of Representatives Standing Committee on Legal and Constitutional Affairs in its report on Article 17.4.7 of the Australia-United States Free Trade Agreement recommended that the Government maintain the existing permitted purposes and exceptions in the *Copyright Act 1968*. Australia. Parliament of Australia, House of Representative Standing Committee on Legal and Constitutional Affairs, *Review of Technological Protection Measures Exceptions* (Feb 2006) 92 (para 4.4) http://www.aph.gov.au/binaries/house/committee/laca/protection/report/fullreport.pdf.

125   Section 116AN(7) of the Act provides an exception for anything lawfully done for the purposes of '(c) performing a statutory function, power or duty' 'by or on behalf of the Commonwealth, a State or a Territory, or an authority of those bodies', which appears to cover s 183 (the Crown use provision).

126   The notion of 'fair dealing' eschews activities that seek a commercial advantage or profit. *Copyright Act 1968* s 132APC contains offence provisions for circumventing an access control technological protection measure where persons are engaged in the conduct with the intention of obtaining a commercial advantage or profit, to which all of the same exceptions apply. The Australian Attorney-General's Department embarked on a *Review of the Technological Protection Measure Exceptions Made Under the Copyright Act 1968* in 2012 with the call for second round submissions by October 2013. Submissions have broadly sought new exceptions to the circumvention of TPMs. As of December 2014, the Department was considering the issues raised in submissions as part of the development of broader online copyright issues. http://www.ag.gov.au/consultations/pages/ReviewofTechnologicalProtectionMeasureexceptionsmadeundertheCopyrightAct1968.aspx.

Contractual and technological restrictions that seek to alter the balance of interests between owners of copyright and users of copyright information established by the *Copyright Act* can be counterproductive in that they may reduce community respect for copyright as a form of property.[128] In the writer's view, the emphasis of concerns by copyright owners against piracy and illegal exploitation of copyright material should be directed at commercial dealings with the material and not the inhibition of access to material via permitted purposes and exceptions.

Conclusion

These reforms of the copyright law are aimed at promoting access to, and the preservation of, copyright information in the possession of government, and to promote government accountability consistent with reforms to federal FOI laws.

However, law reform is not in itself adequate in responding to changes in technology and outlook in the information age. Community desire for open, transparent and accountable government, for government as the preserver of national culture and heritage and for government's ability to act in the national interest in using copyright material, are important values of a modern democracy. Those values are likely to continue although they may be realised through different technology.

Open content licensing practice implemented in a coordinated and consistent way across government is an important complement to law reform to flexibly embrace the demands for access to information and to promote the re-use of that information among the community for their wider economic, political and social benefit.

For the convenience of readers, a summary Table of Recommendations on reform is set out after the Conclusion of this book.

---

127   By way of contrast, s 226E(1) of the New Zealand *Copyright Act 1994* provides: 'Nothing in this Act prevents any person from using a TPM circumvention device to exercise a permitted act under Part 3' (acts permitted in relation to copyright works).

128   David Vaver, 'Intellectual Property: The State of the Art' (2001) 32 *Victoria University of Wellington Law Review* 1—where the author argues that 'for the intellectual property system to survive, it must gain and keep public respect'. He argues that involves 'greater coherence and persuasiveness . . . than the system presently exhibits'.

Conclusion

If this book can be reduced to a single question it is this: ought the needs and status of government be different from private sector institutions that also obtain copyright protection under the law? It has been argued in this book that government cannot be equated to a company and that it rightly has distinct roles and responsibilities that provide it with peculiar needs and status under the *Copyright Act 1968* (Cth). This has long been reflected in the law.

The book has examined the role of government as proprietor, preserver and user of copyright material under the *Copyright Act 1968* and the policy considerations that Australian law should take into account in supporting that role. The focus of this work has been on the Australian federal government that is referred to as the 'Commonwealth' in the *Copyright Act 1968*.

Taking into account the interests of government, its levels of accountability, its unique responsibilities and its diversity, it can be argued that modern government has needs and status quite distinct from private sector institutions. In the writer's view, there are clear and compelling public policy grounds for continuing the recognition of each of the three roles of government under Australian copyright law.

It is clear from the research in this book that the three roles of government have old origins. Since that time, the size and scope of government has changed significantly and the form of government has evolved into a modern liberal democracy. Openness and accountability are now key attributes of democracy. Over time the technology of communication has moved from the introduction of printing to the electronic age and the dissemination of information has moved in importance from the printing press to the omnifarious and omnipresent individual computer. The information age, in many respects, represents the democratisation of knowledge.

Government ownership of copyright is appropriate given the diverse nature of the material government produces and commissions, which in some cases is outside the normal administrative processes of government. While it is commonly argued government ownership of copyright impedes access to government information, open content attribution licensing from government as copyright owner conveniently identifies the source and ownership of information and enables a level of assuredness about the re-use of that information. In particular, material in the public domain may not be sourced and may in itself become the subject of third-party ownership claims, whether in the published edition or in the edited form of the material.[1] Further, such licensing can provide some control over the integrity of material when it is disseminated so that users receive it in its original, unaltered form and, as a consequence, can place appropriate reliance on it.[2] The exercise of government rights in copyright is important in ensuring that the public interest in accessing works of government can, as far as practical, be fully realised.

The archival functions of government are important in promoting open and accountable government and in preserving national culture and heritage. Similarly, the library deposit laws are an important part of the preservation of national cultural life and identity. These values are embodied in the *International Covenant on Civil and Political Rights* and the *International Covenant on Economic, Social and Cultural Rights*. Australia is a party to both.

The Crown use provisions in the *Copyright Act 1968* emanate from a recognition of the needs of government to use copyright material in the exercise of its fundamental responsibilities to the community it serves, such as defence, policing, essential communications and emergency relief, in ensuring the security of its citizens. Since the introduction of s 183A, the provisions have been employed more widely to meet management demands for effective research, review and consideration of material and for government agency coordination and interoperability.[3]

While these three roles of government should be preserved, in the writer's view government copyright law and practice in each of these roles has not responded expeditiously or adequately to the information age and to the desire and the ability of individuals to access information quickly and effectively. Copyright policy embodied in the law and government copyright practice should more properly reflect the collective values of Australian society.[4] Those values should properly include and reflect national governance and cultural values.

Both the law and practice of government copyright has been out of step with public sentiment for greater openness and accountability of government, which is reflected in widening FOI laws and other administrative reforms, in greater engagement with the

---

1   The dissemination of federal US legislation and case law is dominated by private suppliers who strongly assert copyright in their marked up versions of these laws.

2   Victoria. Economic Development and Infrastructure Committee, Parliament of Victoria, *Inquiry into Improving Access to Victorian Public Sector Information and Data: Public Hearings and Transcripts*, Brisbane (12 August 2008) 9 (Professor Anne Fitzgerald) http://www.parliament.vic.gov.au/archive/edic/inquiries/access_to_PSI/transcripts/EDIC_080812_A_Fitzgerald.pdf.

3   'Information interoperability' may be described as 'the ability to transfer and use information in a uniform and efficient manner across multiple organisations and information technology systems'. Australia. Department of Finance and Administration, Australian Government Information Management Office, *Australian Government Information Interoperability Framework (April 2006)* 3 http://www.finance.gov.au/files/2012/04/Information_Interoperability_Framework.pdf.

4   Refer to Susy Frankel, 'From Barbie to Renoir: Intellectual Property and Culture' (2010) 41 *Victoria University of Wellington Law Review* 1, 13 where the author argues that the right way to discuss the limits of intellectual property is to understand and to try and articulate the relationship between intellectual property and culture (that includes expressive values and free speech). This book argues for greater consistency between important social values and copyright law and policy over the three roles of government.

community and in technology that facilitates quick and easy access to, and re-use of, information worldwide.[5] This view is supported by reports here and overseas.[6]

The present age is characterised by the ability of individuals to transfer information freely, and to have quick access to knowledge that used to be difficult or impossible to find. Some estimates suggest that more than a billion people worldwide use the internet today for public and private activities and business and personal reasons.[7] At the end of December 2010, there were more than 10.4 million active internet users in Australia.[8] By December 2012, that figure had increased to almost 12.2 million and by June 2014 to 12.483 million.[9] Far greater access to information and the far greater ability to communicate, share, engage with and disseminate information is in the hands of the individual. This suggests demands for openness and accountability of government are unlikely to diminish.

Government copyright policy, like copyright law reform, should be the subject of public scrutiny and comment. Government licensing policy should cover the three arms of government and the material it covers. As far as possible, it should be consistent across each arm of government and, most importantly, consistent across the executive arms of each government—the departments and agencies that claim Crown copyright ownership. It would be most desirable for the Commonwealth and the States to agree on appropriate policy across their executives and other arms of government in relation to the legal, educational, scientific and various other material produced by them and, at least, on the form the licensing should use. As access to information is more and more internet-based, licensing of that information may be effected through symbols or legends on individual government material and through online portals. Policy should include central portals or central points of access to obtain current information and data on information available to access across government as well as links to the information and licensing terms.

---

5   As the Report of the Information Management Steering Committee on Information Management in the Commonwealth Government stated, not only is access to publicly releasable information a fundamental right of citizens in a democratic society but access to that information is of potential value to individuals, the private sector and other agencies. Australia. Office of Government Information Technology, *Management of Government Information as a National Strategic Resource: Report of the Information Management Steering Committee on Information Management in the Commonwealth Government* (August 1997) xxviii, 34, 35.

6   Refer to Chapter 3, 'International Comparisons with the Australian Law'.

7   SIFT Information Security Services, *Future of the Internet Project: Reliability of the Internet* [7] http://www.archive.dbcde.gov.au/__data/assets/pdf_file/0004/75676/FOTI-Reliability-FinalReport.pdf.

8   Australian Bureau of Statistics, *8153.0 – Internet Activity, Australia, Dec 2010* (1 April 2011) http://www.abs.gov.au/AUSSTATS/abs@.nsf/Lookup/8153.0Main+Features1Dec%202010. Refer also to Department of the Broadband, Communications and the Digital Economy, *09/10 Annual Report (28 September 2010)*, 26 that shows that 47 percent of Australians in 1999 had access to a home computer and of those 22 percent had access to the internet; however in 2007–08, 78 percent had access to a home computer and of those 92 percent were connected to the internet (that is 72 percent of all households).

9   Australian Bureau of Statistics, *8153.0 – Internet Activity, Australia, Dec 2012* (9 April 2013) http://www.abs.gov.au/AUSSTATS/abs@.nsf/Lookup/8153.0Main+Features1December%202012. *8153.0 – Internet Activity, Australia, June 2014* (7 October 2014) http://www.abs.gov.au/ausstats/abs@.nsf/mf/8153.0/.

The development of Creative Commons licences, recognised in more than 70 countries, provides commonly understood and recognised forms of licensing appropriate for most government information. The Australian federal government and three state governments, as well as government-funded institutions, have formally adopted Creative Commons licensing. Material outside the ambit of those licences, for example, for restrictive licensing for sensitive information that traditionally has used legally complex and dense forms of agreements, should also be reformed into common, plainer and electronically-accessible documents. The introduction and use of these licences and the material covered by them should be the subject of open public input and review. In that way, licensing policy may meet the challenges of technological change and changing community outlook and norms.

One danger of licensing policy is that it may be used as a means of transferring the costs of dissemination of government information to the private sector, which, in turn, may reduce government communication activity to reduce costs. Another danger is that it may leave important information to third-party interpretation. Convenient web-based access to PSI (with a consistent regime for licensing across jurisdictions) that makes clear to persons accessing that information their rights to re-use that information, and sensible caching of older information, largely answers these criticisms. Further, there is a fundamental common law duty on the Crown to disseminate works of state, such as legislation, which is the basis of its prerogative right in the nature of copyright. This duty should be preserved and observed. In the writer's view, this early 'push' model should be the basis of a wider policy towards PSI. Governments should maintain their obligations to publish in electronic and, as appropriate, hard-copy form for greater effectiveness and accountability, regardless of the activities of the private sector.

This analysis of government as owner, preserver and user of copyright material also raises questions about the extent to which these interests are distinct from the interests of other owners and users of copyright material under the Act and the extent to which the law should accommodate those interests. As advanced in Chapter 7, the range of government works attracts various copyright protection rationales.[10] The government as preserver and user of copyright material justifies some special provisions in the *Copyright Act 1968*, which reflects its particular status as a social and political institution, although many archival and library provisions apply beyond the government sphere.

This analysis also raises broader questions about copyright policy, embodied in the law, concerning the balance of interests between owners and users of copyright material and the relationship the law has to practice. Copyright treaties prescribe certain minimum standards of protection and the bounds of exceptions to the exclusive rights of copyright owners. Australian copyright law itself seeks to impose a balance between the rights of owners and users of copyright material consistent with these international copyright treaty obligations. However, the public interest in access to, and the re-use of, most government copyright material goes beyond the normative balance presently applied in the law. That public interest involves other legal considerations beyond copyright law.[11]

---

10   Most submissions to the Copyright Law Review Committee supported the retention of government copyright and the Committee itself only recommended its removal in respect of a limited range of judicial, legal and executive materials: Australia. Copyright Law Review Committee, *Crown Copyright* (2005), 35, 138.

Because the law seeks to apply policy to all material protected by copyright, it does not necessarily reflect the different access considerations in every particular material. That, in itself, does not necessarily demand a change in the law, but it does pose compelling reasons for changes in government licensing practice.

The Influence of International Developments

While this book has stressed the public benefit in encouraging access to, and re-use of, PSI and has also stressed the importance of consistency and flexibility in government policy on access to PSI, the international consideration of these questions and of the relationship between copyright and access to information is likely to continue. Thus, national experience is important in developing any international instrument and Australian policy solutions are helpful to that end.

The Organisation for Economic Co-operation and Development's (OECD) *The Seoul Declaration for the Future of the Internet Economy*,[12] included a ministerial declaration[13] on fostering creativity in the development, use and application of the internet and of making PSI and content, including scientific data, and works of cultural heritage more widely accessible in digital format. Ministers also declared that they will facilitate the convergence of digital networks, devices, applications and services, through policies that:

- Uphold the open, decentralised and dynamic nature of the Internet and the development of technical standards that enable its ongoing expansion and contribute to innovation, interoperability, participation and ease of access.[14]

Ministers also welcomed the OECD report *Shaping Policies for the Future of the Internet Economy* and commended 'its consideration by OECD member countries and non-member economies in developing their policies to support the Internet Economy'.[15] Specific policy recommendations of that report included:

- Maximising the availability of public sector information for use and re-use based upon the presumption of openness as the default rule; and
- Encouraging broad non-discriminatory competitive access and conditions for re-use of public sector information by eliminating exclusive arrangements, and

---

11   Above n 4.

12   OECD, *The Seoul Declaration for the Future of the Internet Economy,* OECD Ministerial Meeting on the Future of the Internet Economy, Seoul, South Korea 17–18 June 2008 http://www.oecd-ilibrary.org/science-and-technology/the-seoul-declaration-for-the-future-of-the-internet-economy_230445718605.

13   Adopted by the Australian Minister for Broadband, Communications and the Digital Economy, Senator Stephen Conroy—refer to Senator the Hon Stephen Conroy, Media Release 'Call for Greater Collaboration on e-Security and Cyber Safety' (19 June 2008) http://pandora.nla.gov.au/pan/80090/20130918-1430/www.minister.dbcde.gov.au/conroy/media/media_releases/2008/047.html.

14   Above n 12, 6.

15   Ibid n 12, 9.

removing unnecessary restrictions on the ways in which it can be accessed, used, re-used, combined or shared.
- Improving access to information and content in electronic form and over the Internet.

. . .

- When public sector information is not provided free of charge, pricing it transparently and consistently within and, as far as possible, across public sector organisations so as to facilitate access and re-use and ensure competition.
- When public sector information is not provided free of charge, costs charged should not exceed marginal costs of maintenance and distribution. Any higher pricing should be based on clearly expressed policy grounds.[16]

The reforms of the law and of policy suggested in this book are consistent with the OECD recommendations.

Future Directions

The recommendations of the OECD report *Shaping Policies for the Future of the Internet Economy* recognise that some PSI may not be provided free of charge. In the United Kingdom, the UK Government Licensing Framework includes licences for which a fee is charged.[17] The Queensland GILF Stage 2 report and the Victorian EDIC report recognise that open content licensing is not appropriate for some government information licensing transactions and standard templates should be developed to support those. There may be particular areas of high investment or of commissioned material released by government where the public interest in the licensing of that material will be outweighed by the interests of government in recouping a return on its investment in developing and disseminating that material. However, the basis of decisions to charge fees or withhold licensing permission should be the subject of public comment and review. For example, it may be in the public interest that non-exclusive licensing of this kind of material could be permitted within a limited time rather than embargoed for the period of the whole prospective economic life of the material.

Further, there will be privacy, security and other legitimate grounds for not releasing government information. As argued in this book, such grounds are best determined through the processes of FOI and archival laws.

---

16 OECD, Directorate for Science, Technology and Industry, *Shaping Policies for the Future of the Internet Economy* (June 2008) 21 http://www.oecd.org/internet/ieconomy/40821707.pdf.

17 United Kingdom. The National Archives *UK Government Licensing Framework* (2014) 15 (Licensing where charges apply (The Charged Licence)) http://www.nationalarchives.gov.uk/documents/information-management/uk-government-licensing-framework.pdf or http://www.nationalarchives.gov.uk/information-management/re-using-public-sector-information/licensing-for-re-use/ or http://www.nationalarchives.gov.uk/information-management/re-using-public-sector-information/licensing-for-re-use/ukglf/.

Another factor in the development of copyright policy is the need for government to develop stronger interagency collaboration and communication to better develop policy and to better deliver services as well as to improve regulatory compliance and enforcement. A management concern is to avoid what one United States senator has described as 'the stove pipe syndrome',[18] where one agency does not talk to another and one level of government does not talk to another. The *Australian Government Information Interoperability Framework* report stated that it was a key theme of Australian Government policy that agencies should work together 'to better respond to complex policy challenges and to improve the delivery of services to Australian citizens':[19]

> Agencies are increasingly required to reach across portfolio boundaries to find collaborative, networked and multi-channel approaches to delivering information and services.
>
> . . .
>
> Improving the capability of agencies to confidently manage, transfer and exchange information is critical to achieving the benefits of 'connected' government.[20]

As community interconnectivity increases so does its power to influence government. Consequently, in future, governments are likely to evolve their responsibilities in the light of community needs and pressures. 'Connected government' inevitably requires the reproduction, mashing and communication of copyright works internally.

More efficient service to, and engagement with, the community are likely to require the wider use of non-government copyright material. E-government, online health care and education, and a participative web environment for government are examples of initiatives that are likely to be enhanced through technical innovation and convergence and improved connectivity. Some solutions are proposed in this book on the law dealing with Crown use but there remains the potential of wider usage of copyright material through engagement with the community beyond the fulfilment of statutory obligations. The future of engagement and interaction with government and with access to government information lies in solutions that do not create heavy compliance burdens. Heavy compliance burdens would counteract the efficiencies that the use of ICT technology seeks to produce.

In this writer's view, the balance of interests between copyright owners and government users of copyright information lies in the recording and remuneration of multiple acts comprised in the copyright in works under the Crown use statutory licence, whether by way of multiple copies or by multiple recipients, and to eschew the recording of single instance acts, which may, in any event, fall within the special defences to infringement under

---

18 Tom Daschle, former US Senate majority leader quoted in Ben Macintyre, 'WikiLeaks Dump Alters Rules of Game Forever', *The Australian* (Sydney) (2 December 2010) 8; and by Larry Downes, 'Connect Government Stovepipes' *USATODAY* (online) (6 April 2002) http://www.usatoday.com/news/opinion/2002/06/04/ncguest1.htm.

19 Australia. Department of Finance and Administration, Australian Government Information Management Office, *Australian Government Information Interoperability Framework (April 2006)* 1 http://www.finance.gov.au/files/2012/04/Information_Interoperability_Framework.pdf.

20 Ibid.

the *Copyright Act 1968*. Excluded from this view is subject matter other than works protected under Part IV of the *Copyright Act*—other than published editions of works.

There is a continuing dynamic in the way copyright material is being accessed and re-used, which is exemplified by mashups. This integration or remix of material across media and information from multiple sources—facilitated by software interfaces—demonstrates the creativity and fluidity of the digital age. There is a danger that a stringent and strict approach to rights under copyright law might stifle new forms of creativity that may emanate from technological change. The reforms suggested in this book place a stronger recognition of the public interest in those values, which lie at the heart of the relationship between government and the community, over a stringent and strict approach to rights.[21]

The internet offers new and somewhat unpredictable possibilities with the further development and convergence of information and communications technology. Government can develop a more direct and interactive relationship with its citizens and greater responsiveness and, through example, stimulate creativity and social and economic activity by promoting access to, and re-use of, its own copyright information.

Government copyright law and practice in each of the three governmental roles recognised under the *Copyright Act 1968* has not responded adequately to the information age and to the desire and the ability of individuals to access information quickly and effectively.

The solution offered in this book is reform of the law and of public policy that is in step with access to information policy, the promotion of better communication and interaction with the community, and the enhanced preservation of government and private copyright materials for reasons of government accountability, effective administration and national culture and heritage.

---

21 On 29 June 2012, the Australian Attorney-General gave a reference to the Australian Law Reform Commission for inquiry and report into *Copyright and the Digital Economy*. The Terms of Reference required the Australian Law Reform Commission to report by 30 November 2013 on 'whether the exceptions and statutory licences in the *Copyright Act 1968*, are adequate and appropriate in the digital environment', having regard among other things to 'the importance of the digital economy and the opportunities for innovation leading to national economic and cultural development created by the emergence of new digital technologies'. Australia. Australian Law Reform Commission, *Copyright and the Digital Economy: Final Report* (ALRC Report 122) (November 2013) 7 http://www.alrc.gov.au/publications/copyright-report-122.

Table of Recommendations

Heading of provision	*Copyright Act 1968* (Cth) in force (30 June 2014)	Proposed
Crown copyright ownership in original works and recordings and films made under direction of Crown	s 176(1), s 178(1)	Ambit of 'Commonwealth or State' and 'made by or under the direction of' should be clarified.
Crown copyright in original works first published in Australia under direction of Crown	s 177 ambiguous: operates in one way tantamount to an acquisition of property	Repeal. Replace by equivalent of s 48 of the *Copyright, Designs and Patents Act 1988* (UK). Exclude profit-making activities from the scope of the new provision.
Copyright in statutory instruments and judgments	s 8A, s 182A	Clarify scope of the prerogative right in the nature of copyright, or replace by statutory right. The duty on the Crown to disseminate the laws of the land should be expressed in statutory form.
Use of copyright material for the Crown	s 183	Clarify so that the special defences, e.g. fair dealing for research or study, and s 200AB, can be relied upon by Crown servants during the course of their duties if they do an act for the purposes described. The Crown use provision only applies outside of the operation of the special defences. A provision similar to s 48 of *Copyright, Designs and Patents Act 1988* (UK) to be inserted. Exclude profit-making activities from the scope of the new provision.
Legal deposit	s 201	Expand to cover all media protected by the *Copyright Act 1968* (Cth) and not just the material presently listed within the definition of 'library material' to give greater effect to the policy behind the law.
Reproducing or communicating works for preservation and other purposes	s 51A, s 51AA, s 51B, s 110B, s 110BA	Repeal. Replace by rights to reproduce or communicate for its own 'internal purposes' works housed within it. No limit on number. Internal purposes to be defined inclusively.
Publication of unpublished works	s 51, s 52, s 200AB	Section 51 to be amended to make the period of access to unpublished works under that provision consistent with the period in which these works are open to public inspection. Government to provide open content licence to enable re-use of government copyright works released under the *Freedom of Information Act 1982* (Cth) or under the *Archives Act 1983* (Cth). Amend s 51, s 52 and s 200AB to enable re-use of orphan works contained in the material above where public access under of the *Freedom of Information Act 1982* or *Archives Act 1983* has been given. Section 57 of the *Archives Act 1983* be extended to enable Archives to communicate/publish records online similar to the protection of s 90 and s 91 of the *Freedom of Information Act 1982*.

Heading of provision	*Copyright Act 1968* (Cth) in force (30 June 2014)	Proposed
Exclusions (contractual)		A new provision should be inserted in the *Copyright Act 1968* which renders contractual attempts to limit the application of the special defences under the *Copyright Act 1968* as contrary to public policy and void.
Exclusions (technological)		It would be desirable to widen the special defence exceptions listed in Schedule 10A of the Copyright Regulations 1969 (Cth), at least where there is no commercial advantage or profit, to strengthen the balance of interests between users and owners of copyright material.

Glossary

Access describes being able to find and retrieve information in a way that would otherwise often amount to an infringement of copyright; for example, by reproducing or copying material containing information. Where retrieved information is used to reproduce and build upon it, to use it, for example, for economic gain and for a range of public goods, this is referred to as re-use of information. The two steps are sometimes referred to as rights to access and re-use information. A 2008 OECD recommendation used the term 'better access and wider use and re-use'[1] of PSI. The term 'open content' is also used to describe information that is subject to these two rights. The meaning of 'access' is further described in Chapter 3.

Copyright material means material protected under the Australian *Copyright Act 1968* (Cth), comprising literary, dramatic, musical and artistic works, (collectively referred to as 'works' in the *Copyright Act*) sound recordings, cinematograph films, television and sound broadcasts and published editions of works (collectively referred to as 'subject matter other than works' in the *Copyright Act*).

Crown copyright refers to government copyright in each of its three arms (refer to '**government**'). Part VII of the *Copyright Act 1968*, which is headed 'the Crown', refers to the 'Commonwealth' and 'State', that is, all three arms of government of the Commonwealth and each State. This is further discussed in Chapter 1.

Crown in right of the Commonwealth or 'Crown in right of the State' refers to rights held by the Crown as sovereign in each of those capacities and exercisable by the Crown on advice by the respective executive government. This is further discussed in Chapter 1.

---

1 OECD. *Recommendation of the Council for Enhanced Access and More Effective Use of Public Sector Information,* OECD Ministerial Meeting on the Future of the Internet
Economy, Seoul, South Korea 17–18 Jun 2008 http://www.oecd.org/sti/44384673.pdf;
http://www.oecd.org/sti/oecdrecommendationonpublicsectorinformationpsi.htm. This includes use by the original public sector generator or holder or other public sector bodies and further re-use by business or individuals for commercial or non-commercial purposes. In general, the term 'use' implies this broad spectrum of use and re-use.

Government principally refers to 'the executive government', which is embodied within the terms 'Commonwealth' and 'State' under Part VII of the *Copyright Act 1968* (Cth). The terms 'Commonwealth' and 'State' in Part VII of the *Copyright Act 1968* each refer to all three arms of government—executive, legislative and judicial—but references to one of those arms of government are specifically identified as such.

Prerogative right of the Crown in the nature of copyright or 'prerogative copyright' refers to one of the proprietary rights of the Crown in right of the Commonwealth or several States that are residuary monarchical rights after the growth of responsible government and exercisable on advice by the executive government. The prerogative right of the Crown in the nature of copyright is preserved by s 8A of the *Copyright Act 1968* (Cth). It is described in more detail in Chapter 2.

Legal deposit sometimes referred to as 'library deposit' or 'copyright deposit' means the legal requirement on publishers or disseminators of copyright material to deposit a copy of that material with a library or other body nominated by government.

Public domain means not subject to copyright protection.[2]

Public sector information (PSI) means data, information or content that is generated, created, collected, processed, preserved, maintained, disseminated or funded by (or for) the government or public institutions.[3] The OECD similarly defines PSI as 'information, including information products and services, generated, created, collected, processed, preserved, maintained, disseminated, or funded by or for the government or public institution.'[4]

---

2   This is its traditional meaning. Rufus Pollock uses the term 'Open Data Commons Public Domain' to describe database material in which copyright and moral rights exist but are waived under an open content licence: refer to Online Home of Rufus Pollock, *Open Data Commons Public Domain Dedication and Licence* (PDDL) (15 March 2008) http://opendatacommons.org/licenses/pddl/.

3   Australia. Office of the Australian Information Commissioner, *Open Public Sector Information: from principles to practice – Report on agency implementation of the Principles of open public sector information* (February 2013) 61 http://www.oaic.gov.au/images/documents/migrated/oaic/repository/publications/reports/Open_public_sector_information_from_principles_to_practice_February2013.pdf.

4   OECD. *Recommendation of the Council for Enhanced Access and More Effective Use of Public Sector Information* (30 April 2008) 4 http://www.oecd.org/internet/ieconomy/40826024.pdf.

Appendix: Manuscript Privileges

Plate 1. Grant of the Office of King's Printer in Latin, Greek and Hebrew to Bonham Norton by King James 1 (1612/13). Courtesy The National Archives, United Kingdom. *Patent Rolls: James I*, c66/1966/6 (1612/13).

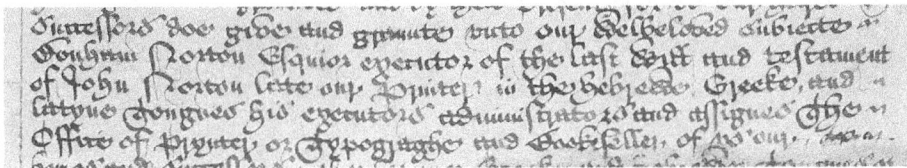

'successors doe give and grante unto our welbeloved subecte Bonham Norton Esquire executor of the last will and testament of John Norton late our Printer in the Hebrew, Greek and latyne tongues his executors administrators and assignes The Office of Printer or Typographer and Bookeseller . . . '

The full grant is shown on the next three pages.

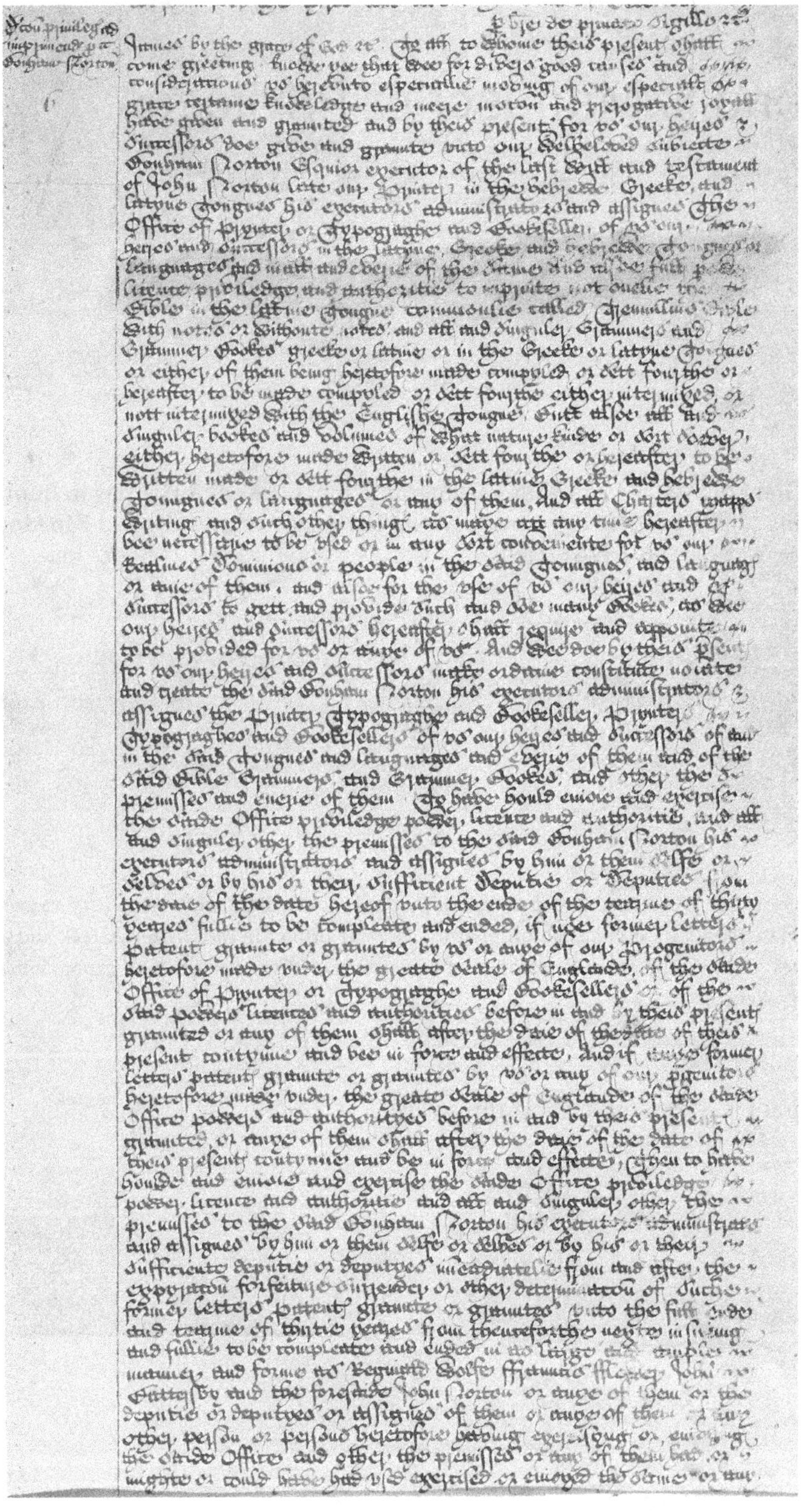

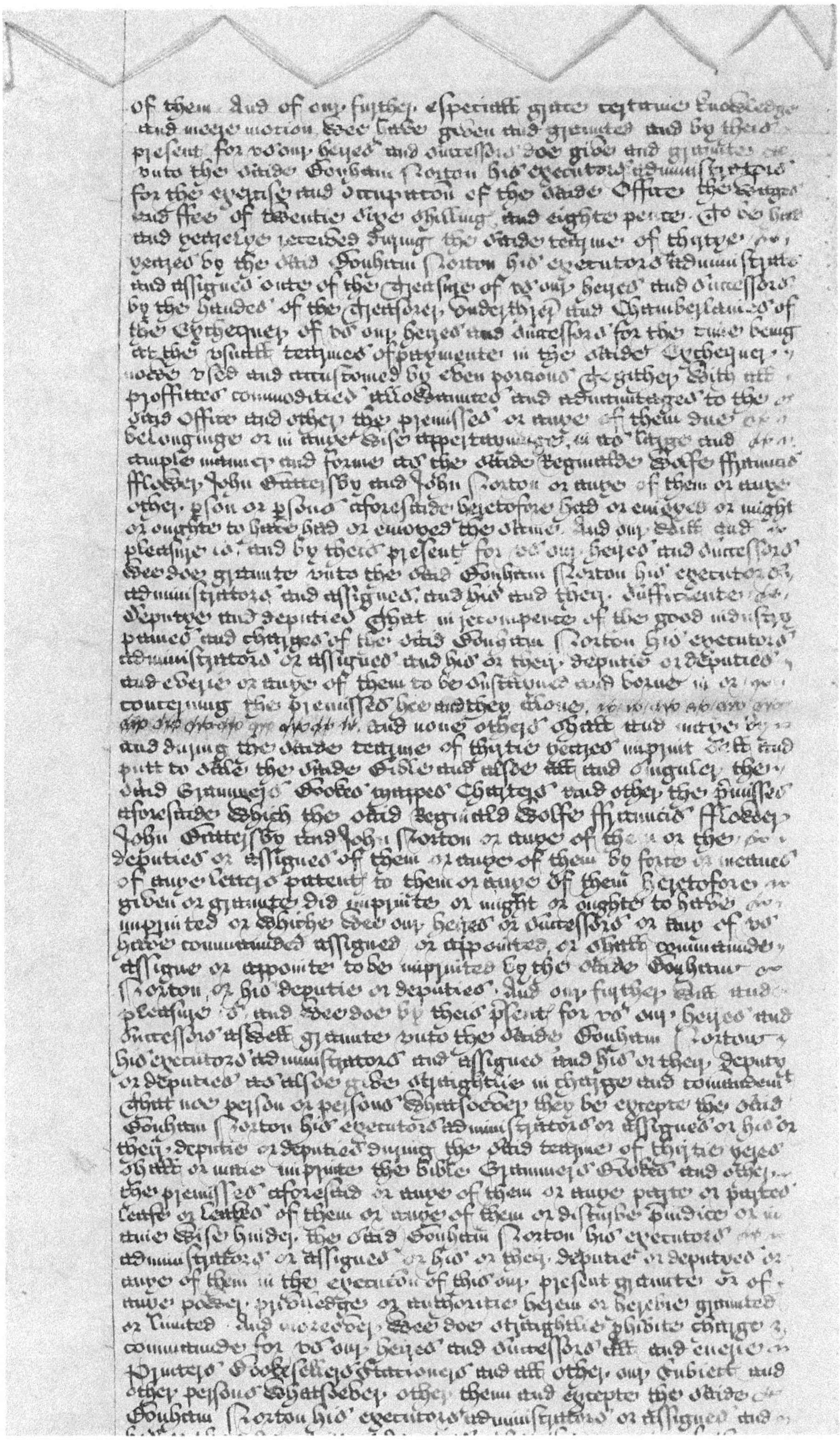

of them and of our further especiall grace certaine knowledge
and mere motion wee have given and graunted and by theis
present[es] for us our heires and successors doe give and graunte
unto the saide William Norton his executours administrators
for the exercise and occupation of the saide Office the wages
and ffees of twentie sixe shillinges and eighte pence To be had
and yerelye receaved during the saide terme of thirtye
yeares by the said William Norton his executors administrators
and assignes oute of the Threasure of us our heires and successors
by the handes of the Threasorer, Underthreasorer and Chamberleines of
the Exchequer of us our heires and successors for the time being
at the usuall termes of paymente in the saide Exchequer
nowe used and accustomed by even portions together with all
proffittes commodities allowaunces and advauntages to the
saide Office and other the premisses or anye of them due
belonginge or in anye wise appertayninge, in as large and
ample manner and forme as the saide Reginalde Wolfe Thomas
fflower John Battersby and John Norton or anye of them or anye
other p[er]son or p[er]sons aforesaide heretofore had or enjoyed or might
or oughte to have had or enjoyed the same. And our will and
pleasure is, and by theis present[es] for us our heires and successors
wee doe graunte unto the said William Norton his executors
administrators and assignes, and his and their sufficiente
deputye and deputies that in recompence of the good industry
paines and charges of the said William Norton his executors
administrators or assignes and his or their deputie or deputies
and everie or anye of them to be sustayned and borne in or
concerning the premisses hee and they alone, [illegible]
[illegible] and none other shall and maye by
and during the saide terme of thirtie yeares imprint sell and
putt to sale the saide Bible and also all and singuler the
said Grammer Bookes [illegible] Chartes and other the premisses
aforesaide which the saide Reginalde Wolfe Thomas fflower
John Battersby and John Norton or anye of them or the
deputies or assignes of them or anye of them by force or vertue
of anye letters pattente to them or anye of them heretofore
given or graunted did imprinte or might or oughte to have
imprinted or which wee our heires or successors or any of us
have commaunded assigned or appointed, or shall commaunde
assigne or appointe to be imprinted by the saide William
Norton, or his deputie or deputies. And our further will and
pleasure is, and wee doe by theis p[re]sent[es] for us our heires and
successors aswell graunte unto the saide William Norton
his executors administrators and assignes and his or their deputy
or deputies as also give streightlie in charge and commaundement
that noe person or persons whatsoever they be excepte the said
William Norton his executors administrators or assignes or his or
their deputie or deputies during the said terme of thirtie yeres
shall or maie imprinte the Bible Grammer Bookes and other
the premisses aforesaid or anye of them or anye parte or partes
leafe or leaves of them or anye of them or disturbe p[re]judice or in
anie wise hinder the said William Norton his executors
administrators or assignes or his or their deputie or deputies or
anye of them in the execucion of this our present graunte or of
anye power priviledge or authoritie herein or hereby graunted
or limited. And moreover wee doe streightlie p[ro]hibite charge and
commaunde for us our heires and successors all and everie
Printers Bookesellers Stationers and all other our Subiectes and
other persons whatsoever other then and excepte the saide
William Norton his executors administrators or assignes and

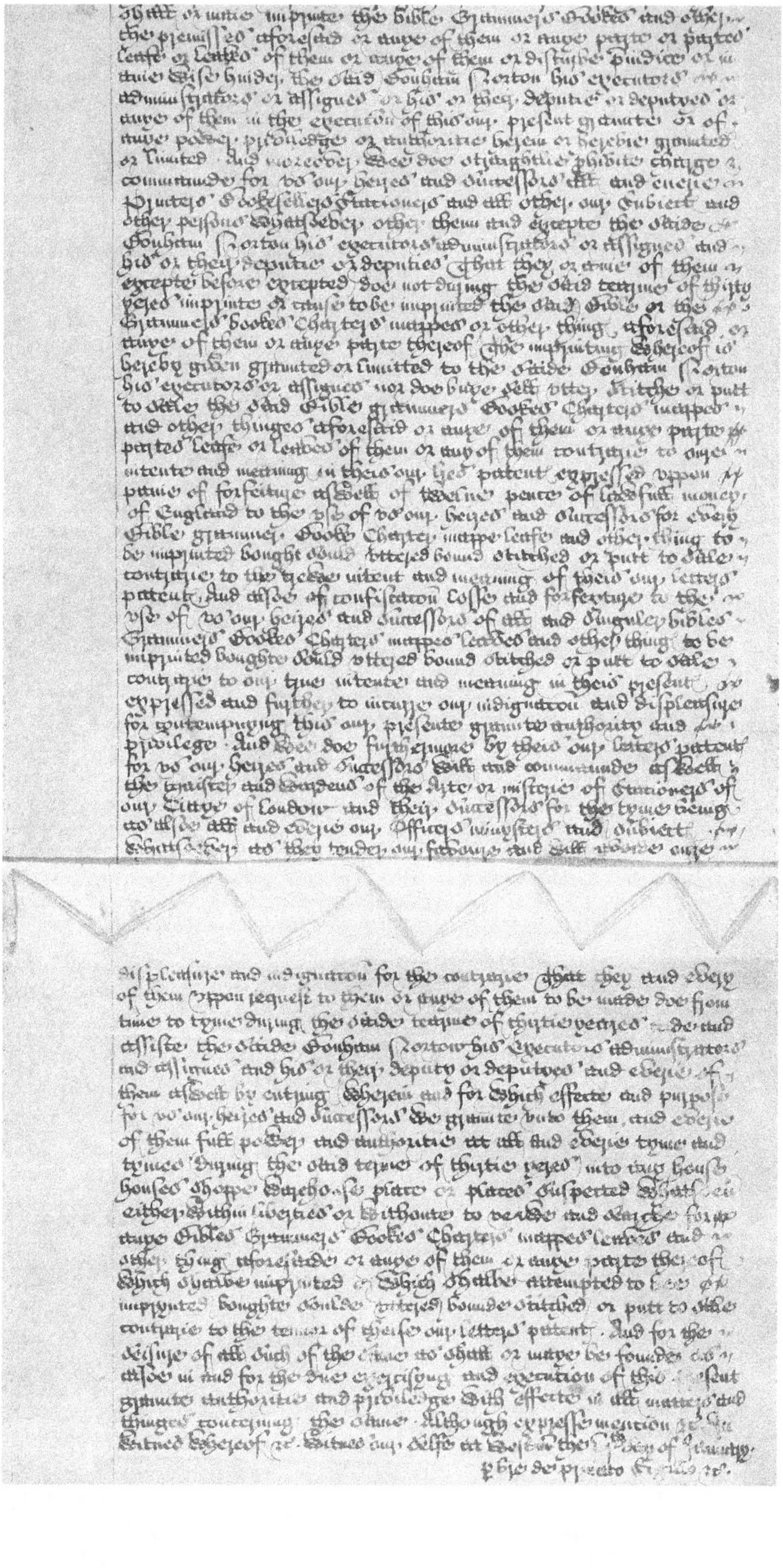

shall or maie imprinte the Bible, Grammers, Bookes and other
the premisses aforesaid or anye of them or anye parte or parted
leafe or leaves of them or anye of them or distribute divide or in
anie wise hinder the said Boughan Norton his executors
administrators or assignes or his or their deputie or deputyes or
anye of them in the execution of this our present graunte or of
anye power priviledge or authoritie herein or herebie graunted
or limited. And moreover wee doe straightlie prohibite chardge &
commaunde for us our heires and successors all and everie
Printers Bookesellers Stationers and all other our subiects and
other persons whatsoever other than and excepte the saide
Boughan Norton his executors administrators or assignes and
his or their deputie or deputies that they or anie of them
excepte before excepted doe not during the said terme of thirty
yeres imprinte or cause to be imprinted the said Bible or the
Grammers Bookes Charters mappes or other thing aforesaid or
anye of them or anye parte thereof the imprinting whereof is
hereby given graunted or limited to the saide Boughan Norton
his executors or assignes nor doe buye sell utter stitche or putt
to sale the said Bible grammers Bookes Charters mappes
and other thinges aforesaid or anye of them or anye parte
parted leafe or leaves of them or any of them contrarie to our
intente and meaning in theis our lres patent expressed uppon
paine of forfeiture aswell of twelve pence of lawfull money
of England to the use of us our heires and successors for every
Bible grammer Booke Charter mappe leafe and other thing to
be imprinted bought solde uttered bound stitched or putt to sale
contrarie to the true intent and meaning of theis our letters
patent, And alsoe of confiscation losse and forfeiture to the
use of us our heires and successors of all and singuler bibles
Grammers Bookes Charters mappes leaves and other thing to be
imprinted boughte solde uttered bound stitched or putt to sale
contrarie to our true intente and meaning in theis present
expressed and further to incurre our indignation and displeasure
for contemptinge this our presente graunte authority and
priviledge And wee doe further give by theis our letters patent
for us our heires and successors will and commaunde aswell
the Maister and Wardens of the Arte or misterie of Stationers of
our Cittye of London and their successors for the tyme being
as alsoe all and everie our Officers ministers and subiects
whatsoever as they tender our favoure and will avoide our
displeasure and indignation for the contrarie that they and every
of them uppon request to them or anye of them to be made doe from
time to tyme during the saide terme of thirtie yeares ayde and
assiste the saide Boughan Norton his executors administrators
and assignes and his or their deputy or deputyes and everie of
them aswell by entring wherein and for which effecte and purpose
for us our heires and successors wee graunte unto them and everie
of them full power and authoritie at all and everie tyme and
tymes during the said terme of thirtie yeres into anye house
houses shoppe warehouse place or places suspected whatsoever
either within liberties or withoute to searche and enquire for
anye Bibles Grammers Bookes Charters mappes leaves and
other thing aforesaide or anye of them or anye parte thereof
which shalbe imprinted or which shalbe attempted to bee
imprynted boughte solde uttered bounde stitched or putt to sale
contrarie to the tenor of theise our letters patent. And for the
seisure of all such of the same as shall or maye be founde as
alsoe in and for the due exercising and execution of this present
graunte authoritie and priviledge with effecte in all matters and
thinges touching the same. Although expresse mention [illegible]
[illegible] whereof &c. Witnes our selfe at Westm the [illegible] day of [illegible]

p bre de privato sigillo &c.

Plate 2. Grant of the Office of King's Printer to John Reeves, George Eyre and Andrew Strahan in reversion by King George III (1799). Courtesy The National Archives, United Kingdom. *Patent Rolls: George III*, c66/3961/13 (1799).

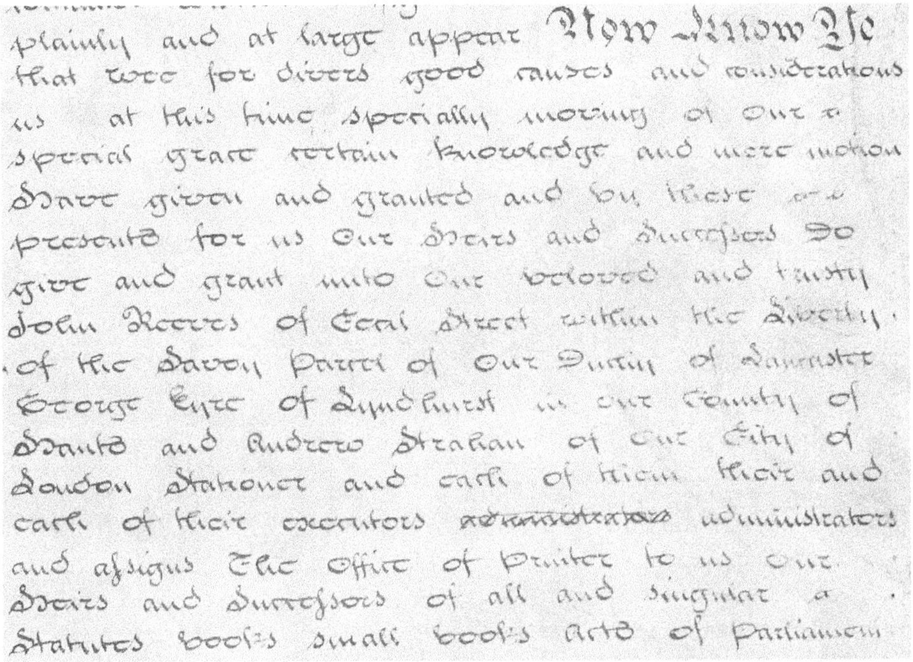
plainly and at large appear Now Know Ye
that wee for divers good causes and considerations
us at this time specially moving of Our
special grace certain knowledge and mere motion
Have given and granted and by these
presents for us Our Heirs and Successors Do
give and grant unto Our beloved and trusty
John Reeves of Cecil Street within the Liberty
of the Savoy Parcel of Our Duchy of Lancaster
George Eyre of Lyndhurst in our County of
Hants and Andrew Strahan of Our City of
London Stationer and each of them their and
each of their executors administrators
and assigns The Office of Printer to us Our
Heirs and Successors of all and singular
Statutes books small books Acts of Parliament

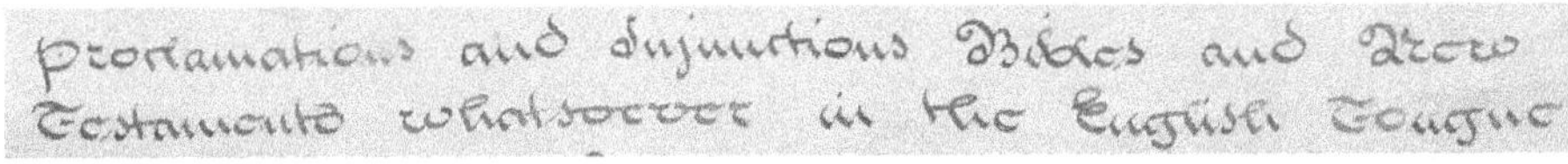
Proclamations and Injunctions Bibles and New
Testaments whatsoever in the English Tongue

'. . . Now Know Ye, that we for divers good causes and considerations us at this time specially moving of our special grace certain knowledge and mere motion, Have given and granted and by these presents for us our Heirs and Successors Do give and grant unto our beloved and trusty John Reeves of Cecil Street within the Liberty of the Savoy Parcel of the Duchy of Lancaster George Eyre of Lyndhurst in our County of Hants and Andrew Strahan of our City of London Stationer and each of them their and each of their executors administrators and assigns The Office of Printer to us our Heirs and Successors of all and singular Statutes books small books Acts of Parliament Proclamations and Injunctions Bibles and New Testaments whatsoever in the English Tongue . . .'

The full grant is shown on the next seven pages.

John Reeves and others
Kings Printer in Reversion

(13)

George the Third by the Grace of God of Great Britain France and Ireland King Defender of the Faith &c To all To whom these Presents shall come Greeting Whereas our Royal Ancestor George the first late King of Great Britain &c by his Letters Patent made under the Great Seal of Great Britain bearing Date at Westminster the thirteenth Day of December in the second Year of his Reign for himself his Heirs and Successors Did give and grant to his beloved and trusty John Baskett of his City of London Bookseller his executors and assigns The Office of Printer to the said late King his Heirs and Successors of all and singular Statutes Books Small Books Acts of Parliament Proclamations and Injunctions and Bibles and New Testaments whatsoever in the English Tongue or in any other Tongue whatsoever of any translation with notes or without notes And also of all Books of Common Prayer and the Administration of the Sacraments and other Rites and Ceremonies of the Church of England in any Volumes whatsoever theretofore printed by the Royal Typographers for the time being or thereafter to be printed by the Command or Privilege or Authority of him his Heirs or Successors and also of all other Books whatsoever which he had commanded or should command or his Heirs or Successors should command to be used for the service of God in the Churches of that part of his Realm of Great Britain called England And of all other Books Volumes and Things whatsoever by whatsoever name term title or meaning or by whatsoever names terms titles or meanings then were named called or distinguished or any of them was named called or distinguished or thereafter should be named called or distinguished theretofore printed by the Royal Typographers for the time

being or then already by the Parliament of Great Britain in the English Tongue or any other mixed tongue published printed or worked off or thereafter to be published worked off or put to the press by the Command Privilege or Authority of him his Heirs or Successors (except only the rudiments of the grammatical institutions of the Latin Tongue To have enjoy occupy and exercise the said Office together with all Profits Commodities and Advantages Preeminences and Privileges to the same Office in any wise belonging or appertaining to the said John Baskett his executors and assigns by him or

belonging or appertaining to the said John
Baskett his executors and assigns by him or
his executors or by his or their sufficient Deputy
or Deputies for the term of Thirty Years to
commence and be computed from and immediately
after the expiration or other determination of the
several and respective estates and interests in
the said Office before that time granted by
Our Royal Predecessor Ann Queen of Great
Britain by her Letters Patent made under her
Seal of Great Britain bearing Date at Westminster
the Thirteenth Day of October in the twelfth year
of her reign to her beloved subjects Benjamin
Tooke and John Barber of her City of London
Booksellers and each of them their and each
of their Executors and Assigns To have enjoy
exercise and occupy the said Office to the said
Benjamin Tooke and John Barber for the term
of thirty Years to commence and be computed
from and immediately after the expiration or
other sooner determination of the several and
respective Estates and interests before that time
granted by Our late Royal Predecessor Charles
the Second late King of England Scotland France
and Ireland by his Letters Patent made under
his Great Seal of England bearing date at
Westminster the twenty fourth Day of December
in the twenty seventh year of his Reign to
his beloved subjects Thomas Newcomb and Henry
Hills To have enjoy exercise and occupy the
said Office to the said Thomas Newcomb and
Henry Hills for the term of thirty Years
which last mentioned term of thirty years began
at and from the tenth Day of January One
thousand seven hundred and nine as by the
said Letters Patent made to the said John
Baskett amongst other things in the same
contained relation being thereunto had will more
plainly and at large appear Now Know Ye
that wee for divers good causes and considerations
us at this time specially moving of our
special grace certain knowledge and mere motion
Have given and granted and by these
presents for us Our Heirs and Successors Do
give and grant unto Our beloved and trusty
John Reeves of Cecil Street within the Liberty
of the Savoy Parcel of Our Duchy of Lancaster
George Eyre of Lyndhurst in our County of
Hants and Andrew Strahan of Our City of
London Stationer and each of them their and
each of their executors administrators administrators
and assigns The Office of Printer to us Our
Heirs and Successors of all and singular
Statutes books small books Acts of Parliament

Proclamations and Injunctions Bibles and New
Testaments whatsoever in the English Tongue
or in any other Tongue whatsoever of any
translation with notes or without notes And also
of all books of Common Prayer and Administration
of the Sacraments and other rites and ceremonies
of the Church of England in any volumes
whatsoever heretofore printed by the Royal
Typographers for the time being or hereafter
to be printed by the Command Privilege or
Authority of us Our Heirs or Successors But
also of all other Books whatsoever which
we have commanded or hereafter shall
command or Our Heirs or Successors shall
command to be used for the service of God
in the Churches of that part of our Realm
of Great Britain called England And of all
other books volumes and things whatsoever by
whatsoever name term title or meaning or by
whatsoever names terms titles or meanings they
are named called or distinguished or any of
them is named called or distinguished or
hereafter shall be named called or distinguished
heretofore printed by the Royal Typographers
for the time being or by the Parliament of
Great Britain in the English Tongue or in any
other mixed Tongue already published printed or
worked off or hereafter to be published worked
off or put to the press by the Command Privilege
or Authority of us Our Heirs or Successors
(except only the rudiments of the grammatical
institutions of the Latin Tongue And them the
said John Reeves George Eyre and Andrew
Strahan and their executors and assigns Printer to
us our Heirs and Successors of all and singular
the premises we make ordain and constitute by
these presents To have enjoy occupy and
exercise the said Office Together with all profits
commodities and advantages preeminences and
privileges to the said Office in any wise
belonging or appertaining To the said John
Reeves George Eyre and Andrew Strahan their
executors and assigns by themselves or by
their sufficient Deputy or Deputies for and
during the term of thirty years to commence
and be computed from and immediately after
the expiration or other ~~sooner~~ determination
of the estate and interest in the said Office
before granted to the said John Baskett his
executors and assigns or when or as soon as
the said Office shall be vacant and shall
happen by any means whatsoever to be in
Our hands in the same manner as if such
grant had not been made And further we

Our hands in the same manner as if such a
grant had not been made And further we
of our more abundant grace certain knowledge
and mere motion Do give and grant to the
said John Reeves George Eyre and Andrew
Strahan and each of them their and each of
their Executors administrators and assigns during
the same term of thirty years last above
mentioned Authority Privilege and faculty of
printing all and all manner of abridgments of
all statutes and Acts of Parliament whatsoever
published or hereafter to be published and in
order that no one do presume to impede or
in any wise disturb the said John Reeves

George Eyre and Andrew Strahan or either of
them their or either of their executors administrators
or assigns during the aforesaid term to them granted
in the said Office in rightfully and duly exercising
their said Office or to do any thing whatsoever
whereby the profits which may accrue to the said
John Reeves George Eyre and Andrew Strahan or
any of them their or either of their executors
administrators or assigns by reason of the said
Office may be diminished we prohibit and
enjoin and by these presents for us our heirs
and successors forbid all and singular the subjects
of us our heirs and successors whatsoever and
wheresoever abiding and all others whatsoever
that neither they nor any of them neither by
themselves or by any other or others during
the said last mentioned term of thirty years
print or cause to be printed within that part
of Our Realm of Great Britain called England
any volume book or work or any volumes or
books or works the printing of which we
by these presents have granted to the
said John Reeves George Eyre and Andrew Strahan
their executors and assigns nor any Bibles or
New Testaments in the English Tongue of any
translation with notes or without notes nor
any books of Common Prayer and Administration
of the Sacraments and other rites and ceremonies
of the Church of England nor any other books
by us our heirs or successors for the every
service of God in the Churches of us our
heirs or successors commanded or to be
commanded to be used nor import or cause
to be imported sell or cause to be sold
any books volumes or works whatsoever in
the English Tongue or in the English mixed
with any other Tongue whatsoever printed in
parts beyond the seas or in foreign parts out
of that part of Our Realm of Great Britain

of that part of Our Realm of Great Britain
called England being such as have been or
may be lawfully printed by the said John
Reeves George Eyre and Andrew Strahan or
either of them their or either of their or
Administrators Executors or assigns or their or
either of their Deputy or Deputys by virtue
of their presents under the penalties and
forfeitures by the Laws and Statutes of this
Realm in that behalf made and provided or
that may be hereafter provided forbidding also
and by these presents for us Our Heirs and
Successors really prohibiting and enjoining that
no other shall in any manner or by any
color or pretext whatsoever presume or dare
to reprint in any manner whatsoever or
purchase elsewhere printed any book or books
or any work or works whatsoever that may
be printed by the said John Reeves George
Eyre and Andrew Strahan or either of them
their or either of their executors administrators
or assigns by virtue of these presents And
Further of Our more abundant grace we
have granted and given licence and by
these presents we do for us Our Heirs and
Successors grant and give licence to the said

John Reeves George Eyre and Andrew Strahan
them and each of them and to their and each
of their executors administrators and assigns to
That they or any of them during the aforesaid
term to them above granted may take retain
and hire workmen in the Art and Mystery of
printing to work in such art or mystery at the
appointment and by the Assignment of the said
John Reeves George Eyre and Andrew Strahan
their executors or assigns for such time or
times during which the said John Reeves
George Eyre and Andrew Strahan their
executors or assigns or any of them shall
want such workmen we have also given
and granted and by these presents for us
Our Heirs and Successors Do give and grant
to the said John Reeves George Eyre and
Andrew Strahan and each of them their and
each of their executors administrators and
assigns for exercising the said Office a fee or
Annuity of six Pounds thirteen shillings and
four pence of lawful money of Great Britain
by the year To Have and annually receive the

four pence of lawful money of Great Britain
by the year TO HAVE and annually receive the
said fee or annuity of six pounds thirteen
shillings and four pence to the said John
Reeves George Eyre and Andrew Strahan their
executors administrators and assigns at the
feasts of Easter and Saint Michael the
Archangel to be paid in equal portions during
the said term of thirty years above by these
presents granted from the treasury of us our
Heirs and Successors at the receipt of Our
Exchequer at Westminster by the hands of the
Commissioners of Our Treasury or the Treasurer
and Chamberlains of us Our Heirs and
Successors for the time being commanding and
by these presents for us our Heirs and
Successors firmly enjoining and ordering all and
singular Mayors Sheriffs Bailiffs Constables Officers
Ministers and Subjects whatsoever of us our
Heirs and Successors that they be from time
to time when there shall be occasion assisting
attendant and aiding as they ought to the said
John Reeves George Eyre and Andrew Strahan
their executors and assigns in the execution of
the aforesaid Office and in the doing of all
and singular the things specified in these
our Letters Patent to be done Provided always
and our will and pleasure nevertheless is
that these our Letters Patent are and shall be
deemed to be made and granted and to be
valid and effectual only upon condition that
the said John Reeves George Eyre and Andrew
Strahan their executors and assigns from time
to time and at all times during the term
hereinbefore granted and when and as often
as they or any of them shall be required by
Our Lord High Treasurer or the Commissioners
of Our Treasury for the time being or at
his or their instance or by his or their orders
print for and supply to us our Heirs or
Successors or in any manner whatsoever for
or on our behalf or for our Service any
of the Articles Matters or Things which by
virtue of these Our Letters Patent and the
Office hereby granted they or any of them

are authorized to print and for or in respect
of the printing and supplying of which they
can or may be intitled to require demand or
receive any price or payment whatsoever over
and above the said fee hereby granted shall
and do accordingly print for and supply to us
Our Heirs and Successors or in such manner
for or on our behalf or for our service all
and every such articles matters and things
respectively at and for such Prices and rates
of payment for the same respectively as to
our said Treasurer or Lords of Our Treasury
for the time being shall appear to be just
and reasonable Lastly wee will and by these
presents for us Our Heirs and Successors do
grant unto the said John Reeves George Eyre
and Andrew Strahan that these Our Letters
Patent or the Inrollment of the same shall be
good firm valid and effectual in the Law
notwithstanding the not rightly or fully reciting
the before recited Letters Patent or the not
naming or the not rightly naming or mentioning
the Office and premises aforesaid or any of
them and notwithstanding any other omission
imperfection defect thing cause or matter or
whatsoever to the contrary thereof in any wise
notwithstanding In Witness & Witness &
the Eighth day of July in the thirty ninth
Year of Our Reign.

By Writ of Privy Seal.

Plate 3. Licence to print to Andrew Strahan and William Woodfall all legal books touching or concerning the common law of England for 40 years commencing on 30 April 1789. Courtesy The National Archives, United Kingdom. *Patent Rolls: George III*, c66/3850/5 (1789).

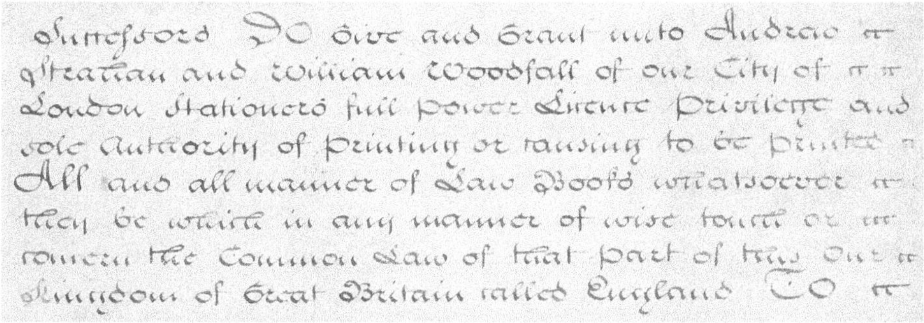
Successors Do give and Grant unto Andrew
Strahan and William Woodfall of our City of
London Stationers full Power Licence Privilege and
sole Authority of Printing or causing to be Printed
All and all manner of Law Books whatsoever
they be which in any manner of wise touch or
concern the Common Law of that part of this Our
Kingdom of Great Britain called England To

'. . . Do give and grant unto Andrew Strahan and William Woodfall of our City of London Stationers full Power Licence Privilege and sole authority of Printing or causing to be Printed All and all manner of Law Books whatsoever they be which in any manner of wise touch or concern the Common Law of that part of this our Kingdom of Great Britain called England . . .'

The full licence is shown on the next two pages.

Andrew Strahan et al.
Licence to print Law
Books ⸺⸺ }

GEORGE the Third by the Grace of God &c TO ALL manner of Printers Booksellers Stationers and all other Our Subjects whatsoever Greeting Know Ye that We for divers good Causes and Considerations us in this behalf moving of Our especial Grace certain knowledge and meer Motion HAVE given and granted and by these presents for us Our Heirs and Successors DO give and grant unto Andrew Strahan and William Woodfall of our City of London Stationers full power Licence Privilege and sole Authority of printing or causing to be printed All and all manner of Law Books whatsoever they be which in any manner of wise touch or concern the Common Law of that part of this Our Kingdom of Great Britain called England TO HOLD exercise and enjoy the said power Licence Privilege and sole Authority hereby by us granted or mentioned or intended to be granted unto the said Andrew Strahan and William Woodfall their Executors Administrators and Assigns for and during the Term of forty years to commence from the Thirtieth Day of April One thousand seven hundred and eighty nine in as full and ample manner and form to all intents and purposes as any person or persons have held and enjoyed or ought of Right to have held or enjoy the same And our express Will and pleasure is AND WE do hereby strictly charge and command all and every person and persons whatsoever that they nor any or either of them presume in any manner of wise to print or cause to be printed any Law Books whatsoever relating to the Common Law of that part of this Our Kingdom of Great Britain called England without the Licence Consent or Agreement of the said Andrew Strahan and William Woodfall their Executors

the Licence Consent or Agreement of the said Andrew Strahan and William Woodfall their Executors or Administrators or Assigns in Writing first had and obtained in that behalf upon pain of forfeiture as well as Twelve Pence in Money for every one of the said Books to the use of Us Our Heirs and Successors as also upon pain of forfeiture of all and every the said Books so to be by them or any of them imprinted contrary to the true meaning of these Our Letters Patent To the use of the said Andrew Strahan and William Woodfall their Executors Administrators or Assigns And further to incur Our High Displeasure for breaking and neglecting this Our present Grant and Privilege And We do also hereby Will and Command all Our Ministers and Subjects whatsoever that they and every of them be aiding encouraging and assisting unto the said Andrew Strahan and William Woodfall their Executors Administrators and Assigns in the due and lawful Execution of the Powers and Privileges hereby granted as they tender Our Pleasure and will answer the contrary at their perils And lastly We do hereby for Us Our Heirs and Successors declare and agree that these Our Letters Patent or the Enrollment or Exemplification thereof shall be in and by all things good firm valid and effectual in the Law to all Intents and purposes and shall be to be construed and adjudged as well in all Our Courts as elsewhere in the most favorable and beneficial sense for the best advantage of the said Andrew Strahan and William Woodfall their Executors Administrators and Assigns according to Our Royal Intent and

purpose hereinbefore declared In Witness &c.
Witness &c. the Twentieth day of August in the Twenty ninth year of our Reign

By Writ of Privy Seal

Works Cited

International Treaties and Declarations

Australia-United States Free Trade Agreement (AUSFTA) (18 May 2004)—(entered into force 1 January 2005) http://www.dfat.gov.au/fta/ausfta/final-text/index.html.

Berne Convention for the Protection of Literary and Artistic Works (Paris Act), opened for signature 24 July 1971, 1161 UNTS 30 (entered into force 15 December 1972) http://www.wipo.int/treaties/en/ip/berne/.

International Convention for the Protection of Performers, Producers of Phonograms and Broadcasting Organisations (Rome Convention) done at Rome on 26 October 1961 http://www.wipo.int/treaties/en/ip/rome/.

International Telecommunications Union / United Nations, *Declaration of Principles: Building the Information Society: a Global Challenge in the New Millennium,* Document WSIS–03/GENEVA/ Doc/4-E 12 December 2003 World Summit on the Information Society Geneva 2003-Tunis 2005 http://www.itu.int/wsis/docs/geneva/official/dop.html.

International Telecommunications Union / United Nations, *Tunis Agenda for the Information Society,* Document WSIS-05/TUNIS/DOC/6 (Rev.1)-E, 18 November 2005, World Summit on the Information Society Geneva 2003-Tunis 2005 http://www.itu.int/wsis/docs2/tunis/off/6rev1.html.

International Telecommunications Union/United Nations, *Tunis Commitment*, Document WSIS-05/ TUNIS/Doc/7-E 18 November 2005, World Summit on the Information Society Geneva 2003-Tunis 2005 http://www.itu.int/wsis/docs2/tunis/off/7.html.

OECD. *Recommendation of the Council for Enhanced Access and More Effective Use of Public Sector Information,* OECD Ministerial Meeting on the Future of the Internet Economy, Seoul, South Korea 17–18 June 2008 http://www.oecd.org/sti/40826024.pdf.

OECD. *The Seoul Declaration for the Future of the Internet Economy*, OECD Ministerial Meeting on the Future of the Internet Economy, Seoul, South Korea 17–18 June 2008 http://www.oecd.org/sti/40839436.pdf.

OECD. Directorate for Science, Technology and Industry, *Shaping Policies for the Future of the Internet Economy* (June 2008) http://www.oecd.org/internet/ieconomy/ 40821707.pdf.

Office of the United Nations High Commissioner for Human Rights, *International Covenant on Civil and Political Rights* (1976) http://treaties.un.org/doc/Publication/UNTS/Volume%20999/volume-999-I-14668-English.pdf or http://www.ohchr.org/en/professionalinterest/pages/ccpr.aspx.

Office of the United Nations High Commissioner for Human Rights, *International Covenant on Economic, Social and Cultural Rights* (1976) http://www.ohchr.org/EN/ProfessionalInterest/Pages/CESCR.aspx.

Open Government Partnership (1970) http://www.opengovpartnership.org/.

UNESCO. *Convention on the Means of Prohibiting and Preventing the Illicit Import, Export and Transfer of Ownership of Cultural Property* (14 November 1970) http://portal.unesco.org/en/ev.php-URL_ID=13039&URL_DO=DO_TOPIC&URL_SECTION=201.html.

United Nations. *Universal Declaration of Human Rights* GA Res 217A (III), UN Doc A/810 at 71 (10 December 1948) http://www.ohchr.org/en/udhr/pages/introduction.aspx.

WIPO Copyright Treaty (WCT) 1996 (entered into force 6 March 2002) http://www.wipo.int/treaties/en/ip/wct/.

World Trade Organization, *Agreement on Trade-Related Aspects of Intellectual Property Rights* (TRIPS Agreement) 1994 (entered into force 1 January 1996) http://www.wto.org/english/tratop_e/trips_e/t_agm0_e.htm.

Guides

Attorney-General's Department (Cth), *Australian Government Intellectual Property Manual* (2012) http://www.ag.gov.au/RightsAndProtections/IntellectualProperty/Documents/IntellectualPropertyManual.pdf.

Attorney-General's Department (Cth), *Guidelines for Licensing Public Sector Information for Australian Government Agencies* (28 February 2012) http://www.ag.gov.au/RightsAndProtections/IntellectualProperty/Documents/GuidelinesforlicensingPSIforAusGovagencies.pdf.

Australian Copyright Council, 'Government and Copyright: A Practical Guide' (2002) *Australian Copyright Council Bulletin* 1.

Australian Copyright Council, *Government: Commonwealth, State and Territory* Information Sheet G062 v 18 (November 2014) http://www.copyright.org.au/ACC_Prod/ACC/Information_Sheets/Government__Commonwealth__State___Territory.aspx.

Australian Copyright Council, *The 'Special Case' or 'Flexible Dealing' Exception: Section 200AB* (2009) http://www.copyright.org.au/acc_prod/ACC/Information_Sheets/Special_Case_or_Flexible_Dealing_Exceptions__Section_200AB.aspx.

Australian Libraries Copyright Committee and Australian Digital Alliance, *A User's Guide to the Flexible Dealing Provision for Libraries, Educational Institutions and Cultural Institutions* (2008) http://digital.org.au/our-work/publication/section-200ab-flexible-dealing-handbook-online.

Cross Jurisdictional Chief Information Officers Committee, *Australian Governments Open Access and Licensing Framework (AusGOAL)* http://www.ausgoal.gov.au/.

Department of Finance (Cth), *Public Governance, Performance and Accountability Act 2013 (PGPA Act) Commonwealth Entities and Companies (189)* 8 December 2014 http://www.finance.gov.au/flipchart/.

EIFL (Electronic Information for Libraries), *eIFL-IP Draft law on copyright Including Model Exceptions and Limitations for Libraries and Their Users* (2014) http://www.eifl.net/system/files/resources/201411/eifl_draft_law_2014.pdf.

Max Planck Institute for Intellectual Property and Competition Law, *Declaration: A Balanced Interpretation of the 'Three Step Test' in Copyright Law* (July 2008) http://www.ip.mpg.de/en/news/declaration_on_the_three_step_test.html.

UNESCO, Jules Larivière, *Guidelines for Legal Deposit Legislation* (2000) IFLA http://unesdoc.unesco.org/images/0012/001214/121413eo.pdf.

Reports, Agreements and Submissions

Australia

Advisory Council on Intellectual Property (Cth), *Review of Crown Use Provisions for Patents and Designs* (November 2005) http://www.acip.gov.au/pdfs/ACIP_Final_Report_Review_of_Crown_Use_Provisions_Archived.pdf.

Advisory Group on Reform of Australian Government Administration, Department of Prime Minister and Cabinet (Cth), *Ahead of the Game: Blueprint for the Reform of the Australian Government Administration* (March 2010) http://apo.org.au/files/Resource/APS_reform_blueprint.pdf.

Attorney-General's Department (Cth), *Agreement between Copyright Agency Limited and the Commonwealth for copying of literary works by the Commonwealth — June 2003* (signed 10 June 2003).

Attorney-General's Department (Cth), *Consultation Paper: Extending Legal Deposit* (Canberra, 2012) http://www.ag.gov.au/consultations/pages/ExtendingLegalDeposit.aspx.

Attorney-General's Department (Cth), *Discussion Paper on the Extension of Legal Deposit* (2007) http://arts.gov.au/sites/default/files/pdfs/legal_deposit_discussion_paper_2007.pdf.

Attorney-General's Department (Cth), *Intellectual Property Principles for Australian Government Agencies* (2010) http://www.ag.gov.au/RightsAndProtections/IntellectualProperty/Documents/StatementofIP-principlesforAusGovagencies.pdf or [1–7] http://www.ag.gov.au/RightsAndProtections/IntellectualProperty/Documents/IntellectualPropertyManual.pdf.

Australian Copyright Council, *Response to Government 2.0 Taskforce Issues Paper* (August 2009) http://gov2.net.au/submissions/australian-copyright-council/index.html.

Australian Government Information Management Office, Department of Finance and Administration (Cth), *Australian Government Information Interoperability Framework (April 2006)* http://www.finance.gov.au/files/2012/04/Information_Interoperability_Framework.pdf.

Australian Government Information Management Office, Department of Finance and Deregulation (Cth), *Commonwealth Library Deposit and Free Issue Schemes (LDS)* (March 2013) http://www.finance.gov.au/librarydeposit/.

Australian Government Information Management Office, Department of Finance and Deregulation (Cth), *Declaration of Open Government* (16 July 2010) Lindsay Tanner http://www.finance.gov.au/blog/2010/07/16/declaration-open-government/.

Australian Government Information Management Office, Department of Finance and Deregulation (Cth), *Engage: Getting on with Government 2.0: Report of the Government 2.0 Taskforce* (December 2009) http://gov2.net.au/report/.

Australian Government Information Management Office, Department of Finance and Deregulation (Cth), *Interacting with Government: Australians' Use and Satisfaction with E-Government Services—2008* http://www.finance.gov.au/publications/interacting-with-government/index.html.

Australian Government Information Management Office, Department of Finance and Deregulation (Cth), *National Government Information Sharing Strategy: Unlocking Government Information Assets to Benefit the Broader Community* (August 2009) http://www.finance.gov.au/files/2012/04/ngiss.pdf.

Australian Government Information Management Office, Department of Finance and Deregulation (Cth), *A National Standards Framework for Government* (August 2009) http://www.finance.gov.au/policy-guides-procurement/national-standards-framework/.

Australian Government Information Management Office, Department of Finance and Deregulation (Cth). *Online Information Service Obligations (OISOs),* AGIMO (2011) http://www.finance.gov.au/agimo-archive/oiso.html.

Australian Government Information Management Office, Department of Finance and Deregulation (Cth), *Review of the Australian Government's Use of Information and Communication Technology* (Sir Peter Gershon 16 October 2008) http://www.finance.gov.au/publications/ICT-Review/docs/Review-of-the-Australian-Governments-Use-of-Information-and-Communication-Technology.pdf.

Australian Law Reform Commission, *Australia's Federal Record: A Review of Archives Act 1983*, Report No 85 (1998).

Australian Law Reform Commission, *Copyright and the Digital Economy: Final Report* (ALRC Report 122) (November 2013) http://www.alrc.gov.au/publications/copyright-report-122

Australian Law Reform Commission, *Keeping Secrets: the Protection of Classified and Security Sensitive Information*, Report 98 (2004).

Australian Law Reform Commission, *Open Government: a review of the Federal Freedom of Information Act 1982*, Report 77 (1995).

Australian National Audit Office, *Intellectual Property Policies and Practices in Commonwealth Agencies Audit Report No 25 2003/2004* (2004) http://www.anao.gov.au/Publications/Audit-Reports/2003-2004/Intellectual-Property-Policies-and-Practices-in-Commonwealth-Agencies.

Australian National Audit Office, *Recordkeeping, Audit Report No 45 2001–02* (1 May 2002) http://www.anao.gov.au/uploads/documents/2001-02_Audit_Report_45.pdf.

Australian National Audit Office, *Recordkeeping in Large Commonwealth Organisations, Audit Report No 7 2003–04* (24 September 2003) http://www.anao.gov.au/uploads/documents/2003-04_Audit_Report_7.pdf.

Copyright Law Committee on Reprographic Reproduction, *Report of the Copyright Law Committee on Reprographic Reproduction* (Franki Committee) (1976).

Copyright Law Review Committee, *Copyright and Contract* (2002).

Copyright Law Review Committee, *Crown Copyright* (2005).

Copyright Law Review Committee, *Simplification of the Copyright Act 1968: Parts 1 and 2* (1998/1999).

Council of Australian Governments, *Competition Principles Agreement—11 April 1995* (as amended to 13 April 2007) http://www.coag.gov.au/node/52.

Cutler & Company Pty Ltd, *Commerce in Content: Building Australia's International Future in Interactive Multimedia Markets*: A Report for the Department of Industry, Science and Technology, CSIRO, and the Broadband Services Expert Group (1994).

Cutler & Company Pty Ltd, *Venturous Australia: Building Strength in Innovation: Report on the Review of the National Innovation System* (the Cutler Report) Report to Senator the Hon Kim Carr, Minister for Innovation, Industry, Science and Research (August 2008) http://www.industry.gov.au/innovation/InnovationPolicy/Pages/Document%20library/NISReport.aspx or http://www.industry.gov.au/innovation/InnovationPolicy/Documents/Policy/NISReport.pdf.

Department of Broadband Communications and the Digital Economy (Cth), *Australia's Digital Economy: Future Directions* (2009) http://pandora.nla.gov.au/pan/102861/20090717-1104/www.dbcde.gov.au/__data/assets/pdf_file/0003/117786/DIGITAL_ECONOMY_FUTURE_DIRECTIONS_FINAL_REPORT.pdf.

Department of Communications, Information Technology and the Arts (Cth), *Unlocking the Potential: Digital Content Industry Action Agenda, Strategic Industry Leaders Group report to the Australian Government* (2005)

Department of Finance and Deregulation (Cth), *Government Response to the Report of the Government 2.0 Taskforce* (May 2010) http://www.finance.gov.au/publications/govresponse20report/ or http://www.finance.gov.au/publications/govresponse20report/doc/Government-Response-to-Gov-2-0-Report.pdf.

Department of Foreign Affairs and Trade (Cth), *Common Core Document—Incorporating the Fifth Report under the International Covenant on Civil and Political Rights and the Fourth Report under the International Covenant on Economic, Social and Cultural Rights* (June 2006) http://dfat.gov.au/international-relations/themes/human-rights/Documents/core_doc.pdf.

Department of Innovation, Industry, Science and Research (Cth), *Powering Ideas: An Innovation Agenda for the 21st Century* (2009) http://apo.org.au/research/powering-ideas-innovation-agenda-21st-century.

Department of Prime Minister and Cabinet (Cth), *Information Policy and E-Governance in the Australian Government: A Report for the Department of the Prime Minister and Cabinet* Dr Ian Reinecke (March 2009) http://www.dpmc.gov.au/publications/information_policy/docs/information_policy_e-governance.pdf.

Department of the Regional Australia Local Government, Arts and Sport (Cth), *Creative Australia: National Cultural Policy* (2013) http://creativeaustralia.arts.gov.au/assets/Creative-Australia-PDF-20130417.pdf.

Fitzgerald, A and Pappalardo, K *Report to the Government 2.0 Taskforce: Project 4 Copyright Law and Intellectual Property* (Dec 2009) http://gov2.net.au/projects/index.html.

House of Representative Standing Committee on Legal and Constitutional Affairs, Parliament of Australia, *Review of Technological Protection Measures Exceptions* (Feb 2006) http://www.aph.gov.au/binaries/house/committee/laca/protection/report/fullreport.pdf.

Intellectual Property and Competition Review Committee (Cth), *Review of Intellectual Property Legislation under the Competition Principles Agreement* (September 2000): Final Report of the Intellectual Property and Competition Review Committee to Senator the Hon Nicholas Minchin, Minister for Industry, Science and Resources, and the Hon Daryl Williams AM QC MP, Attorney-General (Ergas Committee) (2000).

National Library of Australia, *Collection Development Policy* (December 2008) http://www.nla.gov.au/policy/cdp.

National Library of Australia, *Pandora: Online Australian Publications: Selection Guidelines for Archiving and Preservation by the National Library of Australia* (Revised August 2005: updated 13 August 2008) http://pandora.nla.gov.au/selectionguidelines.html.

National Office of the Information Economy, *Better Services, Better Government* (2002) http://www.finance.gov.au/agimo-archive/__data/assets/pdf_file/0016/35503/Better_Services-Better_Gov.pdf.

Office of Government Information Technology (Cth), *Management of Government Information as a National Strategic Resource: Report of the Information Management Steering Committee on Information Management in the Commonwealth Government* (August 1997).

Office of the Australian Information Commissioner, *Open Public Sector Information: from principles to practice – Report on agency implementation of the Principles of open public sector information* (February 2013) http://www.oaic.gov.au/images/documents/migrated/oaic/repository/publications/reports/Open_public_sector_information_from_principles_to_practice_February2013.pdf.

Office of the Australian Information Commissioner, *Principles on Open Public Sector Information* (May 2011) http://www.oaic.gov.au/information-policy/information-policy-resources/information-policy-agency-resources/principles-on-open-public-sector-information or http://www.oaic.gov.au/images/documents/information-policy/information-policy-agency-resources/principles_on_psi_short.pdf.

Office of the Australian Information Commissioner, *Understanding the Value of Public Sector Information in Australia – Issues Paper 2* (November 2011) http://www.oaic.gov.au/information-policy/informationpolicy-engaging-with-you/previous-information-policy-consultations/informationpolicy-issues-paper-2-understanding-the-value-of-public-sector-information-in-australia or http://www.oaic.gov.au/images/documents/information-policy/engaging-with-you/previous-information-policy-consultations/issues-paper-2/issues_paper2_understanding_value_public_sector_information_in_australia.pdf.

Parliament of Australia. *The Joint Select Committee on Parliamentary and Government Publications* (Erwin Committee), Parliamentary Paper 32 (1964).

Phillips, Margaret, *Collecting Australian Online Publications*, version 6 (2003) National Library of Australia http://pandora.nla.gov.au/guidelines.html.

Prices Surveillance Authority (Cth), *Inquiry into the Publication Pricing Policy of the Australian Government Publishing Service*, Report No 47 (1992).

Report of the Committee Appointed by the Attorney-General of the Commonwealth to Consider what Alterations are Desirable in the Copyright Law of the Commonwealth (Spicer Committee) (1959). This Report is sometimes referred to as *Report of the Copyright Law Review Committee* (Spicer Committee) (1959).

SIFT Information Security Services, *Future of the Internet Project: Reliability of the Internet* http://www.archive.dbcde.gov.au/__data/assets/pdf_file/0004/75676/FOTI-Reliability-FinalReport.pdf.

Australian States

ACT, Auditor-General's Office, *Records Management in ACT Government Agencies* (June 2008) http://www.audit.act.gov.au/auditreports/reports2008/Report%203-2008%20-%20Records%20Management.pdf.

Department of Innovation, Industry and Regional Development (Vic), *Whole of Victorian Government Response to the Final Report of the Economic Development and Infrastructure Committee's Inquiry into Improving Access to Victorian Public Sector Information and Data* (2 February 2010) http://www.parliament.vic.gov.au/images/stories/committees/edic/access_to_PSI/Response-to-the-EDIC-Inquiry-into-Improving-Access-to-Victorian-PSI-and-Data.pdf.

Economic Development and Infrastructure Committee, Parliament of Victoria, *Inquiry into Improving Access to Victorian Public Sector Information and Data: Report* (June 2009) Parliamentary Paper No 198, Session 2006–2009 http://www.parliament.vic.gov.au/edic/inquiries/article/1019.

Hodgkinson, S. and Stewart, L, *Victorian State Government E-Government Landscape Scan: Overview*, Version 3.0 http://web.archive.org/web/20091020023848/http://www.egov.vic.gov.au/index.php?env=-innews/detail:m3086-1-1-8-s-0:n-1647-0-0--.

New South Wales Government, *Agreement between the Crown in Right of the State of New South Wales and the Copyright Agency Limited*, dated 14 March 2005 http://www.copyright.com.au/states_territories.htm and the *Interim Rate Agreement between Copyright Agency Limited and Crown in Right of the State of New South Wales* [2009] http://www.lawlink.nsw.gov.au/lawlink/legislation_policy/. These Agreements are referred to in Clauses 3.5–3.6 of the current *Remuneration Agreement between the Crown in Right of the State of New South Wales and Copyright Agency Limited* [2010] http://www.lpclrd.lawlink.nsw.gov.au/lpclrd/lpclrd_copyright/lpclrd_agreements.html.

Northern Territory Government Gazette, No G43 (1996) 'Copyright Policy Concerning Legislation'.

Northern Territory Government Gazette, No G48 (1998) 'Copyright Policy in Judgments of the Courts of the Northern Territory'.

NSW Government Gazette, No 23 (1995) 1087 'Notice: Copyright in judicial decisions' (The Hon John Hannaford)

NSW Government Gazette, No 110 (1996) 6611 'Notice: Copyright in legislation and other material' (The Hon JW Shaw).

Queensland Government, *Queensland Public Sector Intellectual Property Principles* (2013) (Version 2) http://www.qld.gov.au/dsitia/assets/documents/ip-principles.pdf.

Queensland Spatial Information Office, Office of Economic and Statistical Research, Queensland Treasury, *Government Information and Open Content Licensing: An Access and Use Strategy* Government Information Licensing Framework Project Stage 2 Report (October 2006) http://eprints.qut.edu.au/32117/.

State Library of Tasmania, *Legal Deposit* (2014) http://www.linc.tas.gov.au/forpublishers/legaldeposit.

State Records of New South Wales, *Building the Archives: Policy on Records Appraisal and the Identification of State Archives* (June 2001) https://www.records.nsw.gov.au/recordkeeping/rules/policies/building-the-archives.

State Records of New South Wales, *Strategies for Documenting Government Business: The DIRKS Manual* (June 2003) http://www.records.nsw.gov.au/documents/recordkeeping-dirks/DIRKS%20Manual.pdf or http://www.records.nsw.gov.au/recordkeeping/advice/designing-implementing-and-managing-systems/dirks-manual/dirks-manual (June 2003, revised 2007).

Tasmanian Government, *Crown Copyright: Guidelines for Administration v.2.0* http://www.communications.tas.gov.au/channels/publishing/publications/crown_copyright_guidelines_for_administration_v.2.0.

Canada

Department of Industry, Information Highway Advisory Council, *Connection, Community, Content: The Challenge of the Information Highway* (Information Highway Advisory Council Secretariat/Industry Canada, 1995).

Keyes, AA and Brunet, C, *Copyright in Canada: Proposals for a Revision of the Law* (April 1977) (Consumer and Corporate Affairs, Ottawa, 1977).

KPMG Consulting, *Executive Summary: Geospatial Data Policy Study* (March 2001) (Ottawa, 2001) http://www.geos.ed.ac.uk/~gisteac/proceedingsonline/Source%20Book%202004/SDI/National/Canada/Canadian%20Geospatial%20Data%20Policy%20Study%20Executive%20Summary.pdf.

Library and Archives of Canada, *Collection Development Framework* (30 March 2005) http://www.collectionscanada.gc.ca/obj/003024/f2/003024-e.pdf.

Library and Archives of Canada, *Digital Collection Development Policy* (1 Feb 2006) http://www.collectionscanada.gc.ca/collection/003-200-e.html.

Ministry of Industry, *Supporting Culture and Innovation: Report on the Provisions and Operation of the Copyright Act (2002)*.

Treasury Board of Canada Secretariat, *Communications Policy of the Government of Canada* (2006) http://www.tbs-sct.gc.ca/pol/doc-eng.aspx?id=12316.

European Union

Commission of the European Communities, *Guidelines for Improving the Synergy between the Public and Private Sectors in the Information Market,* Directorate-General for Telecommunications, Information Industries and Innovation (1989).

European Commission, *Green Paper—Copyright in the Knowledge Economy* (16 July 2008) http://ec.europa.eu/internal_market/copyright/docs/copyright-infso/greenpaper_en.pdf.

New Zealand

National Library of New Zealand, *Collections Policy* (December 2010) http://www.natlib.govt.nz/about-us/policies-strategy/our-policy-about-collections.

State Services Commission, *New Zealand Government Open Access and Licensing framework (NZ-GOAL)* (Version 1) (August 2010) https://ict.govt.nz/assets/Uploads/Documents/NZGOAL.pdf or http://ict.govt.nz/guidance-and-resources/information-and-data/nzgoal/.

State Services Commission, *Policy Framework for Government Held Information* (1997) http://www.ssc.govt.nz/Documents/policy_framework_for_Government_.htm.

State Services Commission / Tony Ryall, *More Government Information for Reuse* (6 August 2010) http://beehive.govt.nz/release/more-government-information-reuse.

United Kingdom

British Library, *Collection Development Policy* (2011) http://www.bl.uk/aboutus/stratpolprog/coldevpol/index.html.

Cabinet Office, *The Power of Information: An Independent Review by Ed Mayo and Tom Steinberg* (2007) http://www.opsi.gov.uk/advice/poi/index.htm.

Works Cited

Cabinet Office, White Paper: *Future Management of Crown Copyright*, (1999) http://www.opsi.gov.uk/advice/crown-copyright/future-management-of-crown-copyright.pdf.

Copyright and Designs Law: Report of the Committee to Consider the Law on Copyright and Designs (Whitford Committee) Cmnd 6732 (1977).

First Report from the Select Committee on the best means of affording members information to be derived from Public Documents, with a view to economy, facility of access, and clearness of arrangement, (Select Committee on Printed Papers) London 1833, 12 Accounts and Papers (House of Commons).

First Report of the Controller of Her Majesty's Stationery Office (1881).

HM Treasury, *Cross Cutting Review of the Knowledge Economy: Review of Government Information* (2000) http://webarchive.nationalarchives.gov.uk/+/http:/www.hm-treasury.gov.uk/spend_sr00_ccr.htm.

Intellectual Property Office, *Government Policy Statement: Consultation on Modernising Copyright* (July 2012) https://www.gov.uk/government/consultations/copyright.

Intellectual Property Office, *Digital Opportunity: A Review of Intellectual Property and Growth* (Hargreaves Report) (May 2011) http://www.ipo.gov.uk/ipreview-finalreport.pdf or https://www.gov.uk/government/publications/digital-opportunity-review-of-intellectual-property-and-growth.

Intellectual Property Office, *Modernising Copyright: A Modern, Robust and Flexible Framework* (December 2012) http://webarchive.nationalarchives.gov.uk/20140603093549/http://www.ipo.gov.uk/response-2011-copyright-final.pdf.

Intellectual Property Office, *UK Government Response to European Commission's Green Paper—Copyright in the Knowledge Economy* (December 2008) http://webarchive.nationalarchives.gov.uk/20140603093549/http://www.ipo.gov.uk/c-eupaper.pdf.

The National Archives, *UK Government Licensing Framework* (2014) http://www.nationalarchives.gov.uk/information-management/re-using-public-sector-information/licensing-for-re-use/ukglf/ or http://www.nationalarchives.gov.uk/information-management/re-using-public-sector-information/licensing-for-re-use/ or http://www.nationalarchives.gov.uk/documents/information-management/uk-government-licensing-framework.pdf.

Office of Fair Trading, *The Commercial Use of Public Information (CUPI)* (2006) OFT 861 http://webarchive.nationalarchives.gov.uk/20140402142426/http://oft.gov.uk/oftwork/publications/publication-categories/reports/consumer-protection/oft861 or http://www.opsi.gov.uk/advice/poi/oft-cupi.pdf.

Public Record Office, *Calendar of Patent Rolls: Edward VI, Vol V (1547–1553)* (1926).

Public Record Office, *Calendar of Patent Rolls: Philip and Mary Vol 1(1553–1554)* (1937).

Public Record Office, *Calendar of State Papers, Domestic: Charles II, 1660–1685* (HMSO and Longman, 1860–1947) (28 volumes).

Public Record Office, *MSS Calendars and Indexes to the Patent Rolls: 1 Elizabeth I – 7 William IV* (1965).

Report from the Select Committee on King's Printers' Patents, London, 1832, 18 Accounts and Papers (House of Commons) 713 (Sess 1831–1832).

Report from the Select Committee on the Printing done for the House, London 1828, 4 Accounts and Papers (House of Commons) 520 (Sess 1828).

Report from Standing Committee A on the Copyright Bill, House of Commons, (11 July 1911).

Report of the Copyright Committee, (Gregory Committee) Cmnd 8662 (1952).

Second Report of the Controller of Her Majesty's Stationery Office (1887).

Third Report of the Controller of Her Majesty's Stationery Office (1890).

United Nations

Economic and Social Council, *Third Periodic Report: Australia*. 07/23/1998. E/1994/104/Add.22. (State Party Report) Implementation of the International Covenant on Economic, Social and Cultural Rights (15 June 1998) http://www.unhchr.ch/tbs/doc.nsf/0/da87cf0d8cdb87708025678500387c12.

United States of America

Deparment of Justice, Office of Legal Counsel, *Memorandum from Acting Assistant Attorney-General RE: Whether Government Reproduction of Copyrighted Materials Invariably is a 'Fair Use' under Section 107 of the Copyright Act of 1976* (30 April 1999) http://www.loc.gov/flicc/gc/fairuse.html.

Department of State, *Open Government Plan* (Summer 2014) http://www.state.gov/documents/organization/231006.pdf.

Executive Office of the President, Office of Management and Budget, *E-Government Strategy: Simplified Delivery of Services to Citizens* (2002) [1] https://www.whitehouse.gov/sites/default/files/omb/inforeg/egovstrategy.pdf.

Executive Office of the President, Office of Management and Budget, *FY 2007 Report to Congress on Implementation of The E-Government Act of 2002* (1 March 2008) http://www.whitehouse.gov/sites/default/files/omb/assets/omb/inforeg/reports/fy2007_egov_report.pdf.

Executive Office of the President, Office of Management and Budget, *Memorandum for the Heads of Executive Departments and Agencies* from Peter R Orszag Director, Subject: Open Government Directive (8 December 2009 M-10-06) http://www.whitehouse.gov/sites/default/files/omb/assets/memoranda_2010/m10-06.pdf.

Executive Office of the President, Office of Management and Budget, *Memorandum to the Heads of Executive Departments and Agencies: December 16 2005* (from Dep Director Clay Johnson III) http://www.whitehouse.gov/omb/memoranda/fy2006/m06-02.pdf.

Executive Offive of the President, Office of Management and Budget, *OMB Circular A-130 revised* http://www.whitehouse.gov/omb/circulars_a130_a130trans4.

Executive Offive of the President, Office of Management and Budget, *Open Government and Records Management* (12 May 2010) (Cass R Sunstein) http://www.whitehouse.gov/omb/inforeg_speeches/open_government_05122010/.

House of Representatives Committee on the Judiciary, *Legislative History for Copyright Act of 1976: Notes for the Committee on the Judiciary*, House Report No 94-1476 (1976) at Copyright Law Revision (House Report No 94-1476) http://en.wikisource.org/wiki/Copyright_Law_Revision_(House_Report_No._94-1476).

Office of the Director of National Intelligence (US), *Information Sharing Environment Implementation Plan* (November 2006) http://www.fas.org/irp/agency/ise/plan1106.pdf.

Presidential Documents, *Memorandum for the Heads of Executive Departments and Agencies* of 21 January 2009, 74 (15) Federal Register 4683–4 http://www.justice.gov/oip/foia_guide09/presidential-foia.pdf.

Works Cited

United States Government, *The Open Government Partnership: National Action Plan for the United States of America* (20 September 2011) http://www.whitehouse.gov/sites/default/files/us_national_action_plan_final_2.pdf.

The White House, National Security Council, *National Strategy for Information Sharing* (October 2007) http://www.fas.org/sgp/library/infoshare.pdf.

Monographs, Databases and Theses

Arber, E, *A Transcript of the Registers of the Company of Stationers of London 1554–1640* (5 vols) (London, Privately Printed, 1875–1894).

Atkinson, B, *The True History of Copyright* (Sydney University Press, 2007).

Auger, CP, *Information Sources in Grey Literature* (Bowker-Saur, 4th edn, 1998).

Barrington Partridge, RC, *The History of the Legal Deposit of Books throughout the British Empire* (Library Association, 1938).

Bentley, L and Sherman, B, *Intellectual Property Law* (Oxford University Press, 3rd edn, 2009).

Bentley L and Kretschmer M, (eds), *Primary Sources on Copyright (1450–1900)* http://www.copyrighthistory.org.

Blackstone, W, *Commentaries on the Laws of England* (Clarendon Press, 1766).

Chitty, J, *A Treatise on the Law of the Prerogatives of the Crown* (Butterworth and Son, 1820).

Dibdin, T, *Frognall's Edition of Ames' Typographical Antiquities* (William Miller, 1812).

Evatt, HV, *The Royal Prerogative* (Lawbook, 1987).

Fitzgerald, A, *Open Access Policies, Practices and Licensing: A Review of the Literature in Australia and Selected Jurisdictions* (Queensland University of Technology ePrints, 2009).

Fitzgerald, B (ed) *Access to Public Sector Information: Law, Technology & Policy* (Sydney University Press, 2010) 2 vols.

Fitzgerald, B and Atkinson, B (eds), *Copyright Future: Copyright Freedom* (Sydney University Press, 2011).

Fitzgerald B, Fitzgerald A, et al, *Internet and E-Commerce Law, Business and Policy* (Lawbook, 2011).

Frankel, S, *Intellectual Property in New Zealand* (LexisNexis, 2nd edn, 2011).

Garnett, K, Davies, G and Harbottle, G, *Copinger and Skone James on Copyright* (Sweet and Maxwell, 15th edn, 2005).

Gervais, D, *The TRIPS Agreement: Drafting History and Analysis* (Sweet and Maxwell, 3rd edn, 2008).

Gilchrist, JS, *Crown Copyright: An Analysis of Rights Vesting in the Crown under Statute and Common Law and their Interrelationship* (LLM thesis, Monash University, 1983).

Heylen, P, *Cyprianus Anglicus* (London, Printed for A Seile, 1668).

Laslett, P (ed), *John Locke: Two Treatises of Government* (Cambridge University Press, 1988).

Lindgren K, Rothnie WA and Lahore JC, *Copyright and Designs* (LexisNexis Butterworths, 2004–) (looseleaf).

Macray, WD, *Annals of the Bodleian Library* (The Bodleian Library, 2nd edn, 1984) (a reprint of the second edition published in 1890 by Clarendon Press).

Martin, GH and Spufford, P (eds), *The Records of the Nation: The Public Record Office 1938–1988* (The Boydell Press, 1990).

Pearce, DC and Geddes, RS, *Statutory Interpretation in Australia* (LexisNexis Butterworths, 7th edn, 2011).

Plomer, HR, *Wynkyn de Worde & His Contemporaries from the Death of Caxton to 1535* (Grafton & Co, 1925).

Ricketson, S, *The Berne Convention for the Protection of Literary and Artistic Works: 1886–1986* (London Centre for Commercial Law Studies, 1987).

Ricketson, S and Creswell, C, *The Law of Intellectual Property: Copyright, Designs & Confidential Information* (Thomson Legal & Regulatory, 2nd edn, 2002–) (looseleaf).

Scrutton, TE, *The Law of Copyright* (William Clowes and Sons, 3rd edn, 1896).

Wheeler, GW (ed), *Letters of Sir Thomas Bodley to Thomas James* (Clarendon Press, 1926).

Articles and Conference Papers

Bannister, Judith, 'It Ain't What you Say, it's the Way that you Say It. Could Freedom of Political Expression Operate as a Defence to Copyright Infringement in Australia?' (1996) 14 *Copyright Reporter* 22.

Bannon QC, CJ, 'Copyright in Reasons for Judgment and Law Reporting' (1982) *56 Australian Law Journal 59*.

Booth, Keitha, 'New Zealand Policy on Information Access' (Speech delivered at International Summit on Open Access to Public Sector Information, Brisbane 4 March, Canberra 6 March 2008) http://www.osdm.gov.au/Events/182.aspx.

Britton, Miriam, 'Implementing the Public Sector Information Directive' (2012) 34 (2) *European Intellectual Property Review* 75.

Campbell, E and Monotti, A, 'Immunities of Agents of Government from Liability for Infringement of Copyright' (2002) 30 *Federal Law Review* 459.

Cook, John S, 'A Summary View of Government Cost Recovery Policies in Australia and New Zealand Relating to the Supply of Public Sector Information' (2010) *Queensland University of Technology ePrints* http://eprints.qut.edu.au/31609/.

Cox, Noel, 'Copyright in Statutes, Regulations, and Judicial Decisions in Common Law Jurisdictions: Public Ownership or Commercial Enterprise' (2006) 27 (3) *Statute Law Review* 185.

Cunningham, A, *Archives—Encyclopedia of Library and Information Science* (Informaword /Taylor & Francis, 3rd edn, 2010) 1:1 [203] 192–207.

Dmitrieva, I, 'State Ownership of Copyrights in Primary Law Materials' (2000) 23 *Hastings Communications and Entertainment Law Journal* 81.

Drahos, Peter, 'Global Law Reform and Rent Seeking: The Case of Intellectual Property' (1996) 7 (1) *Australian Journal of Corporate Law* 45.

Editorial, 'The Crown and Copyright in Publicly Delivered Judgments' (1982) *56 Australian Law Journal* 326.

Editorial, 'Victoria Licences Copyright in Legislation' (1995) 8 *Australian Intellectual Property Law Bulletin* 11.

Fitzgerald, Brian, Foong, Cheryl and Fitzgerald, Anne, 'Copyright Exceptions beyond the *Copyright Act 1968* (Cth)' (2012) 11 (2) *Canberra Law Review* 160.

Frankel, Susy, 'From Barbie to Renoir: Intellectual Property and Culture' (2010) 41 *Victoria University of Wellington Law Review* 1.

Geiger, Christophe, 'The Role of the Three-Step Test in the Adaptation of the Copyright Law to the Information Society' (2007) *UNESCO e-Copyright Bulletin* (Jan–March 2007) 2 http://portal.unesco.org/culture/en/files/34481/11883823381test_trois_etapes_en.pdf/test_trois_etapes_en.pdf.

Gellman, Robert, 'Twin Evils: Government Copyright and Government Copyright-Like Controls over Government Information' (1995) 45 *Syracuse Law Review* 999.

Gilchrist, John, 'The Office of King's Printer and the Commercial Dissemination of Government Information—Past and Prospect' (2003) 7 *Canberra Law Review* 145.

Gilchrist, John 'Origins and Scope of the Prerogative Right to Print and Publish Certain Works in England' (2012) 11 (2) *Canberra Law Review* 4.

Gilchrist, John, 'The Franki Committee (1976) Report and Statutory Licensing', in Brian Fitzgerald and Benedict Atkinson (eds) *Copyright Future: Copyright Freedom* (Sydney University Press, 2011) 65.

Gilchrist, John, 'The Role of Government as Proprietor and Disseminator of Information' (1996) 7(1) *Australian Journal of Corporate Law* 62.

Gilchrist, John, 'Copyright Deposit, Legal Deposit or Library Deposit?: The Government's Role as Preserver of Copyright Material' (2005) 5(2) *QUT Law and Justice Journal* 177.

Griffith, G, 'Copyright, Privilege and Members of Parliament' (2001) 19 *Copyright Reporter* 4.

Hallam, EM, 'Nine Centuries of Keeping the Public Records', in Martin, GH and Spufford, P (eds), *The Records of the Nation: The Public Record Office 1938–1988* (The Boydell Press, 1990) 23.

Handover, PM, 'The "Wicked" Bible and the King's Printing House, Black Friars', (1958) *Times (London) House Journal* 215.

Haxton, N, 'Law Reporting and Risk Management Citing Unreported Judgments' (1998) 17 *Australian Bar Review* 9.

Heller, JS, 'Copyright Law and American Law Libraries: A 1994 Status Report' (1994) 25 (3) *The Law Librarian* 128.

Hilty, Reto M, 'Declaration on the "Three-Step Test": Where do we go from here?' (2010) 1 *Journal of Intellectual Property, Information Technology and E-Commerce Law* 83 http://www.jipitec.eu/issues/jipitec-1-2-2010/2614/.

Hudson, E, 'The Copyright Amendment Act 2006—The Scope and Likely Impact of New Library Exceptions' (2006) *University of Melbourne Law School Research Series* 5.

Kent, CA, 'The Privatizing of Government Information' (1989) 16 (2) *Government Publications Review* 113.

Missingham, R, 'Case Study: Australian Parliament' (Paper presented at the *Using Creative Commons in the Public Sector* Seminar, Canberra, Parliament House, 26 November 2010).

Mitchell, O, 'Crown Copyright in Legislation', (1991) 21 *Victoria University of Wellington Law Review*, 351.

Monotti, A, 'Nature and Basis of Crown Copyright in Official Publications' (1992) 9 *European Intellectual Property Review* 305.

Mulgan, Richard, 'Everyone "Researches". So Why's the Policy so Bad?' *The Public Sector Informant* (Canberra, March 2009) 6.

National Archives of Australia, 'Kirby's Personal Records Saved' (2010) 38 *Memento* 30.

Nicholson, Donna, 'Case Study: Australian Bureau of Statistics' (Paper presented at the *Using Creative Commons in the Public Sector* Seminar, Canberra, Parliament House, 26 November 2010).

Perry, Mark, 'Acts of Parliament: Privatisation, Promulgation and Crown Copyright—is there a Need for a Royal Royalty?' [1998] *New Zealand Law Review* 493.

Perry, Mark, 'Judges' Reasons for Judgments—To Whom Do They Belong?' (1998) 18 *New Zealand University Law Review* 257.

Piggott, M, 'The History of Australian Record Keeping: A Framework for Research' in BJ McMullin (ed), *Coming Together. Papers from the Seventh Australian Library History Forum* (Melbourne, 1997) 33.

Pollock, Rufus, *Open Data Commons Public Domain Dedication and Licence* (PDDL) (15 March 2008) http://opendatacommons.org/licenses/pddl/.

Robbie, G, 'Crown Copyright—Bete Noire or White Knight?' (1996) 2 *Journal of Information Law and Technology* 1 http://www2.warwick.ac.uk/fac/soc/law/elj/jilt/1996_2/special/robbie.

Rosati, Eleonora, 'The Hargreaves Report and Copyright Licensing: Can National Initiatives Work per se?' (2011) 33 (11) *European Intellectual Property Review* 673.

Sawer, G, 'Copyright in Reports of Legal Proceedings' (1953) 27 *Australian Law Journal* 82.

Spigelman, The Hon JJ, 'Citizens, Consumers and Courts' (2001) 60(4) *Australian Journal of Public Administration* 5.

Sterling, JAL 'Crown Copyright in the United Kingdom and other Commonwealth Countries', 1995 https://lexum.com/conf/dac/en/sterling/sterling.html.

Taggart, M, 'Copyright in Written Reasons for Judgment' (1984) 10 *Sydney Law Review* 319.

Vaver, David, 'Intellectual Property: The State of the Art' (2001) 32 *Victoria University of Wellington Law Review* 1.

Wilenski, PS, 'Small Government and Social Equity' in Glenn Withers (ed) *Bigger or Smaller Government? Papers from the Sixth Symposium of the Academy of Social Sciences in Australia*, Canberra (Academy of Social Sciences in Australia, 1982) 37.

Index

www.ingramcontent.com/pod-product-compliance
Lightning Source LLC
Chambersburg PA
CBHW080550270326
41929CB00019B/3248